Editors/Advisory Boa

Members of the Advisory Board are instrumental in the final selection of articles for each edition of articles for content, level, currentness, and appropriateness provides critical direction to the ea find their careful consideration well reflected in this volume.

Preface

Approximately four-fifths of the world's population lives in the developing world. Because of its large population, as well as its increasing role in the international economy, in frequent conflicts and humanitarian crises, and importance to environmental preservation, the developing world continues to be a focus of international attention. The developing world has also figured prominently in the debate over the economic and cultural effects of globalization. International security concerns also focus on the circumstances in some developing countries that may provide opportunity for terrorists to recruit and operate.

It is also important to recognize that developing countries demonstrate considerable ethnic, cultural, political, and economic diversity, making generalizations about them difficult. Increasing differentiation among these diverse countries further complicates our ability to comprehend the challenges of modernization, development, and globalization that they face. An understanding of these challenges must take into account the combination of internal and external factors that influence issues of peace and security, international trade and finance, debt, poverty, the environment, human rights, and gender The ways in which these issues intersect suggests the need for greater recognition of the connections between industrialized and developing countries, and the need for cooperation to deal with the effects of globalization and interdependence.

There is significant debate regarding the best way to address the developing world's problems. Moreover, the developing world's needs compete for attention on an international agenda that is often dominated by the concerns of industrialized nations and more recently shaped by the war on terrorism. Domestic concerns within the industrial nations also continue to overshadow the plight of the developing world.

This eighteenth edition of *Annual Editions: Developing World* seeks to provide students with an understanding of the diversity and complexity of the developing world and to acquaint them with the challenges that these nations confront. There remains a clear need for greater awareness of the problems that confront the developing world and recognition that the international community must make a commitment to effectively address these issues— especially in an international environment dominated by globalization and the war on terrorism. I hope that this volume contributes to students' knowledge and understanding of current trends and their implications, and serves as a catalyst for further discussion.

Over sixty percent of the articles in this edition are new. I chose articles that I hope are both interesting and informative and that can serve as a basis for further student research and discussion. The units deal with what I regard as the major issues facing the developing world. In addition, I have attempted to suggest similarities and differences between developing countries, the nature of their relationships with the industrialized nations, and the differences in perspective regarding the causes of and approaches to the issues.

I would again like to thank McGraw-Hill for the opportunity to put together a reader on a subject that is the focus of my teaching and research. I would also like to thank those who have sent in the response forms with their comments and suggestions. I have tried to take these into account in preparing the current volume. No book on a topic as broad as the developing world can be comprehensive. There are certainly additional and alternative readings that might be included. Any suggestions for improvement are welcome. Please complete and return the postage-paid article rating form at the end of the book with your comments.

Robert J. Griffiths
Editor

Contents

UNIT 1
Understanding the Developing World

The concepts in bold italics are developed in the article. For further expansion, please refer to the Topic Guide.

UNIT 2
International Political Economy

The concepts in bold italics are developed in the article. For further expansion, please refer to the Topic Guide.

UNIT 3
Conflict and Instability

The concepts in bold italics are developed in the article. For further expansion, please refer to the Topic Guide.

The concepts in bold italics are developed in the article. For further expansion, please refer to the Topic Guide.

The President of the
Democratic Republic
of the Congo

UNIT 4
Political Change

Unit Overview   **128**

The concepts in bold italics are developed in the article. For further expansion, please refer to the Topic Guide.

UNIT 5
Population, Resources, Environment and Health

The concepts in bold italics are developed in the article. For further expansion, please refer to the Topic Guide.

UNIT 6
Women and Development

The concepts in bold italics are developed in the article. For further expansion, please refer to the Topic Guide.

The concepts in bold italics are developed in the article. For further expansion, please refer to the Topic Guide.

Topic Guide

This topic guide suggests how the selections in this book relate to the subjects covered in your course. You may want to use the topics listed on these pages to search the Web more easily.

On the following pages a number of Web sites have been gathered specifically for this book. They are arranged to reflect the units of this *Annual Edition*. You can link to these sites by going to the student online support site at *http://www.mhcls.com/online/*.

ALL THE ARTICLES THAT RELATE TO EACH TOPIC ARE LISTED BELOW THE BOLD-FACED TERM.

Internet References

The following Internet sites have been carefully researched and selected to support the articles found in this reader. The easiest way to access these selected sites is to go to our student online support site at *http://www.mhcls.com/online/*.

AE: Developing World 08/09

The following sites were available at the time of publication. Visit our Web site—we update our student online support site regularly to reflect any changes.

General Sources

Foreign Policy in Focus (FPIF): Progressive Response Index
http://fpif.org/progresp/index_body.html

This index is produced weekly by FPIF, a "think tank without walls," which is an international network of analysts and activists dedicated to "making the U.S. a more responsible global leader and partner by advancing citizen movements and agendas." This index lists volume and issue numbers, dates, and topics covered by the articles.

People & Planet
http://www.peopleandplanet.org

People & Planet is an organization of student groups at universities and colleges across the United Kingdom. Organized in 1969 by students at Oxford University, it is now an independent pressure group campaigning on world poverty, human rights, and the environment.

United Nations System Web Locator
http://www.unsystem.org

This is the Web site for all the organizations in the United Nations family. According to its brief overview, the United Nations, an organization of sovereign nations, provides the machinery to help find solutions to international problems or disputes and to deal with pressing concerns that face people everywhere, including the problems of the developing world, through the UN Development Program at *http://www.undp.org* and UNAIDS at *http://www.unaids.org*.

United States Census Bureau: International Summary Demographic Data
http://www.census.gov/ipc/www/idb/

The International Data Base (IDB) is a computerized data bank containing statistical tables of demographic and socioeconomic data for all countries of the world.

World Health Organization (WHO)
http://www.who.ch

The WHO's objective, according to its Web site, is the attainment by all peoples of the highest possible level of health. Health, as defined in the WHO constitution, is a state of complete physical, mental, and social well-being and not merely the absence of disease or infirmity.

UNIT 1: Understanding the Developing World

Africa Index on Africa
http://www.afrika.no/index/

A complete reference source on Africa is available on this Web site.

African Studies WWW (U. Penn)
http://www.sas.upenn.edu/African_Studies/AS.html

The African Studies Center at the University of Pennsylvania supports this ongoing project that lists online resources related to African Studies.

UNIT 2: International Political Economy

Center for Third World Organizing
http://www.ctwo.org/

The Center for Third World Organizing (CTWO, pronounced "C-2") is a racial justice organization dedicated to building a social justice movement led by people of color. CTWO is a 20-year-old training and resource center that promotes and sustains direct action organizing in communities of color in the United States.

ENTERWeb
http://www.enterweb.org

ENTERWeb is an annotated meta-index and information clearinghouse on enterprise development, business, finance, international trade, and the economy in this age of cyberspace and globalization. The main focus is on micro-, small-, and medium-scale enterprises, cooperatives, and community economic development both in developed and developing countries.

International Monetary Fund (IMF)
http://www.imf.org

The IMF was created to promote international monetary cooperation, to facilitate the expansion and balanced growth of international trade, to promote exchange stability, to assist in the establishment of a multilateral system of payments, to make its general resources temporarily available under adequate safeguards to its members experiencing balance of payments difficulties, and to shorten the duration and lessen the degree of disequilibrium in the international balances of payments of members.

TWN (Third World Network)
http://www.twnside.org.sg/

The Third World Network is an independent, nonprofit international network of organizations and individuals involved in issues relating to development, the Third World, and North-South issues.

U.S. Agency for International Development (USAID)
http://www.usaid.gov

USAID is an independent government agency that provides economic development and humanitarian assistance to advance U.S. economic and political interests overseas.

The World Bank
http://www.worldbank.org

The International Bank for Reconstruction and Development, frequently called the World Bank, was established in July 1944 at the UN Monetary and Financial Conference in Bretton Woods, New Hampshire. The World Bank's goal is to reduce poverty and improve living standards by promoting sustainable growth and investment in people. The bank provides loans, technical assistance, and policy guidance to developing country members to achieve this objective.

UNIT 3: Conflict and Instability

The Carter Center
http://www.cartercenter.org

The Carter Center is dedicated to fighting disease, hunger, poverty, conflict, and oppression through collaborative initiatives in the areas of democratization and development, global health, and urban revitalization.

Center for Strategic and International Studies (CSIS)
http://www.csis.org/

For four decades, the Center for Strategic and International Studies (CSIS) has been dedicated to providing world leaders with strategic insights on, and policy solutions to, current and emerging global issues.

Conflict Research Consortium
http://conflict.colorado.edu/

The site offers links to conflict- and peace-related Internet sites.

Institute for Security Studies
http://www.iss.co.za

This site is South Africa's premier source for information related to African security studies.

Institute for Global communications
http://www.igc.org/peacenet/

PeaceNet promotes dialogue and sharing of information to encourage appropriate dispute resolution, highlights the work of practitioners and organizations, and is a proving ground for ideas and proposals across the range of disciplines within the conflict-resolution field.

Refugees International
http://www.refintl.org

Refugees International provides early warning in crises of mass exodus. It seeks to serve as the advocate of the unrepresented—the refugee. In recent years, Refugees International has moved from its initial focus on Indochinese refugees to global coverage, conducting almost 30 emergency missions in the last 4 years.

UNIT 4: Political Change

Latin American Network Information Center—LANIC
http://www.lanic.utexas.edu

According to Latin Trade, LANIC is "a good clearinghouse for Internet-accessible information on Latin America."

ReliefWeb
http://www.reliefweb.int/w/rwb.nsf

ReliefWeb is the UN's Department of Humanitarian Affairs clearinghouse for international humanitarian emergencies.

World Trade Organization (WTO)
http://www.wto.org

The WTO is promoted as the only international body dealing with the rules of trade between nations. At its heart are the WTO agreements, the legal ground rules for international commerce and for trade policy.

UNIT 5: Population, Resources, Environment and Health

Earth Pledge Foundation
http://www.earthpledge.org

The Earth Pledge Foundation promotes the principles and practices of sustainable development—the need to balance the desire for economic growth with the necessity of environmental protection.

EnviroLink
http://envirolink.org

EnviroLink is committed to promoting a sustainable society by connecting individuals and organizations through the use of the World Wide Web.

Greenpeace
http://www.greenpeace.org

Greenpeace is an international NGO (nongovernmental organization) that is devoted to environmental protection.

Linkages on Environmental Issues and Development
http://www.iisd.ca/linkages/

Linkages is a site provided by the International Institute for Sustainable Development. It is designed to be an electronic clearinghouse for information on past and upcoming international meetings related to both environmental issues and economic development in the developing world.

Population Action International
http://www.populationaction.org

According to its mission statement, Population Action International is dedicated to advancing policies and programs that slow population growth in order to enhance the quality of life for all people.

www.mhcls.com/online/

The Worldwatch Institute
http://www.worldwatch.org

The Worldwatch Institute advocates environmental protection and sustainable development.

UNIT 6: Women and Development

WIDNET: Women in Development NETwork
http://www.focusintl.com/widnet.htm

This site provides a wealth of information about women in development, including the Beijing '95 Conference, WIDNET statistics, and women's studies.

Women Watch/Regional and Country Information
http://www.un.org/womenwatch/

The UN Internet Gateway on the Advancement and Empowerment of Women provides a rich mine of information.

We highly recommend that you review our Web site for expanded information and our other product lines. We are continually updating and adding links to our Web site in order to offer you the most usable and useful information that will support and expand the value of your Annual Editions. You can reach us at: *http://www.mhcls.com/annualeditions/*.

UNIT 1

Understanding the Developing World

Unit Selections

1. **How to Help Poor Countries,** Nancy Birdsall, Dani Rodrik, and Arvind Subramanian
2. **The Utopian Nightmare,** William Easterly
3. **Africa's Village of Dreams,** Sam Rich
4. **Today's Golden Age of Poverty Reduction,** Surjit S. Bhalla
5. **Development as Poison,** Stephen A. Marglin
6. **Why God Is Winning,** Timothy Samuel Shaw and Monica Duffy Toft

Key Points to Consider

- How can wealthy countries contribute to development?

- In what ways must efforts to help the poor be more realistic?

- Has poverty been reduced worldwide? If so, what factors have played a role?

- How will the Millennium Villages Project address poverty?

- Why is this project controversial?

- What constitutes the Western model of development?

- Is the Western model of development transferable to the developing world?

- How have modernization and democratization contributed to the influence of religion worldwide?

Student Web Site
www.mhcls.com/online

Internet References
Further information regarding these Web sites may be found in this book's preface or online.

Africa Index on Africa
http://www.afrika.no/index/
African Studies WWW (U. Penn)
http://www.sas.upenn.edu/African_Studies/AS.html

Parvinder Sethi

The diversity of the countries that make up the developing world has made it difficult to characterize and understand these countries and their role in international affairs. The task has become even more difficult as further differentiation among these countries has occurred. "Developing world" is a catch-all term that lacks precision and explanatory power. It is used to describe a wide range of societies from desperately poor to resource-rich, traditional to modernizing, and authoritarian to democratic. To complicate things even further, there is also controversy over what actually constitutes development. For some, it is economic growth or progress towards democracy; for others it involves greater empowerment and dignity. There are also differing views on why progress toward development has been uneven. The West tends to see the problem as stemming from poor governance, institutional weakness and failure to embrace free-market principles. Critics from the developing world cite the legacy of colonialism and the nature of the international political and economic structures as the reasons for a lack of development. In any case, lumping together the 100-plus nations that make up the developing world obscures the disparities in size, population, resources, forms of government, level of industrialization, distribution of wealth, ethnic diversity, and a host of other indicators that make it difficult to categorize and generalize about this large, diverse group of countries.

Despite their diversity, many nations of the developing world share some characteristics. Developing countries often have large populations, with annual growth rates that often exceed two percent. Poverty continues to be widespread in both rural and urban areas, with rural areas often containing the poorest of the poor. While the majority of the developing world's inhabitants continue to live in the countryside, there is a massive rural-to-urban migration under way, cities are growing rapidly, and some developing countries are approaching urbanization rates in industrialized countries. Wealth is unevenly distributed, making education, employment opportunities, and access to health care luxuries that relatively few can enjoy. Corruption and misman-agement are common. With very few exceptions, these nations share a colonial past that has affected them both politically and economically. Moreover, critics charge that the neocolonial structure of the international economy and the West's political, military, and cultural links with the developing world amount to continued domination.

Developing countries continue to struggle to improve their citizens' living standards. Despite the economic success in some areas, over a billion people live on less than a dollar a day. Although there is some indication (depending on how the data is measured) that the number of poor worldwide is declining, poverty is still a major feature of the developing world. There is also growing economic inequality between the industrial

1

countries and much of the developing world. This is especially true of the poorest countries that have become further marginalized due to their fading strategic importance since the end of the cold war and their limited participation in the global economy. Inequality is also growing within developing countries where elite access to education, capital, and technology has significantly widened the gap between rich and poor.

Although the gap between rich and poor nations persists, some emerging markets have seen significant growth. However, the harsh realities of the global economy were demonstrated during the 1997 Asian financial crisis. Investors remain wary of investing in developing countries and those receiving this investment have taken steps to reduce the risks of more mobile capital. Focus on the relatively few countries that are making progress has further marginalized the large number of developing countries that have not experienced economic growth. The reasons for poor economic performance in many developing countries are complex. Both internal and external factors play a role in the inability of some developing countries to make economic progress. Among the factors are the colonial legacy, continued reliance on the export of primary products, stagnating or declining terms of trade for those primary products, protectionism in the industrialized countries, inadequate foreign aid contributions, debt, as well as weak governance and a lack of regime transparency and accountability. Concerns about the strength of growth in the United States and the rest of the industrialized world has also had a significant impact on the economic prospects of the developing world.

Shortly after independence, a divide between developing and industrialized countries emerged. The basis for this division was the view that the industrialized world continued to dominate and exploit the developing countries. This viewpoint encouraged efforts to alter the international economic order during the 1970s. While the New International Economic Order (NIEO) succumbed to neoliberalism in the 1980s, developing countries still seek solidarity in their interactions with the West. The efforts to extract concessions from the industrialized countries in the negotiations on the Doha trade round illustrate this effort. Moreover, developing countries still view Western prescriptions for development skeptically, and chafe under the Washington Consensus that dictates terms for access to funds from international financial institutions and foreign aid. Some critics suggest that Western development models are detrimental and result in inequitable development and cultural imperialism. In contrast to the developing world's criticism of the West, industrial countries continue to maintain the importance of institution-building, and following the western model that emphasizes a market-oriented approach to development. There is clearly a divergence of opinion between the industrialized countries and the developed world on issues ranging from economic development to governance.

Ultimately the development process will be shaped primarily by the countries experiencing it. The industrialized countries can, however, contribute to this process through trade liberalization, increasing access to technology, and providing more innovative and effective aid, all of which would contribute to a larger role for the developing world in the global economy. Globalization's effects are most readily apparent in relation to economic issues, but the influence of cultural factors, such as religion, are also adding to the complexity of our understanding of the developing world.

How to Help Poor Countries

NANCY BIRDSALL, DANI RODRIK, AND ARVIND SUBRAMANIAN

Getting Development Right

The year 2005 has become the year of development. In September, at the UN Millennium Summit meeting of heads of state, in New York, leaders of wealthy nations will emphasize their commitment to deeper debt relief and increased aid programs for developing countries. The Millennium Development Goals, the centerpiece of the conference's program, call for halving the levels of world poverty and hunger by 2015.

The summit will focus on increasing international aid to 0.7 percent of donors' gross national product to finance a doubling of aid transfers to especially needy areas, particularly in Africa. With respect to global trade, efforts will center on the Doha Round of multilateral trade negotiations and opening markets to important exports (such as cotton) from developing countries. The discussions will thus proceed based on two implicit but critical underlying assumptions: that wealthy nations can materially shape development in the poor world and that their efforts to do so should consist largely of providing resources to and trading opportunities for poor countries.

These assumptions ignore key lessons of the last four decades and of economic history more generally. Development is something largely determined by poor countries themselves, and outsiders can play only a limited role. Developing countries themselves emphasize this point, but in the rich world it is often forgotten. So too is the fact that financial aid and the further opening of wealthy countries' markets are tools with only a limited ability to trigger growth, especially in the poorest countries. The tremendous amount of energy and political capital expended on these efforts in official circles threatens to crowd out attention to other ways in which rich countries could do less harm and more good. A singular focus on aid and market access at the September 2005 Millennium Summit should not leave other potentially rewarding measures on the back burner.

Bootstraps

Consider Nicaragua and Vietnam. Both are poor countries with primarily agricultural economies. Both have suffered from long periods of conflict. And both have benefited from substantial foreign aid. But only Vietnam has reduced poverty dramatically and enjoyed steady economic growth (five percent per capita since 1988). Nicaragua has floundered economically, with per capita growth too modest to make a real dent in the number of poor people.

Vietnam faced a U.S. embargo until 1994, and it is still not a member of the World Trade Organization (WTO). Despite these obstacles, it has found markets for its growing exports of coffee and other agricultural products and has successfully begun diversifying into manufacturing as well, especially of textiles. Nicaragua, on the other hand, benefits from preferential access to the lucrative U.S. market and had several billion dollars of its official debt written off in the 1990s. Yet its coffee and clothing export industries have not been able to compete with Vietnam's.

Why has Vietnam outpaced Nicaragua? The answers are internal: history and economic and political institutions have trumped other factors in determining economic success. Access to the U.S. market and the largesse of Western donors have not been powerful enough to overcome Nicaragua's history of social and economic inequality: land and power there have long been concentrated in the hands of a few elites, and the government has failed to invest enough in infrastructure and public welfare.

The experiences of many other developing countries confirm the importance of specific internal factors. Like Vietnam, neither China nor India—the two emerging superstars of the last quarter century—has benefited from trade preferences. And neither has received much foreign aid compared to countries in Africa and Central America. But by enacting creative domestic reforms, China and India have prospered, and in both countries poverty has plunged.

On the flip side, many African countries have been unable to match Vietnam's success, despite being no poorer or more agrarian. True, education and health indicators have improved markedly in Africa, and some of its countries have achieved macroeconomic stability. But even in the best-performing countries, growth and productivity remain modest, and investment depends completely on foreign aid infusions. It may be tempting to ascribe the rare African successes—Botswana and Mauritius, for example—to high foreign demand for their exports (diamonds and garments, respectively), but that explanation goes only so far. Obviously, both countries would be considerably poorer without access to markets abroad. But what distinguishes them is not the external advantages they enjoy; but their ability to exploit these advantages. Natural resource endowments have often hurt many developing countries: the word "diamond" hardly conjures images of peace and prosperity in the context of Sierra Leone, and oil has been more curse than blessing for Angola, Equatorial Guinea, Nigeria, and many others.

Witness the case of Mexico. It has the advantage of sharing a 2,000-mile border with the world's greatest economic power. Since the North American Free Trade Agreement went into effect in 1994, the United States has given Mexican goods duty-free access to its markets, has made huge investments in the Mexican economy, and has continued to absorb millions of Mexican laborers. During the 1994–95 peso crisis, the U.S. Treasury even underwrote Mexico's financial stability. Outside economic help does not get much better. But since 1992, Mexico's economy has grown at an annual average rate of barely more than one percent per capita. This figure is far less than the rates of the Asian growth superstars. It is also a fraction of Mexico's own growth of 3.6 percent per year in the two decades that preceded its 1982 debt crisis. Access to external markets and resources has not been able to make up for Mexico's internal problems.

A notable exception to the limitations of outside assistance is European Union membership. By offering its poorer eastern and southern neighbors not just aid transfers and market access but the prospect of joining the union, the EU has stimulated deep policy and institutional changes and impressive growth in about 20 countries. But the exception proves the rule: the EU is not just an economic arrangement; it is also a political system in which member states transfer extensive legal powers to the central authority. In return, the center shoulders significant responsibilities for the economic well being of each member.

Unfortunately, accession to the EU or to any other major power is not an option for most of the poorest parts of the world—and increasing the financial resources and trading opportunities for the poorest countries is not a sufficient substitute.

Easy Access

To start, there is the question of market access. Currently, the international trade system is full of inequities. Rich countries place their highest tariffs on imports important to developing countries garments and agriculture, for example. The tariffs escalate as the level of processing increases, discouraging industrialization in the poor countries. In addition, multilateral trade negotiations lack transparency and often exclude developing countries from the real action. Using WTO procedures to settle trade disputes requires money and technical expertise, both of which poor countries lack.

But to say that these flaws seriously hamper development in struggling economies would be to overlook the remarkable success in the last two decades of Vietnam and China in exporting manufactured goods, of Chile in exporting wine and salmon, and most recently of India in exporting services. These countries have achieved success in exporting, despite the impediments. And barriers on manufactured exports from developing countries were even higher when the Asian "tigers" first arrived on the scene in the 1960s and 1970s.

Many argue that agricultural tariffs in particular represent an impediment to poor countries' economic growth. The World Bank and organizations such as Oxfam argue that doing away with agricultural subsidies and protectionism in industrialized nations would significantly reduce poverty in the developing world. European cows, the famous example goes, are richer—receiving $2.50 a day each in subsidies—than one-third of the world's people.

Liberalizing trade in agricultural products would mostly benefit the consumers in wealthy nations.

Yet the reality is that liberalizing agricultural trade would largely benefit the consumers and taxpayers of the wealthy nations. Why? Because agricultural subsidies serve first and foremost to transfer resources from consumers and taxpayers to farmers within the same country. Thus, citizens of developed countries would derive the most benefit from having those subsidies cut. Other countries are affected only insofar as world prices rise. But the big, clear gainers from such price increases would be countries that are large net exporters of agricultural products—rich countries, such as the United States, and middle- income countries, such as Argentina, Brazil, and Thailand.

What about the poorer countries? For one thing, many poor countries are actually net importers of agricultural products, and so they benefit from low world prices. An increase in prices may help the rural poor, who sell the agricultural goods, but it would make the urban poor—the consumers—worse off. Net poverty could still be reduced, but to what extent depends in complicated fashion on the working condition of roads and the markets for fertilizer and other inputs, on how much of the gains are captured by poor farmers versus intermediaries, and on the poverty profile of each country.

Regardless of whether agricultural liberalization increases or decreases poverty, the impact would not be significant. Most studies predict that the effect of such liberalization on world prices would be small. The International Monetary Fund (IMF) estimates that world prices would only rise by 2–8 percent for rice, sugar, and wheat; 4 percent for cotton; and 7 percent for beef. The typical annual variation in the world prices of these commodities is at least one order of magnitude larger.

Take cotton specifically. The largest credible estimate of the impact of the complete removal of U.S. cotton subsidies on world prices is less than 15 percent. How much of an effect could this have on farm incomes in West Africa? There is actually a useful benchmark for comparison. In 1994, the member states of the Communauté Financière Africaine currency zone (in which 14 African countries have had their currencies pegged to the French franc since 1948) devalued their currency from 50 to 100 CFA francs per French franc, effectively doubling the domestic price of cotton exports. If at least some of the resulting price gain had gone to cotton farmers (and not to intermediaries or inflation), the farmers' incomes would have increased in countries such as Burkina Faso and Benin. Indeed, the price gain should have increased income and decreased poverty even more than would the complete removal of U.S. cotton subsidies.

There is little evidence that a significant reduction in rural poverty took place, however. A World Bank study found that poverty in Burkina Faso remained stubbornly high and even increased in parts of the country.

Furthermore, a general reduction of trade barriers in rich countries could leave some of the world's poorest countries worse off. A substantial part of least-developed countries' exports enjoy favorable conditions of access to the markets of rich countries under various preferential trade arrangements. With the end in January 2005 of the long-standing system of quotas on apparel, for example, poor countries such as Bangladesh, Cambodia, and Lesotho, which benefited from preferential arrangements, justifiably have been fearing competition from China and Vietnam. The loss of preferential access for the poorest countries is not a justification for stopping trade liberalization in its tracks. But it is an additional reason to be cautious when estimating the magnitude of poor nations' gains from a trade-centered agenda.

Of course, if global trade and growth were to implode, as in the period between the world wars, international development would receive a serious blow. A healthy multilateral trading system is important to keep the possibility remote, and it can protect the poorest countries from unreasonable bilateral pressures. A successful Doha Round could stimulate trade among developing countries and would signal a political willingness on the part of the international community to keep the system purring and prevent an implosion—even if the actual gains for the poorest countries from trade-barrier reductions would be modest.

More Money?

If not better market access, what about more aid? Boosting assistance to the poorest countries of the world is a central recommendation of the recent reports of the UN Millennium Project and British Prime Minister Tony Blair's commission on Africa, and, along with reduced corruption and better management in poor countries, it is a cornerstone of the strategy envisaged to achieve the Millennium Development Goals.

Aid has accomplished some great things. On the health front, smallpox has been eradicated, infant mortality rates have been lowered, and illnesses such as diarrhea and river blindness have been widely treated. Aid programs have improved women's access to modern contraception in Bangladesh and Egypt and helped increase school enrollment in Uganda and Burkina Faso. Aid also pays for much of the (still-limited) access to AIDS medicines in poor countries. In the last decade, aid has helped restore peace and order after conflicts in places including Bosnia, East Timor, and Sierra Leone. In addition, aid can be a vehicle for policy advice and dialogue between recipients and outsiders. There have even been macroeconomic successes, such as the $1 billion grant that allowed Poland to establish an exchange-rate stabilization fund in 1990. By stabilizing the Polish currency, this relatively small amount of financing provided valuable breathing space for the implementation of broader policy reforms.

What these successes share is that they were narrowly targeted at specific objectives. Assistance does work well, but only when the recipient countries do the right things to help themselves and have the capacity and the leadership to spend the money wisely. Some statistical evidence indicates a link between financial assistance and growth. But aid has not been associated with the sustained increases in productivity and wages that ultimately matter. During the 1990s, for example, countries in sub-Saharan Africa received funding amounting on average to about 12 percent of their GDP, while their average growth rate per capita declined by 0.6 percent per year. Meanwhile, some of today's development successes—such as Chile and Malaysia—relied little on aid. And aid to China and India has been very small.

Aid is only as good as the ability of a developing country to use it effectively.

There are many reasons for the mixed performance of foreign assistance. Donors themselves cause many of the problems. Recipient countries can be overwhelmed by the multiplicity of donors pursuing many, even inconsistent, objectives, disbursing aid to innumerable projects and imposing a plethora of conditions on its use. These factors contribute to rather than offset a poor country's lack of institutional capacity. On top of that, there is the natural volatility and uncertainty of foreign aid, which make it difficult for recipient governments to plan their budgets. For more than a decade, the bureaucracies of donor states and organizations have been unable, despite good intentions and constant resolve, to change the political incentives and constraints that impede the reform of their aid-delivery apparatuses.

Probably more important, however, are institutional deficiencies on the recipients' side. Aid is only as good as the ability of a recipient's economy and government to use it prudently and productively. Thus, the fundamental dilemma: countries most in need of aid are often those least able to use it well. That sets limits on the extent to which large infusions of foreign funds can make a difference. The greatest example of the success of aid—the Marshall Plan—illustrates the importance of homegrown institutional competence. Because the institutions and capabilities of the United Kingdom, France, and Germany survived the war to a large extent, even their war-ravaged economies were able to exploit fully the potential of financial assistance.

This simple point addresses the view that aid is a sine qua non for African development on account of the continent's bad geography and favorable environment for diseases. A country's growth may in fact be hampered by its unsuitability for agriculture; its isolated geography; and its susceptibility to malaria and other tropical diseases. In such cases, it might seem appropriate that donors give more. But adverse geography does not fundamentally alter the fact that the effectiveness of assistance depends on the institutions of the recipient country. At its best, aid has helped nations rebuild after conflicts and assisted in achieving specific objectives. But its role in creating and sustaining key institutions and long-term economic health has been much less clear.

Sins of Commission

To help developing countries help themselves, wealthy nations must begin to lift the burdens they impose on the poor. Currently, the developed world uses international trade agreements to impose costly and onerous obligations on poor countries. The most egregious example has been the WTO'S intellectual property agreement, the Trade-Related Aspects of Intellectual Property Rights (TRIPS). Despite recent efforts to cushion its impact on the poorest countries, TRIPS will make the prices of essential medicines significantly greater, and this at a time when poor countries are being ravaged by one of the worst health epidemics ever known—HIV/AIDS. The price increase means that money from the citizens of poor countries will be transferred directly to wealthy pharmaceutical companies. The resulting revenue, although a significant amount of money for the poor countries, will be a relatively small part of the companies' net total profits—hardly enough to induce extra research and development.

An international community that presides over TRIPS and similar agreements forfeits any claim to being development-friendly. This must change: the rich countries cannot just amend TRIPS; they must abolish it altogether. A simple comparison makes the point clear: major industrial countries such as Italy, Japan, and Switzerland adopted pharmaceuticals patent protection when their per capita income was about $20,000; developing countries will adopt it at income levels of $500 per capita, in the case of the poorest, and $2,000–4,000 for the middle-income countries. By these standards, forcing developing countries to abide by TRIPS is about 50–100 years premature.

But costly obligations are not restricted to TRIPS. Trade agreements between the United States and countries such as Jordan, Morocco, and Vietnam have required the latter to adhere to intellectual property regulations that go beyond TRIPS, further increasing the patent holder's monopoly and restricting access to medicines. Other trade agreements have called for developing countries to open their capital accounts immediately, despite recent experience showing that doing so exposes the countries to the volatility of international capital flows.

Just as crucial for empowering poor countries is providing them with enough space to craft their own economic policy. During the last decade, economists have come to understand that economic development is at once easier and harder than previously thought. Many countries have reduced poverty and generated significant economic growth without the deep, comprehensive structural reform that has been the centerpiece for development institutions over the last quarter century. That is the good news. The bad news is that there are few general economic-policy standards that seem to apply to every country—except for such basic principles as macroeconomic stability, outward orientation, accountable government, and market-based incentives. The hard part is moving beyond these broad objectives and figuring out the appropriate specific policies for each developing country's particular needs. The many poor countries that have made progress on the general standards can better craft their own economic course if they have adequate room for policy autonomy and experimentation. The idea may sound radical, but would China have been better off implementing a garden-variety World Bank structural adjustment program in 1978 instead of its own brand of heterodox gradualism?

Almost all successful cases of development in the last 50 years have been based on creative—and often heterodox—policy innovations. South Korea and Taiwan, for example, combined their outward trade orientations with unorthodox policies: export subsidies, directed credit, patent and copyright infringements, domestic-content requirements on local production, high levels of tariff and nontariff barriers, public ownership of large segments of banking and industry, and restrictions on capital flows, including direct foreign investment. Since the late 1970s, China has also followed a highly unorthodox two-track strategy, violating practically every rule in the book—including, most notably, securing private property rights. India, which raised its economic growth rate in the early 1980s, remained a highly protected economy well into the 1990s. Even Chile—Latin America's apparently "orthodox" standout that managed to achieve both growth and democracy—violated conventional wisdom by subsidizing its nascent export industries and taxing capital inflows.

Conversely, countries that have adhered more strictly to the orthodox structural reform agenda—most notably in Latin America—have fared less well. Since the mid-1980s, virtually all Latin American countries have opened and deregulated their economies, privatized their public enterprises, and allowed unrestricted access to foreign capital. Yet they have grown at a fraction of the pace of the heterodox reformers and have been strongly buffeted by macroeconomic instability.

The contrasting experiences of eastern Asia, China, and India suggest that the secret of poverty-reducing growth lies in creating business opportunities for domestic investors, including the poor, through institutional innovations that are tailored to local political and institutional realities. Ignoring these realities carries the risk that pro-poor policies, even when they are part of apparently sound and well-intentioned IMF and World Bank programs, will be captured by local elites.

Wealthy nations and international development organizations thus should not operate as if the right policies and institutional arrangements are the same across time and space. Yet current WTO rules on subsidies, foreign investment, and patents preclude some of the policy choices made, for example, by South Korea and Taiwan in the past, when rules under the WTO's predecessor, the General Agreement on Tariffs and Trade, were more permissive. What is more, new WTO members typically confront demands to conform their trade and industrial policies to standards that go well beyond existing WTO agreements. The new Basle II international banking standards, better fitted to banks in industrialized nations, risk making it more difficult for banks in developing countries to compete.

To be sure, not all internationally imposed economic discipline is harmful. The principle of transparency, enshrined in international trade agreements and many global financial codes, is fully consistent with policy independence, as long as governments are provided leeway with respect to actual policy content. A well-functioning international economic system does need rules. But international rules should regulate the interface between different policies and institutional regimes, not erase them.

There are signs of change in the rich world's attitude. Some donors, notably the United Kingdom and the United States, the latter with its Millennium Challenge Account, are moving away from attaching explicit, heavy conditions to their grants and loans and are instead screening applicants early to ensure that assistance will be reasonably well spent. The World Bank and other organizations are designing programs with countries in which resources are disbursed not in exchange for policy reform but on the basis of pre-agreed benchmarks of progress—be it reduced inflation, more children finishing primary school, or more completed external audits of government accounts. These changes deserve to be reinforced.

Rich countries also harm their developing counterparts in other ways, most notably with their emissions of greenhouse gases. According to the growing scientific consensus, the costs of climate change will disproportionately burden developing countries. Estimates of these costs, including reduced water availability and agricultural productivity, vary from 4 to 22 percent of poor countries' incomes. Rich nations must quickly lead the way in enacting measures beyond the Kyoto Protocol. A market-based system of tradable emissions rights offers a great opportunity to combine efficiency with equitable treatment for developing countries. Poor nations would be allotted enough emissions to ensure future growth—the same right that the industrial countries have enjoyed for centuries. Market-based trading would guarantee that pollution would be cut where costs are lowest, ensuring maximum efficiency: if costs are lower in India than in the United States, for example, the United States could pay India to pollute less, and India would be financially better off in doing so.

Positive Steps

Wealthy nations can also take positive steps to directly benefit developing countries—specifically, by taking action against corrupt leaders, assisting research and development, and enhancing global labor mobility.

The deepest challenge for countries in the poorest parts of the world, especially Africa, is governance. The African continent has been ravaged both by civil war and conflict and by rapacious leaders who have plundered the natural wealth of their nations. Corrupt rulers and their weak regimes have arguably been the single most important drag on African development. But with increasing democratization, the situation may be starting to improve. And rich countries can play a large role in the reform process, for the simple reason that corruption has two sides—demand and supply. For every leader who demands a bribe, there is usually a multinational company or a Western official offering to pay it. For every pile of illicit wealth, there is usually a European or American financial institution providing

a safe haven for the spoils. The governments of wealthy countries need to take steps to block these activities.

There have been notable strides in the right direction: the British Department for International Development helped found the Extractive Industries Transparency Initiative a few years ago, and the UN and the Organization for Economic Cooperation and Development (OECD) have been working together to address the bribery of officials in developing countries by foreigners. But these efforts do not go far enough.

Many institutions—the OECD and the U.S. government, for example-have laws against bribing foreign officials. But the regulations are often both narrow in scope and weak on enforcement. For example, a loophole in the U.S. laws ("deferred gifts") invites abuse. Some OECD rules damage transparency by protecting banks that hide ill-gotten wealth deposited by leaders of developing countries. Multinational companies and banks need to be more transparent in their dealings with poor-country governments. Preempting corruption must also be made more of a priority. One idea, first proposed by Harvard University's Michael Kremer, is for the international community to categorize certain regimes as corrupt or "odious." Companies that deal with such regimes would risk losing their claims to repayment if later on a lawful government decided to default on the debt passed down by its unlawful predecessor.

Wealthy countries can also spur technological advances that serve the specific interests of developing countries. Because poor countries lack wealthy markets, private companies in the developed world currently have little incentive to devise technologies for them. Hence a Catch-22 results: developing countries remain poor because of limited technological opportunities, while these opportunities remain difficult to create because the countries are poor.

The health sector provides a good example of the current problem. Pharmaceutical firms in industrialized nations conduct 90 percent of their research on diseases prevalent in the rich world—and that affect less than ten percent of the global population. There is little research on diseases endemic in the poorer parts of the world, because there are no market returns for such investments. Yet developing countries badly need medicine for preventing and curing diseases such as AIDS, malaria, and sleeping sickness. Beyond health care, developing countries also need enhanced crops that can better withstand heat, drought, and the salinization of irrigated land, as well as new energy sources that can reduce the rate of tropical deforestation.

Wealthy countries should spur technological advances that help the poor.

There is already a precedent for foreign research acting to undo this technological imbalance—the "green revolution." Agricultural production in the developing world was revolutionized by new varieties of wheat developed at Norman Borlaug's International Maize and Wheat Improvement Center, in Mexico, and new strains of rice cultivated at the International

Rice Research Institute, in the Philippines. Although the green revolution's impact was uneven, benefiting Asia and Latin America more than sub-Saharan Africa, the aggregate effect was nevertheless sizable. In the 1960s, southern Asia witnessed dramatic increases in productivity growth as a result of the new seed varieties. Yale University's Robert Evenson has estimated that the global return on the research on the new strains was more than 40 percent.

The international community needs to learn from this example, so that the resources of wealthy firms can be harnessed to develop important technologies for the world's poorest countries. One simple yet powerful improvement would be for rich-country governments to commit contractually to rewarding the creation of such new technologies—for example, with guaranteed purchase agreements. In effect, the international community would ensure a minimum financial return on private research undertaken for the benefit of developing countries. The Center for Global Development has devised a plan for this kind of advance-market-commitment mechanism to spark research on a malaria vaccine, at an estimated cost of $3 billion. Imagine the benefits of a $50 billion global technology-creation fund, with actual disbursement of the funds taking place over ten years or more. That $50 billion would represent only about five percent of all the financial aid that donors have promised to spend on the poor in the next decade.

Finally, to have a big impact on developing countries, trade negotiators should spend more time improving the cross-border mobility of labor—particularly of low-skill laborers, who typically are at the bottom of the pile. Current WTO negotiations on labor mobility ("mode four" in the trade jargon) focus only on high-skill labor, and even there they have made very little progress. Greater opportunities for poor and less-skilled workers to move across borders would, more than anything else, increase both the efficiency of resource allocation in the world economy and the incomes of the citizens of poor countries.

This fact is based on a simple principle of economics. The loss in efficiency due to segmented (as opposed to integrated) national markets increases with the gap in prices in these different markets, and the loss is further compounded as the gap increases. Now compare price gaps across different types of markets. In markets for goods and capital, quality- and risk-adjusted price gaps from country to country are relatively small—perhaps no more than 50–100 percent. But in labor markets, which suffer from huge border restrictions, wage gaps for similarly skilled workers are enormous—on the order of 500-1,000 percent. That is why even small relaxations of work-visa restrictions generate large income gains for workers from poor countries (as well as for the world economy). What is especially appealing is that the gains in income go directly to the workers, rather than through imperfect distribution channels (as with trade in goods) or through governments (as with aid).

Take, for example, a scheme for temporary work visas amounting to no more than three percent of the rich countries' total labor force. Under the plan, skilled and unskilled workers from poor nations would be allowed employment in rich countries for three to five years, and they would be replaced by a wave of new workers after their time ended and they returned to their home countries. Such a system would easily yield $200 billion annually for the citizens of developing nations. The returnees would also bring home far more benefits than their wages alone: experience, entrepreneurship, funds to invest, and an increased work ethic.

To make sure these benefits are realized, such a regime must generate incentives for the workers to return home. Although remittances can be an important source of income for poor families, they rarely spark or sustain long-term economic development. Designing contract labor schemes that are truly temporary is tricky, but it can be done. Unlike in previous plans, there must be clear incentives to ensure the cooperation of each party—workers, employees, and home and host governments. One possibility: withhold a portion of workers' earnings until they return home. This forced savings scheme would also guarantee that returning workers would have a sizable pool of resources to invest. In addition, there could be penalties—the reduction of worker quotas, say—for home countries with nationals who fail to return. Home governments would thus be motivated to create a hospitable domestic economic and political climate to encourage their people to come back. Of course, even with the best-designed scheme, it is inevitable that the return rate will fall short of 100 percent. Even with this consideration, however, facilitating labor mobility would bring significant gains.

Despite the obvious advantages, is a scheme like this politically feasible in developed countries? If there has been substantial trade liberalization in rich countries, it is not because it has been popular with voters, but largely because the potential beneficiaries have organized successfully and forced their agendas. Multinational firms and financial enterprises have been quick to recognize the link between enhanced market access abroad and increased profits, and they have put the issues on the negotiating agenda. Temporary labor flows, by contrast, have lacked a well-defined constituency in the developed countries. This is not because the benefits would be smaller, but because the potential beneficiaries are not as clearly identifiable. The tide has begun to turn lately as a result of labor shortages in sectors such as high-tech and seasonal agriculture, and because labor inflows would increase the tax base for financing pension benefits for retirees, thereby providing a partial solution to pension shortfalls in pay-as-you-go systems. Moreover, political realities can change—with the right leadership. In the United States, President George W. Bush has already proposed a temporary-worker program, which if designed properly could mark a useful beginning.

There are of course other ways the rich world could contribute to development. Outsiders should play an important role in preventing and resolving conflicts and humanitarian crises in developing countries. Minimizing and eliminating conflict has obvious benefits for human life—and potentially for long-term development. Just as important is stopping arms sales to dangerous governments and halting the drug and illicit diamond trades that often fund rogue groups. Another important issue is the governance of international economic institutions. The democratic deficit of these institutions has increasingly caused a corresponding legitimacy deficit. Insofar as this gap reduces the effectiveness of such organizations, rich countries would be wise to agree to reforms.

New Priorities

The international community must ask itself what really matters for development, so that good intentions can be translated into real benefits for the poorest countries. To a large extent, sustainable progress is in the hands of the poor countries themselves. Internalizing this reality is important for the developing world—and also for the wealthy one, not least because doing so would check the perennial temptation to promise results that cannot be delivered.

That said, this must be clear: developed countries should not abandon the poor to their plight. If, however, rich countries truly aim to help developing countries achieve lasting growth, they must think creatively about the development agenda. If aid is increased and delivered more efficiently and trade inequities are addressed, then the two traditional pillars of development will yield rewards. But these rewards should not be overestimated. Indeed, other courses of action—such as giving poor nations more control over economic policy, financing new development-friendly technologies, and opening up labor markets—could have more significant benefits. It is time to direct the attention of the world's wealthiest countries to other ways of helping the poorest—ways that have been for too long neglected.

NANCY BIRDSALL is President of the Center for Global Development in Washington, D.C. DANI RODRIK is Professor of International Political Economy at Harvard's John F. Kennedy School of Government. ARVIND SUBRAMANIAN is Division Chief in the Research Department of the International Monetary Fund. The views expressed here are their own and not those of their respective institutions.

Reprinted by permission of *Foreign Affairs,* July/August 2005, pp. 136–152. Copyright © 2005 by the Council on Foreign Relations, Inc.

The Utopian Nightmare

This year, economists, politicians, and rock stars in rich countries have pleaded for debt relief and aid for the world's poorest countries. It certainly sounds like the right thing to do. But utopian dreams of alleviating poverty overlook some hard facts. By promising so much, rich-world activists prolong the true nightmare of poverty.

WILLIAM EASTERLY

"The past has prepared all the materials and means in superabundance to well-feed, clothe, lodge, train, educate, employ, amuse, and govern the human race in perpetual progressive prosperity—without war, conflict, or competition between nations or individuals."

These words were not uttered by a hopeful world leader at the most recent Group of 8 (G-8) summit, or by Bono at a rock concert—but they certainly sound familiar. They were written in 1857, when British reformer Robert Owen called upon rich countries, who could "easily induce all the other governments and people to unite with them in practical measures for the general good all through futurity." Owen was laughed out of town as a utopian.

How comforted Owen would be if he were alive in 2005, when some of the most powerful and influential people seem to believe that utopia is back. American President George W. Bush has dispatched the U.S. military to spread democracy throughout the Middle East, G-8 leaders strive to end poverty and disease sometime soon, the World Bank promises development as the path to world peace, and the International Monetary Fund (IMF) is trying to save the environment. In a world where billions of people still suffer, these are certainly appealing dreams. But is this surprising new fondness for utopia just harmless, inspirational rhetoric? Are utopian ambitions the best way to help the poor-world majority?

Unfortunately, no. In reality, they hurt efforts to help the world's poor. What is utopianism? It is promising more than you can deliver. It is seeing an easy and sudden answer to long-standing, complex problems. It is trying to solve everything at once through an administrative apparatus headed by "world leaders." It places too much faith in altruistic cooperation and underestimates self-seeking behavior and conflict. It is expecting great things from schemes designed at the top, but doing nothing to solve the bigger problems at the bottom.

The Year of Living Utopianly

At the dawn of the new millennium, the United Nations realized Robert Owen's dream of bringing together the "Potentates of the Earth" in what the global organization called a Millennium Assembly. These potentates set Millennium Development Goals for 2015, calling for, among other things, dramatic reductions in poverty, child mortality, illiteracy, environmental degradation, AIDS, tuberculosis, malaria, unsafe drinking water, and discrimination against women.

But it is in 2005 that utopia seems to have made its big breakthrough into mainstream discourse. In March, Columbia University Professor Jeffrey Sachs, celebrity economist and intellectual leader of the utopians, published a book called *The End of Poverty,* in which he called for a big push of increased foreign aid to meet the Millennium Development Goals and end the miseries of the poor. Sachs proposes everything from nitrogen-fixing leguminous trees to replenish soil fertility to antiretroviral AIDS therapy, cell phones that provide up-to-date market information to health planners, rainwater harvesting, and battery-charging stations. His U.N. Millennium Project proposed a total of 449 interventions.

British Chancellor of the Exchequer Gordon Brown likewise called in January for a major increase in aid, a "Marshall Plan" for Africa. Brown was so confident he knew how to save the world's poor that he even called for borrowing against future aid commitments to finance massive increases in aid today. At the World Economic Forum in January, British Prime Minister Tony Blair called for a "big, big push" to meet the goals for 2015, and his administration issued a fat report on saving Africa in March. The World Bank and the IMF issued their own weighty document in April about meeting these goals and endorsing the call for a big push, and utopians of the world will reconvene at the U.N. World Summit in September to evaluate progress on the Millennium Development Goals. The G-8 leaders agreed on a plan in June to cancel $40 billion worth of poor-country debt to help facilitate the "push." The IMF might even tap its gold reserves to bolster the effort.

The least likely utopian is George W. Bush, who has shown less interest in vanquishing poverty, but has sought to portray the Iraq misadventure as a step toward universal democracy and world peace. As he modestly put it in his Second Inaugural Address in January 2005, "America, in this young century, proclaims liberty throughout all the world, and to all the inhabitants thereof."

These leaders frequently talk about how easy it is to help the poor. According to Brown, medicine that would prevent half of all malaria deaths costs only 12 cents per person. A bed net to prevent a child from contracting malaria costs only $4. Preventing 5 million child deaths over the next 10 years would cost just an extra $3 for each new mother, says Brown.

The emphasis on these easy solutions emerged as worry about terrorist havens in poor states intersected with the campaigning on the part of Sachs, Bono, rocker Bob Geldof, and the British Labourites. All these factions didn't seem to realize aid workers had been trying for years to end poverty.

All Talk, No Traction

We have already seen the failure of comprehensive utopian packages in the last two decades: the failure of "shock therapy" to convert the former Soviet Union from communism to capitalism and the failure of IMF/World Bank "structural adjustment" to transform nations in Africa, the Middle East, and Latin America into free-market paragons. All of these regions have suffered from poor economic growth since utopian efforts began. In the new millennium, apparently unchastened, the IMF and World Bank are trying something even more ambitious—social, political, economic, and environmental transformation of the poorest nations through Poverty Reduction Strategy Papers. These reports, which the IMF and World Bank require that governments design in consultation with the poor, are comprehensive plans to make poverty vanish in each nation. It is a little unclear how a bureaucratic document can make often undemocratic governments yield some of their power to the poor, or how it will be more successful than previous comprehensive plans that seem modest by comparison.

Indeed, we have seen the failure of what was already a "big push" of foreign aid to Africa. After 43 years and $568 billion (in 2003 dollars) in foreign aid to the continent, Africa remains trapped in economic stagnation. Moreover, after $568 billion, donor officials apparently still have not gotten around to furnishing those 12-cent medicines to children to prevent half of all malaria deaths.

After handing out $568 billion in aid, donor officials apparently still have not gotten around to furnishing those 12-cent medicines.

With all the political and popular support for such ambitious programs, why then do comprehensive packages almost always fail to accomplish much good, much less attain Utopia? They get the political and economic incentives all wrong. The biggest problem is that the rich people paying the bills do not share the same goals as the poor people they are trying to help. The wealthy have weak incentives to get the right amount of the right thing to those who need it; the poor are in no position to complain if they don't. A more subtle problem is that if all of us are collectively responsible for a big world goal, then no single agency or politician is held accountable if the goal is not met. Collective responsibility for world goals works about as well as collective farms in agriculture, and for the same reason.

To make things worse, utopian-driven aid packages have so many different goals that it weakens the accountability and probability of meeting any one goal. The conditional aid loans of the IMF and World Bank (structural adjustment loans) were notorious for their onerous policy and outcome targets, which often numbered in the hundreds. The eight Millennium Development Goals actually have 18 target indicators. The U.N. Millennium Project released a 3,751-page report in January 2005 listing the 449 intermediate steps necessary to meet those 18 final targets. Working for multiple bosses (or goals) doesn't usually work out so well; the bosses each try to get you to work on their goal and not the other boss's goal. Such employees get overworked, overwhelmed, and demoralized—not a bad description of today's working-level staff at the World Bank and other aid agencies.

Top-down strategies such as those envisioned by President Bush, Prime Minister Blair, and Bono also suffer from complex information problems, even when the incentive problems are solved. Planners at the global top simply don't know what, when, and where to give to poor people at the global bottom.

That is not to say that it is impossible to meet multiple goals for multiple customers with multiple agents. The various needs of the rich are met easily enough by a system of decentralized markets and democracy, which utilize feedback from the customers and accountability of the suppliers. Rich, middle-aged men can buy Rogaine to grow hair on their heads, while women can buy Nair to get rid of hair on their legs. No Millennium Development Goal on Body Hair was necessary. The Rogaine and Nair corporations are accountable to their customers for satisfaction. If the customers don't care for the product, the corporations go out of business; if the customers do like the product, corporations have a profit incentive to supply it. Similarly, men and women in wealthy countries can complain to democratically accountable bureaucrats and politicians if garbage collectors do not pick up their discarded Rogaine and Nair bottles. Private markets also specialize; there is no payoff for them to produce a comprehensive product that both removes hair from women's legs and transfers it to men's heads. The irony of the situation is tragically obvious: The cosmetic needs of the rich are met easily, while the much more desperate needs of the poor get lost in centralized, utopian, comprehensive planning.

Poverty Starts at Home

Free markets and democracy are far from an overnight solution to poverty—they require among many other things the bottom-up evolution of the rules of the game, including contract enforcement and fair political competition. Nor can democratic capitalism be imposed by outsiders (as the World Bank, IMF, and U.S. Army should now have learned). The evolution of markets and democracy took many decades in rich countries, and it did not happen through "big pushes" by outsiders, Millennium Development Goals, or Assemblies of World Leaders. Progress in wealthy countries arrived through piecemeal steps, gradual reforms, incremental improvements, and experimental probing, accompanied by gradually accelerating economic growth, rather than through crash programs.

The problems of the poor nations have deep institutional roots at home, where markets don't work well and politicians and civil servants aren't accountable to their citizens. That makes utopian plans even more starry-eyed, as the "big push" must ultimately rely on dysfunctional local institutions. For example, there are many weak links in the chain that leads from Gordon Brown's 12-cent malaria drug to actual health outcomes in poor countries. According to research by Deon Filmer, Jeffrey Hammer, and Lant Pritchett at the World Bank, anywhere from 30 percent to as much as 70 percent of the drugs destined for rural health clinics in several African countries disappear before reaching the clinics. According to one survey in Zimbabwe, pregnant women were reluctant to use public health clinics to give birth because nurses ridiculed them for not having better baby clothes, forced them to wash bed linens soon after delivery, and even hit them to encourage them to push the baby out faster during delivery. And Africa is not alone—nearly all poor countries have problems of corrupt and often unfriendly civil servants, as today's rich countries did earlier in their history. Researchers find that many people in poor countries bypass public health services altogether, in favor of private doctors or folk remedies.

The poor have neither the income nor political power to hold anyone accountable for meeting their needs—they are political and economic orphans. The rich-country public knows little about what is happening to the poor on the ground in struggling countries. The wealthy population mainly just wants to know that "something is being done" about such a tragic problem as world poverty. The utopian plans satisfy the "something-is-being-done" needs of the rich-country public, even if they don't serve the needs of the poor. Likewise, the Bush Doctrine soothes the fears of Americans concerned about evil tyrants, without consulting the poor-country publics on whether they wish to be conquered or democratized.

Letting total aid money stand for accomplishment is like the producers of *Catwoman,* recently voted the worst movie of 2004, bragging about the movie's $100 million production budget.

The "something-is-being-done" syndrome also explains the fixation on money spent on world poverty, rather than how to meet the needs of the poor. True, doubling the relatively trivial proportion of their income that rich Westerners give to poor Africans is a worthy enough cause. But let's not kid ourselves that spending more money on foreign aid accomplishes anything by itself. Letting total aid money stand for accomplishment is like the Hollywood producers of *Catwoman,* recently voted the worst movie of 2004, bragging about their impressive accomplishment of spending $100 million on its production.

The Way Out

Certainly not all aid efforts are futile. Instead of setting utopian goals such as ending world poverty, global leaders should simply concentrate on finding particular interventions that work. Anecdotal and some systematic evidence suggests piecemeal approaches to aid can be successful. Routine childhood immunization combined with measles vaccination in seven southern African nations cut reported measles cases from 60,000 in 1996 to 117 in 2000. Another partnership among aid donors contributed to the near eradication of guinea worm in 20 African and Asian countries where it was endemic. Abhijit Banerjee and Ruimin He at the Massachusetts Institute of Technology list examples of successful aid programs that passed rigorous evaluation: subsidies to families for education and health costs for their children, remedial teaching, uniforms and textbooks, school vouchers, deworming drugs and nutritional supplements, vaccination, HIV prevention, indoor spraying for malaria, bed nets, fertilizer, and clean water.

Of course, finding and maintaining piecemeal approaches that work well requires improving incentives for aid agencies. Better incentives might come from placing more emphasis on the independent evaluation of aid projects. Given the vast sums that are being spent, reliable evaluations remain surprisingly rare. Better incentives could also come from devising means to get more feedback from the poor people that the programs are trying to help, and holding aid agencies accountable when the feedback is negative. It seems more productive to focus on such critical problems in foreign aid rather than simply promising the rich-country public the end of world poverty.

If an aid-financed "big push" will not generate society-wide development, are things hopeless for poor countries? Fortunately, poor countries are making progress on their own, without waiting for the West to save them. The steady improvement in health and education in poor countries (except for the AIDS crisis), the market-driven growth of China and India, the movement toward democracy in Latin America and Africa (even amid continued disappointing economic growth), not to mention earlier successes such as Botswana and the East Asian Tiger economies, offer hope for homegrown and gradual development.

The outpouring of donations for last December's tsunami victims shows that Europeans and Americans have genuine compassion for those in need. Can the rich-country public call their politicians' bluff and refuse to let them get away with utopian dreams as a substitute for the hard slogging of delivering benefits to the poor? Will they hold the aid agencies accountable for getting money to those in need? Will they figure out new ways to give voice to the voiceless? If they asked, they would likely find that the poor are unmoved by utopian dreams. They probably just want those 12-cent medicines.

WILLIAM EASTERLY is professor of economics at New York University, nonresident fellow at the Center for Global Development, and author of *The Elusive Quest for Growth: Economists' Adventures and Misadventures in the Tropics* (Cambridge: MIT Press, 2001).

Africa's Village of Dreams

A small Kenyan village is the laboratory for celebrity economist Jeffrey Sachs's ambitious scheme to lift Africa out of poverty. Can big money buy the continent's poorest people a better future?

SAM RICH

Sauri must be the luckiest village in Africa. The maize is taller, the water cleaner, and the schoolchildren better fed than almost anywhere else south of the Sahara.

Just two years ago, Sauri was an ordinary Kenyan village where poverty, hunger, and illness were facts of everyday life. Now it is an experiment, a prototype "Millennium Village." The idea is simple: Every year for five years, invest roughly $100 for each of the village's 5,000 inhabitants, and see what happens.

The Millennium Villages Project is the brainchild of economist Jeffrey Sachs, the principal architect of the transition from state-owned to market economies in Poland and Russia. His critics and supporters disagree about the success of those efforts, often referred to as "shock therapy," but his role in radical economic reform in the two countries vaulted him to fame. Now he has a new mission: to end poverty in Africa.

Africa has been drip-fed aid for decades, Sachs writes in his 2005 book The End of Poverty, but it has never received enough to make a difference. What money has trickled in has been wasted on overpriced consultants and misspent on humanitarian relief and food aid, not directed at the root causes of poverty. The average African, Sachs says, is caught in a "poverty trap." He farms a small plot for himself and his family, and simply doesn't have enough assets to make a profit. As the population grows, people have less and less land, and grow poorer. When the farmer has to pay school fees for his children or buy medication, he is forced to sell the few assets he has or else go into debt. But if he had some capital, he could invest in his farm, grow enough to harvest a surplus, sell it, and start making money.

It's not this diagnosis of Africa's problems that makes Sachs's theories contentious, but his proposed solution, which might be called shock aid—huge, sudden injections of money into poor areas. Over five years, $2.75 million is being invested in the single village of Sauri, and an equal amount will be sunk into each of another 11 Millennium Village sites that are being established in 10 African countries.

The project is structured around the Millennium Development Goals that the United Nations laid out in 2000 as part of an ambitious plan to reduce global poverty. The UN wants poor countries to meet these benchmarks in health, education, and other sectors by 2015. Halfway there, most countries appear unlikely to meet these targets. However, the first two Millennium Villages—Sauri, which was so designated in 2004, and Koraro, Ethiopia, where efforts were launched in 2005—are on track to surpass them.

Sachs has persuaded Western governments, local governments, businesses, and private donors such as Hollywood stars and international financiers to foot the bill. Under the auspices of the Earth Institute, the project he heads at Columbia University, he has gathered specialists in fields from HIV/AIDS research to soil science to work out master plans for these dozen villages.

Never before has so much money been invested in an African community as small as Sauri. If Sauri succeeds, it could usher in a new era for development in Africa. The hope of Sachs as well as those who head the United Nations Millennium Project, with which he has partnered, is that by 2015, when the Millennium Development Goals still seem far away, these villages will be seen as models whose success can be duplicated across Africa. But if Sauri fails, the West may become yet more disillusioned with aid, and perhaps even reduce what it presently contributes. This is a defining moment in the aid debate.

Last year I paid a visit to Sauri, this village on which so much appears to hang. I'd just finished reading The End of Poverty, and I'll admit I was skeptical about the soundness of spending vast amounts of money in a single small village. But most of all, I was looking for early indications of what this exhibit in the aid argument might show.

I was carried on a bicycle taxi through the dusty streets of Kisumu, Kenya, past vendors selling barbecued maize in front of shacks cobbled together from tin cans beaten flat and nailed onto wooden struts. Occasionally I could make out the faded logo of the U.S. Agency for International Development on the rusted shell of an old vegetable-oil can. As I neared my destination I caught a glimpse of Lake Victoria's shore, where vendors in stalls sell fried tilapia and chunks of boiled maize meal.

Inside a concrete compound at the headquarters of the Millennium Villages Project, development experts sat at computer monitors in glass-walled offices. As I entered, the receptionist at the front desk was on the phone: "You need notebooks? . . . How many? . . .Three hundred, is that all? Right, I'll order them for you tomorrow. You'll get them in a few days."

I've spent the last five years in Africa, where I've worked with outfits ranging from big international nongovernmental organizations to tiny one-man-band agencies, but I've never seen an order made as breezily as this. At most NGOs, the procurement even of stationery entails filling out forms in triplicate and long delays.

There was a tour leaving on the 30-mile trip to Sauri the next day. I imagined trekking around the model village with one of Sachs's celebrity protégés, perhaps Angelina Jolie or Bono, or maybe a millionaire altruist the likes of George Soros, so I was slightly disappointed to find myself at the appointed hour in a Toyota Land Cruiser beside a couple of unglamorous American professors on a brief visit to advise the project.

The air conditioning purred as our driver bumped the Toyota over potholes on the single-lane highway that runs inland from the Kenyan coast through the capital, Nairobi, toward Uganda. Sauri itself lies just off the road, some 200 miles from Nairobi, and the sight of tall, strong stalks of maize was the first indication that we'd arrived. Women in brightly colored headscarves and second-hand clothes imported from America and Europe sold homemade snacks and Coca-Cola from wooden shacks dotting the sides of the red-brown dirt road. The grass behind them was a lush green, giving way to a wall of maize plants beneath a sky heavy with the clouds that hang in the rainy season.

Our four-by-four negotiated footpaths through the maize fields and under acacias. The first stop was Sauri's health clinic, which provided stark reminders of the depth of Sauri's problems and the benefits money can bring. The nurse there told us that each household received mosquito nets at the start of the project, when a sample test of villagers revealed that more than 40 percent had malaria. Now that figure has dropped to 20 percent. Malaria, a debilitating and sometimes deadly disease, is being treated free of charge with Coartem, an expensive drug unavailable in most parts of Kenya. The clinic provides condoms and Depo-Provera contraceptive injections, and there are plans to introduce tests for

HIV, thought to afflict one in four villagers, and to administer anti-retroviral therapy. Outside the clinic was a covered waiting area furnished with benches. It wasn't big enough to accommodate the burden of the clinic's success: a queue of 50 people waiting to see the facility's sole doctor. More than 200 patients arrive for treatment every day. Most walk from villages miles away.

Minutes later, we arrived at the green courtyard of Bar Sauri Primary School. The red-brick buildings with holes for doors and windows house classrooms for more than 600 children. One of the buildings lacked a roof. The teacher seemed embarrassed to tell us that it had blown off in a storm just days before. He knew roofs don't blow off schoolrooms where we come from.

But he was enthusiastic about the school's innovative feeding program. Ten percent of the village's harvest goes toward school lunches for the children, he said. In addition, the Millennium Villages Project buys fruit, meat, and fish to provide students with necessary vitamins and protein. The project has built upon Sauri's own school feeding program, established five years ago for students in the top year. Now the entire student body receives nourishing meals. Since Sauri began the program, its school ranking has risen from just inside the top 200 in the district into the top 10. Improved nutrition means that the students can concentrate better, and they're also healthier and more energetic. Sauri won everything at the regional sports day, the teacher told us. With a proud smile, he recalled, "And not one of our children fainted!"

The next stop was the information technology center. It was just a shack with a nice sign on the outside and a few books inside. One day, when the village is connected to the electricity grid, computers will be bought and Internet access provided. Bridging the digital divide may seem a low priority when Sauri has so many pressing problems. But textbooks are a rare commodity, and an Internet connection will allow students access to unlimited information; their parents will be able to obtain up-to-date reports on crop prices, pesticides, and fertilizers.

We returned to the Land Cruiser and set off to visit another ramshackle brick building with a crude dirt floor. Here, the dozen men and women who constitute the village's agriculture committee make decisions key to the success of the whole project. Improved harvests can support the school feeding program and provide income for farmers. Successful farming should enable the village to continue to grow after the five-year project finishes in 2009.

The project's major contribution to agriculture has been the purchase of fertilizer to increase maize production. Maize, which has been grown for as long as anyone can remember, is the main subsistence crop here, as it is in large parts of Africa. Synthetic fertilizers are far too expensive for the average farmer, but in Sauri the project spends $50,000 a year on them. The chairman of the committee said the maize harvest has increased two and a half times as a result. Now the question is how to store the surplus so that villagers can sell it in the dry season when prices are high.

At the tour's final stop, the professors stayed in the Land Cruiser to apply more sunscreen. Outside, I found a cement block with a tap jutting out of it. A water and sanitation expert at the site explained that this was an outlet for a filtered spring, and that purified drinking water is supplied to 50 taps around the village. In neighboring villages, long queues form by a single borehole that slops out murky water, which must be boiled over a charcoal stove before it is potable.

The tour over, the professors drove off, but I decided to stay. Clearly, the Millennium Villages Project has achieved some great things, but I didn't feel I'd seen the full picture. As the light fell, I walked toward the guesthouse by the main highway. A woman was handing out cobs of corn to some kids, and offered me one too. We sat on a bench to eat it and watched the steady stream of lorries roll by, carrying imported goods from the Kenyan port of Mombasa into Uganda, 40 miles up the road. The returning lorries moved faster: They were usually empty. None of them stopped in Sauri.

There are two schools of thought about development. The "macro" school, with its emphasis on national-level economic policy, aims at developing an entire society by changing government policies and encouraging investment. This is often called a top-down approach, because people at the top are making decisions for the benefit of those at the grass roots. This is the work of many economists and other academic specialists as well as organizations such as the World Bank and the International Monetary Fund.

Then there's the "micro" school, oriented toward community development, which advocates working with one group of people at a time, trying to solve particular problems by providing training and minimal investment. This bottom-up approach is the domain of most NGOs and charities.

Though these two schools have the same general objectives, their adherents rarely interact and seemingly speak different languages. What's interesting about the Millennium Villages Project is that it is essentially a micro project run by experts from the macro school, such as Sachs.

But Sachs is no ordinary economist. His charisma and fundraising ability are legendary. He convinced Bono, the lead singer of U2 and a well-known activist in his own right, to write the introduction to The End of Poverty. In it, Bono describes traveling with Sachs as the economist enthused about development. Bono modestly portrays himself as the smart, clean-cut geek hanging on the words of the wild-haired creative guy.

It was Sachs's influence and initiative that spawned the Millennium Villages Project. In 2004, after a visit to Sauri as a special adviser to Kofi Annan, then secretary-general of the UN, he wrote an open letter in which he outlined a plan of action for the village that he had developed with the Earth Institute and the UN Millennium Project. He called on donors to support the plan: "The rich world needs to wake from its slumber."

Even Sachs's harshest critic, New York University professor and former World Bank economist William Easterly, has described Sachs as "the economist as rock star." But Sachs's fan base doesn't rescue his theories, in Easterly's opinion. He points out that the idea of investing vast sums of money to close the poverty gap in Africa was tried in the 1950s and '60s, and failed. He says that Sachs's book peddles an "administrative central plan" in which the UN secretary-general "would supervise and coordinate thousands of international civil servants and technocratic experts to solve the problems of every poor village and city slum everywhere." The solutions Easterly favors instead include measures designed to improve accountability and reduce corruption, and specific investments aimed at tackling one problem at a time. In his eyes, Sachs is a utopian. Sachs dismisses Easterly as a "can't do" economist.

But economists aren't Sachs's only critics; others within the micro school he wants to win over are asking questions, too. They want to make sure communities such as Sauri are not simply passive recipients of handouts from donors and lectures from experts, but are actively involved in making decisions about their own development. This is what they mean when they talk about empowerment. Any development project can bring temporary benefits. The trick is to ensure that a community is not enjoying a honeymoon that ends when the project does, but is making changes on which it can continue to build. They want sustainability.

When I tried to ask questions on the tour about these issues, I received some evasive answers. Millennium Villages staffers and Sauri residents seemed reluctant to criticize the project. This is a common problem in areas that receive a good deal of aid: Workers on the project don't want to criticize their employers, and villagers don't want to bite the hand that's feeding them. Would the crop yields and health care in Sauri be better in 10 years' time? Did the villagers believe the changes the project had bought were valuable? Would they be able to keep them up when the money ran out, and did they want to? I decided to spend a few more days in Sauri and talk to the villagers themselves.

I crossed the highway and walked into the village to meet one of Sachs's graduate students, a researcher from Columbia University. When I caught up with him, he was wearing a yellow T-shirt that said "Jeff Sachs Is My Home Boy." I'd run into him earlier in the day, and he had offered to take me to the home of a Sauri resident, Ben Bunde.

When we arrived at Bunde's house, he and his friends were seated under a tree on wooden benches that seemed to grow from the soil in which they were planted. The group was hunched over bits of scrap paper densely covered in hand-writing. They had decided to start up a publication called The Sauri Times, and the Millennium Villages Project had helped fund the first print run.

"There are so many stories to be told about Sauri," Bunde said. "The problem is which ones to tell."

When I asked him how Sauri had changed in the last two years, he leaned back, laughing, and said, "The girls have better haircuts now." There are more hair salons, he said, warming to his subject, and the girls are all getting braids. For the first time, people are selling French fries on the side of the highway. People are more generous, too. "A funeral is a big event in the village, with lots of food. In the old days we would get rice and beans, but now we get meat and soup too." There was so much excitement when the project started that mothers named their babies "Millennium."

I mentioned the elections that took place at the start of the project. Committees of about a dozen villagers for health, education, agriculture, and other key sectors were elected on the advice of project coordinators. The committees' role is to decide how the Millennium Villages money should be spent, and to empower Sauri as a result. But Bunde didn't seem to have confidence in the elections or the committees.

"Few people took part, and they didn't know who to vote for. . . . What would Sachs say if he knew about the witchcraft that took place before the elections? The Kalanya were scaring people to vote for them. In Kenya, we have the Kikuyu factor—the Kikuyu are the dominant tribe. Here in Sauri, we have the Kalanya factor. The Kalanya are the dominant clan. Kalanya elders head all the committees, and yet many of them are uneducated and illiterate. And yet here," he said, gesturing at the young journalists around him, "we have some clever, educated people."

Bunde argued that "clanism" was fostering nepotism and other forms of favoritism. As an example, he cited one of the buildings at the new clinic, which was so badly constructed that it has been condemned. And he hinted at other forms of corruption. There were rumors that the clinic was charging patients from outside Sauri. Civil servants and police in neighboring villages were allegedly using their influence to get their children into Sauri's school.

There was fighting both within and between committees, he continued, and this had delayed development in the village. In the early days of the project, he said, Sachs had ceremoniously handed over the keys to a truck that was to be used to take goods to market and as an ambulance. But because of power struggles over it, the truck hadn't been used or seen in the village since.

Bunde said that there wasn't enough education of Sauri's people at the start of the project. After receiving free fertilizer and mosquito nets, some villagers sold them to people in the surrounding communities the very next day and then conspired to get more fertilizer and nets.

When I asked if he planned to put any of these stories in The Sauri Times, he shook his head. "No, we don't want the donors to pull out!"

In the end, Bunde questioned whether outside experts really understand the problems in Sauri. While life had improved in the years since the Millennium Village experiment began,

Bunde wondered fearfully what will happen when the project ends, "because we have become so dependent." Change, he said, needs to be led from inside the village. "As we say here, only the wearer knows where the shoe pinches."

At breakfast the next morning in the courtyard of the guesthouse, I ran into one of the project coordinators, who agreed to chat with me if he could remain anonymous.

On the tour, our guide had emphasized that the elected committees make all the decisions about how Sauri is run and how aid money is spent. I asked the coordinator if there was tension between what the project's representatives wanted to do with the money and what the committees wanted.

"Yes," he said. "We provided the inputs like the fertilizers, and so the committees just sat back. There were mistakes made on entry to Sauri. There was not enough sensitization. . . . Now the problem is [that] the project is moving so fast, the committees can't keep up."

Lack of education, or "sensitization," both within the committees and in the village generally, has caused problems, the project coordinator observed. The villagers often disappoint their benefactors. When project officials want to implement a change, they advise the committees. But the committees sometimes move slowly, because there's not enough support for a particular proposal either within the committee or in the village as a whole. In the surrounding villages to which the project has been expanded, there has been more education, but he doubted that there has been enough.

The basic inputs of the project have also changed. In Sauri, he said, the amount of fertilizer given to farmers was based on plot size. But this scheme was contrary to traditional community practice because its effects were thought to exacerbate existing inequalities and were often divisive. At the new Millennium Villages Project sites, each farmer will be given the same amount of fertilizer.

From Sauri, I walked half a mile down some railway tracks to the neighboring village of Yala, passing the old, dilapidated train station. Even though only one train passes by a week, the station's colonial-era ornamental gardens are still tended with care.

The local government is based in Yala, and I wanted to find out how its members viewed the new Sauri. A hand-painted sign pointed to a small, spare room, where the paint peeled under a corrugated-iron roof. There I found Richard Odunga, a resident of Sauri and Yala's town clerk. His secretary sat next door in front of a typewriter.

Odunga owns a big plot, uses the fertilizer, and has sold a lot of maize. When I asked him if he'd been able to save money, he sighed. He has been forced to support family members who live outside of Sauri. They ask him for help with school fees and medication, and have drained all his maize profits.

He said relations between the local government and project organizers have been strained. "At first, there was no consultation with government. Later, they realized we were a stakeholder and they needed our assistance." Project leaders initially wanted to build not just a clinic but a hospital in Sauri, before the government pointed out that there was already a hospital just a few kilometers away. The project wanted help from government in electrifying Sauri and grading its roads. Two years on, work has started on the roads, but there is still no connection to the national power grid.

Odunga wondered what will remain after the project finishes. When I asked if the community had started contributing to the project yet, he said, "There is some cost sharing, but it's at a minimum level." Who will pay for the clinic after the project ends? he asked. But villagers will at least benefit from the training they've received: "Skills. That's the most important thing."

A couple of days later, I met a senior official working on the Millennium Villages Project for the UN who has a background in community development, as Sachs, he noted, does not. This official, too, would only talk if he were not identified.

The Millennium Villages Project, he said, "has made all the classic development mistakes. . . . If you give away tons of fertilizer, it's predictable that much of it will end up on the open market. If you put millions [of dollars] in a small place, you're going to have problems."

Encouraging farmers to grow maize is the wrong strategy, he argued. "It just means you move from being food insecure for 11 months of the year to food insecure for just nine months of the year."

Growing only maize year after year depletes the soil. It's also a high-risk strategy, he said, as the entire crop may fail. The price of maize has dropped dramatically around Sauri, he noted, as the village's crop yields have improved and supply has increased. Maize is a subsistence crop that has fed Sauri families for years, but, he contended, its price is too low to make it a cash crop. He is trying to push the project to spend more time touting vegetable crops that fetch good prices at market, such as onions, tomatoes, and cabbages.

In this official's opinion, the project could be more effective if it pushed for some macroeconomic changes, rather than concentrate all its efforts in the village. For instance, farmers in Kenya don't buy fertilizer because it costs three times as much as it does in Europe, he said. If the Kenyan government eased taxes and import duties on fertilizer, "a lot more farmers would buy it."

Many UN officials I spoke to criticized the Sauri project, but none would speak openly. It was clear that dissenting voices were not welcomed, as an e-mail I received from one made plain: "Unfortunately I'm already in a lot of trouble for talking about what every good scientist should be talking about. The current environment is one in which scientists can no longer speak openly and expect to keep their jobs."

The Millennium Villages Project is being launched in locations in Kenya, Ethiopia, Ghana, Malawi, Mali, Nigeria, Senegal, Tanzania, Rwanda, and Uganda. Each cluster of villages will be transformed thanks to the investment of nearly $3 million over five years. The sheer scale of investment in the Millennium Villages Project is difficult to convey. The sums involved are not just bigger than those for other community development projects in Africa; they are hundreds of times bigger.

But is this level of investment really plausible for all of Africa? In Kenya alone, aid from abroad would need to increase 10 times, from $100 million to $1 billion, to blanket the whole of the country with the amounts equivalent to what is spent in Millennium Villages.

Sachs says that if the West spent the 0.7 percent of its gross national product on aid set as a goal by the Monterrey Consensus in 2002, this could start to become a reality. This assumes that all the additional aid would go to Africa, and not, as is often the case, to projects in more developed countries such as those of the former Soviet bloc. Currently, only a few countries, such as Denmark, Sweden, and the Netherlands, are reaching the 0.7 percent mark; the United States gives about 0.2 percent of GNP in aid. It justifies its contribution by pointing out that it's still giving more in absolute terms than any other nation—in fact, it gives more than the world's next two biggest economies, Germany and Japan, put together.

The scale of the Millennium Villages Project makes it seem a different breed entirely from most micro programs, which go into a village with modest funds to achieve a specific goal. They may give a farmer a single cow bred in the West for its high milk yield, and train him to look after it. The farmer passes his first calves on to a neighbor and trains him, and gradually the benefits extend to the wider community. The idea is to create a cycle of development that doesn't require extra money. The progress in this kind of program may be slow, but it's much easier to pinpoint what's working and what's not, to figure out why, and to adapt as necessary.

Sauri has achieved more than such projects could ever reasonably hope to, but it's not yet a model village. Instead, Sauri remains Africa in microcosm. All the fundamental problems that exist in Africa still exist in Sauri; in some eases, these problems are magnified.

The village's political framework is confused. Sauri now has two governments in conflict with each other: the committees and the existing local government. The project's committees have introduced a new layer of bureaucracy, and their vastly superior resources have weakened the local government's power. Further, committees are accused of working against each other, and of being corrupt, slow, and unwieldy. Their representatives are said to have been chosen for their ethnic ties and standing in society, rather than their political acumen. As in many parts of Africa, it's unclear which decisions are made by government and which by donors.

Sauri faces the same economic challenges it always has. Most farmers are still growing subsistence crops and depleting their soils. They could instead be growing crops for market or investing in livestock. Low-cost improvements in farming techniques, such as the use of manure and other organic methods that are more sustainable in the long run, are only beginning to be promoted. Growth will be slow because taxation, bad roads, and a lack of electricity need to be addressed at a national level.

Villagers are clearly enjoying better health as a result of the project. The simple extension of a school feeding program has improved students' performance and could serve as a model for schools across Africa. The clinic has transformed health care: The incidence of malaria has decreased, family planning has increased, and soon anti-retroviral treatments will be available to people with HIV and AIDS. But when the project ends, the funds for the clinic and the doctor, the mosquito nets, and the anti-retrovirals will dry up. In three years, the Kenyan government will face the difficult choice between continuing to fund one model clinic in Sauri or cutting the budget considerably.

And Sauri still must contend with the divisions that are typical throughout Kenya: between ethnic groups, men and women, young and old. Witchcraft was employed to influence the outcome of the elections. The practice of wife inheritance remains common, indicative of a wider set of gender issues. These kinds of cultural problems can't be solved with handouts, but only with subtler interventions.

This is not to say that Sauri cannot change, or that investment in the village is wasted. But if Sauri is to become a useful model for development on a bigger scale, and not just another development expert's white elephant, Sachs and others working on the project must acknowledge that they are still learning about Africa. Sauri is not yet a success.

Lasting changes in Sauri will come about not through distribution of commodities, but through education for children and training for adults. To put it another way, give a man a mosquito net, and when it rips, he'll come and ask for another one. But show him how using a mosquito net benefits his health and how it will save him money on medication in the long run, and he might just go out and buy one for himself.

SAM RICH is a development consultant who has worked on community and international development projects in East Africa for nongovernmental organizations, governments, and the World Bank.

Today's Golden Age of Poverty Reduction

The story the World Bank and other agencies don't want you to know.

SURJIT S. BHALLA

Have we just witnessed history? The last twenty years have been good for growth in the developing countries and have been very good for poverty reduction—indeed, the best ever. More than a billion people have been moved out of poverty, defined according to the dollar a day measure. From about 1.3 billion poor in 1980, poverty in 2000 was close to 500 million. In no other period in history has the number of poor people declined, let alone declined by such historic proportions.

Calculations of poverty reduction go back to at least 1820, but calculations of the decline in the number of poor are unfair to history. Because of health improvements, life expectancy has improved enormously over the last two hundred years. This has enhanced population growth for all levels of income, poor and rich alike. With each succeeding generation, reductions in poverty have become more difficult. A better index, therefore, of historical performance is the fraction of people in poverty. Chart 1 compares the pace of poverty reduction since 1820. The share of population in absolute poverty has declined at a rate of approximately 4 percentage points every twenty years for the 130-year period, 1820 to 1950. Between 1950 and 1980, the pace increased to a rate of 14 percentage points for each twenty years. But the golden age for the poor has been the period post-1980. During this age, the record is of an astonishingly large 20 percentage point plus decline.

What happened? In large part, Asia, the continent given up for "dead" by most economists, came alive. (Gunnar Myrdal won a Nobel prize for his pessimistic work on Asian poverty, *Asian Drama: An Inquiry into the Poverty of Nations*.) More accurately, the two population giants, India and China, reversed course on economic policy. The China conversion story is well known. Not as well known is the fact that until about 1980, the Indian policy regime was as "controlled" as China. So both economies changed at approximately the same time (1978–1980); both started to open up, reduce tariffs, and embrace markets. The rest is history. In 1980, the poverty head count ratio in India and China was 50 and 60 percent, respectively. By 2000,

the poverty ratios in both economies were in the range 10 to 25 percent. The number of people moved out of poverty in these two countries alone was about a billion. This is history—an upliftment of 20 percent of the developing world's population. That is approximately the entire population share of the two other continents where poor people reside, Latin America and sub-Saharan Africa.

> **The golden age for the poor has been the period post-1980. The record is of an astonishingly large 20 percentage point plus decline . . . This is history.**

What has made this possible? Though detractors remain, there were at least three important developments in the world economy: first, more than 1.5 billion individuals in the developing world witnessed an increase in political liberties, as measured by Freedom House. This means that governments today have a lesser chance of survival if they pursue anti-growth policies. For some time now, the confusing "Confucian" hypothesis has prevailed in the world, positing that East Asian economies such as Korea and China grew fast because they had able dictatorships (an oxymoron). This correlation conveniently ignores the fact that most African and Latin American countries also had dictatorships and have not grown particularly fast. Political liberties enhance growth prospects because they limit the tenure of bad governments.

The second important development has been in terms of reversing ostrich-like closed tendencies. Tariff rates in developing economies are less than a third of the levels prevailing in 1980, and the absolute level of such tariffs today is less than 10 percent. This means that industrialists have to earn profits the old-fashioned way—by being efficient. Less chances for bribery of politicians and bureaucrats means better allocation of resources. Low tariffs means pressure from international and domestic consumers for higher efficiency and lower prices that lead to higher growth. How bad was it before and how much has policy changed? Well, the magnitude of change can be appreciated from the fact that as late as 1991, India proudly announced that the peak tariff rate had been reduced to 180 percent!

As late as 1991, India proudly announced that the peak tariff rate had been reduced to 180 percent!

The increased efficiency in production leads to increased trade, which in turn leads to faster growth, and the cycle continues. This is the third happy happening in poor countries. The share of trade in developing economies expanded; this share (fraction of GDP accounted for by exports and imports) was 20 percent in 1960, 30 percent in 1980 and 53 percent in 2000.

Developing (and all) world income inequality not only has improved over the last twenty years, but done so for the first time ever.

It is believed that history would have been even better if somehow the poor countries had been able to control population growth. This belief no longer reflects the recent transformation. A centuries-old phenomenon, associated with all countries, is that with development, fertility rates (number of children ever born per woman) decline, and labor force participation

of women increases, and both fuel each other. This is indeed what has happened in China. India, and most poor Bangladesh is today less than three, and in China and Iran less than two. The population growth rate in India today is close to 1.4 percent annually. The new story in the world today is not population growth, but the great fertility decline. It is coming soon to your favorite poor country.

What's Wrong with Markets?

The "practice" of markets has been the major factor behind historical rates of poverty reduction. But the practice of capitalism and/or enhancement of markets is widely considered a four-letter word (according to those professing political correctness).

The basic complaint against capitalism or "markets" is that while it can and does generate extra growth, it does leave a lot to be desired in terms of inequality. The much-too-often-heard and erroneous refrain is that under capitalism, the rich get richer and the poor get poorer. But like the invisible hand, this deemed politically correct adversity is nowhere to be seen. Indeed, the data are consistent with the alternate explanation—growth is good for poverty reduction. An old truism, but some-what surprisingly, one that needs to be emphasized every second day.

Just last year, the two leading development institutions in the world came out with reports on the importance of inequality change for reduction of poverty. The presumption, and conclusion, was that inequality deterioration had led to considerable welfare loss for the poor, i.e., if inequality had not worsened, world poverty would have been reduced more. The first part of the statement is wrong—developing (and all) world income inequality not only has improved over the last twenty years, but done so for the first time ever (Chart 2). Over the long 130-year period from 1820 to 1980, developing world inequality increased (consumption inequality peaks in 1980); only in

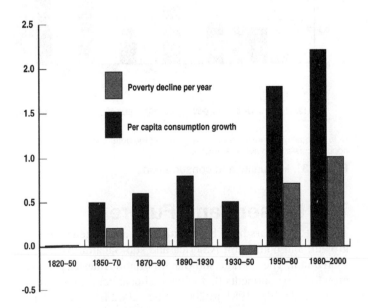

Note: The figures represent annual averages.

Figure 1 Consumption growth and the pace of poverty reduction.

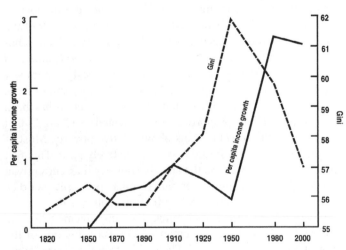

Note: The Gini represents the level of inequality in the designated years; per capita growth is average annual growth between two periods.

Figure 2 Developing world: Inequality and per capita income growth.

the last twenty years has it shown some decline. Not incoincidentally, inequality started declining when average per capita growth in the poorest countries (such as India and China) started exceeding average growth in the rich countries around 1980.

Political liberties enhance growth prospects because they limit the tenure of bad governments.

Yet another (and more heuristic) indicator of inequality change is the excess growth experienced by the bottom 40 percent of the population. When this "excess" growth is negative, inequality has worsened. For example, between 1950 and 1980, average per capita consumption growth in developing economies was 1.8 percent annually: the bottom 40 percent had an average growth rate of 1.6 percent per year. So excess growth for this group was –0.2 percent per year (Chart 3). But globalization during the 1980–2000 period (the one severely criticized for worsening inequality) actually shows the poor reflecting a higher growth than average; 3.1 percent annually versus 2.2 percent, an excess growth of 0.9 percent per year.

The new story in the world today is not population growth, but the great fertility decline. It is coming soon to your favorite poor country.

Fast poverty reduction and improving inequality is not the news one obtains from a cursory perusal of major international newspapers, or the outpourings of international organizations dedicated to the removal of absolute poverty. The chorus: poverty reduction, especially in the last twenty years, has been a failure. Indeed, according to the World Bank, the number of poor in the world barely budged between 1.2 billion in 1990 and 1.1 billion in 2001. This deemed lack of poverty reduction has been the mantra (see Joseph Stiglitz's book, *Globalization and Its Discontents*), and the cause has been variously but mostly attributed to "capitalistic growth" models. History shows these conclusions as false. In my view, poverty reduction has been of such gargantuan proportions (as indicated in Chart 1) that it is time for the world to think about relative poverty. Most of the present poor, and future poor, are relatively poor. This fact should be recognized, and the absolute poverty line, currently at $1.08 1993 purchasing power parity dollars per capita per day, needs to be raised to about $2 (2005 PPP) dollars a day.

Given this historical and miraculous improvement for the world's poor, the question remains: Why isn't this one of the biggest stories of our time? There are several reasons, some good, some perverse, for this disconnect between rock band political correctness and economic reality. It could be argued that by constantly downplaying the success in poverty reduction, the poor of the world would actually gain more resources

to redress their poverty. Extended, this argument means that agencies such as the World Bank can actually lobby the rich governments to give more money for poverty alleviation.

The average sub-Saharan/Latin America per capita growth (two continents that witnessed near zero growth for the long two decades 1981 to 2002) since 2002 has been over 2.5 percent annually.

Extended further, the assumption is that aid monies will be "correctly" allocated to the needy in poor countries. Even if all this is done, the extra money gained due to drawing attention to the world's poor by down-playing poverty achievements has still not reached the poor. That involves the assumption that developing country governments will actually deliver money meant for the poor to the poor. Anybody who buys this sequence of probabilities is "knowledge-proof" about the political reality in the developing world. There maybe such buyers of snake oil in rich countries, but developing country practitioners know better. As far back as 1985, the then-Indian Prime Minister Rajiv Gandhi announced that only 15 percent of every rupee meant for the poor ever reached the poor, the reality has only worsened since then.

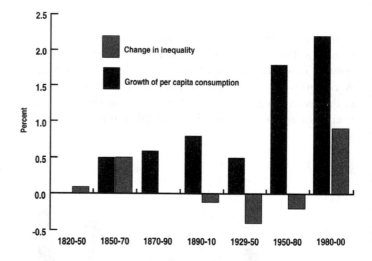

Note: Inequality change is the excess growth of the bottom 40 percent of the population relative to average growth.

Figure 3 Inequality and consumption.

The Present and Future

The last few years have been witness to a resurgence in world growth; and both Latin America and sub-Saharan Africa have shared in it. The average sub-Saharan/Latin America per capita growth (two continents that witnessed near zero growth for the long two decades 1981 to 2002) since 2002 has been over 2.5 percent annually; for Asian (and eastern European economies), the growth has been in excess of 6 percent annually! For developed economies the growth has been close to 2 percent. Surely, this is the golden age for poverty reduction.

But such an age is not recognized by most analysts and most definitely not by international organizations like the World Bank and United Nations. The question does arise: was the growth made possible by state interventions or by the "capitalistic market"? Phrased differently, what are the lessons for Africa from all of this history? Is it Communism that did it? Or was it dictatorship? Or was it enlightened state intervention as argued by some? In all of this heartburning, let us also not forget about the "bad" globalization period—so "bad" that it has helped move close to a billion people out of poverty in the last twenty sweet years. The growth did it, not government intervention, benign or otherwise. And growth for the poor was helped by a decline in world inequality, as poor countries grew faster than rich countries.

Sources

Bhalla, Surjit S. 2002. *Imagine There's No Country: Poverty. Inequality and Growth in the Era of Globalization.* Institute for International Economics.

Bhalla, Surjit S. 2006. *Second Among Equals: The Middle Class Kingdoms of India and China.* Forthcoming.

Bourguignon, François, and Christian Morrisson. 2002. Inequality Among World Citizens: 1820–1992. *American Economic Review,* September, 727–44.

SURJIT S. BHALLA is the head of the hedge fund Oxus Research & Investments in New Delhi, India. He has previously worked for the World Bank, Goldman Sachs and Deutsche Bank.

From *The International Economy,* Spring 2006, pp. 22–25, 58. Copyright © 2006 by The International Economy. Reprinted by permission.

Development as Poison
Rethinking the Western Model of Modernity

Stephen A. Marglin

*A*t the beginning of Annie Hall, Woody Allen tells a story about two women returning from a vacation in New York's Catskill Mountains. They meet a friend and immediately start complaining: "The food was terrible," the first woman says, "I think they were trying to poison us." The second adds, "Yes, and the portions were so small." That is my take on development: the portions are small, and they are poisonous. This is not to make light of the very real gains that have come with development. In the past three decades, infant and child mortality have fallen by 66 percent in Indonesia and Peru, by 75 percent in Iran and Turkey, and by 80 percent in Arab oil-producing states. In most parts of the world, children not only have a greater probability of surviving into adulthood, they also have more to eat than their parents did—not to mention better access to schools and doctors and a prospect of work lives of considerably less drudgery.

Nonetheless, for those most in need, the portions are indeed small. Malnutrition and hunger persist alongside the tremendous riches that have come with development and globalization. In South Asia almost a quarter of the population is undernourished and in sub-Saharan Africa, more than a third. The outrage of anti-globalization protestors in Seattle, Genoa, Washington, and Prague was directed against the meagerness of the portions, and rightly so.

But more disturbing than the meagerness of development's portions is its deadliness. Whereas other critics highlight the distributional issues that compromise development, my emphasis is rather on the terms of the project itself, which involve the destruction of indigenous cultures and communities. This result is more than a side-effect of development; it is central to the underlying values and assumptions of the entire Western development enterprise.

The White Man's Burden

Along with the technologies of production, healthcare, and education, development has spread the culture of the modern West all over the world, and thereby undermined other ways of seeing, understanding, and being. By culture I mean something more than artistic sensibility or intellectual refinement. "Culture" is used here the way anthropologists understand the term, to mean the totality of patterns of behavior and belief that characterize a specific society. Outside the modern West, culture is sustained through community, the set of connections that bind people to one another economically, socially, politically, and spiritually. Traditional communities are not simply about shared spaces, but about shared participation and experience in producing and exchanging goods and services, in governing, entertaining and mourning, and in the physical, moral, and spiritual life of the community. The culture of the modern West, which values the market as the primary organizing principle of life, undermines these traditional communities just as it has undermined community in the West itself over the last 400 years.

The West thinks it does the world a favor by exporting its culture along with the technologies that the non-Western world wants and needs. This is not a recent idea. A century ago, Rudyard Kipling, the poet laureate of British imperialism, captured this sentiment in the phrase "White Man's burden," which portrayed imperialism as an altruistic effort to bring the benefits of Western rule to uncivilized peoples. Political imperialism died in the wake of World War II, but cultural imperialism is still alive and well. Neither practitioners nor theorists speak today of the white man's burden—no development expert of the 21st century hankers after clubs or golf courses that exclude local folk from membership. Expatriate development experts now work with local people, but their collaborators are themselves formed for the most part by Western culture and values and have more in common with the West than they do with their own people. Foreign advisers—along with their local collaborators—are still missionaries, missionaries for progress as the West defines the term. As our forbears saw imperialism, so we see development.

There are in fact two views of development and its relationship to culture, as seen from the vantage point of the modern West. In one, culture is only a thin veneer over a common, universal behavior based on rational calculation and maximization of individual self interest. On this view, which is probably the view of most economists, the Indian subsistence-oriented peasant is no less calculating, no less competitive, than the US commercial farmer.

Cultural imperialism is still alive and well. . . . Foreign advisers ... are still missionaries, missionaries for progress as the West defines the term. As our forebears saw imperialism, so we see development.

There is a second approach which, far from minimizing cultural differences, emphasizes them. Cultures, implicitly or explicitly, are ranked along with income and wealth on a linear scale. As the West is richer, Western culture is more progressive, more developed. Indeed, the process of development is seen as the transformation of backward, traditional, cultural practices into modern practice, the practice of the West, the better to facilitate the growth of production and income.

What these two views share is confidence in the cultural superiority of the modern West. The first, in the guise of denying culture, attributes to other cultures Western values and practices. The second, in the guise of affirming culture, posits an inclined plane of history (to use a favorite phrase of the Indian political psychologist Ashis Nandy) along which the rest of the world is, and ought to be, struggling to catch up with us. Both agree on the need for "development." In the first view, the Other is a miniature adult, and development means the tender nurturing by the market to form the miniature Indian or African into a full-size Westerner. In the second, the Other is a child who needs structural transformation and cultural improvement to become an adult.

Both conceptions of development make sense in the context of individual people precisely because there is an agreed-upon standard of adult behavior against which progress can be measured. Or at least there was until two decades ago when the psychologist Carol Gilligan challenged the conventional wisdom of a single standard of individual development. Gilligan's book *In A Different Voice* argued that the prevailing standards of personal development were male standards. According to these standards, personal development was measured by progress from intuitive, inarticulate, cooperative, contextual, and personal modes of behavior toward rational, principled, competitive, universal, and impersonal modes of behavior, that is, from "weak" modes generally regarded as feminine and based on experience to "strong" modes regarded as masculine and based on algorithm.

Drawing from Gilligan's study, it becomes clear that on an international level, the development of nation-states is seen the same way. What appear to be universally agreed upon guidelines to which developing societies must conform are actually impositions of Western standards through cultural imperialism. Gilligan did for the study of personal development what must be done for economic development: allowing for difference. Just as the development of individuals should be seen as the flowering of that which is special and unique within each of us—a process by which an acorn becomes an oak rather than being obliged to become a maple—so the development of peoples should be conceived as the flowering of what is special and unique within each culture. This is not to argue for a cultural relativism in which all beliefs and practices sanctioned by some culture are equally valid on a moral, aesthetic, or practical plane. But it is to reject the universality claimed by Western beliefs and practices.

Of course, some might ask what the loss of a culture here or there matters if it is the price of material progress, but there are two flaws to this argument. First, cultural destruction is not necessarily a corollary of the technologies that extend life and improve its quality. Western technology can be decoupled from the entailments of Western culture. Second, if I am wrong about this, I would ask, as Jesus does in the account of Saint Mark, "[W]hat shall it profit a man, if he shall gain the whole world, and lose his own soul?" For all the material progress that the West has achieved, it has paid a high price through the weakening to the breaking point of communal ties. We in the West have much to learn, and the cultures that are being destroyed in the name of progress are perhaps the best resource we have for restoring balance to our own lives. The advantage of taking a critical stance with respect to our own culture is that we become more ready to enter into a genuine dialogue with other ways of being and believing.

The Culture of the Modern West

Culture is in the last analysis a set of assumptions, often unconsciously held, about people and how they relate to one another. The assumptions of modern Western culture can be described under five headings: individualism, self interest, the privileging of "rationality," unlimited wants, and the rise of the moral and legal claims of the nation-state on the individual.

Individualism is the notion that society can and should be understood as a collection of autonomous individuals, that groups—with the exception of the nation-state—have no normative significance as groups; that all behavior, policy, and even ethical judgment should be reduced to their effects on individuals. All individuals play the game of life on equal terms, even if they start with different amounts of physical strength, intellectual capacity, or capital assets. The playing field is level even if the players are not equal. These individuals are taken as given in many important ways rather than as works in progress. For example, preferences are accepted as given and cover everything from views about the relative merits of different flavors of ice cream to views about the relative merits of prostitution, casual sex, sex among friends, and sex within committed relationships. In an excess of democratic zeal, the children of the 20th century have extended the notion of radical subjectivism to the whole domain of preferences: one set of "preferences" is as good as another.

Self-interest is the idea that individuals make choices to further their own benefit. There is no room here for duty, right, or obligation, and that is a good thing, too. Adam Smith's best remembered contribution to economics, for better or worse, is the idea of a harmony that emerges from the pursuit of self-interest. It should be noted that while individualism is a prior condition for self-interest—there is no place for self-interest

Insurance

Spending on Insurance Premiums

Region	Percent of Global Premium Market
North America	**37.32**
Canada	1.91
United States	35.41
Latin America	**1.67**
Brazil	0.51
Mexico	0.4
Europe	**31.93**
France	4.99
Germany	5.06
UK	9.7
Asia	**26.46**
China	0.79
India	0.41
Japan	20.62
Africa	**1.03**
South Africa	0.87
Oceania	**1.59**
Australia	1.46

http://www.internationalinsurance.org

without the self—the converse does not hold. Individualism does not necessarily imply self-interest.

The third assumption is that one kind of knowledge is superior to others. The modern West privileges the algorithmic over the experiential, elevating knowledge that can be logically deduced from what are regarded as self-evident first principles over what is learned from intuition and authority, from touch and feel. In the stronger form of this ideology, the algorithmic is not only privileged but recognized as the sole legitimate form of knowledge. Other knowledge is mere belief, becoming legitimate only when verified by algorithmic methods.

Fourth is unlimited wants. It is human nature that we always want more than we have and that there is, consequently, never enough. The possibilities of abundance are always one step beyond our reach. Despite the enormous growth in production and consumption, we are as much in thrall to the economy as our parents, grandparents, and great-grandparents. Most US families find one income inadequate for their needs, not only at the bottom of the distribution—where falling real wages have eroded the standard of living over the past 25 years—but also in the middle and upper ranges of the distribution. Economics, which encapsulates in stark form the assumptions of the modern West, is frequently defined as the study of the allocation of limited resources among unlimited wants.

Finally, the assumption of modern Western culture is that the nation-state is the preeminent social grouping and moral authority. Worn out by fratricidal wars of religion, early mod-

ern Europe moved firmly in the direction of making one's relationship to God a private matter—a taste or preference among many. Language, shared commitments, and a defined territory would, it was hoped, be a less divisive basis for social identity than religion had proven to be.

An Economical Society

Each of these dimensions of modern Western culture is in tension with its opposite. Organic or holistic conceptions of society exist side by side with individualism. Altruism and fairness are opposed to self interest. Experiential knowledge exists, whether we recognize it or not, alongside algorithmic knowledge. Measuring who we are by what we have has been continually resisted by the small voice within that calls us to be our better selves. The modern nation-state claims, but does not receive, unconditional loyalty.

So the sway of modern Western culture is partial and incomplete even within the geographical boundaries of the West. And a good thing too, since no society organized on the principles outlined above could last five minutes, much less the 400 years that modernity has been in the ascendant. But make no mistake—modernity is the dominant culture in the West and increasingly so throughout the world. One has only to examine the assumptions that underlie contemporary economic thought—both stated and unstated—to confirm this assessment. Economics is simply the formalization of the assumptions of modern Western culture. That both teachers and students of economics accept these assumptions uncritically speaks volumes about the extent to which they hold sway.

It is not surprising then that a culture characterized in this way is a culture in which the market is the organizing principle of social life. Note my choice of words, "the market" and "social life," not markets and economic life. Markets have been with us since time out of mind, but the market, the idea of markets as a system for organizing production and exchange, is a distinctly modern invention, which grew in tandem with the cultural assumption of the self-interested, algorithmic individual who pursues wants without limit, an individual who owes allegiance only to the nation-state.

There is no sense in trying to resolve the chicken-egg problem of which came first. Suffice it to say that we can hardly have the market without the assumptions that justify a market system—and the market system can function acceptably only when the assumptions of the modern West are widely shared. Conversely, once these assumptions are prevalent, markets appear to be a "natural" way to organize life.

Markets and Communities

If people and society were as the culture of the modern West assumes, then market and community would occupy separate ideological spaces, and would co-exist or not as people chose. However, contrary to the assumptions of individualism, the individual does not encounter society as a fully formed human being. We are constantly being shaped by our experiences, and in a society organized in terms of markets, we are formed by our experiences in the market. Markets organize not only the production and distribution of things; they also organize the production of people.

The rise of the market system is thus bound up with the loss of community. Economists do not deny this, but rather put a market friendly spin on the destruction of community: impersonal markets accomplish more efficiently what the connections of social solidarity, reciprocity, and other redistributive institutions do in the absence of markets. Take fire insurance, for example. I pay a premium of, say, US$200 per year, and if my barn burns down, the insurance company pays me US$60,000 to rebuild it. A simple market transaction replaces the more cumbersome method of gathering my neighbors for a barn-raising, as rural US communities used to do. For the economist, it is a virtue that the more efficient institution drives out the less efficient. In terms of building barns with a minimal expenditure of resources, insurance may indeed be more efficient than gathering the community each time somebody's barn burns down. But in terms of maintaining the community, insurance is woefully lacking. Barn-raisings foster mutual interdependence: I rely on my neighbors economically—as well as in other ways—and they rely on me. Markets substitute impersonal relationships mediated by goods and services for the personal relationships of reciprocity and the like.

Why does community suffer if it is not reinforced by mutual economic dependence? Does not the relaxation of economic ties rather free up energy for other ways of connecting, as the English economist Dennis Robertson once suggested early in the 20th century? In a reflective mood toward the end of his life, Sir Dennis asked, "What does the economist economize?" His answer: "[T]hat scarce resource Love, which we know, just as well as anybody else, to be the most precious thing in the world." By using the impersonal relationships of markets to do the work of fulfilling our material needs, we economize on our higher faculties of affection, our capacity for reciprocity and personal obligation—love, in Robertsonian shorthand—which can then be devoted to higher ends.

In the end, his protests to the contrary notwithstanding, Sir Dennis knew more about banking than about love. Robertson made the mistake of thinking that love, like a loaf of bread, gets used up as it is used. Not all goods are "private" goods like bread. There are also "public" or "collective" goods which are not consumed when used by one person. A lighthouse is the canonical example: my use of the light does not diminish its availability to you. Love is a *hyper* public good: it actually increases by being used and indeed may shrink to nothing if left unused for any length of time.

Economics is simply the formalization of the assumptions of modern Western culture. That both teachers and students of economics accept these assumptions uncritically speaks volumes about the extent to which they hold sway.

If love is not scarce in the way that bread is, it is not sensible to design social institutions to economize on it. On the contrary, it makes sense to design social institutions to draw out and develop the community's stock of love. It is only when we focus on barns rather than on the people raising barns that insurance appears to be a more effective way of coping with disaster than is a community-wide barn-raising. The Amish, who are descendants of 18th century immigrants to the United States, are perhaps unique in the United States for their attention to fostering community; they forbid insurance precisely because they understand that the market relationship between an individual and the insurance company undermines the mutual dependence of the individuals that forms the basis of the community. For the Amish, barn-raisings are not exercises in nostalgia, but the cement which holds the community together.

Indeed, community cannot be viewed as just another good subject to the dynamics of market supply and demand that people can choose or not as they please, according to the same market test that applies to brands of soda or flavors of ice cream. Rather, the maintenance of community must be a collective responsibility for two reasons. The first is the so-called "free rider" problem. To return to the insurance example, my decision to purchase fire insurance rather than participate in the give and take of barn raising with my neighbors has the side effect—the "externality" in economics jargon—of lessening my involvement with the community. If I am the only one to act this way, this effect may be small with no harm done. But when all of us opt for insurance and leave caring for the community to others, there will be no others to care, and the community will disintegrate. In the case of insurance, I buy insurance because it is more convenient, and—acting in isolation—I can reasonably say to myself that my action hardly undermines the community. But when we all do so, the cement of mutual obligation is weakened to the point that it no longer supports the community.

The free rider problem is well understood by economists, and the assumption that such problems are absent is part of the standard fine print in the warranty that economists provide for the market. A second, deeper, problem cannot so easily be translated into the language of economics. The market creates more subtle externalities that include effects on beliefs, values, and behaviors—a class of externalities which are ignored in the standard framework of economics in which individual "preferences" are assumed to be unchanging. An Amishman's decision to insure his barn undermines the mutual dependence of the Amish not only by making him less dependent on the community, but also by subverting the beliefs that sustain this dependence. For once interdependence is undermined, the community is no longer valued; the process of undermining interdependence is self-validating.

Thus, the existence of such externalities means that community survival cannot be left to the spontaneous initiatives of its members acting in accord with the individual maximizing model. Furthermore, this problem is magnified when the externalities involve feedback from actions to values, beliefs, and then to behavior. If a community is to survive, it must structure the interactions of its members to strengthen ways of being and

27

knowing which support community. It will have to constrain the market when the market undermines community.

A Different Development

There are two lessons here. The first is that there should be mechanisms for local communities to decide, as the Amish routinely do, which innovations in organization and technology are compatible with the core values the community wishes to preserve. This does not mean the blind preservation of whatever has been sanctioned by time and the existing distribution of power. Nor does it mean an idyllic, conflict-free path to the future. But recognizing the value as well as the fragility of community would be a giant step forward in giving people a real opportunity to make their portions less meager and avoiding the poison.

The second lesson is for practitioners and theorists of development. What many Westerners see simply as liberating people from superstition, ignorance, and the oppression of tradition, is fostering values, behaviors, and beliefs that are highly problematic for our own culture. Only arrogance and a supreme failure of the imagination cause us to see them as universal rather than as the product of a particular history. Again, this is not to argue that "anything goes." It is instead a call for sensitivity, for entering into a dialogue that involves listening instead of dictating—not so that we can better implement our own agenda, but so that we can genuinely learn that which modernity has made us forget.

STEPHEN A. MARGLIN is Walter S. Barker Professor of Economics at Harvard University.

Why God Is Winning

Religion was supposed to fade away as globalization and freedom spread. Instead, it's booming around the world, often deciding who gets elected. And the divine intervention is just beginning. Democracy is giving people a voice, and more and more, they want to talk about God.

Timothy Samuel Shah and Monica Duffy Toft

After Hamas won a decisive victory in January's Palestinian elections, one of its supporters replaced the national flag that flew over parliament with its emerald-green banner heralding, "There is no God but God, and Muhammad is His Prophet." In Washington, few expected the religious party to take power. "I don't know anyone who wasn't caught off guard," said U.S. Secretary of State Condoleezza Rice. More surprises followed. Days after the Prophet's banner was unfurled in Ramallah, thousands of Muslims mounted a vigorous, sometimes violent, defense of the Prophet's honor in cities as far flung as Beirut, Jakarta, London, and New Delhi. Outraged by cartoons of Muhammad originally published in Denmark, Islamic groups, governments, and individuals staged demonstrations, boycotts, and embassy attacks.

On their own, these events appeared to be sudden eruptions of "Muslim rage." In fact, they were only the most recent outbreaks of a deep undercurrent that has been gathering force for decades and extends far beyond the Muslim world. Global politics is increasingly marked by what could be called "prophetic politics." Voices claiming transcendent authority are filling public spaces and winning key political contests. These movements come in very different forms and employ widely varying tools. But whether the field of battle is democratic elections or the more inchoate struggle for global public opinion, religious groups are increasingly competitive. In contest after contest, when people are given a choice between the sacred and the secular, faith prevails.

God is on a winning streak. It was reflected in the 1979 Iranian Revolution, the rise of the Taliban in Afghanistan, the Shia revival and religious strife in postwar Iraq, and Hamas's recent victory in Palestine. But not all the thunderbolts have been hurled by Allah. The struggle against apartheid in South Africa in the 1980s and early 1990s was strengthened by prominent Christian leaders such as Archbishop Desmond Tutu. Hindu nationalists in India stunned the international community when they unseated India's ruling party in 1998 and then tested nuclear weapons. American evangelicals continue to surprise the U.S. foreign-policy establishment with their activism and influence on issues such as religious freedom, sex trafficking, Sudan, and AIDS in Africa. Indeed, evangelicals have emerged as such a powerful force that religion was a stronger predictor of vote choice in the 2004 U.S. presidential election than was gender, age, or class.

The spread of democracy, far from checking the power of militant religious activists, will probably only enhance the reach of prophetic political movements, many of which will emerge from democratic processes more organized, more popular, and more legitimate than before—but quite possibly no less violent. Democracy is giving the world's peoples their voice, and they want to talk about God.

Divine Intervention

It did not always seem this way. In April 1966, *Time* ran a cover story that asked, "Is God Dead?" It was a fair question. Secularism dominated world politics in the mid-1960s. The conventional wisdom shared by many intellectual and political elites was that modernization would inevitably extinguish religion's vitality. But if 1966 was the zenith of secularism's self-confidence, the next year marked the beginning of the end of its global hegemony. In 1967, the leader of secular Arab nationalism, Gamal Abdel Nasser, suffered a humiliating defeat at the hands of the Israeli Army. By the end of the 1970s, Iran's Ayatollah Khomeini, avowedly "born-again" U.S. President Jimmy Carter, television evangelist Jerry Falwell, and Pope John Paul II were all walking the world stage. A decade later, rosary-wielding Solidarity members in Poland and Kalashnikov-toting mujahedin in Afghanistan helped defeat atheistic Soviet Communism. A dozen years later, 19 hijackers screaming "God is great" transformed world politics. Today, the secular pan-Arabism of Nasser has given way to the millenarian pan-Islamism of Iranian President Mahmoud Ahmadinejad, whose religious harangues against America and Israel resonate with millions of Muslims, Sunni and Shia alike. "We increasingly see that people around the world are flocking towards a main focal point—that is the Almighty God," Ahmadinejad declared in his recent letter to President Bush.

The modern world has in fact proven hospitable to religious belief. The world is indeed more modern: It enjoys more political freedom, more democracy, and more education than perhaps at any time in history. According to Freedom House, the number of "free" and "partly free" countries jumped from 93 in 1975 to 147 in 2005. UNESCO estimates that adult literacy rates doubled in sub-Saharan Africa, Arab countries, and South and West Asia between 1970 and 2000. The average share of people in developing countries living on less than a dollar a day fell from 28 percent to 22 percent between 1990 and 2002, according to World Bank estimates.

If people are wealthier, more educated, and enjoy greater political freedom, one might assume they would also have become more secular. They haven't. In fact, the period in which economic and political modernization has been most intense—the last 30 to 40 years—has witnessed a jump in religious vitality around the world. The world's largest religions have expanded at a rate that exceeds global population growth. Consider the two largest Christian faiths, Catholicism and Protestantism, and the two largest non-Christian religions, Islam and Hinduism. According to the *World Christian Encyclopedia,* a greater proportion of the world's population adhered to these religious systems in 2000 than a century earlier. At the beginning of the 20th century, a bare majority of the world's people, precisely 50 percent, were Catholic, Protestant, Muslim, or Hindu. At the beginning of the 21st century, nearly 64 percent belonged to these four religious groupings, and the proportion may be close to 70 percent by 2025. The World Values Survey, which covers 85 percent of the world's population, confirms religion's growing vitality. According to scholars Ronald Inglehart and Pippa Norris, "the world as a whole now has more people with traditional religious views than ever before—and they constitute a growing proportion of the world's population."

Not only is religious observance spreading, it is becoming more devout. The most populous and fastest-growing countries in the world, including the United States, are witnessing marked increases in religiosity. In Brazil, China, Nigeria, Russia, South Africa, and the United States, religiosity became more vigorous between 1990 and 2001. Between 1987 and 1997, surveys by the Times Mirror Center and the Pew Research Center registered increases of 10 percent or more in the proportions of Americans surveyed who "strongly agreed" that God existed, that they would have to answer for their sins before God, that God performs miracles, and that prayer was an important part of their daily life. Even in Europe, a secular stronghold, there have been surprising upticks in religiosity.

God's comeback is in no small part due to the global expansion of freedom. Thanks to the "third wave" of democratization between the mid-1970s and early 1990s, as well as smaller waves of freedom since, people in dozens of countries have been empowered to shape their public lives in ways that were inconceivable in the 1950s and 1960s. A pattern emerged as they exercised their new political freedoms. In country after country, politically empowered groups began to challenge the secular constraints imposed by the first generation of modernizing, postindependence leaders. Often, as in communist countries, secular straitjackets had been imposed by sheer coercion; in other cases, as in Atatürk's Turkey, Nehru's India, and Nasser's Egypt, secularism retained legitimacy because elites considered it essential to national integration and modernization—and because of the sheer charisma of these countries' founding fathers. In Latin America, right-wing dictatorships, sometimes in cahoots with the Catholic Church, imposed restrictions that severely limited grassroots religious influences, particularly from "liberation theology" and Protestant "sects."

As politics liberalized in countries like India, Mexico, Nigeria, Turkey, and Indonesia in the late 1990s, religion's influence on political life increased dramatically. Even in the United States, evangelicals exercised a growing influence on the Republican Party in the 1980s and 1990s, partly because the presidential nomination process depended more on popular primaries and less on the decisions of traditional party leaders. Where political systems reflect people's values, they usually reflect people's strong religious beliefs.

Many observers are quick to dismiss religion's advance into the political sphere as the product of elites manipulating sacred symbols to mobilize the masses. In fact, the marriage of religion with politics is often welcomed, if not demanded, by people around the world. In a 2002 Pew Global Attitudes survey, 91 percent of Nigerians and 76 percent of Bangladeshis surveyed agreed that religious leaders should be more involved in politics. A June 2004 six-nation survey reported that "most Arabs polled said that they wanted the clergy to play a bigger role in politics." In the same survey, majorities or pluralities in Morocco, Saudi Arabia, Jordan, and the United Arab Emirates cited Islam as their primary identity, trumping nationality. The collapse of the quasi-secular Baathist dictatorship in Iraq released religious and ethnic allegiances and has helped Islam play a dominant role in the country's political life, including in its recently adopted constitution. As right- and left-wing dictatorships have declined in Latin America and democratization has deepened, evangelicals have become an influential voting bloc in numerous countries, including Brazil, Guatemala, and Nicaragua.

The New Orthodoxies

Far from stamping out religion, modernization has spawned a new generation of savvy and technologically adept religious movements, including Evangelical Protestantism in America, "Hindutva" in India, Salafist and Wahhabi Islam in the Middle East, Pentecostalism in Africa and Latin America, and Opus Dei and the charismatic movement in the Catholic Church. The most dynamic religiosity today is not so much "old-time religion" as it is radical, modern, and conservative. Today's religious upsurge is less a return of religious orthodoxy than an explosion of "neo-orthodoxies."

A common denominator of these neo-orthodoxies is the deployment of sophisticated and politically capable organizations. These modern organizations effectively marshal specialized institutions as well as the latest technologies to recruit new members, strengthen connections with old ones, deliver social services, and press their agenda in the public sphere. The Vishwa Hindu Parishad, founded in 1964, "saffronized" large swaths of India through its religious and social activism and laid the groundwork for the Bharatiya Janata Party's electoral successes in the 1990s. Similar groups in the Islamic world include the Muslim Brotherhood in Egypt and Jordan, Hamas in the Palestinian territories, Hezbollah in Lebanon, and the Nahdlatul Ulama in Indonesia. In Brazil, Pentecostals have organized their own legislative caucus, representing 10 percent of congresspeople. Religious communities are also developing remarkable transnational capabilities, appealing to foreign governments and international bodies deemed sympathetic to their cause.

Today's neo-orthodoxies may effectively use the tools of the modern world, but how compatible are they with modern democracy? Religious radicals, after all, can quickly short-circuit democracy by winning power and then excluding non-believers. Just as dangerous, politicized religion can spark civil conflict. Since 2000, 43 percent of civil wars have been religious (only a quarter were religiously inspired in the 1940s and 50s). Extreme religious ideology is, of course, a leading motivation for most transnational terrorist attacks.

The scorecard isn't all negative, however. Religion has mobilized millions of people to oppose authoritarian regimes, inaugurate democratic transitions, support human rights, and relieve human suffering. In the 20th century, religious movements helped end colonial rule and usher in democracy in Latin America, Eastern Europe, sub-Saharan Africa, and Asia. The post-Vatican II Catholic Church played a crucial role by opposing authoritarian regimes and legitimating the democratic aspirations of the masses.

Today's religious movements, however, may not have as much success in promoting sustainable freedom. Catholicism's highly centralized and organized character made it an effective competitor with the state, and its institutional tradition helped it adapt to democratic politics. Islam and Pentecostalism, by contrast, are not centralized under a single leadership or doctrine that can respond coherently to fast-moving social or political events. Local religious authorities are often tempted to radicalize in order to compensate for their weakness vis-à-vis the state or to challenge more established figures. The trajectory of the young cleric Moqtada al-Sadr in postwar Iraq is not unusual. The lack of a higher authority for religious elites might explain why most religious civil wars since 1940—34 of 42—have involved Islam, with 9 of these being Muslim versus Muslim. We need look no further than Iraq today to see religious authorities successfully challenging the forces of secularism—but also violently competing with each other. Even in a long-standing democracy like India, the political trajectory of Hindu nationalism has demonstrated that democratic institutions do not necessarily moderate these instincts: Where radical Hindu nationalists have had the right mix of opportunities and incentives, they have used religious violence to win elections, most dramatically in the state of Gujarat.

The belief that outbreaks of politicized religion are temporary detours on the road to secularization was plausible in 1976, 1986, or even 1996. Today, the argument is untenable. As a framework for explaining and predicting the course of global politics, secularism is increasingly unsound. God is winning in global politics. And modernization, democratization, and globalization have only made him stronger.

TIMOTHY SAMUEL SHAH is senior fellow in religion and world affairs at the Pew Forum on Religion & Public Life. **MONICA DUFFY TOFT** is associate professor of public policy at the John F. Kennedy School of Government and assistant director of the John M. Olin Institute for Strategic Studies at Harvard University.

From *Foreign Policy*, July/August 2006. Copyright © 2006 by the Carnegie Endowment for International Peace. Reprinted with permission. www.foreignpolicy.com

UNIT 2
International Political Economy

Unit Selections

Key Points to Consider

- In what ways have developing countries increased their share of the global economy? How do they continue to lag behind?

- How does the Indian model of development differ? What must India also do to increase prosperity?

- How are emerging economies challenging the industrial countries?

- What are the prospects for successful completion of the Doha Round of international trade talks?

- How is the global trading system unbalanced?

- How have cotton subsidies hurt poor cotton-producing countries?

- How are rich countries doing with their pledge to increase aid to the developing countries?

- How do NGOs influence the effectiveness of aid?

- In what ways can foreign aid be made more effective?

- How could international food aid be provided more inexpensively?

- How might education gains be improved in the developing world?

- What controversies have emerged regarding microcredit?

Student Web Site
www.mhcls.com/online

Internet Reference
Further information regarding this Web site may be found in this book's preface or online.

Center for Third World Organizing
  http://www.ctwo.org/

Economic issues are among the developing world's most pressing concerns. Economic growth and stability are essential to progress on the variety of problems confronting developing countries. While the developing world is playing a larger role in the global economy, many countries continue to struggle to achieve consistent economic growth. From their incorporation into the international economic system during colonialism to the present, the majority of developing countries have been primarily suppliers of raw materials, agricultural products, and inexpensive labor. Dependence on commodity exports has meant that developing countries have had to deal with fluctuating, and frequently declining, prices for their exports. At the same time, prices for imports have remained constant or have increased. At best, this decline in the terms of trade has made development planning difficult; at worst, it has led to economic stagnation and decline.

With some significant exceptions, developing nations have had limited success in breaking out of this dilemma by diversifying their economies. Moreover, agricultural subsidies have inhibited the ability of developing countries to take advantage of lower commodity production costs. Efforts at industrialization and export of light manufactured goods have led to competition with less efficient industries in the industrialized world. The response of industrialized countries has often been protectionism and demands for trade reciprocity, which can overwhelm markets in developing countries. Although the World Trade Organization (WTO) was established to standardize trade regulations and increase international trade, critics charge that the WTO continues to disadvantage developing countries and remains dominated by the wealthy industrial countries. The developing world also asserts that they are often shut out of trade negotiations, must accept deals dictated by the wealthy countries, and that they lack sufficient resources to effectively participate in the wide range of forums and negotiations that take place around the world.

Moreover, developing countries charge that the industrialized countries are selective in their efforts to dismantle trade barriers and emphasize trade issues that reflect only their interests. Delegates from poor countries walked out of the 2003 WTO ministerial meeting in Cancún, Mexico to protest rich countries' reluctance to eliminate agricultural subsidies and their efforts to dominate the agenda. The 2005 Hong Kong WTO ministerial meeting also made little progress on a comprehensive international trade agreement. A successful conclusion to the Doha round rests on the willingness of both industrialized and developing countries to make concessions, but prospects for this, do not look promising.

The economic situation in the developing world, however, is not entirely attributable to colonial legacy and protectionism on the part of industrialized countries. Developing countries have sometimes constructed their own trade barriers. Evidence suggests that developing countries would benefit from dismantling their trade barriers even if the industrialized countries do not reciprocate. This may become even more important with the end of preferential trade arrangements.

Industrialization schemes involving heavy government direction were often ill-conceived or resulted in corruption and mismanagement. Industrialized countries frequently point to these inefficiencies in calling for market-oriented reforms, but the emphasis on privatization does not adequately recognize the role of the state in developing countries' economies and privatization may result in foreign control of important sectors of the economy as well as a loss of jobs.

Debt has further compounded economic problems for many developing countries. During the 1970s, developing countries' prior economic performance and the availability of petrodollars encouraged extensive commercial lending. Developing countries sought these loans to fill the gap between revenues from exports and foreign aid, and development expenditures. The second oil price hike in the late 1970s, declining export earnings, and worldwide recession in the early 1980s left many developing countries unable to meet their debt obligations. The commercial banks weathered the crisis, and some actually showed a profit. Commercial lending declined in the aftermath of the debt crisis and international financial institutions became the lenders of last resort for many developing countries. Access to World Bank and International Monetary Fund financing became conditional on the adoption of structural adjustment programs that involved steps such as reduced public expenditures, devaluation of currencies, and export promotion, all geared to debt reduction. The consequences of these programs have been painful for developing countries. Declining public services, higher prices, and greater reliance on the exploitation of resources have resulted.

The poorest countries in particular have struggled with heavy debt burdens, and the IMF and World Bank have come under increasing criticism for their programs in the developing world. Though these institutions have made efforts to shift the emphasis to poverty reduction, some critics charge that the reforms are superficial, that the international financial institutions lack accountability, and that developing countries do not have adequate influence in decision-making. Although eliminating the debt of the world's poorest countries and providing substantially more aid were a major focus of the G-8 summit in July 2005, the 2006 Commitment to Development Index indicates that rich countries' rhetoric about dramatic increases in aid has not been matched by reality.

Globalization has complicated international economic circumstances, and views differ regarding benefits and costs of this trend for the developing world. Advocates claim that closer economic integration, especially trade and financial liberalization, increases economic prosperity in developing countries and encourages good governance, transparency, and accountability. Critics respond that globalization's requirements, as determined by the powerful nations and reinforced through the international financial institutions, impose difficult and perhaps counterproductive policies on struggling economies. They also charge that globalization undermines workers' rights and encourages environmental degradation. Moreover, most of the benefits of globalization have gone to those countries that were already growing—leaving the poorest even further behind.

In part due to the realization that poverty in the developing world contributes to the despair and resentment that leads some to terrorism, there has been increased attention focused on foreign aid. There is considerable debate on how to make any increased aid more effective. In addition to aid, attention has also focused on microcredit schemes modeled after the Grameen Bank founded by Nobel prize-winner Muhammad Yunus. As the effectiveness of this strategy has been demonstrated it has been widely copied. As these initiatives have expanded, however, so has the controversy over the best model for lending to the poor.

Climbing Back

The economies of what used to be called the "third world" are regaining their ancient pre-eminence

Since their industrial revolutions in the 19th century, the rich countries of the "first world" have dominated the global economy. By one measure at least, that era may be over. According to estimates by *The Economist,* in 2005 the combined output of emerging (or developing) economies rose above half of the global total.

This figure has been calculated from the International Monetary Fund's World Economic Outlook database. We have adjusted the IMF's numbers in two ways. First, we have taken account of China's recent upward revision of its GDP by 17%. Second, we include the newly industrialized Asian economies (South Korea, Taiwan, Hong Kong and Singapore). These countries might well now be classed as developed, but should surely be counted in any estimate of the long-term success of developing countries. If you exclude countries once they prosper, developing economies' share will never increase.

We have used the IMF's method of converting national GDPs into dollars using purchasing-power parities (PPPs) instead of market exchange rates. The latter can distort the relative size of economies, not only because currencies fluctuate, but also because prices are lower in poorer economies (so a dollar of spending in China, say, is worth a lot more than it is in America).

The prices of traded goods tend to be similar to those in developed economies, but the prices of non-tradable products, such as housing and haircuts, are generally much lower. As a result, converting a poor country's GDP into dollars at market exchange rates could understate the size of its economy and its living standards. This is why the IMF uses PPPs, which take account of international differences in prices of the same goods and services, to provide a more accurate measure of the purchasing power of each country's inhabitants.

It makes a big difference. Measured at market exchange rates, developing economies' share of global output has fallen over the past quarter-century, to just 26% last year. Measured at PPP, it has (more realistically) risen, to just over half. Perhaps the best evidence of the flaw in current-dollar figures is that they suggest developing Asia's share of world output was barely higher in 2000 than in 1980, even though it had been by far the world's fastest growing region. The effect of growth was distorted by currency movements.

Admittedly, calculating PPPs is tricky. They are based on surveys of prices around the world. But as Keynes used to say, "It is better to be roughly right than precisely wrong." Using PPPs provides a more realistic estimate of the balance of output between rich and poor countries. But they are not always appropriate. Trade and financial flows, which, unlike the bulk of GDP, are transacted at market exchange rates, should be converted at those rates into dollars. For businesses too, market exchange rates are relevant for converting foreign revenues and profits into dollars.

But even when measured by market exchange rates emerging economies are flexing their muscles. Last year, their combined GDP grew in current dollar terms by $1.6 trillion, more than the $1.4 trillion increase of developed economies. And there is more to this than just China and India: these two countries together accounted for only one-fifth of the total increase in emerging economies' GDP last year.

Of course, with half the world's output but five-sixths of its population, emerging economies still have incomes per head far lower than the rich world. But by a wide range of gauges they are looming larger. Their share of exports has jumped to 42%, from 20% in 1970. Over the past five years, they have accounted for more than half of the growth in world exports. Emerging economies are now sitting on two-thirds of the world's foreign-exchange reserves and they consume 47% of the world's oil. On the other hand, their stockmarkets still account for only 14% of global capitalization.

Emerging economies have also become increasingly important markets for companies from the rich world. Developed economies' trade with developing countries is growing twice as fast as their trade with one another. Over half of the total exports of America, the euro area and Japan now go to emerging economies. The EU exports twice as much to them as it does to America and Japan combined.

As You Were

The growing clout of emerging economies is in fact returning them to the position they held for most of history. Before the steam engine and the power loom gave Britain its industrial lead, today's emerging economies dominated world output. Estimates by Angus Maddison, an economic historian, suggest that in the 18 centuries until 1820 they produced, on average, around 80% of the total. But they were then left behind by Europe's technological revolution. By the early 20th century their share had fallen to 40%.

The term "emerging market" was coined 25 years ago by the International Finance Corporation, the private-sector arm of the World Bank. For much of the time since, "submerging" has been more apt: look at the succession of crises, from Latin America to East Asia and Russia, in the past decade or so.

Now emerging economies are on the rebound, enjoying their best performance for decades. All 32 economies tracked each week by *The Economist* (see pages 104–106 and our Web site) grew in 2005, for the second year running. In every previous year since the 1970s, at least one emerging economy suffered a recession, if not a severe financial crisis. In the past three years, their growth has averaged more than 6%, compared with 2.4% in rich economies. The IMF forecasts that in the next five years they will roll along at just under 6%, twice as fast as developed economies. Extrapolation is risky, but if this relative pace were sustained, in 20 years' time emerging economies would account for two-thirds of global output. Is this likely?

It stands a good chance. Most emerging economies are today in much stronger health, leaving them better able to withstand adverse global shocks. Their economic policies have matured: most have cut inflation, thanks to stricter monetary and fiscal policies; they have generally shifted towards more flexible exchange rates; and many are now running current-account surpluses and have built up weighty foreign-exchange reserves. Structural reforms to open up markets and to strengthen financial systems are also helping to improve the efficiency of investment.

This week the Institute of International Finance, a bankers' association, said that net private capital flows to emerging markets hit a record $358 billion in 2005. But most countries no longer need this money to finance current-account deficits. Unlike many previous booms, their current expansion has been financed largely by domestic saving rather than debt: their average ratio of foreign debt to exports has fallen from 174% in 1998 to 82% last year.

Beware of Hiccups

However, some of the recent boom in emerging economies is due to three factors that may be unsustainable. First, rising commodity prices have given a fillip to producing countries, such as Russia, Brazil and South Africa. Second, low interest rates have reduced debt-service costs—especially important for Latin America, where the debt-to-export ratio is twice as high as the average for emerging economies. And last, exports have been boosted by America's strong import demand. This favorable environment cannot last: interest rates are rising, and American consumers cannot keep spending more than they earn. Emerging economies' energy-intensive heavy industries are also vulnerable to high oil prices. A saving grace is that these risks partly offset each other. A slump in American demand would reduce both interest rates and oil prices.

Perhaps the biggest risk is that the boom may encourage complacency and reform fatigue. Yet further action is needed, from greater fiscal discipline to more flexible exchange rates.

The future expansion of emerging economies will not follow a straight line. It is unavoidable that emerging economies are more prone to economic ups and downs and financial bubbles, as America was during its entry on to the global stage in the late 19th century. However, the long-run prospects for emerging economies as a whole look excellent, so long as their move towards free and open markets and sound fiscal and monetary policies continues. Get these basics right, and developing countries ought to outpace advanced economies. Because they start with much less capital per worker than developed economies, there is huge scope for boosting productivity by importing western machines and know-how.

Confirmation that emerging economies are grabbing a bigger slice of global output will frighten many people in the rich world. It shouldn't: living standards depend on absolute not relative growth. Emerging economies' spurt is boosting global output, not substituting for growth elsewhere. Their vim is fuelling growth in the rich world just when graying populations might otherwise cause it to slow—not only by importing from developed countries, but also by supplying cheaper consumer goods, by allowing multinational firms to exploit bigger economies of scale, and by encouraging a better allocation of resources through increased competition. It is surely better for today's rich countries to have a smaller share of a fast-growing global economy than a bigger one of a stagnant world.

The India Model
An Economy Unshackled

GURCHARAN DAS

Although the world has just discovered it, India's economic success is far from new. After three postindependence decades of meager progress, the country's economy grew at 6 percent a year from 1980 to 2002 and at 7.5 percent a year from 2002 to 2006—making it one of the world's best-performing economies for a quarter century. In the past two decades, the size of the middle class has quadrupled (to almost 250 million people), and 1 percent of the country's poor have crossed the poverty line every year. At the same time, population growth has slowed from the historic rate of 2.2 percent a year to 1.7 percent today—meaning that growth has brought large per capita income gains, from $1,178 to $3,051 (in terms of purchasing-power parity) since 1980. India is now the world's fourth-largest economy. Soon it will surpass Japan to become the third-largest.

The notable thing about India's rise is not that it is new, but that its path has been unique. Rather than adopting the classic Asian strategy—exporting labor-intensive, low-priced manufactured goods to the West—India has retied on its domestic market more than exports, consumption more than investment, services more than industry, and high-tech more than low-skilled manufacturing. This approach has meant that the Indian economy has been mostly insulated from global downturns, showing a degree of stability that is as impressive as the rate of its expansion. The consumption-driven model is also more people-friendly than other development strategies. As a result, inequality has increased much less in India than in other developing nations. (Its Gini index, a measure of income inequality on a scale of zero to 100, is 33, compared to 41 for the United States, 45 for China, and 59 for Brazil.) Moreover, 30 to 40 percent of GDP growth is due to rising productivity—a true sign of an economy's health and progress—rather than to increases in the amount of capital or labor.

But what is most remarkable is that rather than rising with the help of the state, India is in many ways rising despite the state. The entrepreneur is clearly at the center of India's success story. India now boasts highly competitive private companies, a booming stock market, and a modern, well-disciplined financial sector. And since 1991 especially, the Indian state has been gradually moving out of the way—not graciously, but kicked and dragged into implementing economic reforms. It has lowered trade barriers and tax rates, broken state monopolies, unshackled industry, encouraged competition, and opened up to the rest of the world. The pace has been slow, but the reforms are starting to add up.

India is poised at a key moment in its history. Rapid growth will likely continue—and even accelerate. But India cannot take this for granted. Public debt is high, which discourages investment in needed infrastructure. Overly strict labor laws, though they cover only 10 percent of the work force, have the perverse effect of discouraging employers from hiring new workers. The public sector, although much smaller than China's, is still too large and inefficient—a major drag on growth and employment and a burden for consumers. And although India is successfully generating high-end, capital- and knowledge-intensive manufacturing, it has failed to create a broad-based, labor-intensive industrial revolution—meaning that gains in employment have not been commensurate with overall growth. Its rural population, meanwhile, suffers from the consequences of state-induced production and distribution distortions in agriculture that result in farmers' getting only 20 to 30 percent of the retail price of fruits and vegetables (versus the 40 to 50 percent farmers in the United States get).

India can take advantage of this moment to remove the remaining obstacles that have prevented it from realizing its full potential. Or it can continue smugly along, confident that it will get there eventually—but 20 years late. The most difficult reforms are not yet done, and already there are signs of complacency.

A 100-Year Tale

For half a century before independence, the Indian economy was stagnant. Between 1900 and 1950, economic growth averaged 0.8 percent a year—exactly the same rate as population growth, resulting in no increase in per capita income. In the first decades after independence, economic growth picked up, averaging 3.5 percent from 1950 to 1980. But population growth accelerated as well. The net effect on per capita income was an average annual increase of just 1.3 percent.

Indians mournfully called this "the Hindu rate of growth." Of course, it had nothing to do with Hinduism and everything to do with the Fabian socialist policies of Prime Minister Jawaharlal Nehru and his imperious daughter, Prime Minister Indira Gandhi, who oversaw India's darkest economic decades. Father and daughter shackled the energies of the Indian people under a mixed economy that combined the worst features of capitalism and socialism. Their *model* was inward-looking and import-substituting rather than outward-looking and export-promoting, and it denied India a share in the prosperity that a massive expansion in global trade brought in the post-World War II era. (Average per capita growth for the developing world as a whole was almost 3 percent from 1950 to 1980, more than double India's rate.) Nehru set up an inefficient and monopolistic public sector, over-regulated private enterprise with the most stringent price and production controls in the world, and discouraged foreign investment—thereby causing India to lose out on the benefits of both foreign technology and foreign competition. His approach also pampered organized labor to the point of significantly lowering productivity and ignored the education of India's children.

But even this system could have delivered more had it been better implemented. It did not have to degenerate into a "license-permit-quota raj," as Chakravarthi Rajagopalachari first put it in the late 1950s. Although Indians blame ideology (and sometimes democracy) for their failings, the truth is that a mundane inability to implement policy—reflecting a bias for thought and against action—may have been even more damaging.

In the 1980s, the government's attitude toward the private sector began to change, thanks in part to the underappreciated efforts of Prime Minister Rajiv Gandhi. Modest liberal reforms—especially lowering marginal tax rates and tariffs and giving some leeway to manufacturers—spurred an increase in growth to 5.6 percent. But the policies of the 1980s were also profligate and brought India to the point of fiscal crisis by the start of the 1990s. Fortunately, that crisis triggered the critical reforms of 1991, which finally allowed India's integration into the global economy—and laid the groundwork for the high growth of today. The chief architect of those reforms was the finance minister, Manmohan Singh, who is now prime minister. He lowered tariffs and other trade barriers, scrapped industrial licensing, reduced tax rates, devalued the rupee, opened India to foreign investment, and rolled back currency controls. Many of these measures were gradual, but they signaled a decisive break with India's dirigiste past. The economy returned the favor immediately: growth rose, inflation plummeted, and exports and currency reserves shot up.

To appreciate the magnitude of the change after 1980, recall that the West's Industrial Revolution took place in the context of 3 percent GDP growth and 1.1 percent per capita income growth. If India's economy were still growing at the pre-1980 level, then its per capita income would reach present U.S. levels only by 2250; but if it continues to grow at the post-1980 average, it will reach that level by 2066—a gain of 184 years.

Peculiar Revolution

India has improved its competitiveness considerably since 1991: there has been a telecommunications revolution, interest rates have come down, capital is plentiful (although risk-averse managers of state-owned banks still refuse to lend to small entrepreneurs), highways and ports have improved, and real estate markets are becoming transparent. More than 100 Indian companies now have a market capitalization of over a billion dollars, and some of these—including Bharat Forge, Jet Airways, Infosys Technologies, Reliance Infocomm, Tata Motors, and Wipro Technologies—are likely to become competitive global brands soon. Foreigners have invested in over 1,000 Indian companies

via the stock market. Of the Fortune 500 companies, 125 now have research and development bases in India—a testament to its human capital. And high-tech manufacturing has taken off. All these changes have disciplined the banking sector. Bad loans now account for less than 2 percent of all loans (compared to 20 percent in China), even though none of India's shoddy state-owned banks has so far been privatized.

For now, growth is being driven by services and domestic consumption. Consumption accounts for 64 percent of India's GDP, Compared to 58 percent for Europe, 55 percent for Japan, and 42 percent for China. That consumption might be a virtue embarrasses many Indians, with their ascetic streak, but, as the economist Stephen Roach of Morgan Stanley puts it, "India's consumption-led approach to growth may be better balanced than the resource-mobilization model of China."

The contrast between India's entrepreneur-driven growth and China's state-centered model is stark. China's success is largely based on exports by state enterprises or foreign companies. Beijing remains highly suspicious of entrepreneurs. Only 10 percent of credit goes to the private sector in China, even though the private sector employs 40 percent of the Chinese work force. In India, entrepreneurs get more than 80 percent of all loans. Whereas Jet Airways, in operation since 1993, has become the undisputed leader of India's skies, China's first private airline, Okay Airways, started flying only in February 2005.

What has been peculiar about India's development so far is that high growth has not been accompanied by a labor-intensive industrial revolution that could transform the lives of the tens of millions of Indians still trapped in rural poverty. Many Indians watch mesmerized as China seems to create an endless flow of low-end manufacturing jobs by exporting goods such as toys and clothes and as their better-educated compatriots export knowledge services to the rest of the world. They wonder fearfully if India is going to skip an industrial revolution altogether, jumping straight from an agricultural economy to a service economy. Economies in the rest of the world evolved from agriculture to industry to services. India appears to have a weak middle step. Services now account for more than 50 percent of India's GDP, whereas agriculture's share is 22 percent, and industry's share is only 27 percent (versus 46 percent in China). And within industry, India's strength is high-tech, high-skilled manufacturing.

Even the most fervent advocates of service-based growth do not question the desirability of creating more manufacturing jobs. The failure of India to achieve a broad industrial transformation stems in part from bad policies. After India's independence, Nehru attempted a state-directed industrial revolution. Since he did not trust the private sector, he tried to replace the entrepreneur with the government-and predictably failed. He shackled private enterprise with byzantine controls and denied autonomy to the public sector. Perhaps the most egregious policy was reserving around 800 industries, designated "small-scale industries" (SSI), for tiny companies that were unable to compete against the large firms of competitor nations. Large firms were barred from making products such as pencils, boot polish, candles, shoes, garments, and toys—all the products that helped East Asia create millions of jobs. Even since 1991, Indian governments nave been afraid to touch this "SSI holy cow" for fear of a backlash from the SSI lobby. Fortunately, that lobby has turned out to be mostly a phantom—little more than the bureaucrats who kept scaring politicians by warning of a backlash. Over the past five years, the government has been pruning the list of protected industries incrementally with no adverse reaction.

In the short term, the best way for India to improve the lot of the rural poor might be to promote a second green revolution. Unlike in manufacturing, India has a competitive advantage in agriculture, with plenty of arable land, sunshine, and water. To achieve such a change, however, India would need to shift its focus from peasant farming to agribusiness and encourage private capital to move from urban to rural areas. It would need to lift onerous distribution controls, allow large retailers to contract directly with farmers invest in irrigation, and permit the consolidation of fragmented holdings.

Indian entrepreneurs also still farce a range of obstacles, many of them the result of lingering bad policies. Electric power is less reliable and more expensive in India than in competitor nations. Checkpoints keep trucks waiting for hours. Taxes and import duties have come down, but the cascading effect Of indirect taxes will continue to burden Indian manufacturers until a uniform goods-and-services tax is implemented. Stringent labor law continue to deter entrepreneurs from hiring workers. The "license raj" may be gone, but an "inspector raj" is alive and well; the "midnight knock" from an excise, customs, labor, or factory inspector still haunts the smaller entrepreneur. Some of these problems will hopefully diminish with the planned designation of new "economic zones," which promise a reduced regulatory burden.

Economic history teaches that the Industrial Revolution as it was experienced by the West was usually led by one industry. It was textile exports in the United Kingdom, railways in the United States. India, too, may have found the engine that could fuel its takeoff and transform its economy: providing white-collar services that are outsourced by companies in the rest of the world. Software and business-process outsourcing exports have grown from practically nothing to $20 billion and are expected to reach $35 billion by 2008. The constraining factor is likely to be not demand but the ability of India's educational system to produce enough quality English-speaking graduates.

Meanwhile, high-tech manufacturing, a sector where India is already demonstrating considerable strength, will also begin to expand. Perhaps in a decade, the distinction between China as "the world's workshop" and India as "the world's back office" will slowly fade as India's manufacturing and China's services catch up.

Rising Despite the State

It is an amazing spectacle to see prosperity beginning to spread in today's India even in the presence of appalling governance. In the midst of a booming private economy, Indians despair over the lack of the simplest public goods. It used to be the opposite: during India's socialist days, Indians worried about economic growth but were proud of their world-class judiciary; bureaucracy, and police force. But now, the old centralized bureaucratic Indian state is in steady decline. Where it is desperately needed—in providing basic education, health care, and drinking water—it has

performed appallingly. Where it is not needed, it has only started to give up its habit of stifling private enterprise.

Labor laws, for example, still make it almost impossible to lay off a worker—as the infamous case of Uttam Nakate illustrates. In early 1984, Nakate was found at 11:40 AM sleeping soundly on the floor of the factory in Pune where he worked. His employer let him off with a warning. But he was caught napping again and again. On the fourth occasion, the factory began disciplinary proceedings against him, and after five months of hearings, he was found guilty and sacked. But Nakate went to a labor court and pleaded that he was a victim of an unfair trade practice. The court agreed and forced the factory to take him back and pay him 50 percent of his lost wages. Only 17 years later, after appeals to the Bombay High Court and the national Supreme Court, did the factory finally win the right to fire an employee who had repeatedly been caught sleeping on the job.

Aside from highlighting the problem of India's lethargic legal system, Nakate's case dramatizes how the country's labor laws actually reduce employment, by making employers afraid to hire workers in the first place. The rules protect existing unionized workers—sometimes referred to as the "labor aristocracy"—at the expense of everyone else. At this point, the labor aristocracy comprises only 10 percent of the Indian work force.

No single institution has come to disappoint Indians more than their bureaucracy. In the 1950s, Indians bought into the cruel myth, promulgated by Nehru, that India's bureaucracy was its "steel frame," supposedly a means of guaranteeing stability and continuity after the British raj. Indians also accepted that a powerful civil service was needed to keep a diverse country together and administer the vast regulatory framework of Nehru's "mixed economy." But in the holy name of socialism, the Indian bureaucracy created thousands of controls and stifled enterprise for 40 years. India may have had some excellent business—even though civil servants, but none really understood they had the power to ruin it.

Today, Indians believe that their bureaucracy has become a prime obstacle to development, blocking instead of shepherding economic reforms. They think of bureaucrats as self-serving, obstructive, and corrupt, protected by labor laws and lifetime contracts that render them completely unaccountable. To be sure, there are examples of good performance—the building of the Delhi Metro or the expansion of the national highway system—but these only underscore how often most of the bureaucracy fails. To make matters worse, the term of any one civil servant in a particular job is getting shorter, thanks to an increase in capricious transfers. Prime Minister Singh has instituted a new appraisal system for the top bureaucracy, but it has not done much.

The Indian bureaucracy is a haven of mental power. It still attracts many of the brightest students in the country, who are admitted on the basis of a difficult exam. But despite their very high IQs, most bureaucrats fail as managers. One of the reasons is the bureaucracy's perverse incentive system; another is poor training in implementation. Indians tend to blame ideology or democracy for their failures, but the real problem is that they value ideas over accomplishment. Great strides are being made on the Delhi Metro not because the project was brilliantly conceived but because its leader sets clear, measurable goals, monitors day-to-day progress, and persistently removes obstacles. Most Indian politicians and civil servants, in contrast, fail to plan their projects well, monitor them, or follow through on them: their performance failures mostly have to do with poor execution.

The government's most damaging failure is in public education. Consider one particularly telling statistic: according to a recent study by Harvard University's Michael Kremer, one out of four teachers in India's government elementary schools is absent and one out of two present is not teaching at any given time. Even as the famed Indian Institutes of Technology have acquired a global reputation, less than half of the children in fourth-level classes in Mumbai can do first-level math. It has gotten so bad that even poor Indians have begun to pull their kids out of government schools and enroll them in private schools, which charge $1 to $3 a month in fees and which are spreading rapidly in slums and villages across India. (Private schools in India range from expensive boarding schools for the elite to low-end teaching shops in markets.) Although teachers' salaries are on average considerably lower in private schools, their students perform much better. A recent national study led by Pratham, an Indian nongovernmental organization, found that even in small villages, 16 percent of children are now in private primary schools. These kids scored 10 percent higher on verbal and math exams than their peers in public schools.

India's educational establishment, horrified by the exodus out of the public educational system, lambastes private schools and wants to close them down. NIIT Technologies, a private company with 4,000 "learning centers," has trained four million students and helped fuel India's information technology revolution in the 1990s, but it has not been accredited by the government. Ironically, legislators finally acknowledged the state's failure to deliver education a few months ago when they pushed through Parliament a law making it mandatory for private schools to reserve spots for students from low castes. As with so many aspects of India's success story, Indians are finding solutions to their problems without waiting for the government.

The same dismal story is being repeated in health and water services, which are also de facto privatized. The share of private spending on health care in India is double that in the United States. Private wells account for nearly all new irrigation capacity in the country. In a city like New Delhi, private citizens cope with an irregular water supply by privately contributing more than half the total cost of the city's water supply. At government health centers, meanwhile, 40 percent of doctors and a third of nurses are absent at any given time. According to a study by Jishnu Das and Jeffrey Hammer, of the World Bank, there is a 50 percent chance that a doctor at such a center will recommend a positively harmful therapy.

How does one explain the discrepancy between the government's supposed commitment to universal elementary education, health care, and sanitation and the fact that more and more people are embracing private solutions? One answer is that the Indian bureaucratic and political establishments are caught in a time warp, clinging to the belief that the state and the civil service must be relied on to meet people's needs. What they did not anticipate is that politicians in India's democracy would capture the bureaucracy and use the system to create jobs and revenue for friends and supporters. The Indian state no longer generates public goods. Instead, it creates private benefits for those who control it. Consequently, the Indian state has become so "riddled with perverse incentives . . . that accountability is almost impossible," as the political scientist Pratap Bhanu Mehta reported. In a recent study of India's public services, the activist and author Samuel Paul concluded that "the quality of governance is appalling."

There are many sensible steps that can be taken to improve governance. Focusing on outcomes rather than internal procedures would help, as would delegating responsibility to service providers. But what is more important is for the Indian establishment to jettison its faith in, as the political scientist James Scott puts it, "bureaucratic high modernism" and recognize that the government's job is to govern rather than to run everything. Government may have to finance primary services such as health care and education, but the providers of those services must be accountable to the citizen as though to a customer (instead of to bosses in the bureaucratic hierarchy).

None of the solutions being debated in India will bring accountability without this change in mindset. Fortunately, the people of India have already made the mental leap. The middle class withdrew from the state system long ago. Now, even the poor are depending more and more on private services. The government merely needs to catch up.

Reform School

India's Current government is led by a dream team of reformers—most notably Prime Minister Singh, a chief architect of the liberalization of 1991. Singh's left-wing-associated National Congress Party was swept into power two years ago even though the incumbent BJP (Bharatiya Janata Party) had presided over an era of unprecedented growth. The left boasted that the election was a revolt of the poor against the rich. In reality, however, it was an anti-incumbent backlash—specifically, a vote against the previous government's poor record in providing basic services. What matters to the rickshaw driver is that the police officer does not extort a sixth of his daily earnings. The farmer wants a clear title to his land without having to bribe the village headman, and his wife wants the doctor to be there when she takes her sick child to the health center. These are the areas where government touches most people's lives, and the sobering lesson from India's 2004 elections is that high growth and smart macroeconomic reforms are not enough in a democracy.

Still, the left saw the Congress victory as an opportunity. Unfortunately, it stands rigidly against reform and for the status quo, supporting labor laws that benefit 10 percent of workers at the expense of the other 90 percent and endorsing the same protectionist policies that the extreme right also backs—policies that harm consumers and favor producers. Thus, Singh and his reformist allies often seem to be sitting, frustrated, on the sidelines. For example, the new government has pushed through Parliament the National Rural Employment Guarantee Act, which many fear will simply become the biggest "loot for work" program in India's history. Although some of the original backers of the bill may have had good intentions, most legislators saw it as an opportunity for corruption. India's experience with job-creation schemes is that their benefits usually do not reach the poor; and they rarely create permanent assets even when they are supposed to: the shoddy new road inevitably gets washed away in the next monsoon. There is also the worry that the additional 1 percent of GDP borrowed from the banks to finance this program will crowd out private investment, push up interest rates, lower the economy's growth rate, and, saddest of all, actually reduce genuine employment.

Singh knows that India's economic success has not been equally shared. Cities have done better than villages. Some states have done better than others. The economy has not created jobs commensurate with its rate of growth. Only a small fraction of Indians are employed in the modern, unionized sector. Thirty-six million are reportedly unemployed. But Singh also knows that one of the primary reasons for these failures is rigid labor laws—which he wants to reform, if only the left would let him.

Singh's challenge is to get the majority of Indians united behind reform. One of the reasons that the pace of reform has been so slow is that none of India's leaders has ever bothered to explain to voters why reform is good and just how it will help the poor. (Chinese leaders do not face this problem, which is peculiar to democracies.) Not educating their constituents is the great failure of India's reformers. But it is not too late for Singh and the reformers in his administration—most notably Finance Minister Palaniappan Chidambaram and the head of the Planning Commission, Montek Singh Ahluwalia—to start appearing on television to conduct lessons in basic economics. If the reformers could convert the media and some members of Parliament, the bureaucracy, and the judiciary to their cause, Indians would be less likely to fall hostage to the seductive rhetoric of the left. If they were to admit honestly that the ideas India followed from 1950 to 1990 were wrong, people would respect them. If they were to explain that India's past regulations suppressed the people and were among the causes of poverty, people would understand.

People Power

Shashi Kumar is 29 years old and comes from a tiny village in Bihar, India's most backward and feudal state. His grandfather was a low-caste sharecropper in good times and a day laborer in bad ones. His family was so poor that they did not eat some nights. But Kumar's father somehow managed to get a job in a transport company in Darbhanga, and his mother began to teach in a private school, where Kumar was educated at no cost under her watchful eye. Determined that her son should escape the indignities of Bihar, she tutored him at night, got him into a college, and, when he finished, gave him a railway ticket for New Delhi.

Kumar is now a junior executive in a call center in Gurgaon that serves customers in the United States. He lives in a nice flat, which he bought last year with a mortgage, drives an Indica car, and sends his daughter to a good private school. He is an average, affable young Indian, and like so many of his kind he has a sense of life's possibilities. Prior to 1991, the realization of these possibilities was open only to those with a government job. If you got an education and did not get into the government, you faced a nightmare that was called "educated unemployment." But now, Kumar says, anyone with an education, computer skills, and some English can make it.

India's greatness lies in its self-reliant and resilient people. They are able to pull themselves up and survive, even flourish, when the state fails to deliver. When teachers and doctors do not show up at government primary schools and health centers, Indians just open up cheap private schools and clinics in the slums and get on with it. Indian entrepreneurs claim that they are hardier because they have had to fight not only their competitors but also state inspectors. In short, India's society has triumphed over the state.

But in the long run, the state cannot merely withdraw. Markets do not work in a vacuum. They need a network of regulations and institutions; they need umpires to settle disputes. These institutions do not just spring up; they take time to develop. The Indian state's greatest achievements lie in the noneconomic sphere. The state has held the world's most diverse country together in relative peace for 57 years. It has started to put a modern institutional framework in place. It has held free and fair elections without interruption. Of its 3.5 million village legislators, 1.2 million are women. These are proud achievements for an often bungling state with disastrous implementation skills and a terrible record at day-to-day governance.

Moreover, some of the most important post-1991 reforms have been successful because of the regulatory institutions established by the state. Even though the reforms have been slow, imperfect, and incomplete, they have been consistent and in one direction. And it takes courage, frankly, to give up power, as the Indian state has done for the past 15 years. The stubborn persistence of democracy is itself one of the Indian state's proudest achievements. Time and again, Indian democracy has shown itself to be resilient and enduring—giving a lie to the old prejudice that the poor are incapable of the kind of self-discipline and sobriety that make for effective self-government. To be sure, it is an infuriating democracy, plagued by poor governance and fragile institutions that have failed to deriver basic public goods. But India's economic success has been all the more remarkable for its issuing from such a democracy.

Still, the poor state of governance reminds Indians of how far they are from being a truly great nation. They will reach such greatness only when every Indian has access to a good school, a working health clinic, and clean drinking water. Fortunately, half of India's population is under 25 years old. Based on current growth trends, India should be able to absorb an increasing number of people into its labor force. And it will not have to worry about the problems of an aging population. This will translate into what economists call a "demographic dividend," which will help India reach a level of prosperity at which, for the first time in its history, a majority of its citizens will not have to worry about basic needs. Yet India cannot take its golden age of growth for granted. If it does not continue down its path of reform—and start to work on bringing governance up to par with the private economy—then a critical opportunity will have been lost.

GURCHARAN DAS is former CEO of Procter & Gamble India and the author of *India Unbound: The Social and Economic Revolution From Independence to the Global Information Age.*

Industrial Revolution 2.0

In the corner offices of New York and Tokyo, business leaders cling to the notion that their designs, technologies, and brands are cutting edge. Increasingly, however, that just isn't so. In industries ranging from steel and cement to automobiles and electronics, "Third World companies" are poised to overtake their Western rivals. Get ready for the biggest firms you've never heard of to become household names.

ANTOINE VAN AGTMAEL

For a few minutes, I held the future in my hand. The third-generation cell phone in my palm made a BlackBerry look like a Model T Ford. Looking down at the color video screen, I could see the person on the other end of the line. The gadget, which fit easily into my pocket, could check local traffic, broadcast breaking television news, and play interactive computer games across continents. Internet and e-mail access were a foregone conclusion. So were downloading music and watching video clips.

None of this would be all that surprising were it not for where I was standing. I wasn't visiting Apple Computers in Cupertino, California, or Nokia headquarters outside Helsinki. It was January 2005, and I was in Taiwan, standing in the research lab of High Tech Computer Corporation (HTC). The innovative Taiwanese company employs 1,100 research engineers, invented the iPAQ pocket organizer (which it sold to Hewlett-Packard), and developed a series of advanced handheld phones for companies such as Palm, Verizon, and Vodafone. All around me were young, smart, ambitious engineers. They represented the cream of the crop of Taiwanese universities with, in some cases, years of experience in international firms. They were hard at work testing everything from sound quality in a sophisticated acoustics studio to the scratch resistance of newly developed synthetic materials.

I was being shown not just the prototype of a new smart phone but the prototype of a new kind of company—savvy, global, and, most important, well ahead of its nearest competitors in the United States and Europe. My experience in Taiwan is not that unusual. From Asia to Latin America, companies that many still regard as "Third World" makers of cheap Electronics or producers of raw materials are emerging as competitive firms capable of attaining world-class status. Only a decade ago, the attention of the international business community was focused on a new economy backed by hot tech firms in California and Tokyo. But

the reality of the current global dynamic is that, more likely than not, the next Microsoft or General Electric will come from the "new economies" of Asia, Latin America, and Eastern Europe, not the United States, Europe, or Japan.

Today, emerging-market countries account for 85 percent of the world's population but generate just 20 percent of global gross national product. By 2035, however, the combined economies of emerging markets will be larger than (and by the middle of this century, nearly double) the economies of the United States, Western Europe, or Japan. The reality of globalization—which is only slowly and reluctantly sinking in—is that outsourcing means more than having "cheap labor" toil away in mines, factories, and call centers on behalf of Western corporations. Yet in the West, business leaders and government officials cling to the notion that their companies lead the world in technology, design, and marketing prowess.

Just as the Industrial Revolution turned American companies from imitators to innovators, emerging-market multinationals will do the same.

Increasingly, that just isn't so. South Korea's Samsung is now a better recognized brand than is Japan's Sony. Its research and development budget is larger than that of America's Intel. And its 2005 profits exceeded those of Dell, Motorola, Nokia, and Philips, Mexico's CEMEX is now the largest cement company in the United States, the second largest in the United Kingdom, and the third largest in the world. The gas reserves of Russian giant Gazprom are larger than those of all the major oil companies combined, and its market capitalization—or total stock value—is larger than that of Microsoft. South Korean engineers are helping U.S. steel companies modernize their outdated plants. New proprietary drugs are being developed in Indian and Slovenian labs, where researchers are no longer content to turn out high volumes of low-cost generics for sale in the United States and Europe. New inventions in consumer electronics and wireless technology are moving from Asia to the United States and Europe, not just the other way around.

The growth in emerging-market companies has been nothing short of astounding. In 1988, there were just 20 companies in emerging markets' with sales topping $1 billion. Last year, there were 270, including at least 38 with sales exceeding $10 billion. In 1981, the total value of all stocks listed on stock exchanges in emerging markets was $80 billion. That was less than the market capitalization of the largest emerging-market firm, Samsung, in 2005. Over the past quarter century, the total market capitalization of emerging markets as a group has risen to more than $5 trillion. Twenty-five years ago, portfolio investors had invested less than a few hundred-million dollars in emerging-market firms. Today, annual portfolio investment flows of more than $60 billion constitute the leading edge of a trend. Fifty-eight of the Fortune 500 top global corporations are from emerging markets, and many of them are more profitable than their peers in the West. The era of emerging-market companies being nothing more than unsophisticated makers of low-cost, low-tech products has ended.

Lifting the Veil

Most people are blissfully unaware that companies from emerging markets already play a major part in their lives by making much of what they eat, drink, and wear. One reason that these new multinationals have flown below the radar of so many executives, as well as the general public, is that companies such as Taiwan-based Yue Yuen and Hon Hai remain deliberately hidden in the shadows. Even though Yue Yuen produces the actual shoes for Nike and Hon Hai makes much of what can be found inside Dell computers, Apple iPods, and Sony PlayStations, the bigger brands continue to control the distribution and marketing. When will they remove their veil? These firms' prevailing invisibility—a conscious stealth strategy in some cases—does not mean that they are powerless, less profitable, or that they will be content to have a low profile forever. It won't be long before the biggest companies you have never heard of become household names.

Companies like Samsung, LG, and Hyundai, all based in South Korea, began by making products efficiently and cheaply. Now, they have recognized brand names, a high-quality image, world-class technology, and appealing designs. China's Haier, the country's leading producer of household appliances, is following in their footsteps. In fact, it is already better known than GE, Sony, or Toyota by hundreds of millions of consumers in China, India, and other emerging markets. Firms such as Haier have not relied on big brand names to reach consumers in the United States and Europe. Instead, they used niche products such as small refrigerators and wine coolers to get their lines into big-box stores such as Walmart. And as time goes on, more

emerging-market firms will overtake the long-established Western companies that they now supply.

That has already happened in a number of industries ranging from semiconductors to beer. Samsung now holds the No. 1 global market position not only in semiconductors used in hard disks and flash memory cards but also in flat-screen monitors used for computers and televisions. In 2004, China's Lenovo purchased IBM's ThinkPad brand. In a wholly different industry, Brazilian investment bankers merged domestic beer companies in 1999 and then swapped shares with Europe's largest beer giant, Interbrew, to form a new entity that is now managed by a Brazilian CEO. Meanwhile, Corona beer, produced by Mexico's Modelo, is now the leading imported beer brand in the United States. Elsewhere, the global supply chain is turning upside-down, with Western companies selling components and services to multinationals from emerging markets. GE, for instance, sells jet engines to Brazilian plane manufacturer Embraer. Other smart firms will soon follow suit. Just as the rise of the United States after the Industrial Revolution turned American companies from imitators into innovators, emerging-market multinationals will increasingly do the same.

For many of these firms, the road to success included weathering global financial crises. These economic shocks squeezed out many emerging-market companies. The ensuing Darwinian struggle for survival left only battle-hardened firms still standing. As newcomers, emerging multinationals had to fight for shelf space against preconceived notions of inferior product quality (a bias that wasn't always without justification). When the financial crises were over, a few world-class companies had carved out leading roles. Today, more than 25 emerging-market multinationals have attained a leading global market share in their respective industries. Fifteen command the No. 1 market share—and they are no longer limited to a narrow slice of low-tech industries. The truth is, emerging multinationals now maintain dominant market positions in some of the world's fastest-growing industries. Consider Samsung, which is the global market leader in flash memory cards used in iPods, cameras, and mobile phones. The memory card market was worth $370 million in 2000. This year, it is valued at $13 billion. In fact, more than half of all emerging-market companies of world-class status operate in capital-intensive or technology-oriented industries, where high rates of spending on research and development are required to remain competitive.

Nothing to Lose

But the road to success has not been easy. Emerging-market multinationals did not succeed simply by following textbook practices and solutions. Contrary to popular belief, it is unconventional thinking, adaptability, a global mind-set, and disciplined ambition—not natural resources or the advantage of lowcost labor—that have been the crucial ingredients for their success. As newcomers, emerging-market firms could only wrestle away market share from deeply entrenched incumbents through audacious solutions. Their success hinged upon novel thinking that was widely ridiculed by competitors from the rich world. In many cases, emerging multinationals became

From Small-Time to Prime-Time

A growing number of companies in emerging markets now enjoy the No. 1 global market share for their products. Here's a look at some of the industries they dominate.

Company	Industry	Country
Samsung Electronics	Flat-screen televisions	South Korea
Aracruz Celulose	Market pulp for paper products	Brazil
Sasol	Synthetic fuels	South Africa
TSMC	Logic semiconductors	Taiwan
Yue Yuen	Athletic and casual shoes	Hong Kong
MISC	Liquified natural gas shipping	Malaysia
Embraer	Regional jet aircraft	Brazil
Gazprom	Natural gas	Russia
Hon Hai	Electronics manufacturing by contract	Taiwan
Tenaris	Oil pipes	Argentina

successful only by following the opposite of tried and true textbook policies. Two of the best examples are Taiwan's HTC and Argentina's Tenaris.

By the 1990s, Taiwanese companies had carved out a leading position in notebook computers and various PC accessories. But they were way behind on smaller, more cutting-edge personal digital assistants (PDAS) and smart phones. Until 1997, that is, when a group of Taiwanese engineers got together and decided that the future was elsewhere. Instead of making knockoff organizers or cheap cell phones, the engineers at HTC designed the stylish iPAQ, the first PDA to challenge Palm's unrivaled position. The iPAQ had elements that Palm and other manufacturers had studiously avoided—a Microsoft operating system, an Intel chip, and a Sony screen, all technologies that mobile companies had hitherto considered inferior. But HTC recognized that wireless technology would soon turn PDAS into pocket PCs, combining cell phones with e-mail and Internet access. That insight helped them land a contract to become the primary manufacturer of the Treo PDA and inspired them to embark on a leapfrogging Effort by designing a whole series of versatile handhelds and smart phones that eventually became the chief Windows-based competitors of BlackBerry.

A similarly innovative approach was taken in Argentina by oil-pipe manufacturer Siderca. Realizing that government protection had led to technological mediocrity and a poor global image, Siderca CEO Paolo Rocca decided that global oil giants wanted more than top-quality pipes. They wanted suppliers that could react quickly to their needs anywhere in the world, able to deliver a pipe to a remote oil well in the middle of Nigeria on short notice. Siderca already had loose alliances with companies in Brazil, Italy, Japan, Mexico, and Romania. Rocca transformed this ad hoc group of companies into a well-oiled machine that was able to integrate researchers from far-flung subsidiaries to invent sophisticated pipes that were increasingly in demand for deep-ocean and arctic drilling operations. He also introduced high-tech systems that enabled the company to deliver its pipes "just in time" to the major oil companies, a feat that took leading, rich-world players such as Mannesmann several years to match. When Rocca was finished, the small "club" of traditional Western oil-pipe makers had lost its stranglehold on the market.

Emerging markets now control the bulk of the world's foreign exchange reserves and energy resources.

Other examples abound. Take Aracruz, in Brazil. The company used eucalyptus trees to make market pulp, even though it had generally been looked down upon before as "filler pulp" while the "real" pulp was made from slow-growing pine trees. In Mexico, CEMEX began a global acquisition spree by taking over two Spanish cement producers after it was locked out of the U.S. market by anti-dumping laws. The company's CEO, Lorenzo Zambrano, says, "For Spaniards, the idea of a Mexican company coming to Spain and changing top management was unthinkable."

Superior execution and an obsession with quality are now hallmarks of virtually all of the world-class companies based in emerging markets. That has helped feed a mind-set in which emerging multi-nationals are no longer content with being viewed as leading Chinese, Korean, Mexican, or Taiwanese companies. They aspire to be global, and this aspiration is rapidly becoming a reality.

Back to the Future?

Those who recall the Cold War may be forgiven for entertaining a sense of déjà vu. The launch of Sputnik in 1957 prompted anxieties that the West was falling behind. Two decades later, the overwhelming success of Japanese firms Toyota and Sony resulted in alarmed cries that "the Japanese are winning." Similar calls, proclaiming that the Chinese and the Indians are winning, can be heard today. But those who speak of winners and losers are regarding the global economy as a zero-sum game. There is ample reason to believe that is not the case—not based on naive internationalism, but on the well-justified belief that, in the current global economic order, both sides can come out ahead.

Many emerging multinationals are already owned by shareholders from all over the world. Foreign shareholders own 52 percent of Samsung, 71 percent of CEMEX, 57 percent of Hon Hai, and 54 percent of India-based Infosys. As a group, emerging multinationals can claim about 50 percent of their ownership as being foreign. Emerging multinationals are also becoming significant employers in the United States and Europe, as well as attractive prospective employers for business school graduates and scientists. More than 30,000 people in the United States and Europe work for CEMEX, many more than the company employs in Mexico. Its management meetings are conducted in English, because more than half of the firm's employees do not speak Spanish. Hyundai just opened a plant in Alabama, creating 2,000 American jobs; its regional suppliers employ an additional 5,500 workers. Haier makes most of its refrigerators for the U.S. market at a plant in North Carolina.

Of course, the road ahead for these emerging-market winners will not be without setbacks. Motorola's Razr cell phone has already helped the firm recover much of the ground it lost to Samsung. CEMEX's aggressive acquisition strategy may have worked, but the takeover bids of other emerging multinationals have failed, including Haier's bid to buy Maytag. Others have fallen flat, such as the Taiwanese company BenQ's failure to turn around Germany's Siemens Mobile. The very fact that the Latin and Asian financial crises are receding in memory and that new public offerings by Chinese and Russian companies are often oversubscribed could tempt these emerging competitors to rest on their laurels. An unexpected crisis or decline in China's growth could deliver a blow to the economy that many consider the anchor of the developing world. And a growing list of innovative companies—such as Amazon, Apple, Google, Qualcomm, and Toyota, with its new hybrid car in Japan—reveals that the rich world's creativity is far from dead.

Still, the larger trends are clear. In recent years, it has become apparent that the dominance of the United States as a superpower is resulting in its deepening dependence on foreign money, foreign resources, foreign professionals, and, increasingly, foreign technology. Only 25 years ago, most sophisticated investors scoffed at the notion of investing even a tiny portion of respectable retirement funds or endowments in developing-world companies. Just as the conventional wisdom then wrongly depicted emerging markets as "Third World," today it is all too common to underestimate the leading companies from these markets. Emerging markets now control the bulk of the world's foreign exchange reserves and energy resources. They are growing faster than the United States and many European countries (and have been for decades). Most have budget and trade surpluses, and a few are even recognized as major economic powers.

Standing inside a research lab in China, South Korea, or Taiwan, it is painfully clear just how stymieing Western protectionism has been for Western companies. Such measures led to a false sense of security, a reluctance to streamline, and a lack of innovative thinking in industries ranging from steel and automobiles, to electronics and cement. As Western firms spent the 1980s and 90s protecting themselves from foreign exports, emerging multinationals built campuses of bright, young software engineers in India and incredibly efficient mining operations in Brazil and Chile. Instead of denying the new reality, the West must formulate a creative response to this global shift of power. That task is now the central economic challenge of our time.

ANTOINE VAN AGTMAEL, known for coining the term "emerging markets," is founder and chief investment officer of Emerging Markets Management L.L.C. He is the author of *The Emerging Markets Century: How a New Breed of World Class Companies is Taking over the World* (New York: Free Press, 2007).

The Protection Racket

**Development activists finally realize that free trade
is not evil. When do they plan to tell the poor?**

Arvind Panagariya

It has been encouraging to watch advocates for the world's poor become more sophisticated about the benefits of trade liberalization in recent years. It is now rare to find groups, such as Public Citizen, that are against all forms of liberalization. Most, including Oxfam, Christian Aid, and ActionAid, agree that poor countries would benefit if rich countries lowered their trade barriers. What remains puzzling is why these same organizations resist following their logic any further. Why do those speaking on behalf of the poor fail to realize that developing countries will also benefit from their own liberalization? Why do so many otherwise knowledgeable voices still recommend that developing countries practice poor-world protectionism?

Development activists are slow to accept that liberalization by poor countries—even if rich countries don't respond in kind—increases exports and thereby strengthens developing-country economies. For instance, when Bangladesh lowers its trade barriers, it makes the domestic market less profitable in relation to the world market, therefore encouraging its people to export more. Opening the door to world markets can also usher in new technology and bring out the best in a country's entrepreneurs by encouraging competition with the world's most efficient suppliers of high-quality products.

South Korea's and India's roads to development are good examples of the choice many poor countries face today. Until 1960, the two countries tried to grow by protecting fragile national industries. Then South Korea switched to an export-oriented strategy and proceeded to dismantle trade restrictions across the board. The results weren't long in coming. Seoul produced impressive annual growth rates of 23.7 percent in exports, 18 percent in imports, and 6.3 percent in per capita income between 1961 and 1980. The country's exports as a proportion of gross domestic product (GDP) jumped from 5.3 to 33.1 percent during the same period.

India, on the other hand, toyed with liberalization in the 1960s but never got serious about encouraging its exporters or eliminating restrictions on imports. The government kept an array of domestic industries on life support, without regard to their inefficiency or comparative advantage. India's trade regime was so repressive that (excluding cereal and oil) its imports as a percentage of GDP fell from 7 percent in 1958 to just 3 percent in 1976. Despite stable politics and a highly capable bureaucracy, India saw its per capita GDP grow at a slothful 1.1 percent between 1961 and 1980.

It's tough to find an example of a developing country that has grown rapidly while maintaining high trade barriers. Some have argued that India's and China's recent growth spurts buck the trend. True, protectionist policies were in place when the two countries began to grow rapidly, but they sustained their booms only through massive trade liberalization. And because the liberalization occurred over at least 20 years, the two countries managed to escape some of the most painful social side effects.

Unable to muster empirical support for their positions, today's apologists for protectionism contend that agriculture—now the critical trade issue—is somehow different. Successive Indian commerce ministers, for example, have argued that they cannot risk the lives of the 650 million Indians who depend on agriculture for their livelihood. Oxfam has made similar arguments about countries such as Vietnam and Ghana. Acknowledging that economic liberalization must proceed gradually and with proper safety nets for dislocated farmers hardly supports the protectionist position. There is no reason to believe that the benefits that flow from competition in every other industry do not exist in agriculture, too. Yes, rich countries massively subsidize their own agriculture. But poor countries lose from their trade barriers with or without rich-country subsidies.

Chile's agricultural exports, for example, grew from $1.2 billion to $4.9 billion between 1991 and 2001 as it liberalized. Even India, which has only half-heartedly opened its agricultural sector by removing export restrictions and eliminating exchange-rate overvaluation, saw its agricultural exports rise from $3.4 billion in 1991 to $7.4 billion in 2004. Importantly, this expansion occurred without a significant reduction in agricultural trade barriers in developed country markets.

It's an illusion to believe that rich countries will simply lift their trade barriers without demanding the same of their trading partners in the developing world. Recent history is evidence enough. In 1965, developed countries committed to eliminating trade barriers that were particularly harmful to poor economies.

Yet, with the developing countries opting out of direct negotiations, barriers to imports of agricultural products, textiles, and clothing rose rather than declined. It was only when developing countries joined the Uruguay Round of trade talks through what is now the World Trade Organization that developed countries abolished import quotas on textiles and clothing.

Like South Korea and India before them, today's poorest countries face a choice. They can either wait in vain for rich countries to unilaterally drop their trade barriers, take the time to negotiate mutual concessions, or liberalize their own markets—regardless of what the rich countries do. Getting developed countries to simultaneously liberalize will allow developing countries to multiply the benefits of their own liberalization, but that welcome prospect shouldn't be cause for delay. Unilateralism may be harmful when it comes to matters of peace and war, but when it comes to trade and development, it can be all to the good.

ARVIND PANAGARIYA is professor of economics at Columbia University.

Social Justice and Global Trade

JOSEPH STIGLITZ

The history of recent trade meetings—from Seattle to Daha to Cancun to Hong Kong—shows that something is wrong with the global trading system. Behind the discontent are some facts and theories.

The facts: Current economic arrangements disadvantage the poor. Tariff levels by the advanced industrial countries against the developing countries are four times higher than against the developed countries. The last round of trade negotiations, the Uruguay Round, actually left the poorest countries worse off. While the developing countries were forced to open up their markets and eliminate subsidies, the advanced developed countries continued to subsidize agriculture and kept trade barriers against those products which are central to the economies of the developing world.

Indeed, the tariff structures are designed to make it more difficult for developing countries to move up the value-added chain—to transition, for instance, from producing raw agricultural produce to processed foods. As tariffs have come down, America has increasingly resorted to the use of nontariff barriers as the new forms of protectionism. Trade agreements do not eliminate protectionist sentiments or the willingness of governments to attempt to protect producer and worker interests.

The theories: Trade liberalization leads to economic growth, benefiting all. This is the prevalent mantra. Political leaders champion liberalization. Those who oppose it are cast as behind the times, trying to roll back history.

Yet the fact that so many seem to have been hurt so much by globalization seems to belie their claims. Or more accurately, it has shown that the process of "liberalization"—the details of the trade agreements—make a great deal of difference.

That Mexico has done so poorly under NAFTA has not helped the case for liberalization. If there ever was a free trade agreement that should have promoted growth, that was it, for it opened up to Mexico the largest market of the world. But growth in the decade since has been slower than in the decades before 1980, and the poorest in the country, the corn farmers, have been particularly hurt by subsidized American corn.

The fact of the matter is that the economics of trade liberalization are far more complicated than political leaders have portrayed them. There are some circumstances in which trade liberalization brings enormous benefits—when there are good risk markets, when there is full employment, when an economy is mature. But none of these conditions are satisfied in developing countries. With full employment, a worker who loses his job to new imports quickly finds another; and the movement from low-productivity protected sectors to high-productivity export sectors leads to growth and increased wages. But if there is high unemployment, a worker who loses his job may remain unemployed. A move from a low-productivity, protected sector to the unemployment pool does not increase growth, but it does increase poverty. Liberalization can expose countries to enormous risks, and poor countries—and especially the poor people in those countries—are ill equipped to cope with those risks.

Perhaps most importantly, successful development means going stagnant traditional sectors with low productivity to more modern sectors with faster increases in productivity. But without protection, developing countries cannot compete in the modern sector. They are condemned to remain in the low growth part of the global economy. South Korea understood this. Thirty-five years ago, those who advocated free trade essentially told Korea to stick with rice farming. But Korea knew that even if it were successful in improving productivity in rice farming, it would be a poor country. It had to industrialize.

What are we to make of the oft-quoted studies that show that countries that have liberalized more have grown faster? Put aside the numerous statistical problems that plague almost all such "cross-country" studies. Most of the studies that claim that liberalization leads to growth do no such thing. They show that countries that have traded more have grown more. Studies that focus directly on liberalization—that is, what happens when countries take away trade barriers—present a less convincing picture that liberalization is good for growth.

But we know which countries around the world have grown the fastest: they are the countries of East Asia, and their growth was based on export-driven trade. They did not pursue policies of unfettered liberalization. Indeed, they actively intervened in markets to encourage exports, and only took away trade barriers as their exports grew. They avoided the pitfall described earlier of individuals moving from low-productivity sectors into zero productivity unemployment by maintaining their economies at close to full employment.

The point is that no country approaches liberalization as an abstract concept that it might or might not buy in to for the good of the world. Every country wants to know: For a country with its unemployment rate, with its characteristics, with its financial markets, will liberalization lead to faster growth?

If the economics are nuanced, the politics are simple. Trade negotiations provide a field day for special interests. Their agenda is also straightforward: Exporters want others' markets opened up; those threatened by competition do not. Trade negotiators pay little attention to principles (though they work hard to clothe their position under the guise of principle). They pay attention to campaign contributions and votes.

In the most recent trade talks, for example, enormous attention has been focused on developed countries' protection of their agricultural sectors—protections that exist because of the power of vested agricultural interests there. Such protectionism has become emblematic of the hypocrisy of the West in preaching free trade yet practicing something quite different. Some 25,000 rich American cotton farmers, reliant on government subsidies for cotton, divide among themselves some $3 billion to $4 billion a year, leading to higher production and lower prices. The damage that these subsidies wreak on some 10 million cotton farmers eking out a subsistence living in sub-Saharan Africa is enormous. Yet the United States seems willing to put the interests of 25,000 American cotton farmers above that of the global trading system and the well-being of millions in the developing world. It is understandable if those in the developing world respond with anger.

The anger is increased by America's almost cynical attitude in "marketing" its offers. For instance, at the Hong Kong meeting, U.S. trade officials reportedly offered to eliminate import restrictions on cotton but refused to do anything about subsidies. The cotton subsidies actually allow the U.S. to export cotton. When a country can export a particular commodity, it does little good to allow imports of that commodity. America, to great fanfare, has made an offer worth essentially zero to the developing countries and berated them for not taking it up on its "generous" offer.

At home, the Bush administration might be working harder to provide greater access to low-cost drugs. In trade negotiations, though, it takes the side of drug companies, arguing for stronger intellectual property protection, even if the protection of pharmaceutical-company patents means unnecessary deaths for hundreds of thousands of people who cannot afford the monopoly prices but could be treated if generic medicines were made available.

The international community has announced its commitment to helping the developing countries reduce poverty by half by 2015. There have been enormous efforts at increasing aid and debt relief. But developing countries do not want just a hand out; they want a hand up. They need and want enhanced opportunities for earning a living. That is what a true development round would provide.

In short, trade liberalization should be "asymmetric," but it needs to be asymmetric in a precisely opposite way to its present configuration. Today, liberalization discriminates against developing countries. It needs to discriminate in their favor. Europe has shown the way by opening up its economy to the poorest countries of the world in an initiative called Everything But Arms. Partly because of complicated regulations ("rules of origin"), however, the amount of increased trade that this policy has led to has been very disappointing thus far. Because agricul-

ture is still highly subsidized and restricted, some call the policy "Everything But Farms." There is a need for this initiative to be broadened. Doing this would help the poor enormously and cost the rich little. In fact, the advanced industrial countries as a whole would be better off, and special interests in these countries would suffer.

There is, in fact, abroad agenda of trade liberalization (going well beyond agriculture) that would help the developing countries. But trade is too important to be left to trade ministers. If the global trade regime is to reflect common shared values, then negotiations over the terms of that trade regime cannot be left to ministers who, at least in most countries, are more beholden to corporate and special interests than almost any other ministry. In the last round, trade ministers negotiated over the terms of the intellectual property agreement. This is a subject of enormous concern to almost everyone in today's society. With excessively strong intellectual property rights, one can have monopolies raising prices and Stirling innovation. Poor countries will not have access to life-saving medicines. That was why both the Office of Science and Technology Policy and the Council of Economic Advisers opposed the TRIPS (intellectual property) provisions of the Uruguay Round. It reflected the interests of America's drug and entertainment industries, not the most important producers of knowledge, those in academia. And it certainly did not reflect the interests of users, either in the developed or less-developed countries. But the negotiations were conducted in secret, in Geneva. The U.S. trade representative (like most other trade ministers) was not an expert in intellectual property; he received his short course from the drug companies, and he quickly learned how to espouse their views. The agreement reflected this one-sided perspective.

Several reforms in the structure of trade talks are likely to lead to better outcomes. The first is that the basic way in which trade talks are approached should be changed. Now, it is a clear negotiation. Each country seeks to get the best deal for its firms. This stands in marked contrast to how legislation in all other arenas of public policy is approached. Typically, we ask what our objectives are, and how we can best achieve them. Around those themes, of course, there are negotiations. There are often large differences in views both about what should be the objectives and how best to achieve them. If we began trade talks from this position of debate and inquiry, we could arrive at a picture of what a true development round look like.

Thinking of the task of the WTO as creating a legal framework reflecting principles of fairness, social justice and efficiency—akin to how we think about domestic rules and regulations governing economic behavior—helps us think about what other reforms are needed. We simply need to think about how we attempt to improve the quality of domestic democratic processes and legislation by increasing, for instance, transparency and other governance reforms.

Transparency is essential so there can be more open debate about the merits of various proposals and a chance to put a check on the abuses special interests. Clearly, had there been more transparency and open debate, the excesses in intellectual property protection of the Uruguay Round might have been avoided.

As more and more countries have demanded a voice in trade negotiations, there is often nostalgia for the old system in which four partners (the U.S., EU, Canada and Japan) could hammer out a deal. There are complaints that the current system with so many members is simply unworkable. We have learned how to deal with this problem in other contexts, however, using the principles of representation. We must form a governing council with representatives of various "groups"—a group of the least developed countries, of the agricultural exporting countries, etc. Each representative makes sure that the concerns of his or her constituency are heard. Such a system would be far better than the current "green room" procedures wherein certain countries are put together (in the green room) to negotiate a whole or part of the deal.

Finally, trade talks need to have more focus. Issues like intellectual property should never heven have been part of the Uruguay Round. There already was an international institution dealing with matters of intellectual property. It is not only that trade ministers are ill-equipped to understand what is at issue, and they are therefore subject to undue influence from the special interests that have long held sway over trade ministries. Broadening the agenda also puts developing countries at a particular disadvantage, because they do not have the resources to engage on a broad front of issues.

The most important changes are, however, not institutional changes, but changes in mindset. There should be an effort on the part of each of the countries to think about what kind of international rules and regulations would contribute to a global trading system that would be fair and efficient, and that would promote development.

Fifteen years ago, there was a great deal of optimism about the benefits which globalization and trade would bring to all countries. It has brought enormous benefits to some countries; but not to all. Some have even been made worse off. Development is hard enough. An unfair trade regime makes it even more difficult. Reforming the WTO would not guarantee that we would get a fair and efficient global trade regime, but it would enhance the chances that trade and globalization come closer to living up to their potential for enhancing the welfare of everyone.

Mr. Stiglitz is a professor of economics at Columbia University. In 2001, he was awarded the Nobel Prize in economics.

Cotton: The Huge Moral Issue

World cotton prices have dropped to an historic low: the reason being the immoral continuation of EU and US trade subsidies that allow non-competitive and inefficient farming to continue. While the recent WTO meeting in Hong Kong failed to resolve the issue, the livelihoods of West Africa's 12 million cotton farmers will soon be destroyed if subsidies are not slashed. This is a huge moral issue.

KATE ESHELBY

Seydou, dressed in a ripped T-shirt that hangs off his shoulders, looked at me blankly as I questioned him about the effects of US subsidies on his only source of income, cotton farming. "I don't know about cotton in the US but I know cotton prices have fallen here in Burkina Faso," he lamented.

The farmers working in the cotton fields of Burkina Faso, often in remote locations, have little knowledge of the intricacies of world markets. What they do know is that the price they receive for their cotton harvests—essential for basic necessities such as medicines and school fees—is dropping fast.

The end of cotton farming in Burkina Faso and other cotton producing West African countries is rapidly approaching. World cotton prices have dropped to an historic low: the reason being the immoral continuation of EU and US trade subsidies that allow non-competitive and inefficient farming to continue.

Cotton subsidies in richer countries cause over production, artificially distorting world markets. And who suffers? The poor countries, whose economies are wholly dependent on the cotton trade.

In Burkina Faso, a former French colony in West Africa, cotton is the country's main cash crop. It is the primary source of foreign income, making up one-third of export earnings, and the lifeblood for the majority of farmers. Here cotton is grown on small, family-owned farms, seldom bigger than five hectares. One farmer, called Yacouba, explains: "I also grow maize and groundnuts on the farm, to feed my family, but cotton is my only source of cash."

In contrast, US cotton operations are enormous and yet, unlike Burkina Faso, cotton is a minimal proportion of its GDP. Ironically, the US subsidies are concentrated on the biggest, and richest, farms. One such farm based in Arkansas has 40,000 acres of cotton and receives subsidies equivalent to the average income of 25,000 people in Burkina Faso.

The benefits of subsidies only reach a small number of people in the US and other Western countries, whereas two million people in Burkina Faso, one of the world's poorest countries with few other natural resources, depend on cotton for survival.

The farms in Burkina Faso are very productive, it is cheaper and more economical to grow cotton there than in the US. "I have to take out loans each year to buy enough insecticides and fertilisers for my cotton," says Yacouba. "They are very expensive so we have to work hard to ensure we get a good harvest. Each year I worry whether I will earn enough to pay back the loans." Burkinabe farmers are forced to be efficient, also prevailing against climatic uncertainties and limited infrastructure—all this, with no support from subsidies.

Fields are prepared by plough and both seed planting and picking are done by hand, which explains why cotton is also vital for providing jobs—being very labour intensive. Yacouba explains: "My family works on the farm throughout the year, but during harvesting we bring in extra help." Pickers are dotted around the fields surrounding him, plucking the cotton balls from the shoulder-high plants. Some of the women have children tied to their backs and the sacks of cotton are steadily placed under the shade of a giant baobab tree. This scene is in stark contrast to the US where huge, computerised harvesters pick the cotton and aerial spraying administers the chemicals required.

The meeting (in mid-December 2005) of the World Trade Organisation (WTO) in Hong Kong was to address this farcical situation as part of the Doha "development" talks. But nothing much came out of it. Burkina Faso is still resting its hopes on cotton subsidies being eliminated, or at least reduced, in order to save its fundamental crop from demise. The Doha negotiations, launched in 2001, are intended to show that trade could benefit the world's poor. But subsidies are a global injustice, and create major imbalances in world trade—it is argued they should only be available for products that are not exported, and targeted towards family and small-scale farmers.

The US gives approximately $3.4bn a year in subsidies to its 25,000 cotton farmers; this is more than the entire GDP of Burkina Faso. Subsidies dramatically increased in the US after the 2002 Farm Act and as a result US cotton production has recently reached historic highs. It is now the world's second largest cotton producer, after China, and the biggest exporter—an easy achievement because US cotton prices no longer bear any relation to production costs.

Current world cotton prices are in decline due to global over-production, fuelled by agricultural subsidies. EU and US taxpayers and consumers pay farmers billions of dollars to over-produce for a stagnant market. These surpluses are then dumped overseas, often in developing countries, destroying their markets and driving down world prices.

The livelihoods of West Africa's 12 million cotton farmers will soon be destroyed if subsidies are not slashed. This is a huge moral issue. It is simple—Burkina Faso cannot compete against heavily subsidised exports.

In March 2004, a WTO panel ruled that the majority of US cotton subsidies were illegal. The WTO agreements state that "domestic support should have no, or at most minimal trade-distorting effects on production." The US tried to appeal against this decision but it was overruled.

If Africa took just 1% more in world trade, it would earn $70bn more annually—three times what it now receives in aid. In 2003, Burkina Faso received $10m in US aid, but lost $13.7m in cotton export earnings, as a result of US subsidies. No country ever grew rich on charity, it is trade that holds the key to generating wealth. Fair trade would give the Burkinabe cotton farmers a decent opportunity to make a living by selling their produce, at a decent price, to the richer world; enabling them to work their way out of poverty.

The US was legally required to eliminate all trade-distorting subsidies by 21 September 2005, according to a WTO ruling. President George Bush keeps saying he will cut subsidies, but actions are louder than words. The delay is partly due to a long-standing arm wrestle between the US and the EU, neither of whom will budge. The British prime minister, Tony Blair, does seem to want to abolish EU subsidies, but the French argue that subsidies are not even negotiable. Despite four years of haggling, negotiators are still at loggerheads. Numerous reports have been compiled, many meetings held and yet scant progress has been made—and things are only getting worse for the Burkinabe cotton farmers.

"Both the US and EU brag about their boldness, but the actual reform they propose is minuscule, tiny fractions of their massive farm support. The negotiations have recently moved into the finger-pointing phase in which rich countries criticise the inadequacy of each other's proposals. Meanwhile, poor countries await something real," says Issaka Ouandago, from Oxfam's office in Burkina Faso.

Oxfam has been supporting the struggle of African cotton farmers in their campaign known as the "Big Noise", and are hoping to gather a petition of one million signatures against cotton subsidies. "We can only hope the US reform their subsidy programmes and stop dumping cheap cotton onto the world market," Ouandago continues. "Despite their WTO commitments to reduce trade-distorting subsidies, the EU and US have used loopholes and creative accounting to continue. Such practices are undermining the fragile national economics of countries that depend on cotton."

The rich countries have to come forward with more, otherwise the Doha Round will achieve nothing, as the meeting in Hong Kong proved—although developing countries have less political power, they are still capable of blocking the negotiations if they don't get what they want. In the last WTO meeting, held in Geneva, July 2004, negotiations on US cotton subsidies were supposed to be kept separate from broader agricultural negotiations—this did not happen. It was a blow for Burkina Faso and other West Africa countries who produce mainly cotton and are less interested in other commodities. A subcommittee on cotton was set up to "review" the situation, but the EU and US have not taken this committee seriously.

With the emergence of the G20 alliance, some developing countries, such as India and Brazil, are now powerful enough to resist pressures, but African countries have previously never been centre stage. West African cotton producers are, however, becoming far stronger as a group. "We have become more united to make our voice heard. Our aim is to gather all African cotton producers together," explains Yao, a member of the National Union of Cotton Producers in Burkina Faso.

The only reason Burkinabe cotton farmers are still surviving is that producer prices have been maintained at a minimum level-175 CFA per kg of cotton seed is the minimum price the farmers need to break even, prices never go below this, despite being above current world prices.

In recent years, the Burkinabe cotton companies used their profits from previous harvests to support the farmers; these savings are now depleted. The full effects of world prices have, therefore, not yet been felt by the farmers, the worst is to come—once the prices are forced to drop below this minimum, the farmers can no longer survive.

Leaving the house of Seydou, I wonder about his fate. A pile of bright-white cotton sits drying in the glaring sun, in front of his mud house. Inside the walls are bare, except for a single cross; a bundle of clothes hang from a rope and a pile of maize is stacked in the corner. "I cannot afford to buy things because cotton prices keep fluctuating," he says. "I know cotton grows well here but prices are down so I cannot send my youngest son to school. This makes me sad. I know his only chance of a good future is school."

In Burkina Faso, cotton is the country's biggest interest and essential to its economy, so it prays that cotton is addressed more seriously and given the attention it deserves. As the sun sets, the workers leave the fields, holding sacks of cotton above their heads. A donkey cart trundles by, carrying a mound of cotton—kicking up a trail of red earth. Their livelihoods depend on the decisions made at the WTO.

From *New African*, January 2006, pp. 26–28. Copyright © 2006 by IC Publications Ltd. Reprinted by permission.

"We Need Trade Justice, Not Free Trade"

PETER HARDSTAFF

Fairtrade is both a way for consumers to take individual positive action in solidarity with the poor and a way to introduce people to wider development issues.

But buying Fairtrade products should be seen as part, rather than the sum total, of the action needed to address global poverty. That is why many of the organisations which have been involved in the fair-trade movement over the years have been campaigning to change international trade rules. And, judging by events at the World Trade Organisation (WTO), there is much still to do.

This month, the stalled Doha round of international trade talks officially resumed, but there is little to celebrate in this. In fact, these are dangerous times for poor countries in the WTO. The signs are that the major trade powers are trying to stitch up a deal among themselves and present it as a fait accompli to the poorest countries. The really bad news is that what is on the table will not only not benefit these poor countries, it may do great harm.

Although many developing countries were reticent about the launch of the Doha round back in November 2001, there was huge political pressure to "do something" multilateral in the wake of the 11 September 2001 attacks. The spin merchants at the WTO decided to call the new round of trade talks a "development round," but they are struggling to maintain this façade. Several detailed studies have come to light showing that the kind of deal on the table will benefit a few rich countries; most, if not all, developing countries will lose out.

Sandra Polaski of the Carnegie Endowment for International Peace, for example, believes her research disproves the commonly held view that agricultural liberalisation benefits developing countries, and that it therefore had to be the key to achieving the development goals of the Doha round. "In fact," she has written, "agricultural liberalisation benefits only a relatively small subset of developing countries."

Her study shows that those benefiting include Brazil, Argentina, most of the rest of Latin America, South Africa and some south-east Asian countries, notably Thailand. However, the losers in agricultural liberalisation include many of the world's poorest nations, including Bangladesh, the countries of East Africa and the rest of sub-Saharan Africa. The Middle East, North Africa, Vietnam, Mexico, India and China also end up worse off.

Even the World Bank has revised downwards its estimates of developing-country "gains" from the round—which it now projects to be in the region of just $16bn—and again points towards the bulk of these gains going to the larger developing countries.

The sting in the tail, even for the likes of Brazil and South Africa, is that the benefits could be far outweighed by the costs of opening markets in the manufacturing sector; another recent study estimates these could be up to $63bn.

Poor countries in the WTO understand the situation only too well. As one African delegate commented on the restarting of talks: "Resumption? This is a false resumption. The process is to legitimise the deal that the US and EU may come up with."

The last round of trade talks—the so-called Uruguay round—was criticised as a stitch-up between the US and EU. The main difference now is that India and Brazil may end up also being party to a deal that is then passed to the rest of the WTO membership in expectation that they would rather sign than be perceived as responsible for the round "failing".

The world desperately needs a democratic global system that regulates international trade for the benefit of the environment and development, but this is not it.

Multilateralism and multilateral rules are important. We do not want a world of unilateral trade policies based on the "might is right" exercise of political and economic clout, yet something is badly wrong with the rules that are being created and with the way in which they are being created.

The European Union and the US must both reform their agricultural subsidies. But just as important, if not more so, is to give developing countries the right to use policies of the kind that rich countries were once able to develop. This means, for example, the ability to use tariffs to help fledgling industries grow and it means effective regulation of foreign investors.

We also need to see a change in the way trade talks are conducted. Poor countries deserve to have their say rather than being presented with stitched-up deals that it is politically difficult for them to refuse. In short, what we need is trade justice, not free trade.

PETER HARDSTAFF is head of policy at the World Development Movement www.wdm.org.uk

Ranking the Rich

Poverty is blamed for everything from terrorism to bird flu. Rich nations have never sounded more committed to stamping it out. Is it all just hot air? The fourth annual CGD/ FP Commitment to Development Index ranks 21 rich nations on whether they're working to end global poverty—or just making it worse.

Last year was dubbed the "Year of Development." Leaders of the world's richest nations made impassioned pleas to help the poor at a summit in Gleneagles, Scotland. At the World Economic Forum in Davos, French President Jacques Chirac proposed an airline ticket tax to fund foreign aid. At a world trade summit in Hong Kong in December, rich countries offered to phase out subsidies for their agricultural exports. U2 rocker-activist Bono jetted everywhere from Nigeria to the National Prayer Breakfast in Washington, touting The One Campaign to end global poverty, and movie stars donned insignia bracelets in support of his cause. "There can be no excuse, no defense, no justification for the plight of millions of our fellow human beings," British Prime Minister Tony Blair said in March. "There should be nothing that stands in the way of our changing it."

But are the world's richest countries actually making things better for those most in need? Each year the Center for Global Development and FOREIGN POLICY look past the rhetoric to measure how rich country governments are helping or hurting poor countries. How much aid are they giving? How high are their trade barriers against imports such as cotton from Mali or sugar from Brazil? Are they working to slow global warming? Are they making the world's sea lanes safe for global trade? To find out, the index ranks 21 nations by assessing their policies and practices across seven areas of government action: foreign aid, trade, investment, migration, environment, security, and technology.

In large part, the deeds of the last year did not live up to the talk. In most policy areas that matter for poor countries, a majority of rich-country governments either failed to follow words with meaningful action—or they simply remained silent. At Gleneagles, British and American negotiators pushed through an agreement to "drop the debt" for up to 40 poor, mostly African countries. It may sound extraordinarily generous, but this debt relief package equals a mere 1 percent increase in aid. The Group of Eight (G-8) industrialized nations also "committed" themselves to "substantially reducing" subsidies and tariffs that protect their farmers at the expense of farmers in poor countries. Again, it may have sounded good, but the G-8's offer, spelled out later in the year, was only equivalent to cutting the European Union's import barriers by 1 percent. The feebleness of the offer is one reason why world trade negotiations remain hopelessly deadlocked. No development news of the past year commanded more headlines than immigration. In the United States, millions of Latin American migrants marched in the streets and boycotted their jobs in an effort to draw attention to the positive contributions they make to America's economy. In France, demonstrations in the Paris suburbs turned violent as the country's interior minister, Nicolas Sarkozy, announced he might deport tens of thousands of immigrants back to their home countries. Yet this hotly debated issue was followed by precious little action. Prime Minister Blair convened a Commission for Africa, but it studiously avoided talking about how Britain could make it easier for someone from Kenya or Ghana to immigrate, get a job, develop skills, and send money home. In the United States, immigration legislation brewed in the U.S. Congress, but then stalled. And the subject was equally taboo for French politicians.

A less publicized event of 2005 was the notable growth in total foreign aid given by rich countries. It shot to a record $106.5 billion, thanks largely to reconstruction efforts in Iraq. But some $19 billion of that aid came in the form of the cancellation of old loans to Iraq and Nigeria. These write-offs, though long overdue, put little new money in the hands of Iraqis and Nigerians. These aid figures should also be kept in perspective. Consider that India and China added some $400 billion to their combined economic output last year alone. That's proof that internal, not external, forces more often drive economic development. China's export of goods and India's export of services to rich countries have helped produce economic growth and poverty reduction so rapid that the Millennium Development Goal of a 50 percent cut in the number of people living on $1 a day has probably already been met on a global level.

Internal factors may drive development, but external ones can facilitate it—or stand in the way. That point was made by Andrew Natsios, the former head of the U.S. Agency for International Development, when he challenged America's longstanding food aid program before stepping down in January. Natsios criticized a law that requires the U.S. government to buy food from U.S. farmers, ship it on American boats, and deliver it to famine-stricken regions via U.S.-based organizations. The U.S. government must deliver food aid this way even when it depresses local

And the Winner Is . . .

This year, the Netherlands beat Denmark to take the No. 1 ranking in the index. A new policy to limit imports of illegally cut timber from tropical nations and its support for an international effort to control bribery helped land the country in the winner's circle this year.

But the main reason the Netherlands came out on top is because others stumbled. The Danes, who have historically been among the index's best performers, registered the largest overall drop. Copenhagen was hurt by a shrinking of its foreign aid spending by 14 percent between 2001 and 2004, while its economy grew by 9 percent. New Zealand also fell, as the number of immigrants it admitted from developing countries plunged from 48,000 in 2001 to 29,000 last year.

One country that made strides this year is Japan, which has finished dead last every year since the index was launched in 2003. It reportedly put an end to a long-held practice of lobbying poor-country governments against enforcing labor, human rights, and environmental standards for Japanese-owned factories. The United States improved its score, due in part to falling farm subsidies and rising foreign aid. Spain posted the most spectacular gains, thanks to a migration policy that makes it easier for immigrants to enter and work legally.

For the 21 rich countries as a whole, the overall trend continues to be one of little change. The average score for all the index countries climbed modestly from 5.0 in 2003 to 5.3 in 2005, then fell slightly to 5.2 this year. Still, twice as many countries have seen their score improve as have seen their score decline in the past four years. That's an encouraging trend, because development is about more than just giving money; it's about the rich and powerful taking responsibility for policies that affect the poor and powerless.

CDI Performance over Time

Country	2003	2004	2005	2006	Change 2003 2006	Rank by Improvement
Spain	3.9	4.4	4.7	4.8	+0.9	1
United Kingdom	4.6	4.8	5.3	5.1	+0.5	2
United States	4.5	4.9	5.0	5.0	+0.5	2
Japan	2.7	2.9	2.8	3.1	+0.4	4
Portugal	4.4	4.9	4.9	4.8	+0.4	4
Sweden	5.9	6.5	6.6	6.3	+0.4	4
Canada	4.9	5.1	5.3	5.2	+0.3	7
Greece	3.7	3.9	4.1	4.0	+0.3	7
Ireland	4.7	4.8	4.9	5.0	+0.3	7
Italy	4.0	4.2	4.5	4.3	+0.3	7
Norway	5.9	6.1	6.2	6.2	+0.3	7
Finland	5.2	5.4	5.6	5.4	+0.2	12
Austria	5.3	5.4	5.4	5.4	+0.1	13
Belgium	4.8	4.6	4.9	4.9	+0.1	13
Switzerland	5.3	5.0	5.1	5.2	0.1	15
France	4.7	4.8	4.8	4.6	0.1	15
Germany	5.4	5.3	5.5	5.3	0.1	15
Netherlands	6.7	6.7	6.8	6.6	0.1	15
Australia	5.8	5.7	5.7	5.5	0.3	19
New Zealand	5.9	5.6	5.6	5.6	0.3	19
Denmark	7.0	6.9	6.7	6.4	0.6	21
Average	5.0	5.1	5.3	5.2	+0.3	

food prices, pushing more farmers into poverty, and even when it could buy food from farmers just outside a famine zone for much less. Some nongovernmental organizations that get a large fraction of their funding from the program defended the status quo, arguing that dropping the "made in America" requirement would undermine the program's support among American farmers and shippers. Congress quickly axed Natsios's proposal for reform. That the U.S. government must pay off American interests to feed the starving is a sad commentary on how low the commitment to development may still be.

It also helps explain why the United States finishes 13th in this year's index. The Netherlands, meanwhile, ranks first on the strength of its generous aid-giving, falling greenhouse gas emissions, and support for investment in developing countries. Japan improved, but remains in last place as the rich country least committed to helping the poor. It might seem strange that small nations such as the Netherlands beat out large economies such as Japan and the United States. But the index measures how well countries are living up to their potential. In truth, even the Dutch could do better. They are party, for instance, to Europe's Common Agricultural Policy, which effectively levies a 40 percent tax on farm imports from poor countries. That certainly doesn't help the world's poorest countries, no matter what anyone says.

Commitment to Development Index 2006

2006 rank	Country	Aid	Trade	Investment	Migration	Environment	Security	Technology	Average
1	Netherlands	8.5	6.2	7.8	4.8	7.5	6.1	5.3	6.6
2	Denmark	10.0	5.9	5.3	5.0	6.1	6.9	5.5	6.4
3	Sweden	9.8	6.1	6.2	4.8	7.0	4.9	5.4	6.3
4	Norway	9.3	1.2	8.0	4.6	6.1	8.1	5.9	6.2
5	New Zealand	2.2	7.6	3.7	6.9	6.4	7.4	4.9	5.6
6	Australia	2.5	6.4	6.9	6.4	3.9	8.1	4.6	5.5
7	Finland	3.9	6.1	6.2	2.7	6.7	6.3	6.3	5.4
7	Austria	2.7	5.9	3.3	10.5	6.2	4.5	4.5	5.4
9	Germany	3.3	5.9	6.8	6.2	6.7	3.7	4.3	5.3
10	Canada	3.3	6.8	7.7	4.7	4.5	3.0	6.6	5.2
10	Switzerland	4.8	3.1	7.2	9.5	5.3	1.6	5.1	5.2
12	United Kingdom	4.6	5.9	8.6	2.6	7.8	1.6	4.5	5.1
13	United States	2.2	7.4	6.9	4.6	3.2	5.9	5.0	5.0
13	Ireland	5.9	5.7	2.5	4.6	7.5	5.9	3.0	5.0
15	Belgium	5.1	5.9	6.5	2.6	6.6	3.4	4.5	4.9
16	Portugal	2.3	6.1	6.2	1.4	6.4	6.2	5.1	4.8
16	Spain	2.5	6.0	6.7	5.2	3.8	3.5	6.1	4.8
18	France	4.1	6.0	5.9	2.6	6.1	0.5	6.9	4.6
19	Italy	1.6	6.1	5.5	3.2	4.8	3.9	5.1	4.3
20	Greece	2.7	5.9	4.0	1.7	5.2	5.0	3.0	4.0
21	Japan	1.1	−0.4	5.6	1.7	4.3	2.8	6.3	3.1

Wasting Aid in Iraq

Last year was a record-smasher for foreign aid. Total aid given by index countries climbed 31.4 percent in 2005, to $106.5 billion. Not surprisingly, flows to Iraq accounted for most of this increase. This sharp rise in generosity, however, is not as much a cause for celebration as it might appear. Rarely has so much been given, and so little received.

Some $6.3 billion of the 2005 aid total was U.S. aid to Iraq, probably the largest single-year transfer between two countries since the Marshall Plan. But the index counts aid to Iraq at just 10 cents on the dollar, because the World Bank puts the country ahead of only Somalia when it comes to combating corruption and enforcing the rule of law. Sadly, events in 2005 confirmed fears about the country's rampant graft and violence. Senior Iraqi government officials estimate that as much as 30 percent of the country's budget is lost to corruption—ranging from bribery to padded contracts and influence peddling. It isn't just the Iraqis who are poor administrators. Even the U.S. government estimates that

$8.8 billion disappeared during the first 14 months that the Coalition Provisional Authority ran Iraq. As of early 2005, at least 40 percent of U.S. reconstruction aid was spent on security. "I'd say that 60, maybe even 70 percent [of what] we see as reconstruction aid goes into nonproductive expenditures," says Ali Allawi, Iraq's minister of finance.

Nor are donors as generous as they would have us believe. Of the reported aid to Iraq, $14 billion came in the form of debt relief. Back in the 1980s when Saddam Hussein had warmer ties with the United States, France, and other Western governments, he borrowed heavily from them. The loans went bad after the 1991 Gulf War. But, on paper, interest and penalties piled up until the formal write-off of the debts in late 2004. Although long overdue, in reality this debt relief put almost no additional cash into the coffers of the new Iraqi government, because most of the debts would never have been repaid anyway. Commitment? Yes. Development? Hardly.

The Government Trough

Rich countries spend $84 billion a year subsidizing their farmers. That's nearly as much as they spend on foreign aid, which is about $29 a year for each of the world's 2.7 billion people who live on less than $2 a day. Poor people often get less assistance than the rich world's farm animals. The European Union, for example, doles out almost $30 per year for each sheep living there. In Norway and Switzerland, each cow gets nearly $1,000 of the government's money a year. These subsidies push down global agricultural prices and undermine farmers in poorer countries. Bellying up to the government's trough has never been so costly.

Subsidies per Head per Year (in U.S. $)

Country	Cattle	Chickens	Pigs	Sheep	Aid per poor person in developing world
EU 15	$179.28	1¢	$9.24	$28.93	$16.11
Australia	$17.12	39¢	$6.49	94¢	54¢
Canada	$68.59	15¢	$18.99	0¢	95¢
Japan	$163.23	21¢	$3.92	0¢	$2.38
New Zealand	$2.66	13¢	$2.14	19¢	8¢
Norway	$965.72	$1.48	$39.98	$94.06	83¢
Switzerland	$987.58	$7.83	$139.62	$16.11	61¢
United States	$29.06	58¢	$9.03	$4.12	$7.67
All	$92.59	38¢	$10.58	$12.85	$29.17

Hooray for High Gas Prices

The price of oil has tripled since 2002. That has rich people in the developed world complaining. But for poor countries, it's good news when the rich world pays high prices at the pump. That's because higher gas prices encourage more fuel-efficient cars, less driving, and, ultimately, slower global warming. Poor countries are the most vulnerable to the consequences of climate change, including rising sea levels, floods, and the spread of infectious diseases. The United Nations, for instance, estimates that a mere 1.5-foot rise in sea level could flood more than 6,000 square miles of Bangladesh, displacing 12 million people.

Because taxes on gasoline are one factor that drives up prices, the higher a country's gas taxes, the better it does in the index. The United States, Canada, and Australia have the cheapest gas among the 21 index countries, mainly due to low government taxes. Their citizens also consume the most fuel. For instance, U.S. gasoline taxes average just 39 cents per gallon, whereas in Europe they range between $2.56 and $4.18 a gallon. When gas taxes are low, it is the poor in developing countries who pay the heaviest price.

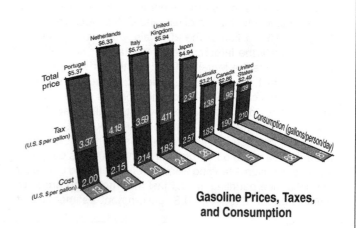

Gasoline Prices, Taxes, and Consumption

Development Begins at the Ballot Box

Democracy has its virtues. Democratic nations, for instance, rarely go to war against each other. Nobel laureate economist Amartya Sen has noted that democracies tend to avoid famines. In the 1960s, while China's Great Leap Forward killed 30 million people, democratic India found ways to feed its growing population. To this list of democratic virtues, the index can add one more: A commitment to democracy at home means a greater commitment to development abroad.

At the World Bank, researchers have built a measure of the quality of democracy, which they call "Voice and Accountability." It is a mathematical synthesis of expert judgments gathered by groups including Freedom House and the Economist Intelligence Unit, which measures elements of democracy such as free and fair elections and how much the government represses dissent. Governments in wealthy countries haven't been shy about using these scores to make favorable comparisons between themselves and developing countries.

But the mirror is equally revealing when turned the other way. When the World Bank's data are compared to the index,

it is clear that the more accountable a government is to its own people, the more it does for those to whom it is not accountable. It's not just that a handful of Nordic nations give lots of foreign aid. In fact, as Jörg Faust of the German Development Institute has found, the pattern persists when aid is dropped from the index. The Netherlands, for instance, not only gives aid generously, but is reducing its greenhouse emissions, has put in place policies that support investment in developing countries, and actively contributes to peacekeeping operations around the globe. At the opposite extreme, Japan, which has the second-least accountable government after Greece, has a small aid program and high barriers to workers and agricultural imports from poor countries.

This pattern likely stems from the fact that in wealthy democracies with less accountable governments, special interests hold more sway. They divert government spending away from foreign aid, force aid to be "tied" to spending on donor-country companies, and promote self-interested trade barriers. Development may take place abroad, but the index shows that it often begins at home.

Democracy at Home, Development Abroad

More democracy means a greater commitment to development.

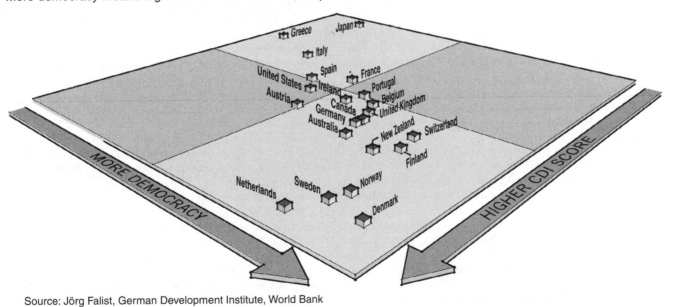

Source: Jörg Falist, German Development Institute, World Bank

Foreign Aid II

This Kind of 'Help' Is Just No Help at All

Aid agencies are not living up to their responsibilities. The new age missionaries seem to have become more of a contributor than a solution to Africa's crises

MICHAEL HOLMAN

The multi-billion dollar aid industry has largely failed in Africa. Not only have they failed along with others in the aid industry, most nongovernmental organisations (NGOs) have become part of the problem. Not that they will admit their failure. They refuse to share the blame for the grim record. Instead they have closed ranks—along with UN development agencies and bilateral agencies—and all sing from the same hymn sheet: 'Aid works', they claim. 'Give us even more money and we will complete the job. . .'

They would say that, wouldn't they? The alternative is far too uncomfortable. The rapid growth of NGOs dealing with Africa has given them enormous power, but they have been slow to adapt to their responsibilities.

Increasingly, NGOs are becoming the spending agents of government development agencies, and are losing their independence. One consequence of their increasing role in Africa has been the atrophy of the muscles of the State in Africa, which in turn erodes loyalty to the State—and I think this goes to the heart of the problems that beset Africa, from corruption to low domestic savings.

The growth of the foreign NGO movement (as distinct from local NGOs) began in the 1970s, and has expanded from a few hundred to tens of thousands today.

It was a response to Africa's deepening crisis—debt, disease, war and disaster. Initially it was a humanitarian response, literally 'first aid'. It soon widened to broad development assistance: from helping to run railways to supplying health clinics, and staffing policy-making teams in government.

But the type of NGO aid, and the attitudes attached to it, reflected ideological battles—socialism versus capitalism, to put it crudely—that NGOs had lost at home and instead fought abroad in states such as Tanzania and Zambia.

As crisis deepened, the number of agencies rose

Today they still fight these battles over water privatization, for example. NGOs are outraged that water should be sold for a profit,
overlooking the fact that from Lagos to Luanda, the poor already pay for their water.

The NGOs' role in telecommunications and deregulation—which led to the growth in mobile phones, independent radio stations, and the Internet—has been negative. Yet these three developments have done more to democratise Africa than anything else.

Meanwhile, NGOs have tapped into a huge reservoir of support and compassion for Africa, and persuaded the public to put its money where the NGO mouth is.

Their domestic public relations strategy is outstanding: look at the professional NGO lobby behind the pop stars at Gleneagles G8 meeting last year. The aid agencies were there in strength, promoting their solutions for Africa's ills, rallying their troops and rattling collection boxes. There is a lot of new aid money to rattle for: billions and billions of dollars, if Britain's Tony Blair and Gordon Brown get their well-intentioned way.

Since 1971 Africa has received more than \$350bn in aid; in 2004 it was \$15bn, and the Gleneagles' intention is to double this. Nobody knows what proportion of aid passes through NGO hands but it is substantial and getting bigger.

While Africa's crisis has deepened and its problems have multiplied, so the number of foreign NGOs has risen. The more NGOs around, the steeper a country's economic decline. And the NGO staff don't come cheap.

An estimated \$4bn is spent annually on recruiting some 100,000 expatriates in Africa, many of them for jobs with NGOs. The result is that there are more foreigners working in Africa than there were at independence five decades ago. They are helping to run everything from ministries to mines, working as policy-makers and performing heroics on the front line against poverty.

Yet Africa's management capacity is weaker today, according to the World Bank, than in the 1960s. The greatest danger to Africa is that it lacks the skills that are needed to manage its own recovery.

As foreigners arrive to take up short-term contracts, each year about 70,000 skilled Africans—doctors, engineers, nurses—leave to work abroad. Western governments should ask whether the growth of NGOs is not only a symptom of Africa's crisis, but perhaps part of the cause. Why are there so many NGOs? How do they coordinate? Where do they get their money? Do they train their staff, and if so what are they taught? What proportions of funds comes from official aid agencies, which increasingly use the NGOs as a conduit?

Some tough questions for the west

How effectively do the NGOs spend it? Who monitors the spending? Are they adept at spinning the aid story at home, while lacking professionalism in the field? In short, do the NGOs have power and influence without responsibility?

Of course, no one can feel anything but admiration for emergency humanitarian missions, such as the International Red Cross or Oxfam's front-line troops. Today the NGO role usually goes well beyond first aid assistance to people in dire distress. They are important to the development of the region where they are based. However, neither the NGOs nor the official agencies are prepared to accept a share of the blame for Africa's development disaster.

Kenya is a case in point. Forty years after independence and billions of dollars of aid and countless hours of NGO work, the country is miserably worse off. The government itself acknowledges that nearly six in every ten people subsist on less than two dollars a day, and the figure is rising.

It is easy to forget that Kenya is a poor country: it has no mineral resources; two-thirds of the land is arid or semi arid. In a good year of rain, it can feed itself. But good years are the exception and that is not going to change.

Meanwhile the population has doubled in 25 years. There are more mouths to feed and the shambas (farms) are becoming smaller and less viable as they get sub-divided. North-east Kenya is worst hit, and much of the food aid is going there.

Have the donors, by providing food over the past four decades, effectively subsidised the people living there, or encouraged families to move there from other parts of Kenya and so helped create the very problem they now seek funds to alleviate? We all know what food aid can do to local agriculture.

Also, by providing food, medicine and shelter, the NGOs may be ensuring that the government of Kenya doesn't have to bear the consequences of its incompetent, corrupt mismanagement. This undermines the relationship between the State and the citizen, with profound consequences.

There is an unwritten contract between the State and the citizen. The State should provide security, the rule of law, and basic services—in return, the citizen has a loyalty to the State and pays taxes. But if the State does not deliver, why should citizens be loyal? Instead the loyalty goes to the clan, the tribe, the region.

What is the role of aid workers in all this? By going beyond first aid and taking over services (the World Food Programme, for example,

---

10 Ways of Prospering Without Aid

1. **ENCOURAGE IDEAS** The high cost of books in Africa is a de facto tax on ideas. Publishers in rich countries should allow African publishers to print a limited run of their books. If the authors forgo royalties and publishers co-operate, locally printed versions could sell at a fifth of the foreign price.

2. **MAKE FOREIGN NGOS COMPETE** NGOs should work more with the private sector: much of their development work should be open to tender. Companies running large projects should include a social component (primary education or healthcare) that the voluntary agencies would tender for and operate.

3. **THE PRIVATE SECTOR SHOULD BUILD INFRASTURCTURE** In Kenya, the potholed Nairobi-Mombasa road should be rebuilt under a build-operate-transfer scheme. The construction company operates the project for an agreed period before handling it to the state.

4. **CHARGE FOR PROFESSIONALS' VISAS** Professionals who emigrate from Africa, whether doctors or dentists, engineers or lawyers, should have to pay a market rate for the privilege of a visa which allows them to work abroad. The money raised should be used in the emigrants' countries of origin to train replacements.

5. **CHOCOLATE MUST CONTAIN MORE COCOA** Double the minimum amount of cocoa required to make chocolate under current trade rules. Cocoa prices will rise and chocolate will taste better.

6. **PROMOTE AFRICAN MUSIC** Africa needs a Nashville-style centre to promote its music and attract more commercial backing. It would be a centre for the production of great music and would train managers and musicians.

7. **MAKE AID CONDITIONAL ON IMPROVING THE BUSINESS CLIMATE** The latest International Finance Corporation's report on impediments to business shows that registering a company in Kenya takes ten times longer than in Hong Kong and requires five stages, compared to two. This is repeated across Africa, whether registering a business, selling property or recovering a debt.

8. **ABOLISH TAXES ON COMPUTERS EXPORTED TO AFRICA** Privatisation, deregulation and the emergence of democracy go hand in hand. Computers are critical to this development. In return, African governments would end import levies on computers.

9. **FAIR TAXES ON COFFEE AND FAIR RETURNS FOR FARMERS** Imported raw coffee is taxed at a third of the rate of processed beans, the first stage in a trading system that ensures that less than 0.2% of the value of processed coffee is retained by the growers themselves. Reforming this tax will benefit Africa's growers and their families, some 60m people. There should also be better marketing and packaging for Africa's products. East Africa's coffee producers now use attractive vacuum-sealed, foil packets but in Congo a fine soap made from pure palm oil is sold wrapped in newspaper and in northern Uganda, mangoes rot on the ground because no one can dry and package them to international standards. Foreign retailers should share their expertise with African traders.

10. **GIVE POWER TO AFRICA'S WOMEN** Disenfranchise African men for 5 years.

—Michael Holman and Andrew Rugasira

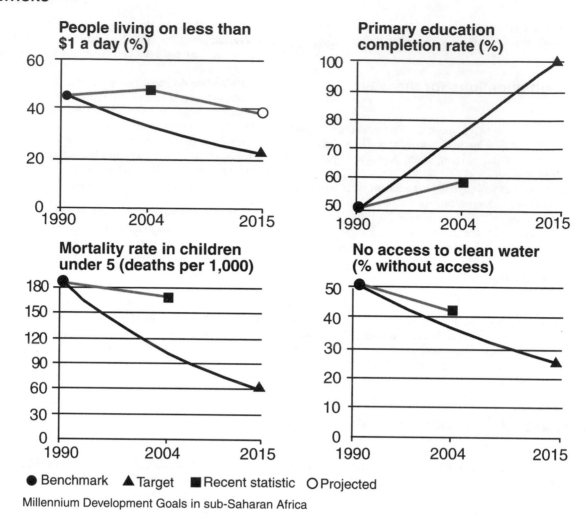

Millennium Development Goals in sub-Saharan Africa

assists in the management of Kenya railways) the NGOs ensure that the State is cushioned from the consequences of its incompetence.

The NGOs also assist in weakening the State, and contribute to its decline under a system of tribal barons who call themselves cabinet ministers. Yet the belief that NGOs can circumvent corrupt governments, which they helped create, is at the heart of the argument of those who defend increases in British aid to Kenya.

Britain's Development Minister Hilary Benn argues: "Just because poor people live in a country where corruption is a serious problem, does that mean they do not deserve our assistance if it can be effective? . . .Our support to Kenya will mean textbooks in its primary schools and 11m treated bed-nets, saving lives." Minister Benn not only fails to understand the root causes of corruption but he also fails to understand how corruption works, day after day, in Kenya. Textbooks or bed-nets, they cannot avoid being tainted.

The process begins when the consignments arrive at Kenyatta airport and the first pay-off comes when they have to be cleared through customs. It continues when they pass through the numerous police road-blocks en route to their destination. And when they arrive, they are used as patronage or leverage.

Far from challenging conventional wisdom, many NGOs have become little more than an arm of official donor policy.

One of Africa's most encouraging developments in recent years has been the growth in civil society, but foreign NGOs have played only a modest part.

Two policy shifts, reluctantly made by African governments, have boosted local democracy: state-controlled television and radio was deregulated, and the telecommunications sector is being privatised.

More information became available, mobile phone ownership soared, and the Internet took off.

But many NGOs are still rooted in an ideological past, fighting battles on African soil which have been long lost at home, in which privatisation, profit and the private sector are all treated with deep suspicion.

Aid isn't working, but the aid lobby pretends it is. They do so by treating Africa as one vast Potemkin village. The term goes back to Catherine the Great. One of her generals, Gregori Potemkin, had elaborate fake villages constructed in advance of her tours of the Ukraine and the Crimea.

The term—Potemkin village—today means something that appears elaborate to impressive but in fact lacks substance. In Africa, realities on the continent are concealed by a Potemkin like structure.

Africa's Potemkin village has been erected by well-meaning outsiders. Reality is either distorted or hidden behind false assumptions, phoney statistics, and misleading language.

Schools without books, airports without runways

So when we read about the post-independence developments in Africa—in health, or education, or the damage wrought by war or famine—we use and read words involving concepts that seem familiar. But these words have a substance, a meaning, or an implication that is inappropriate in Africa, however suitable they are in Europe. So we'll

Why Statistics Are Damn Lies and Dangerous Too

There are just a handful of African countries which maintain reliable statistics. Yet the World Bank and UNDP report, with great precision, about levels of literacy across the continent, or the number of children at school, or radios per head, or maternal death rates.

Official accounts tell us that Africa's GDP has been measured, more or less accurately, and it has fallen or risen by remarkably precise percentages, over or below another remarkably precise percentage—the rate of population increase.

The truth is we really do not know very much about the state of the continent. None of us—Afro-pessimists or Afro-optimists—know how many Africans have access to secure shelter, or clean water, or indeed how many Africans live on the continent, or the rate at which the overall number increases.

We do know that Africa's most populous nation is Nigeria. But we do not know whether there are 100m or 150m Nigerians. The last reliable census was conducted before independence, more than 40 years ago, and more recent efforts are distorted by religious allegiances and financial demands.

We have no idea how many people live in Congo—the last census was in the 1950s. We do know that many people have died, directly or indirectly, in the war there. But when an aid agency says over 3m have died, it is sucking its thumb. There is no way of testing whether the claim is accurate. All it means is that a great many people have perished.

We just don't know. But we pretend to know, or are fooled by bogus statistics.

Aiding and abetting this deception is a cocoon of comfort for visitors, especially journalists, diplomats, businessmen and aid workers. An insulated environment created by business-class travel, five-star hotels, four-wheel drive vehicles, mobile phones, and laptop computers. Living and working in this cocoon creates an illusion of progress, but only for this elite.

The reality on the ground is very different. Conditions for most Africans have got worse over the years due to war, neglect and mismanagement.

Do statistics and assumptions based on guesswork make any difference?

Yes, because Western policy on Africa is built on these false assumptions, using these blunt tools, Ever since the World Bank rang the alarm bell I the early 1980s, warning of Africa's deepening crisis', these non-words, flawed concepts and spurious statistics have been at the heart of Western policy analysis.

Western politicians are reluctant to concede that the policies they have been implementing, costing voters billions of aid dollars, may not work. Indeed, the policies may be part of the problem, and not part of the solution.

Far from admitting defeat, the politicians declare victory. They use a shaky set of so-called 'facts' to reach the conclusion that aid is working, that Africa is recovering—slowly, erratically, perhaps—but recovering nonetheless.

read or send reports that refer to villages, clinics, schools, universities, and airports and we will refer to rises or falls in GDP, or the number of Africans subsisting on a dollar or less a day. Yet all too often we are talking about non-villages or un-schools or ex-airports.

What we don't have are words for an airport without a runway, or schools without classrooms, universities without books. Or prime ministers without power, or presidents without a civil service. Or central bank governors without banking systems, and finance ministers without finance.

Yet the assumption is that in Africa these institutions exist and function, roughly in accordance with their counterparts in Europe. We might acknowledge that the "hospital" may be short of medicine. But we assume that it is there, just as we assume that the finance minister has powers he can exercise.

We erect fantastical superstructures, for example, called development plans, using statistics that are no more than extrapolations, built on assumptions, which in turn are based on information from the colonial era. Reality across Africa is different.

We should be worried by the accuracy and quality of reporting on Africa.

When reality is not an objective appraisal, when it becomes what we, who work in or on Africa—journalists, diplomats, aid workers—think it is, or think it should be, we are doomed to make mistakes.

Sometimes, through ignorance, or because the agents of Western policy are out of their depth, a dangerous new reality is created. The NGOs did this in Congo in the mid-1990s, when their warnings of refugees heading for the eastern border became a self-fulfilling prophecy. Refugees gathered by the scores of thousands on the eastern border, having walked there because they knew from their radios that food from donors awaited them.

Although most governments and commentators accept the importance of the private sector in development, NGOs remain suspicious if not downright hostile. A functional partnership between business and the NGOs seems far away.

It's not just that Africa has gone backwards, it is the way the rest of the world has gone forwards which is not understood. The international flow of goods, services, capital and labour dwarfs our imaginings. There's a good reason why Britain is no longer a manufacturer (more efficient producers in Asia), why services are becoming tradable (more productive workers in India), why the huge US current account deficit doesn't matter (inward capital flows), and why developed countries want Malawian doctors and nurses (losing their own elsewhere, or not producing them in the first place).

These developments—like corruption and capital flight—have big implications for Africa. NGO people still don't get this. Not many people do.

Making Aid Work

The end of the cold war and progress toward a new aid architecture should make aid more effective

MARK SUNDBERG AND ALAN GELB

Too much of the $300 million in aid to Africa since 1980 has vanished into a sinkhole of fraud, malfeasance and waste.

—Sharon LaFraniere,
New York Times, July 2005

. . . Reality is broadly the opposite of current popular beliefs. Aid has not been wasted: it has kept African economies afloat through disturbed times.

—Paul Collier,
"What Can We Expect from
More Aid to Africa?" May 2006

Since 1960 nearly $650 billion in aid (in 2004 prices) has been provided to sub-Saharan African (SSA) countries by the OECD Development Assistance Committee (DAC) countries. And this number would be even higher if contributions from emerging non-DAC donors, such as China, India, and some of the Gulf states, were added to the total. Has all this aid been gainfully used to promote sustainable growth and development? This is difficult to answer because the links between foreign aid and countries' development are complex. However, the likely answer is, on the whole, "No." Historically, most aid has not been used very well. Much of it was never intended for development to begin with, and a large share went to war-torn and politically unstable countries where development gains have subsequently been lost. However, there is good reason to believe that substantive changes are taking place and that "more and better aid" is now going to finance development programs.

The Changing Aid Picture

Total aid to Africa (defined as sub-Saharan Africa in this article) from rich countries represents the bulk of reported net financial flows to the continent, accounting for between 40 percent and 90 percent in any given year since 1970. While equity and foreign direct investments have grown significantly since the mid-1990s, they are highly concentrated in a small number of countries. For most countries, official development assistance (ODA) is still the largest single source of capital inflows, contributing nearly half of all net capital flows (see Figure 1). Following a major decline in the mid-1990s that coincided with the end of the cold war, aid has begun to increase again, although it is still below earlier levels. Per capita aid flows are particularly striking. They declined to $24 per capita in 1999 (nearly half the level seen in the late 1980s) but have since increased to about $37 per capita (see Figure 2).

People typically think of aid as financing for development. But a large amount of aid is not intended for this purpose. OECD countries count a wide range of financing items as ODA, including such special-purpose items as costs linked to program administration, emergency and food assistance, technical cooperation, and debt relief. What remain are "non-special-purpose grants" that constitute what taxpayers typically consider foreign aid: financing for education, infrastructure, and health projects,

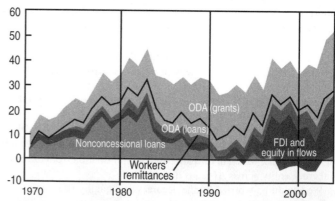

Figure 1   Where the money comes from.   ODA still outranks all other sources. (reported net capital flows to sub-Saharan Africa; billion 2004 dollars)

Sources: OECD-DAC; and World Bank, *Global Development Finance* (2006).

Note: Negative net nonconcessional loans are the reasons for the dips into negative numbers, but positive FDI and equity inflows more than offset those negative net flows.

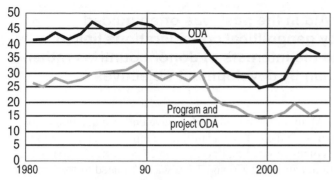

Figure 2   The impact of realpolitik on aid flows.   Aid took a significant dip after the end of the cold war and is only now recovering. (net per capita real ODA flows to SSA; 2004 dollars)

Source: OECD-DAC database.

Note. Program and project ODA refers to total net ODA less special-purpose grants (technical cooperation grants, food and emergency relief, and *bilateral* debt forgiveness grants). Multilateral debt forgiveness grants are included because we assume multilateral debts were being serviced, making debt forgiveness equivalent to program aid.

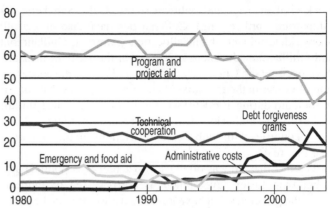

Figure 3   The changing landscape of aid to Africa.   The share of program and project aid has taken a big fall.

(percent of net ODA by aid instrument)

Source: OECD-DAC database.

Note. Aid categories follow OECD-DAC definitions. Program and project ODA refers to total net ODA less special-purpose grants (technical cooperation grants, food and emergency relief, and all debt forgiveness). Administrative costs are for bilateral ODA only and have been imputed for Africa based on global levels. Administrative costs are not reported by multilateral agencies. Debt relief before 1999 was small (less than 1 percent of ODA) and cannot be distinguished by recipient region.

as well as budget support for general financing needs. Over time, this share of aid going to *project and program support* has fallen. In per capita terms, the decline in project and program aid during the 1990s was significant, and it has not yet recovered.

Many factors have contributed to reducing the share of aid that finances development projects. The decline by more than one-third in the share of program and project aid in total ODA—from 63 percent to 41 percent—has coincided with increases in the share of administrative costs, debt relief, and emergency aid (see Figure 3). *Technical cooperation,* much of it spent on foreign advisors, has historically been the second largest component of aid—even though finance for training programs, analytic reports, and expert advice may never actually cross the borders of the donor country. Its share has declined but is still about one-fifth of total ODA, valued at $4.5 billion to Africa in 2004.

Administrative costs on bilateral aid have increased from an average of 5 percent to nearly 5 percent of assistance, in part because of the proliferation of agencies and countries involved in delivering aid—whereas 2 agencies and 10 countries provided aid to Africa in 1960, these numbers had increased to 16 agencies and 31 countries reporting to the DAC by 2004. Measures of donors' administrative costs do not take into account the enormous administrative burden placed on the countries that receive aid. One informal estimate based on a survey of high-level policymakers suggested that as much as half of senior bureaucrats' time in African countries is taken up in dealing with requirements of the aid system and visiting bilateral and multilateral delegations (World Bank, 2000).

Debt relief has increased fivefold since the late 1980s and today makes up 20 percent of all ODA. It is recorded as a special-purpose grant in the OECD-DAC system, which reflects the intent to make most debt relief *additional* to new ODA commitments. Valuing debt relief is quite difficult and warrants further work to improve measurement. But relief on liabilities that are not being (and often cannot be) serviced does not provide a

new flow of resources for development, although it does reduce debt overhang. That said, relief for debt that is being serviced and clearly constitutes a claim on future resources may provide a future dollar-for-dollar cash-flow equivalent.

Emergency and food aid has also increased significantly, nearly doubling from 7 percent to 13 percent of total ODA since 1980. This type of aid is helpful in a crisis but does not generally contribute to financing long-term development.

Finally, a further practice that reduces the value of official aid is the tying of aid to donor country exports or firms. Tied aid is estimated to be 11–30 percent less valuable than untied aid because of price differentials between what donor country firms charge and what would be available in the market (UN, 2005). Throughout the 1980s, more than half of all aid was tied in this way. There are indications that the share of tied aid is declining, but several donors no longer report how much of their aid is tied, making this difficult to confirm. However, based on what data are available, the UN estimates that tied aid reduced the value of bilateral aid sent to Africa by $1.6–2.3 billion (out of a total of $17 billion) in 2003.

In sum, less than one-fourth of bilateral aid and 38 percent of total aid is provided as financing that can be directly used for projects and programs to build infrastructure, educate children, or reduce the spread of infectious disease. This excludes debt relief, a portion of which provides additional resources. In other words, development finance in the traditional sense is far less than what is reported as aid.

Where Has the Aid Gone?

Aid has often been criticized for flowing to dictators and corrupt regimes with little interest in national development. And there is evidence that, during the cold war, aid was often provided for geopolitical reasons and sometimes even favored regimes with weak civil liberties and political rights (Gelb, Sundberg, and Fitzpatrick, forthcoming). Colonial ties have also historically been a determinant of aid allocation (Amprou, Guillaumont, and Guillaumont-Jeanneney, 2005). On the basis of measures developed by the University of Maryland to rate the concentration of power in the executive, known as "Polity IV," about half of total aid during 1960–90 went to countries that had "unlimited executive authority." Only 10 percent went to more democratic countries with "substantial restrictions on the executive" (see Figure 4).

The fact that aid was often used to achieve geopolitical aims rather than foster development is corroborated by evidence about the principles that have guided aid allocation in the past—as measured by the extent to which countries and multilateral organizations based their decisions to give aid on need (poverty) and good management and governance (policy). Figure 5 shows aid selectivity trends since 1977. Both bilateral and multilateral aid demonstrate weak policy selectivity through 1991: aid was allocated with little weight placed on management and governance capacity. Poverty selectivity was also very low and even perverse for bilateral donors—that is to say, higher levels of poverty did not drive larger aid allocations. For multilateral donors, this was also true in the late 1970s, but selectivity improved in the 1980s.

A great deal of aid was also allocated to countries that became politically unstable or endured civil conflict—in fact, 28 countries in Africa have experienced a total of 100 military coups or coup attempts since 1975, and 22 countries have experienced conflict during the past 30 years. From 1980 to 2002, one-fourth of all aid to Africa went to countries experiencing conflict. Nearly one-fifth of total aid went to countries later torn by conflicts that eroded prior development gains.

> **"Aid in the past was often guided by geopolitical considerations linked to the interests of donor countries rather than by development objectives."**

Many of the countries that have endured autocratic governments, civil conflict, and military coups have also seen high levels of unrecorded capital flight. In 25 countries in Africa, capital flight between 1970 and 1996 was estimated to total $193 billion compared with $178 billion in external debt, suggesting that several countries in Africa are, ironically, net creditors to rich countries (Boyce and Ndikumana, 2001). This is not to say that aid was the source of capital flight, but much of it was provided to countries from which capital flight was rampant.

Some Encouraging Trends

The good news is that in several respects these trends are changing significantly, which portends well for better-quality and more effective aid in the future. Several developments help to underscore this. First, *aid is now going to governments with*

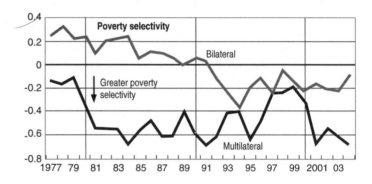

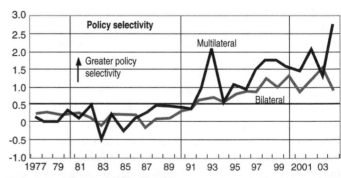

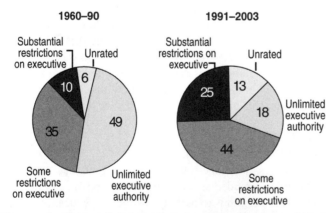

1960–90   **1991–2003**

Figure 4 From dictatorships to democracies. Aid increasingly goes to countries with more executive accountability. (aid and checks on executive authority, average annual percent of net ODA)

Sources: Gelb, Sundberg, and Fitzpatrick (forthcoming). ODA data are from OECD-DAC. Polity IV ratings are from University of Maryland.

Note: Unlimited executive authority = Polity IV scores of 1–2; some restrictions on executive authority = 3–4; substantial restrictions on executive authority = 5–7, where 7 is the highest score (mature democracy). Unrated countries are those in anarchy or transition or under foreign interruption (for instance, occupation by a foreign power).

Figure 5 Seasons for giving aid. Donors are now more likely to emphasize need and democratic values when deciding where to send aid.

(log elasticity of aid to GDP per capita (purchasing power parity))

Source: Authors' calculations.

Note: A positive and rising value for the policy indicator shows allocations to countries with better governance (as measured by the World Bank's country Policy and Institutional Assessment (CPIA) index), whereas a negative and falling value of the poverty indicator (using income per capita as a proxy) indicates greater allocations to poor countries.

better civil liberties and political rights. This is due both to greater aid selectivity and to the spread of democratic institutions and multiparty elections in Africa. Aid to countries with unlimited executive authority has fallen from nearly half to 18 percent, and the share of aid to countries with more democratic systems and checks and balances that place restrictions on the executive has nearly tripled.

Second, *policy and poverty selectivity have improved significantly.* The trend is most marked for multilateral donors, but bilateral donors are also placing much more importance on the quality of governance and overall policies in their aid decisions. These considerations have been made explicit in the performance-based allocation systems used by the multilateral development banks and by several bilateral donors.

Third, *there is a clear recognition of the need to improve aid quality* by reducing the number of agencies involved in disbursing aid, harmonizing aid procedures to reduce compliance costs for the recipients, eliminating tied aid, and aligning aid priorities with the countries' own policy priorities. The OECD's 2005 Paris Declaration on Aid Effectiveness is a key step in this direction. The *Global Monitoring Report 2006* (World Bank and IMF, 2006), which covers the performance of donors, developing countries, and the international financial institutions and their key responsibilities under the Monterrey Accord, is a further step toward mutual accountability.

Fourth, governance indicators suggest that *many countries have improved public resource management by strengthening fiduciary oversight.* The public financial management indicators that are being tracked for countries receiving debt relief under the enhanced Heavily Indebted Poor Countries Initiative show that many countries have improved their public expenditure management since 1999, and more indicators are being developed to track performance in other governance areas.

Finally, there is evidence of a *reversal in the high level of capital flight from Africa,* which has removed enormous amounts of much-needed financing for development. As political instability subsides and more countries turn to multiparty elections, and as growth picks up and income levels improve, domestic residents repatriate more assets (Collier, Hoeffler, and Pattillo, 2004).

In summary, aid in the past was often guided by geopolitical considerations linked to the interests of donor countries rather than by development objectives. Not surprisingly, much of it was used to finance governments that did not have development as their first priority. Furthermore, much aid was not in a form that could be used to finance development (emergency relief and technical assistance are two examples). But changes since the mid-1990s hold clear promise for improving aid quality and effectiveness. The harmonization and alignment of aid under the 2005 Paris Declaration on Aid Effectiveness, as well as the trend toward improved aid allocation selectivity on the basis of need and policy quality, provide evidence of this. This "new aid architecture" can be simply described as aligning aid with country-owned poverty reduction strategies to finance priority social and infrastructural investments, conditional on delivering measurable results. New non-DAC donors and emerging donors, such as China and India, should also learn from DAC donor experience and improve aid alignment in order to enhance the impact of their aid.

References

Amprou, Jacky, Patrick Guillaumont, and Sylviane Guillaumont-Jeanneney, 2005, *Aid Selectivity According to Augmented Criteria* (Clermont-Ferrand, France: Centre d'Etudes et de Recherches sur le Développement International).

Boyce, James, and Léonce Ndikumana, 2001, "Is Africa a Net Creditor? New Estimates of Capital Flight from Severely Indebted Sub-Saharan African Countries, 1970–1996," *Journal of Development Studies,* Vol. 38 (December), pp. 27–56.

Collier, Paul, Anke Hoeffler, and Catherine Pattillo, 2004, "Africa's Exodus: Capital Flight and the Brain Drain as Portfolio Decisions," *Journal of African Economies,* Vol. 13, AERC Supplement 2, pp. ii15–ii54.

Dollar, David, and Victoria Levin, 2004, "The Increasing Selectivity of Foreign Aid, 1984–2002," Policy Research Working Paper No. 3299 (World Bank: Washington).

Gelb, Alan, Mark Sundberg, and Brendan Fitzpatrick, forthcoming, "Aid to Sub-Saharan Africa: Whither $650 Billion?" Development Economics Department (World Bank: Washington).

Organization for Economic Cooperation and Development, 2005, *Making Poverty Reduction Work: OECD's Role in Development Partnership* (Paris: OECD-DAC).

———, Paris Declaration on Aid Effectiveness; http://www.oecd.org/document/18/0,2340,en_26493236398_35401554_1_1_1_1,00.html

United Nations, 2005, *Human Development Report: International Cooperation at a Crossroads: Aid, Trade and Security in an Unequal World* (New York).

World Bank, 2000, *Can Africa Claim the 21st Century?* (Washington).

——— and International Monetary Fund, 2006, *Global Monitoring Report 2006: Strengthening Mutual Accountability—Aid, Trade and Governance* (Washington).

MARK SUNDBERG is a Lead Economist, and **ALAN GELB** is Director of Development Policy, at the World Bank.

Food Sovereignty: Ending World Hunger in Our Time

FREDERIC MOUSSEAU AND ANURADHA MITTAL

This past Thanksgiving, while millions of Americans sat at a table overflowing with food, more than thirty children died each minute around the world due to hunger related causes.

Certainly hunger isn't a result of food scarcity. In fact, *abundance* best describes the world's food supply. World agriculture produces 17 percent more calories per person today than it did thirty years ago, despite a 70 percent population increase. This is enough food to provide every person worldwide with at least 2,720 kilocalories a day.

International food aid, the most publicized instrument in the campaign against hunger, was initiated in 1954, and yet hunger is a bigger crisis now than ever before. Chronic hunger affects over 852 million people across the globe, and its victims include 6.5 million children who die from hunger related causes each year—one every five seconds. While millions of tons of food are shipped as food aid to the global south, apart from some specific disaster and war situations, this doesn't serve the hungry and malnourished whose numbers increase by 4.5 million each year.

So who then benefits the most from food aid? Specific crop lobbies, U.S. shipping companies, and NGO and relief organizations are some of the top winners. For example, Horizon Milling, a joint venture of Cargill Inc. and CHS Inc., has since 1995 sold to the U.S. government $1.09 billion of grain for food aid operations. The second player, the shipping industry, is supported by the 1985 Farm Bill, which requires that at least 75 percent of U.S. food aid be shipped by U.S. vessels. And the main U.S-based relief and development organizations rely highly on in-kind U.S. food aid for either direct food interventions or for funding of other activities. On average the main U.S.-based relief groups rely on the sale of food aid in developing countries for 30 percent of their resources.

This preferential treatment to food produced in the United States and for U.S. shipping companies makes U.S. food aid the most expensive in the world. The premiums paid to suppliers and shippers raise the cost of food aid by over 100 percent compared to local purchases. As reported in the *New York Times,* food delivered by NGOs and the World Food Program (WFP) in 2004 cost only 40 percent of the U.S. food aid budget. The rest was pocketed by suppliers.

In addition, this requirement delays delivery of emergency food aid by an average of nearly five months. In fact, most times, aid is too little and too late. It was appalling to see images of victims of starvation in Niger hit the Western media in July 2005, when the food shortage had been announced nearly a year before without triggering a response that could have prevented or ameliorated a famine. The severity of the situation was known in October 2004 when Niger's government and the WFP appealed for international support. Four months after its first appeal WFP had received only 10 percent of the required funding. According to Jan England, humanitarian coordinator for the United Nations, in October 2004 $1.00 per day could save a child's life whereas $80.00 dollars per day was required in July 2005.

Recognizing this, the European Union procures a majority of its food aid—90 percent in 2004—from developing countries. Canada increased local and regional purchases from 10 percent to 50 percent in September 2005. The United States is the only donor nation that has avoided local and regional purchases.

The White House and USAID have proposed to spend in 2006 one quarter of its food aid budget to buy food grown by local or regional producers. However, both House and Senate leaders have rejected this recommendation. Virginia Republican Bob Goodlatte, chair of the House Agriculture Committee, has gone on to warn that buying food aid overseas would erode congressional support for famine-fighting programs: "It must come from American farmers so it will circulate through the American economy." Instead of prioritizing feeding starving stomachs, Congress' focus remains fixed on fattening pockets of agribusiness and shipping companies.

A joint poll conducted by the *Washington Post,* Harvard University, and the Kaiser Family Foundation asked Americans which area of federal expenditure they thought was the largest. Sixty-four percent of the respondents said it was foreign aid, which in fact constitutes less than one half of one percent of the federal budget. Their response isn't surprising, though, given the number of people who are generously contributing to relief efforts from New Orleans to Niger. But Americans could do even more by challenging the lawmakers who have been blinded by corporate America's interests.

Food aid needs drastic changes if we really want to diminish world hunger. If kept separate from trade and other political interests and supported by a consistent aid budget, the replacement of in-kind food aid with local and triangular purchases would double the amount of food available. The current U.S. food aid budgets could be cut in half without a decrease in the overall volume delivered if the food were procured locally.

More importantly, a study on food aid—*Food Aid or Food Sovereignty? Ending World Hunger in Our Time*—conducted recently by the Oakland Institute, shows that while the European and Canadian shift to local purchases is good it doesn't necessarily promote food security in developing countries. The study recommends that, first, local procurement of food aid must prioritize small-scale farmers, given the dumping of subsidized food as aid adversely affects local agricultural capacity and erodes farmers' livelihoods.

Since most low-income, food-deficit countries (LDCs) specialize in non-food exportable commodities like coffee, cocoa, tea, and tobacco, the top ten list of WFP suppliers include, instead of LDCs, a number of "more advanced" developing countries, such as Brazil and South Africa, which specialize in industrial production of exportable food commodities. For example, in 2005 South Africa will be the origin of most WFP purchases for interventions in Southern Africa, and triangular purchases will consist of cereals produced by large-scale commercial farmers and agribusinesses. Small-scale farmers in Mozambique will also produce a surplus in 2005, yet they are unlikely to supply food to the WFP because of higher marketing costs due to the country's poor road and storage infrastructure.

Another factor that requires emphasis be put on purchases from small farmers locally is the fact that large companies dominate export trade in developing countries. Two corporations—Cargill, the United States' largest privately owned corporation and Archer Daniels Midland (ADM)—control 75 percent of the global grain trade. These corporations dominate the agricultural sector of many developing countries. For instance, Nestlé controls 80 percent of milk production in Peru. Cargill Paraguay sells more than 30 percent of the total production of soy, wheat, and corn of the country.

In the aftermath of the devastating tsunami that struck Indonesia in 2004, local farmers groups organized a farmer's network to supply fresh food to the affected populations of Banda Aceh, demonstrating the feasibility of addressing acute emergency needs with food produced locally by small producers. In the West Bank, WFP buys olive oil from destitute farmers who have been cut off from their markets by the separation wall. This type of local purchase requires flexible and decentralized procurement systems and eventually benefits local agriculture and reduces the need for food aid in the long run.

Second, donors must not only review their procurement system and dissociate food aid from their national interests but also increase the amount of resources for agriculture and rural development which have been cut by half from $5.14 billion to $2.22 billion in the past two decades. Examples from situations of extreme hunger around the world have proven that, in the long run, policies that emphasize helping affected countries develop their own agricultural sectors actually help feed more people and decrease developing countries' dependence on aid programs.

Third, it is essential that strategies are put in place to reduce food aid needs over the long term. This requires support for national policies that are built on the foundation of food sovereignty and support small farmers through land redistribution, extension services, and support for the production of staple food rather than cash crops. In addition, the protection of prices and markets and the management of national food stocks will be essential to mitigate the effects of the fluctuations of national food production on producers and consumers, thereby reducing the need for food aid.

Under the dictates of the international financial institutions, marketing boards, which stabilized prices and managed national food stocks, have been systematically dismantled in many developing countries. These state-run institutions emphasized self-sufficiency, thereby reducing the need for food imports. This allowed governments to buy agricultural commodities from farmers, keep them in a rolling stock, and release them into the market in the event of a bad harvest in the following years. Marketing boards also organized the redistribution of food from surplus to deficit areas of the country. Preventing price volatility, they protected both producers and consumers against sharp rises or drops in prices. Today in Niger or in Malawi, as pointed out by the humanitarian relief organization Doctors Without Borders, the root cause of hunger is poverty, and the group is distributing food to those who are too poor to buy food. In the absence of price controls, the poor have seen price increases of 100 to 200 percent during the lean periods.

During the 1990s Indonesia signed the General Agreement on Tariffs and Trade (GATT) which reduced state intervention in food production and opened up domestic markets to foreign imports. By the end of the 1990s Indonesia became a large importer of rice and one of the largest recipients of food aid. In 2002 the government reintroduced tariffs and imposed tighter control on rice imports. Bulog, the state agency whose role had shrunk in the 1990s, was again put in charge of stabilizing the market and acting as a safety net. Decentralized and operating countrywide, the agency not only supplied the market with rice during lean seasons and periods of high prices but also redistributed surpluses to regions that encountered staple food deficits. In 2004 the country became self-sufficient in the production of rice for the first time in twenty years and had to ban imports to protect its market and producers.

Zimbabwe underwent a similar experience in the 1990s. Under structural adjustment, extreme poverty increased by 50 percent between 1990 and 1995. Recognizing that agricultural growth did not benefit the poor, but rather large-scale farmers and agribusinesses, the government decided to return its market and safety net function to its Grain Marketing Board, which had almost been eliminated following the recommendations of the International Monetary Fund and the World Bank. Affected by severe food shortages over the past three years, Zimbabwe has been able to import and distribute over one million tons of food through its board.

Some would say that this is an idealistic vision. But the world is desperate for answers. The worst is happening right now from Niger to Malawi. So the next time we sit down to an over-flowing banquet we must face some simple questions: do we want freedom from hunger or freedom to trade? Do we want a corporate-profit steered world as that envisioned by Cargill and Continental or do we want strong native cultures proud of their ability to feed their people?

FREDERIC MOUSSEAU is the senior fellow and **ANURADHA MITTAL** is the executive director at the Oakland Institute, a policy think tank whose mission is to promote fair debate and increase public participation by bringing dynamic new voices into policy debates on critical economic and social issues. To order a copy of the food aid report, contact them at info@oaklandinstitute.org (www.oaklandinstitute.org).

Crisis of Credibility
The Declining Power of the International Monetary Fund

Walden Bello and Shalmali Guttal

Bangkok—What a difference two decades make! In 1985, the International Monetary Fund (IMF) and the World Bank stood at the pinnacle of their power. Taking advantage of the Third World debt crisis of the early 1980s, both institutions were in the midst of instituting radical free market reforms via "structural adjustment programs"—a cookie-cutter package of economic policies including deregulation, privatization, cuts in government spending and emphasis on exports—in more than 70 developing countries.

Ten years later, in 1995, the IMF stood unchallenged as the centerpiece of the global financial system and was launching its ambitious drive to make capital account liberalization—a requirement that countries remove all restrictions on inflows and outflows of capital—one of the articles of association of the Fund.

But by 2005, the credibility of the IMF was in shreds.

The Unraveling of the IMF

Distant, feared and arrogant, the IMF met what amounted to its Stalingrad in Asia in the late 1990s. East Asian economies were then widely heralded as the leaders of the global economy in the twenty-first century, economies whose average rate of growth would remain at 6 to 8 percent far into the future. When these economies crashed in the summer of 1997, the impact on the reigning ideology of globalization was massive. Perhaps the most shocking aspect of the crisis for people in the developing world was the social impact: over a million people in Thailand and some 21 million people in Indonesia found themselves impoverished in just a few weeks.

Suddenly, the IMF was widely discredited, seen as the architect of the capital account liberalization that created the crisis, and of the severe contraction that followed. The IMF was responsible too in large part for the worsening of that contraction, as it demanded countries plunged into depression restrain government spending—exactly the opposite of sound advice for an economy in contraction.

Throughout the developing world, the January 1998 picture of Michel Camdessus, then the IMF managing director, arms folded, standing over Indonesian President Suharto signing an IMF agreement mandating harsh conditions of stabilization became an icon of Third World subjugation to a much hated suzerain.

So unpopular was the IMF that in Thailand, Thaksin Shinawatra and his Thai Rak Thai political party ran against it and the administration that had sponsored its policies in 2001, winning a lopsided victory for them and with it, inauguration of anti-IMF expansionary policies that revived the Thai economy.

In Malaysia, Prime Minister Mohamad Mahathir defied the IMF by imposing capital controls, a move that raised a howl from speculative investors but one that ultimately won the grudging admission of the IMF itself as having stabilized an economy in serious crisis.

Indeed, an IMF assessment eventually admitted—though in euphemistic terms—that its whole approach to the Asian financial crisis of fiscal tightening to stabilize exchange rates and restore investor confidence along the way was mistaken: "The thrust of fiscal policy . . . turned out to be substantially different . . . because . . . the original assumptions for economic growth, capital flows, and exchange rates . . . were proved drastically wrong."

The Fund's close association with the interests of the United States—it is often viewed as a vassal of the U.S. Treasury Department—further discredited the Fund.

One of the episodes during the Asian financial crisis that exposed the IMF as being essentially a tool of the United States was the battle over Japan's proposal for an "Asian Monetary Fund." Tokyo proposed the fund, with a possible capitalization of $100 billion, in August 1997, when Southeast Asian currencies were in a free fall. The idea was to create a multipurpose fund that would assist Asian economies in defending their currencies against speculators, provide emergency balance of payments financing and make available long-term funding for economic adjustment purposes. As outlined by Japanese Foreign Ministry officials, notably the influential Ministry of Finance official Eisuke Sakakibara, the Asian Monetary Fund (AMF) would be more flexible than the IMF, by requiring a "less uniform, perhaps less stringent, set of required policy reforms as conditions for receiving help." Not surprisingly, the AMF proposal drew strong support from Southeast Asian governments.

Just as predictably, the AMF aroused strong opposition from both the IMF and the United States. At the IMF-World Bank annual meeting in Hong Kong in September 1997, IMF Managing Director Michel Camdessus and his U.S. deputy Stanley Fischer argued that the AMF, by serving as an alternate source of financing, would subvert the IMF's ability to secure tough economic reforms from Asian countries in financial trouble. Analyst Eric Altbach claims that some U.S. officials "saw the AMF as more than just a bad idea; they interpreted it as a threat to America's influence in Asia. Not surprisingly, Washington made considerable efforts to kill Tokyo's proposal." Unwilling to lead an Asian coalition against U.S. wishes, Japan abandoned the proposal that might have prevented the collapse of the Asian economies. The episode left many Asians very resentful of both the IMF and the United States.

Revisiting Structural Adjustment

The Fund's performance during the Asian financial crisis led to a widespread reappraisal of the Fund's role in the Third World in the 1980s and early 1990s, when the IMF, along with the World Bank, became the main instrument for the imposition of "market friendly" structural adjustment programs in over 70 developing and post-socialist economies.

After more than a decade and a half of such policies, it was hard to point to more than a handful of successes, among them the very questionable case of Pinochet's Chile.

Poverty and inequality in most adjusted economies had increased. Beyond that, structural adjustment institutionalized stagnation in Africa, Latin America and other parts of the Third World. A study by the Center for Economic and Policy Research shows that 77 percent of countries for which data is available saw their per capita rate of growth fall significantly during the period 1980–2000. In Latin America, income expanded by 75 percent during the 1960s and 1970s, when the region's economies were relatively closed, but grew by only 6 percent in the past two decades. A more global comparison has been attempted by Robert Pollin, and this showed that, excluding China from the equation, the overall growth rate in developing countries during the interventionist "developmental state" era (1961–80) was 5.5 percent, compared to 2.6 percent in the structural adjustment era. In terms of the growth rate of income per capita, the figures were 3.2 percent in the developmental state era and 0.7 in the subsequent two decades.

By the late 1990s, the Fund could no longer pretend that structural adjustment had not been a massive disaster in Africa, Latin America and South Asia. During the World Bank-IMF meetings in September 1999, the Fund conceded failure by renaming the Enhanced Structural Adjustment Facility (ESAF) the "Poverty Reduction and Growth Facility" (PRGF). It promised to learn from the World Bank by making the elimination of poverty the "centerpiece" of its programs. But this was too little, too late, and too incredible.

Indeed, among the key consequences of the IMF's calamitous record in East Asia and the developing world was that it brought the long simmering conflict within the U.S. elite over the role of the Fund to a boil. The U.S. right denounced the Fund for promoting "moral hazard," that is, irresponsible lending that ensured private foreign creditors that they would be paid back no matter what. Some, including former U.S. Treasury Secretary George Shultz, called for the IMF's abolition. Meanwhile, orthodox liberals like Jeffrey Sachs and Jagdish Bhagwati attacked the Fund for being a threat to global macroeconomic stability and prosperity. Late in 1998, a rare conservative-liberal alliance in the U.S. Congress came within a hair's breath of denying the IMF a $14.5 billion contribution. With arm-twisting on the part of the Clinton administration, the contribution was secured, but it was clear that the long-time internationalist consensus among U.S. elites that had propped up the Fund for over five decades was unraveling.

IMF Reform: Promise versus Reality

As the crisis of legitimacy of the IMF worsened, the agency felt the need for reform acutely. Reform of the international financial architecture, debt relief and the approach to financing development topped the agenda.

Calls for a new global financial architecture to reduce the volatility of the trillions of dollars shooting around the world in pursuit of narrow but significant interest rate differentials came from many quarters. The United States argued that the current architecture was basically sound, and that there was no need for major reforms. Though there were differences on some details, this position was shared by the other members of the G-7 group of rich countries.

This approach advocated increased transparency in government finances and national banking laws, tougher bankruptcy laws to eliminate moral hazard, and greater inflow of foreign capital to re-capitalize shattered banks and "stabilize" the local financial system. This latter measure translated in concrete terms into enabling foreign banks to freely buy up local institutions or set up fully owned subsidiaries.

The G-7 also trumpeted the creation of a "Financial Stability Forum." As originally proposed, this body had no representation from the developing economies. When this generated criticism, the G-7 issued an invitation to Singapore and Hong Kong to join the body. The developing countries were still not satisfied, however, leading the G-7 to create the G-20, with more representation from the developing countries.

More than three quarters of countries saw their per capita growth rate fall significantly during the period of IMF dominance.

Wall Street and other financial centers, as well as their government allies, strongly resisted Tobin taxes (taxes on currency trades across borders) or similar controls designed to slow down capital flows by imposing fees on them at various points in the global financial network. Even when the IMF admitted that capital controls worked to stabilize the Malaysian economy during the 1997 financial crisis, it remained generally opposed to capital controls. The IMF refused to endorse even the gentlest capital controls, like the Chilean *encaja,* which sought to deter capital volatility by taxing capital inflows that did not remain in the country for a designated period of time and thus avoid volatile movements that could destabilize an economy.

When it came to the role of the IMF in financial crisis management, the G-7 supported the expansion of the powers of the IMF despite its poor record. They gave the Fund the authority to push private creditors to carry some of the costs of a rescue program, that is, to "bail them in" instead of bailing them out, an approach that was tried out in the Korean financial crisis. This was a modest response to clamor on both the right and the left that the Fund had encouraged future acts of irresponsible lending by private creditors by bailing out previous bad loans.

The G-7 also authorized the creation of a "contingency credit line" that would be made available to countries that are about to be subjected to speculative attack. Access to these funds would be dependent on a country's track record for observing good macroeconomic fundamentals, as traditionally stipulated by the Fund.

The only problem was that no one wanted to take advantage of this pre-crisis credit line, rightly worried that speculative investors would view such a move as a sign of crisis, rush to take their capital out of the country, and so precipitate the crisis that the pre-crisis credit line was supposed to avert in the first place.

Probably the most far-reaching proposal came, surprisingly, from the U.S. deputy director of the Fund, Ann Krueger. At the height of the Argentine crisis in 2002, Krueger proposed an orderly work-out process similar to Chapter 11 bankruptcy proceedings in the United States: the "Sovereign Debt Restructuring Mechanism."

A government suffering a financial crisis would apply for IMF protection. If the IMF found that the country was dealing with its creditors "in good faith," it would grant a standstill in its payments to them. Protected in this fashion, the debtor country would negotiate new terms of repayment to its creditors, with the IMF providing it with emergency funding to finance its imports of goods and services. The IMF then would oversee the creation of some sort of tribunal independent of the Fund that would adjudicate disputes between the debtor and the creditors, and among creditors, and come out with a debt restructuring program that would be binding on everybody.

Debt cancellation advocates generally applauded the idea of a bankruptcy-type process for debtor countries, but they remained strongly critical of Krueger's proposal. In Krueger's design, the IMF would maintain a great deal of authority to decide when countries were eligible to enter the bankruptcy process and to certify if they had adopted "sound" economic plans for recovery. This scheme might have actually intensified IMF control over poor country economies, they feared.

More decisive opposition to Krueger's proposal came from a different quarter: powerful interests in the U.S. government and financial community were dead set against it. The day after Krueger made her proposal public, John Taylor, the international undersecretary of the U.S. Treasury, registered his disagreement, saying that the "most practical and broadly acceptable reform would be to have sovereign borrowers and their creditors put a package of new clauses in the debt contracts." In other words, maintain the *status quo,* where the creditors tend to unite and have tremendous advantage over the debtor.

Krueger apparently had the support of Secretary of the Treasury Paul O'Neill. But when O'Neill was fired by President Bush in December 2002, Krueger lost her strongest supporter. At its April 2003 meeting of the IMF's International Monetary and Finance Committee, the United States squelched the proposal.

The lack of any real movement in reforming the international financial architecture prompted warnings, by of all people, Robert Rubin, that "[f]inancial crises have continued to rock emerging markets and are likely to remain a factor in the decades ahead."

The IMF Blinks

The low state to which the fortunes of the IMF had sunk in the estimate of its once compliant pupils in the developing world was illustrated most significantly by the case of Argentina.

After defaulting on $100 billion of its $140 billion debt, Argentina's economy collapsed in 2002. Then Nestor Kirchner was elected president in 2003. Kirchner told holders of Argentine bonds that it would repay them—but only after writing off 75 to 90 percent of the value of the bonds. He also played hardball with the IMF, telling the Fund, in March 2004, that the country would not repay a $3.3 billion installment due the IMF unless it approved a similar amount of new lending to Buenos Aires.

According to Stratfor, an agency specializing in political risk analysis, the future of the IMF was at stake in the negotiations: "If Argentina walks away from its private and multilateral debts successfully—meaning that it doesn't collapse economically when it is shut out of international markets after repudiating the debt—then other countries might soon take the same path. This could finish what little institutional geopolitical relevance the IMF has left."

The IMF blinked. Kirchner stuck to his guns on his radically devalued payment to foreign bondholders, one of the Fund's key constituencies, and the Fund came up with a new multibillion dollar loan for his government.

WALDEN BELLO and **SHALMALI GUTTAL** are members of the staff of Focus on the Global South, a Bangkok-based analysis and advocacy institute focusing on issues of trade, development and security. Many of the themes touched on in this article are further developed in Bello's most recent book, *Dilemmas of Domination: the Unmaking of the American Empire* (New York: Henry Holt and Company, 2005).

From *Multinational Monitor,* July/August 2005, pp. 19–22. Copyright © 2005 by Essential Information. Reprinted by permission.

Without Consent: Global Capital Mobility and Democracy

JEFF FAUX

Shortly after he became the first general secretary of the World Trade Organization, Renato Ruggiero observed, "We are no longer writing the rules of interaction among separate national economies. We are writing the constitution of a single global economy."

The word constitution—with its implication of world government—shocked some international trade officials. Like a reference to sex at a Victorian dinner table by an otherwise respectable gentleman, it was resolutely ignored by the business press and the policy academics, whose public commentary acts as a Greek chorus for what George Soros so aptly named "free-market fundamentalistism." The WTO, sings the chorus, is *not* a constitution. Its purpose is "free trade," an arrangement that presumably requires less, not more, government.

Yet Ruggiero was simply acknowledging the obvious. Markets are not found in a state of nature. They are human creations, defined by enforceable rules. Even the most primitive markets require rules for what constitutes private property, valid contracts, weights and measures, and so on. And they always reflect a social contract.

In modern, civilized economies, rules are enforced by public institutions—legislatures, courts, regulatory agencies, central banks. The social contract includes protection of labor, the environment, and public health from the brutalities of unconstrained capitalism.

The precise content of a market's rules has major consequences for who gets to be rich and who gets to be poor. Therefore, all markets have a *politics*. Political science, as a famous American scholar once observed, is the study of "who gets what."

When markets expand their boundaries, so must the rules. In our own history, advances in technology, business organization, and westward migration expanded the U.S. economy from a series of regional markets, regulated by state governments, to a continental economy regulated primarily by the federal government. Note that the federal government did not just impose rules on trade *among* the states, but market rules *within* the states as well. Because we had a Constitution guaranteeing some form of democracy and a Bill of Rights, the new rules were subject to

public debate. Political parties evolved around class-based conflicts over land settlement, the gold standard, anti-trust, child labor, social security, environmental protections, and so forth.

Today, technology, business organization, and migration are relentlessly expanding markets beyond the capacity of individual nation-states to regulate them. Because business must have rules, a constitution for the global market is being written—at the World Trade Organization, the International Monetary Fund, and the World Bank. Befitting a world dominated by one superpower, the U.S. Treasury and the Pentagon play leadership roles. Because there is no prior framework of democracy or accountability, the new constitution is being written piecemeal, in secret, and publicly unacknowledged, except for an occasional slip of the tongue, as in the case of Ruggiero.

Who Decides?

But if all rule-setting generates politics, what are the politics of the setting of the new rules for the global economy? Who gets to decide "who gets what?"

To the typical reader of the world's major newspapers or watcher of the nightly news, the rules for a borderless economy seem to be set by a sort of parliament of nations, where finance ministers at the IMF, trade ministers at the WTO, and economic ministers at the World Bank pursue their national interests. Interestingly enough, the new constitution is not being written at the United Nations, which is presumably our principal world legislature.

This notion of "national" interests dominates the language of globalization. Thus, the reports from the recent WTO meetings in Cancun speak of *U.S. interests* vs. *Brazil's interests* vs. *South Africa's interests,* and so on. . . . The implication of this language is that when George W. Bush or Lula or Thabo Mbeki turns his gaze to foreign economic affairs, the domestic conflict over "who gets what" stops at the border.

National interests are then aggregated into international blocs. Global economic politics is presented as a conflict between rich countries and poor countries, the North and the South, the producers of raw materials and the producers of software.

Yet, as the late Michael Harrington once remarked, there are poor people in rich countries and rich people in poor countries. And just as politics in an expanding American economy developed around class and other interests across state lines, a similar process is going on in the current globalizing economy.

The individuals who negotiate trade and investment agreements and who sit on the boards of the IMF, the World Bank, and international financial agencies formally represent different national interests. But they increasingly act as agents for an international class interest as well. Globalization has created a global elite—people with mutual economic interests regardless of nationality. They include the leaders of multinational corporations and their financiers, their political partners, and their clients and retainers among the punditry, the military, the international bureaucracies, and the academy.

After a speech I gave a few years ago at the Council on Foreign Relations in New York, a retired State Department official bluntly underlined the fundamental reality. "What you don't understand," he said, "is that when we negotiate economic agreements with these poorer countries, we are negotiating with people from the same class. That is, people whose interests are like ours."

I call this global governing class the Party of Davos, after the Swiss site of one of the annual conferences of the global elite. As Adam Smith reminded us, "People of the same trade seldom meet together, even for merriment and diversion, but the conversation ends in a conspiracy against the public." We should expect no less when people from different countries with the same interests meet at the global economy's watering holes for merriment, diversion . . . and conspiracy. It would be odd if it were otherwise. So it should be no surprise that the rules of the global market written by the Party of Davos protect and promote the positions of its membership—those who control large amounts of capital. The rules thus encourage trade deregulation, privatization, weakening of unions, financial market liberalization, and a general shredding of the social contract.

This is not to say that the world's governing class is always of exactly one mind, or that nationality plays no role in the pursuit of self-interest. Bankers in Miami see the world differently than bankers in Portland, Oregon. Those in London have a different perspective from those in Singapore. But when it comes to protecting the generic rights of capital, the elites of Miami, Portland, London, and Singapore are united.

Accordingly, issues of concern to other classes are, by joint agreement, left out of the agendas of the IMF, the WTO, and other international forums, and therefore out of the concerns of the global constitution. These include the rights of labor, the protection of the environment, public health, community stability . . . and of course, democracy and accountability.

These interests are championed by the minor party in the politics of global markets. Let us call it the Party of Porto Alegre, the original Brazilian site of the World Social Forum. This is the party of the opposition. It includes many labor unions, environmental organizations, religious and human rights activists, indigenous groups, and their many sympathizers around the world. They first came together at the WTO meeting in Seattle in the last weeks of the twentieth century when they crashed the party of the Party of Davos.

The often bizarre television images that the world sees of the street activists of the Party of Porto Alegre harassing the Party of Davos from one meeting of the IMF or the WTO to another are distortions designed to ridicule any opposition to Davos's hegemony. Yet, the images do capture an important part of their relationship. The goal of the Party of Davos is to escape popular constraints on capital and the goal of the Party of Porto Alegre is to constrain it—making it subject to democracy and accountability. This is why the constitution of the new world order is not being written at the United Nations. The UN is too unwieldy, too transparent, and too susceptible to Porto Alegre-ish sentiments.

Whatever separate goals its members might pursue, the common agenda of the Party of Davos is to break the bargaining power of labor. By labor, I do not mean just labor unions, but the vast majority of the people on this planet who must work in order to live—from industrial and service workers in advanced countries to rural laborers and marginal peasants in the most economically backward corners of the globe. The bargaining between labor and capital—which takes place within the firm and in a society's political life—is what makes up the "social contract" that is required in order to legitimize the unequal distribution of income, wealth, and power that markets generate.

Still, Davos makes a moral claim. It is that an emphasis on the distribution of wealth actually makes the poor worse off. In contrast, says Davos, deregulated capitalism makes for faster economic growth, and that growth improves life for everyone—especially the poor.

The Davos Record

We now have been at Davos's neoliberal program for twenty years, time enough to evaluate this claim. Of course, in a world of roughly two hundred separate nations and six billion people, measuring anything on a global scale is very tricky, particularly when the policies pursued by the different economies have not been uniform. But some things seem clear.

Most important, after two decades of neoliberalism, global economic growth has slowed from the previous twenty years. From 1960 to 1980, world gross domestic product grew at an average rate of 4.6 percent annually. In the following two decades, under increasing free trade and deregulation, growth in the world economy slowed to less than 2.9 percent annually. Moreover, those fast-growing countries that provide the most weight in the aggregate numbers—China and India—were the most resistant to the advice of the bankers, the international bureaucrats, and the army of consultants who work for the Party of Davos.

The trends on poverty and inequality are more difficult to sort out. But it appears that if one eliminates China and India—who represent 38 percent of the world's population—from the calculation, world poverty has not improved very much. Inequality among nations has certainly gotten worse. And inequality within nations seems to have increased in Latin America, Africa, Eastern and Central Europe, Central Asia. All but five industrialized countries (Denmark, Luxembourg, the Netherlands, Spain, and Switzerland) saw inequality increase while France saw no change in inequality. A recent analysis by Christian E. Weller, Robert E. Scott, and Adam S. Hersh of the Economic Policy Institute reports that the median income of the richest 10 percent of the world's people were 70 times that of the poorest 10 percent in 1980, and 122 times in 1999.

Competent scholars argue over these numbers, but one thing is obvious to all but the hopelessly ideological: the last twenty years have not produced the surge in living standards that neoliberalism's champions promised would flow from the liberation of capital from social constraints and the weakening of the bargaining power of the world's working people. Even then-World Bank president James Wolfensohn in 1999 was moved to admit, "At the level of people, the system isn't working," suggesting that there are other "levels" at which the system is working perfectly well.

The NAFTA Model

One place to see the process more clearly is here on our own continent, where in January the North American Free Trade Agreement (NAFTA) will be ten years old.

Like the WTO, NAFTA does more than just govern trade among its three members—Canada, Mexico, and the United States. If NAFTA had only been concerned with free trade, the agreement could have been written on a few pages. Instead, NAFTA is a thousand-page template for the constitution of an emerging continental economy.

In fact, NAFTA was a model for the WTO. It is the explicit template for the proposed Free Trade Agreement of the Americas, the Central American Free Trade Agreement, and the Asia-Pacific Economic Cooperation Forum. And it is the inspiration of the economic portion of the Bush administration's September 2002 National Security Strategy, openly referred to by its intellectual supporters as an agenda for "empire."

The vision of economic integration embodied in NAFTA differs from the vision of the other major model of regional market integration—the European Union. The development of the EU has been based on the understanding that common political institutions are the inevitable consequence of common economies. Every major step of the process was, and still is, transparent—subject to fiery public debates over the rules, particularly over the balance between individual rights, local sovereignty, and market efficiency.

In contrast, the constitution of the single North American market was merchandized to the citizens and legislators of each of the three countries as a simple, narrow, stand-alone agreement on foreign trade.

NAFTA does, of course, promote increased trade between Canada, Mexico, and the United States. Its text lays out a timetable for the elimination of customs barriers on everything from vegetables to truck transportation. But it is also as much an investment agreement as a trade agreement. The document binds each nation to extraordinary protection of the other member states' investors. It requires governments to guarantee the repatriation of profits in hard currency. Its Chapter 11 gives private investors the right to bring suit against governments over laws that might endanger future profits (defined as "tantamount to expropriation"). It inhibits efforts by national governments to liberalize the ownership of intellectual property. Disputes are settled in secret by tribunals of experts, many of whom are employed privately as corporate lawyers and consultants.

The result is a framework for the governance of the continental economy that curtails domestic powers of popularly elected government. NAFTA restricts the public sector's freedom of action in taxation, procurement, and capital market policies. Under NAFTA, corporations have forced state and provincial governments in each country to rescind environmental regulations. United Parcel Service is currently charging that Canada's government-owned postal service violates UPS's NAFTA-given right to provide private mail service. Little by little, policy proposals in all three nations now must pass the test of whether they are "NAFTA compatible."

In effect, NAFTA is a constitution that recognizes only one citizen—the multinational corporate investor. Governments will be punished for infringing on the rights of investors, whose protection is guaranteed. But governments may diminish, even abolish, the civil rights of workers or the claims of the environment with impunity. In contrast to the detailed protections for investors in NAFTA itself, the fig-leaf "side agreements" covering labor and the environment are weak and unenforceable.

Had this formula been proposed as the governing constitution of Canada, Mexico, or the United States, the electorates of each nation would have no doubt overwhelmingly rejected it. But, by defining the debate over its adoption as a dispute between abstract notions of "free trade" and "protectionism," the promoters of NAFTA diverted attention from the larger political significance of the agreement.

To be sure, there was protectionist opposition to NAFTA in all three nations. But the traditional politics of previous trade battles, in which industrial sectors—including employers, workers, and communities—who might lose from freer trade were pitted against industrial sectors that might win, was muted. The investor protections of NAFTA split off the interests of large U.S. employers from their workers by allowing firms to shift production to lower cost Mexico. Thus, U.S. auto firms' chief executive officers supported the treaty while U.S. auto workers opposed it.

The conflict over NAFTA thus reflected a new, class-based politics of trade. The opposition was led not by industrial "losers," but by the social movements—labor, environmentalists, consumers and nationalists in all three countries who were alarmed over the potential loss of national sovereignty and the domestic social contract.

The central claim for NAFTA was Davosian: the agreement would create a sustained economic boom in Mexico that would more than compensate for any social costs. One typical prediction, by a U.S. undersecretary of commerce, was that Mexico would grow, "between a supercharged 6 percent a year, worthy of Asia's tigers, and a startling 12 percent per year comparable to China's recent economic growth." The growth would lift the country's poor (more than 40 percent of Mexicans live on less than $2 a day) into the middle class.

The Mexican boom, in turn, would bring economic benefits to the United States and, to a lesser extent, Canada. First, the immigration of undocumented Mexican workers would diminish, if not disappear. In 1990, then-president of Mexico Carlos Salinas asked an American audience, "Where do you want Mexicans working, in Mexico or in the United States?" Second, NAFTA would create a new middle-class market in Mexico for the more expensive goods produced in the United States and Canada.

NAFTA at Ten

It is now painfully obvious that the promise of greater economic growth was not fulfilled. Over the last ten years, Mexico's growth has been at best half of what it needs to create enough jobs for its expanding labor force. Since 2000, Mexico has scarcely grown at all. The record would have been worse but for the unsustainable U.S. boom in the late 1990s which boosted Mexican exports. Since the mid-1980s, when the neoliberal reforms began, growth has fallen to less than a third of the 3.4 percent rate at which Mexico grew in the years of the 1960s and 1970s—the so-called "bad old days" of government industrial policies and import substitution.

While the economic benefits fell short, the human and social costs of the continent-wide reallocation of investment rose dramatically. These costs included the destruction of livelihood of millions of workers, particularly in Mexican agricultural labor and U.S. manufacturing. On both sides of the border, the promises made to these working populations were abandoned almost as soon as the ink was dry on the agreement. For example, Mexican farmers were promised that they would receive generous financial and technical assistance to help them meet competition from U.S. agribusiness. But after the treaty was signed, funding for farm programs dropped dramatically. Meanwhile, the U.S. government massively increased subsidies for corn, wheat, livestock, dairy products, and other farm products exported to Mexico. This, "comparative advantage" enabled U.S. agribusiness to drive thousands of small Mexican farmers out of their own markets. When the displaced campesinos and their families arrived in nearby cities, few jobs were waiting. NAFTA concentrated growth along Mexico's northern border, where the Mexican government keeps unions out so that the *maquiladora* factories can process and assemble goods for export to the United States with workers who are desperate, pliable, and even cheaper than elsewhere in Mexico. Between 1994 and 2000, *maquiladora* employment doubled while employment in the rest of the country stagnated.

In the absence of labor and environmental protections, the expanding sweatshops of the north created a social and ecological nightmare. Rural migrants overwhelmed the already inadequate housing, health, and public-safety infrastructures, spreading shantytowns, pollution, and crime. *Maquiladora* managers often hire large numbers of women, whom they believe are more docile and more dexterous than men at assembly work. Earnings are typically about $55 a week for forty-five hours—not enough for survival in an area where acute shortages of basic services have raised the cost of living. Families break up as men cross the border in search of jobs, leaving women vulnerable to the social chaos.

An Amnesty International report on the border town of Ciudad Juárez, where hundreds of young women have been killed, quotes the director of the city's only rape crisis center (annual budget: $4,500): "This city has become a place to murder and dump women. [Authorities] are not interested in solving these cases because these women are young and poor and dispensable."

In the United States, workers were betrayed by major multinational firms that had assured the U.S. Congress that their interest in NAFTA was solely in the middle-class Mexican market. Once the agreement was signed, these same firms began to shift production south of the border, eliminating hundreds of thousands of jobs in the United States. Clearly, the object of their desire was the low-wage Mexican worker, not the mythical high-wage Mexican consumer.

The net effect was to undercut wage levels on both sides of the border. Indeed, despite the shift of manufacturing to Mexico, average real wages in Mexican manufacturing in January 2003 were some 9 percent below their January 1994 level. No doubt some Mexicans have benefited from cheaper prices of expensive U.S. and Canadian goods. But in a country where the poverty rate is above 50 percent, the basic cost of living for most people seems to have gotten worse. For example, in December 1994, the minimum wage (currently $4.20 per day) bought 44.9 pounds of tortillas. Today it buys 18.6 pounds. In December 1994, it bought 24.5 litres of gas for cooking and heating. Today it buys seven.

So the dangerous migration across the border continues. "If you're going to improve your life, you have to go to the United States," said a neighbor of one of the nineteen undocumented Mexican migrants found asphyxiated in a Houston-bound truck in May 2003.

The failure of NAFTA to produce sufficient growth to absorb its own labor force should not have been a surprise. The conventional economic argument for free trade is not that it promotes growth, but that the reallocation of capital among the lines of comparative advantage promotes efficiency gains in the form of lower prices. Freer trade can produce such gains, but most efforts to measure them consistently produce small numbers.

Recently, the World Bank estimated that the Doha round agenda would add roughly $160 billion in static gains—the gains consistent with free trade theory—to the GDP of the world's developing nations. The number was used in the chorus of recrimination against the third world nations for letting the meeting in Cancún fail. Yet, a closer look at the estimates shows that they completely ignore any costs of dislocation, unemployment, and the loss of markets by local producers. Even so, these "gross" gains represent an increase of only 1.5 percent of GDP by the year 2015. Harvard economist Dani Rodrik has observed that "no widely accepted model attributes to postwar trade liberalization more than a tiny fraction of the increased prosperity of advanced industrial countries."

Frightened by the disputed election of 1988 that almost installed a leftist president, elites in both countries wanted to make it much harder for a future populist Mexican government to pursue redistribution politics. It was a shared objective: inasmuch as the ownership of assets in a single market is commingled, there is little practical distinction between the rights of Canadian, U.S., or Mexican multinational investors. Moreover, NAFTA created new opportunities for Mexican business elites to broker privatized assets to foreign investors at enormous profit. For example, an investment group headed by the well-connected Roberto Hernandez bought Mexico's second largest commercial bank from the government for $3.1 billion and resold it to Citicorp for $12.5 billion. Foreign investors now own more than 85 percent of the Mexican banking system, yet credit available to Mexican business has actually shrunk.

The problem of Mexican growth will not disappear with the revival of the U.S. economy. Mexico's temporary faster growth in the late 1990s was a function of an extraordinary boom in the United States that we now know was unsustainable. With generous injections of fiscal stimulus, U.S. growth may accelerate for a while, but the chances of a return to those years of excessive speculation are remote. With the U.S. trade deficit now expanding to worrisome levels, policymakers may soon be looking for more ways to limit imports. The ominous shifting of production from Mexican *maquiladoras* to even lower cost China is further evidence that the assumption that Mexico's needed growth would automatically flow from free trade was naïve.

In many developing countries, the largest part of Mexico's economic problem lies not in restricted export markets, but in the stifling maldistribution of wealth and power that restricts internal growth. The rich pay hardly any taxes. Despite the image of Mexico as a country with a strong state, the public revenue is 19 percent of GDP, compared with the more than 30 percent that the presumably more conservative American public sector takes.

Seeking an Alternative

The alternatives thus far presented by the Party of Porto Alegre seem to be caught in a web of contradictions. For example, at the same time that demonstrators demand that the IMF and other world institutions respect local sovereignty and end efforts to impose the neoliberal model, they demand that a wide variety of their own rules—independence for indigenous tribes, gender and racial equality, priority for small farmers, environmental regulations—be imposed on sovereign nations

Moreover, the Party of Porto Alegre is caught in a Catch-22 situation:

- Social justice requires global political institutions to regulate the global market
- Global political institutions are dominated by the Party of Davos
- The Party of Davos is hostile to social justice

The Party of Porto Alegre is thus forced back into a defense of national sovereignty as the only available instrument for achieving social justice. Yet sovereignty is steadily eroding under the relentless pressure of global markets. Moreover, nationalist politics undercut the cross-border cooperation needed to balance the cross-border political reach of business and finance.

Nationalism perpetuates the myth that national identity is the only factor in determining whether one wins or loses in the global economy. It obscures the common interests of working families in all countries when faced with the alliances of investors that now dominate the global marketplace.

Still, human rights and social justice will become part of the "constitution" of the global marketplace only when enough nation-states demand it. Therefore, the global opposition must pursue a common global program for working people that reinforces their national struggles for economic and social equity. Such a program would support national democratic movements and leaders who understand that national social contracts cannot be maintained in a global market that lacks one of its own, and that a global social contract cannot be established in the absence of effective social democracy at the national level.

The creation of a true global alternative requires a perspective through which the interests of workers in all countries are linked. In a global marketplace, workers' living standards increasingly rise and fall together. When workers in Brazil win a wage increase, it raises the bargaining power of workers in Germany. When workers in Indonesia improve their working conditions, workers in Nigeria benefit. Likewise, when the social safety net is strengthened in one country it helps those struggling for human economic and social rights in other countries as well.

In a world of countries desperate for investment, the development of a global political movement powerful enough to bring the investor class to the bargaining table is clearly a long way off. But, with a nod to Margaret Thatcher, there is no alternative.

I believe that it is time for us to concentrate on a feasible project—the building of a model of cross-border solidarity among the ordinary people of our own continent.

A Modest Continental Proposal

Despite the failure of NAFTA to deliver on the promises of its architects, it is here to stay. Every day more intracontinental connections in finance, marketing, production, and other business networks are being hardwired for a consolidated North American market. Almost 70 percent of U.S. imports from Mexico are within the same firm or related firms producing the same final product. Ford pick-up trucks are now assembled in Cuautitlan, Mexico, with engines from Windsor, Ontario, and transmissions from Livonia, Michigan. Labor markets are relentlessly merging, for professionals as well as migrant workers.

Post- 9/11 border security concerns in the U.S. slowed down the process. But commerce will prevail, and is now above pre-9/11 levels. Ultimately, the War on Terrorism is more likely to constrict the political freedoms of North Americans than the freedom of money and goods to cross their borders.

Moreover, the writing of the North American constitution continues. Out of the public eye, trigovernmental task forces and committees are discussing proposals ranging from guest-worker programs to continental transportation systems and the privatization of Canadian water and Mexican oil. Think-tanks, new academic institutes, and business associations are debating ideas about the harmonization of taxes and regulation, monetary policies, and a single currency. As the former Canadian ambassador to the United States recently commented, "Few days go by without new ideas for keeping NAFTA." The shared assumption is that the necessary political governance of the North American economy can be achieved by stealth, by grafting new agreements onto the basic NAFTA framework without stirring up public concerns over sovereignty and accountability.

But, sooner rather than later, the question of NAFTA's future must become part of the domestic politics of each nation. We need a process in which electorates of all three countries share an honest dialogue over the common future that was denied them in the first NAFTA debate.

In all three countries, the sense that globalization is beyond the influence of the majority of people has disempowered the public discussion of how to shape a common future. A focus on the question, "What do we want North America to look like ten or twenty years from now?" might be a way to revive that discussion and eventually generate the basis for a new and more comprehensive bargain among all people of the three countries.

Shortly after his election, Mexican president Vicente Fox suggested that NAFTA countries adopt a version of the European Union's program for investment in poorer areas. Mexico—even more so than the poorest nations of Western Europe—needs substantial investment in education, health, and infrastructure to create sufficient jobs for its people.

Fox's proposal was rejected in both Washington and Ottawa. It may be time to revive that suggestion to create a new Grand Bargain. In return for long-term financial assistance for Mexico's public investment, the working people of Canada and the United States would get an agreement on enforceable labor and environmental standards, so that as Mexico grows, wage levels and working conditions will rise—creating a middle-class market in Mexico and preventing the undercutting of labor standards north of the border. It could also build a middle-class constituency for modern tax, legal and public administration systems. The credible prospect of widely shared prosperity in Mexico that is creating enough jobs for its people would, in turn, make it easier to achieve a satisfactory accord on migration.

Debate over a new bargain might also recognize that democracy is incompatible with Chapter 11 and other NAFTA provisions that undermine the authority of the local public sector. And it might initiate an honest effort to apply the principles of sustainability to the continent's economic growth.

A continent-wide project for economic and social justice has another great advantage. It could provide a way to work out a model for the governance of a global economy that reconciles the tension between the relentless drive of technology to expand the boundaries of the market and the human needs of a decent society. Focusing on building such a decent society in our own continental neighborhood could also help redirect our political energies away from the temptation of global empire.

Just perhaps, if we could achieve economic integration with social justice between two first world societies and one third world society on this continent, we might have something to contribute to the development of a just and prosperous global society.

JEFF FAUX was the founder, and is now Distinguished Fellow, of the Economic Policy Institute. This article is adapted from a paper delivered at the Villanova University Conference on Catholic Social Teaching and Globalization in November 2003.

UNIT 3
Conflict and Instability

Unit Selections

Key Points to Consider

- What factors account for the decline in conflict worldwide?

- Who are the various actors in Iraq's civil war?

- What are the regional implications of the Iraq war?

- Why is progress in Afghanistan in jeopardy?

- What are the sources of instability in Pakistan?

- What is the motivation behind India's Naxalite rebellion?

- Is there reason to be hopeful that the situation in Darfur will improve?

- What are the challenges to successful UN peacekeeping?

- What are the advantages and disadvantages of the International Criminal Court?

Student Web Site
www.mhcls.com/online

Internet References
Further information regarding these Web sites may be found in this book's preface or online.

The Carter Center
http://www.cartercenter.org
Center for Strategic and International Studies (CSIS)
http://www.csis.org/
Conflict Research Consortium
http://conflict.colorado.edu/
Institute for Security Studies
http://www.iss.co.za
Institute for Global communications
http://www.igc.org/peacenet/
Refugees International
http://www.refintl.org

While evidence points to a decline in conflict worldwide, conflict and instability in the developing world remain major threats to international peace and security. Conflict stems from a combination of sources including ethnic and religious diversity, nationalism, the struggle for state control, and competition for resources. In some cases, boundaries that date from the colonial era encompass diverse groups. Such diversity can increase tension among groups competing for scarce resources and opportunities. When some groups benefit or are perceived as enjoying privileges at the expense of others, ethnicity can offer a convenient vehicle around which to organize and mobilize. Moreover, ethnic politics lends itself to manipulation both by regimes that are seeking to protect privileges, maintain order, or retain power; and those that are challenging existing governments. In a politically and ethnically charged atmosphere, conflict and instability often result as groups vie to gain control of a state apparatus that can extract resources and allocate benefits. Early literature on modernization and development speculated that as developing societies progressed from traditional to modern, primary attachments such as ethnicity and religious affiliation would fade and be replaced by new forms of identification. Clearly, however, ethnicity remains a potent force, as does religion. Ethnic politics and the emergence of religious radicalism demonstrate that such attachments have survived the drive toward modernization. While ethnicity has certainly played a role in many recent conflicts, conflicts over power and resources may be mistakenly viewed as ethnic in nature. In any case, these conflicts generate economic disruption, population migration, environmental degradation, and may also draw other countries into the fighting. Failing states also contribute to the potential for conflict. They can offer a haven for terrorists and criminals to operate and the spill-over from conflict in these states can widen instability.

Initially inspired and encouraged by the theocratic regime in Iran, Islamists have not only pushed for the establishment of governments based on Islamic law, but have engaged in a wider struggle with what they regard as the threat of western cultural dominance. Radical Islamic groups that advocate a more rigid and violent interpretation of Islam have increasingly challenged more mainstream Islamic thought. These radicals are driven by hatred of the West and the United States in particular, and have engaged in several high profile operations such as the 1998 East African embassy bombings and the September 11th attacks. Although there is a tendency to equate Islam with terrorism, it is a mistake to link the two. A deeper understanding of the various strands of Islamic thought is required to separate legitimate efforts to challenge repressive regimes and forge an alternative to western forms of political organization, from radicals who pervert Islam and use terrorism as a tactic.

Whatever the cause, there is no shortage of tension and conflict around the world. Prospects for peace between the Israelis and Palestinians were dealt a blow with the victory of the Islamist group

Hugo Rami/IRIN

Hamas in the 2006 Palestinian parliamentary elections. The war in Iraq has become a complex civil war pitting several different actors against one another. The Iraq war has also had a major regional impact. The Taliban pose a renewed security threat in Afghanistan, where the Karzai government is having difficulty consolidating gains in the face of growing NATO unease with its mission, a booming opium trade, and tensions with Pakistan. Pakistan itself faces increasing polarization on several fronts. India's Naxalite movement demonstrates that ideology remains a source of conflict. Meanwhile, the nuclear weapons programs of Iran and North Korea have heightened tensions with the United States and illustrate the growing problem of nuclear proliferation. Africa continues to be particularly conflict-prone. Zimbabwe is sliding further into economic disaster and instability. Darfur remains a focus of world-wide concern. Arab militias supported by the government have carried out deadly attacks against black residents causing hundreds of thousands of deaths, generating as many as a million refugees, and creating a spill-over effect in neighboring countries. Efforts to end the suffering have been unsuccessful so far, but there is growing pressure on Sudan to halt the conflict. Somalia's long chaos took a new turn with Ethiopian intervention in support of the interim government against the Union of Islamic Courts. Peacekeeping efforts in both Darfur and Somalia demonstrate the challenges of deploying troops under international auspices and the need for some sort of rapid reaction force to react more quickly to crises.

Although conflict may have declined worldwide, the threats to peace and stability in the developing world remain complicated and dangerous, and clearly have the potential to threaten international security. These circumstances require a greater effort to understand and resolve conflicts, whatever their source.

The End of War?

Explaining 15 years of diminishing violence.

GREGG EASTERBROOK

Daily explosions in Iraq, massacres in Sudan, the Koreas staring at each other through artillery barrels, a Hobbesian war of all against all in eastern Congo—combat plagues human society as it has, perhaps, since our distant forebears realized that a tree limb could be used as a club. But here is something you would never guess from watching the news: War has entered a cycle of decline. Combat in Iraq and in a few other places is an exception to a significant global trend that has gone nearly unnoticed—namely that, for about 15 years, there have been steadily fewer armed conflicts worldwide. In fact, it is possible that a person's chance of dying because of war has, in the last decade or more, become the lowest in human history.

Five years ago, two academics—Monty Marshall, research director at the Center for Global Policy at George Mason University, and Ted Robert Gurr, a professor of government at the University of Maryland—spent months compiling all available data on the frequency and death toll of twentieth-century combat, expecting to find an ever-worsening ledger of blood and destruction. Instead, they found, after the terrible years of World Wars I and II, a global increase in war from the 1960s through the mid-'80s. But this was followed by a steady, nearly uninterrupted decline beginning in 1991. They also found a steady global rise since the mid-'80s in factors that reduce armed conflict—economic prosperity, free elections, stable central governments, better communication, more "peacemaking institutions," and increased international engagement. Marshall and Gurr, along with Deepa Khosla, published their results as a 2001 report, *Peace and Conflict,* for the Center for International Development and Conflict Management at the University of Maryland. At the time, I remember reading that report and thinking, "Wow, this is one of the hottest things I have ever held in my hands." I expected that evidence of a decline in war would trigger a sensation. Instead it received almost no notice.

"After the first report came out, we wanted to brief some United Nations officials, but everyone at the United Nations just laughed at us. They could not believe war was declining, because this went against political expectations," Marshall says. Of course, 2001 was the year of September 11. But, despite the battles in Afghanistan, the Philippines, and elsewhere that were ignited by Islamist terrorism and the West's response, a second edition of *Peace and Conflict,* published in 2003, showed the total number of wars and armed conflicts continued to decline. A third edition of the study, published last week, shows that, despite the invasion of Iraq and other outbreaks of fighting, the overall decline of war continues. This even as the global population keeps rising, which might be expected to lead to more war, not less.

In his prescient 1989 book, *Retreat from Doomsday,* Ohio State University political scientist John Mueller, in addition to predicting that the Soviet Union was about to collapse—the Berlin Wall fell just after the book was published—declared that great-nation war had become "obsolete" and might never occur again. One reason the Soviet Union was about to collapse, Mueller wrote, was that its leaders had structured Soviet society around the eighteenth-century assumption of endless great-power fighting, but great-power war had become archaic, and no society with war as its organizing principle can endure any longer. So far, this theory has been right on the money. It is worth noting that the first emerging great power of the new century, China, though prone to making threatening statements about Taiwan, spends relatively little on its military.

Last year Mueller published a follow-up book, *The Remnants of War,* which argues that fighting below the level of great-power conflict—small-state wars, civil wars, ethnic combat, and clashes among private armies—is also waning. *Retreat from Doomsday* and *The Remnants of War* are brilliantly original and urgent books. Combat is not an inevitable result of international discord and human malevolence, Mueller believes. War, rather, is "merely an idea"—and a really bad idea, like dueling or slavery. This bad idea "has been grafted onto human existence" and can be excised. Yes, the end of war has been predicted before, prominently by H.G. Wells in 1915, and horrible bloodshed followed. But could the predictions be right this time?

First, the numbers. The University of Maryland studies find the number of wars and armed conflicts worldwide peaked in 1991 at 51, which may represent the most wars happening simultaneously at any point in history. Since 1991, the number has fallen steadily. There were 26 armed conflicts in 2000 and 25 in 2002, even after the Al Qaeda attack on the United States and the U.S. counterattack against Afghanistan. By 2004, Marshall and Gurr's latest study shows, the number of armed conflicts in the world had declined to 20, even after the invasion of Iraq. All told, there were less than half as many wars in 2004 as there were in 1991.

Marshall and Gurr also have a second ranking, gauging the magnitude of fighting. This section of the report is more subjective. Everyone agrees that the worst moment for human conflict was World War II; but how to rank, say, the current separatist fighting in Indonesia versus, say, the Algerian war of independence is more speculative. Nevertheless, the *Peace and Conflict* studies name 1991 as the peak post-World War II year for totality of global fighting, giving that year a ranking of 179 on a scale that rates the extent and destructiveness of combat. By 2000, in spite of war in the Balkans and genocide in Rwanda, the number had fallen to 97; by 2002 to 81; and, at the end of 2004, it stood at 65. This suggests the extent and intensity of global combat is now less than half what it was 15 years ago.

How can war be in such decline when evening newscasts are filled with images of carnage? One reason fighting seems to be everywhere is that, with the ubiquity of 24-hour cable news and the Internet, we see many more images of conflict than before. A mere decade ago, the rebellion in Eritrea occurred with almost no world notice; the tirelessly globe-trotting Robert Kaplan wrote of meeting with Eritrean rebels who told him they hoped that at least spy satellites were trained on their region so that someone, somewhere, would know of their struggle. Today, fighting in Iraq, Sudan, and other places is elaborately reported on, with a wealth of visual details supplied by minicams and even camera-enabled cell phones. News organizations must prominently report fighting, of course. But the fact that we now see so many visuals of combat and conflict creates the impression that these problems are increasing: Actually, it is the reporting of the problems that is increasing, while the problems themselves are in decline. Television, especially, likes to emphasize war because pictures of fighting, soldiers, and military hardware are inherently more compelling to viewers than images of, say, water-purification projects. Reports of violence and destruction are rarely balanced with reports about the overwhelming majority of the Earth's population not being harmed.

Mueller calculates that about 200 million people were killed in the twentieth century by warfare, other violent conflicts, and government actions associated with war, such as the Holocaust. About twelve billion people lived during that century, meaning that a person of the twentieth century had a 1 to 2 percent chance of dying as the result of international war, ethnic fighting, or government-run genocide. A 1 to 2 percent chance, Mueller notes, is also an American's lifetime chance of dying in an automobile accident. The risk varies depending on where you live and who you are, of course; Mueller notes that, during the twentieth century, Armenians, Cambodians, Jews, kulaks, and some others had a far higher chance of death by war or government persecution than the global average. Yet, with war now in decline, for the moment men and women worldwide stand in more danger from cars and highways than from war and combat. World Health Organization statistics back this: In 2000, for example, 300,000 people died in combat or for war-related reasons (such as disease or malnutrition caused by war), while 1.2 million worldwide died in traffic accidents. That 300,000 people perished because of war in 2000 is a terrible toll, but it represents just .005 percent of those alive in that year.

This low global risk of death from war probably differs greatly from most of the world's past. In prehistory, tribal and small-group violence may have been endemic. Steven LeBlanc, a Harvard University archeologist, asserts in his 2003 book about the human past, *Constant Battles*, that warfare was a steady feature of primordial society. LeBlanc notes that, when the aboriginal societies of New Guinea were first observed by Europeans in the 1930s, one male in four died by violence; traditional New Guinean society was organized around endless tribal combat. Unremitting warfare characterized much of the history of Europe, the Middle East, and other regions; perhaps one-fifth of the German population died during the Thirty Years War, for instance. Now the world is in a period in which less than one ten-thousandth of its population dies from fighting in a year. The sheer number of people who are *not* being harmed by warfare is without precedent.

Next consider a wonderful fact: Global military spending is also in decline. Stated in current dollars, annual global military spending peaked in 1985, at $1.3 trillion, and has been falling since, to slightly over $1 trillion in 2004, according to the Center for Defense Information, a nonpartisan Washington research organization. Since the global population has risen by one-fifth during this period, military spending might have been expected to rise. Instead, relative to population growth, military spending has declined by a full third. In current dollars, the world spent $260 per capita on arms in 1985 and $167 in 2004.

The striking decline in global military spending has also received no attention from the press, which continues to promote the notion of a world staggering under the weight of instruments of destruction. Only a few nations, most prominently the United States, have increased their defense spending in the last decade. Today, the United States accounts for

44 percent of world military spending; if current trends continue, with many nations reducing defense spending while the United States continues to increase such spending as its military is restructured for new global anti-terrorism and peacekeeping roles, it is not out of the question that, in the future, the United States will spend more on arms and soldiers than the rest of the world combined.

Declining global military spending is exactly what one would expect to find if war itself were in decline. The peak year in global military spending came only shortly before the peak year for wars, 1991. There's an obvious chicken-or-egg question, whether military spending has fallen because wars are rarer or whether wars are rarer because military spending has fallen. Either way, both trend lines point in the right direction. This is an extremely favorable development, particularly for the world's poor—the less developing nations squander on arms, the more they can invest in improving daily lives of their citizens.

What is causing war to decline? The most powerful factor must be the end of the cold war, which has both lowered international tensions and withdrawn U.S. and Soviet support from proxy armies in the developing world. Fighting in poor nations is sustained by outside supplies of arms. To be sure, there remain significant stocks of small arms in the developing world—particularly millions of assault rifles. But, with international arms shipments waning and heavy weapons, such as artillery, becoming harder to obtain in many developing nations, factions in developing-world conflicts are more likely to sue for peace. For example, the long, violent conflict in Angola was sustained by a weird mix of Soviet, American, Cuban, and South African arms shipments to a potpourri of factions. When all these nations stopped supplying arms to the Angolan combatants, the leaders of the factions grudgingly came to the conference table.

During the cold war, Marshall notes, it was common for Westerners to say there was peace because no fighting affected the West. Actually, global conflict rose steadily during the cold war, but could be observed only in the developing world. After the cold war ended, many in the West wrung their hands about a supposed outbreak of "disorder" and ethnic hostilities. Actually, both problems went into decline following the cold war, but only then began to be noticed in the West, with confrontation with the Soviet empire no longer an issue.

Another reason for less war is the rise of peacekeeping. The world spends more every year on peacekeeping, and peacekeeping is turning out to be an excellent investment. Many thousands of U.N., NATO, American, and other soldiers and peacekeeping units now walk the streets in troubled parts of the world, at a cost of at least $3 billion annually. Peacekeeping has not been without its problems; peacekeepers have been accused of paying very young girls for sex in Bosnia and Africa, and NATO bears collective shame for refusing support to the Dutch peacekeeping unit that might have prevented the Srebrenica massacre of 1995. But, overall, peacekeeping is working. Dollar for dollar, it is far more effective at preventing fighting than purchasing complex weapons systems. A recent study from the notoriously gloomy RAND Corporation found that most U.N. peacekeeping efforts have been successful.

Peacekeeping is just one way in which the United Nations has made a significant contribution to the decline of war. American commentators love to disparage the organization in that big cereal-box building on the East River, and, of course, the United Nations has manifold faults. Yet we should not lose track of the fact that the global security system envisioned by the U.N. charter appears to be taking effect. Great-power military tensions are at the lowest level in centuries; wealthy nations are increasingly pressured by international diplomacy not to encourage war by client states; and much of the world respects U.N. guidance. Related to this, the rise in "international engagement," or the involvement of the world community in local disputes, increasingly mitigates against war.

The spread of democracy has made another significant contribution to the decline of war. In 1975, only one-third of the world's nations held true multiparty elections; today two-thirds do, and the proportion continues to rise. In the last two decades, some 80 countries have joined the democratic column, while hardly any moved in the opposite direction. Increasingly, developing-world leaders observe the simple fact that the free nations are the strongest and richest ones, and this creates a powerful argument for the expansion of freedom. Theorists at least as far back as Immanuel Kant have posited that democratic societies would be much less likely to make war than other kinds of states. So far, this has proved true: Democracy-against-democracy fighting has been extremely rare. Prosperity and democracy tend to be mutually reinforcing. Now prosperity is rising in most of the world, amplifying the trend toward freedom. As ever-more nations become democracies, ever-less war can be expected, which is exactly what is being observed.

For the great-power nations, the arrival of nuclear deterrence is an obvious factor in the decline of war. The atomic bomb debuted in 1945, and the last great-power fighting, between the United States and China, concluded not long after, in 1953. From 1871 to 1914, Europe enjoyed nearly half a century without war; the current 52-year great-power peace is the longest period without great-power war since the modern state system emerged. Of course, it is possible that nuclear deterrence will backfire and lead to a conflagration beyond imagination in its horrors. But, even at the height of the cold war, the United States and the Soviet

Union never seriously contemplated a nuclear exchange. If it didn't happen then, it seems unlikely for the future.

In turn, lack of war among great nations sets an example for the developing world. When the leading nations routinely attacked neighbors or rivals, governments of emerging states dreamed of the day when they, too, could issue orders to armies of conquest. Now that the leading nations rarely use military force—and instead emphasize economic competition—developing countries imitate that model. This makes the global economy more turbulent, but reduces war.

In *The Remnants of War,* Mueller argues that most fighting in the world today happens because many developing nations lack "capable government" that can contain ethnic conflict or prevent terrorist groups, militias, and criminal gangs from operating. Through around 1500, he reminds us, Europe, too, lacked capable government: Criminal gangs and private armies roamed the countryside. As European governments became competent, and as police and courts grew more respected, legitimate government gradually vanquished thug elements from most of European life. Mueller thinks this same progression of events is beginning in much of the developing world. Government and civil institutions in India, for example, are becoming more professional and less corrupt—one reason why that highly populous nation is not falling apart, as so many predicted it would. Interstate war is in substantial decline; if civil wars, ethnic strife, and private army fighting also go into decline, war may be ungrafted from the human experience.

I s it possible to believe that war is declining, owing to the spread of enlightenment? This seems the riskiest claim. Human nature has let us down many times before. Some have argued that militarism as a philosophy was destroyed in World War II, when the states that were utterly dedicated to martial organization and violent conquest were not only beaten but reduced to rubble by free nations that initially wanted no part of the fight. World War II did represent the triumph of freedom over militarism. But memories are short: It is unrealistic to suppose that no nation will ever be seduced by militarism again.

Yet the last half-century has seen an increase in great nations acting in an enlightened manner toward one another. Prior to this period, the losing sides in wars were usually punished; consider the Versailles Treaty, whose punitive terms helped set in motion the Nazi takeover of Germany. After World War II, the victors did not punish Germany and Japan, which made reasonably smooth returns to prosperity and acceptance by the family of nations. Following the end of the cold war, the losers—the former Soviet Union and China—have seen their national conditions improve, if fitfully; their reentry into the family of nations has gone reasonably well and has been encouraged, if not actively aided, by their former adversaries. Not punishing the vanquished should diminish the odds of future war, since there are no

generations who suffer from the victor's terms, become bitter, and want vengeance.

Antiwar sentiment is only about a century old in Western culture, and Mueller thinks its rise has not been given sufficient due. As recently as the Civil War in the United States and World War I in Europe, it was common to view war as inevitable and to be fatalistic about the power of government to order men to march to their deaths. A spooky number of thinkers even adulated war as a desirable condition. Kant, who loved democracy, nevertheless wrote that war is "sublime" and that "prolonged peace favors the predominance of a mere commercial spirit, and with it a debasing self-interest, cowardice and effeminacy." Alexis De Tocqueville said that war "enlarges the mind of a people." Igor Stravinsky called war "necessary for human progress." In 1895, Oliver Wendell Holmes Jr. told the graduating class of Harvard that one of the highest expressions of honor was "the faith . . . which leads a soldier to throw away his life in obedience to a blindly accepted duty."

Around the turn of the twentieth century, a counterview arose—that war is usually absurd. One of the bestselling books of late-nineteenth-century Europe, *Lay Down Your Arms!,* was an antiwar novel. Organized draft resistance in the United Kingdom during World War I was a new force in European politics. England slept during the '30s in part because public antiwar sentiment was intense. By the time the U.S. government abolished the draft at the end of the Vietnam War, there was strong feeling in the United States that families would no longer tolerate being compelled to give up their children for war. Today, that feeling has spread even to Russia, such a short time ago a totalitarian, militaristic state. As average family size has decreased across the Western world, families have invested more in each child; this should discourage militarism. Family size has started to decrease in the developing world, too, so the same dynamic may take effect in poor nations.

There is even a chance that the ascent of economics to its pinnacle position in modern life reduces war. Nations interconnected by trade may be less willing to fight each other: If China and the United States ever fought, both nations might see their economies collapse. It is true that, in the decades leading up to World War I, some thought rising trade would prevent war. But today's circumstances are very different from those of the fin de siècle. Before World War I, great powers still maintained the grand illusion that there could be war without general devastation; World Wars I and II were started by governments that thought they could come out ahead by fighting. Today, no major government appears to believe that war is the best path to nationalistic or monetary profit; trade seems much more promising.

The late economist Julian Simon proposed that, in a knowledge-based economy, people and their brainpower are more important than physical resources, and thus the lives of a country's citizens are worth more than any object that might be seized in war. Simon's was a highly optimistic view—he assumed governments are grounded in reason—and yet there is a chance this vision will be realized. Already, most Western nations have achieved a condition in which citizens' lives possess greater economic value than any place or thing an army might gain by combat. As knowledge-based economics spreads throughout the world, physical resources may mean steadily less, while life means steadily more. That's, well, enlightenment.

In his 1993 book, *A History of Warfare,* the military historian John Keegan recognized the early signs that combat and armed conflict had entered a cycle of decline. War "may well be ceasing to commend itself to human beings as a desirable or productive, let alone rational, means of reconciling their discontents," Keegan wrote. Now there are 15 years of positive developments supporting the idea. Fifteen years is not all that long. Many things could still go badly wrong; there could be ghastly surprises in store. But, for the moment, the trends have never been more auspicious: Swords really are being beaten into plowshares and spears into pruning hooks. The world ought to take notice.

From *The New Republic,* May 30, 2005, pp. 18–21. Copyright © 2005 by The New Republic, LLC. Reprinted by permission of The New Republic.

Iraq's Civil War

"The US and Iraqi governments' reluctance to accept the designation 'civil war' does not alter the reality on the ground."

AHMED S. HASHIM

"We are not in a civil war. Iraq will never be in a civil war. The violence is in decrease and our security ability is increasing. What you see is an atmosphere of reconciliation." So insisted Iraqi Prime Minister Nuri al-Maliki on August 28, 2006. But violent events before and since have brutally contradicted his statement. Iraq is in a civil war.

First, there is the now depressingly familiar Iraqi-on-Iraqi violence between Shiites and Sunnis, which grew to serious levels following the destruction by Sunni extremists of the Shiite shrine of Al- Askariya in Samarra on February 22. In the month of October alone, the United Nations reported that 3,709 Iraqis were killed, largely as a result of sectarian conflict. On November 22, in the deadliest sectarian attack in Baghdad since the US-led invasion, explosions from five car bombs and a mortar shell tore through crowded intersections and marketplaces in the Shiite district of Sadr City, killing more than 200 people and wounding approximately 250.

Sadr City is populated by constituents of the powerful maverick politician Moktada al-Sadr. The inevitable response by Shiites came the following day when gunmen from the Mahdi Army, a powerful militia created by Sadr in 2003, launched a series of attacks on Sunni mosques, including the famous Abu Hanifa Mosque in central Baghdad. Half a dozen Sunnis reportedly were doused in kerosene and set on fire by gunmen while security forces stood by. This cycle of sectarian conflict was well under way when the prime minister insisted there was no civil war.

Second, Iraq has witnessed serious intra-sectarian strife, adding another twist to a situation that has been described, accurately, as one of complex violence. The past year saw deadly internecine fighting among the Sunnis, between what might be referred to as mainstream (for want of a better word) Iraqi insurgents—that is, nationalists, former Baathists, and tribal militants—and Sunni religious extremists and foreign jihadists associated with Al Qaeda in Iraq (AQI). And even as

Maliki was talking of national reconciliation in late August, firefights were erupting between the Shiite Mahdi militia and Iraqi government forces. The latter forces, largely made up of Shiite personnel, reportedly suffered two dozen deaths in the town of Diwaniya at the hands of Mahdi Army gunmen.

Third, the Sunni insurgency continues. While the prime minister was offering his assurances, that weekend eight US soldiers died at the hands of Sunni insurgents, and there was a brief mutiny of a British-trained Iraqi army unit in a southern province. The troops mutinied because they had been told they were to deploy to Baghdad.

Finally, in addition to the bloodshed between Sunnis and Shiites, within sects, and between insurgents and security forces, a more general but equally calamitous insecurity, including widespread organized crime, has deepened across much of Iraq, including the capital. All of these trends reflect a state of affairs in Iraq that has deteriorated throughout the past year, belying Maliki's claims of national reconciliation.

Indeed, the level and extent of violence in 2006 were the worst since the 2003 invasion. Hope that their nation can turn things around and advance toward some form of stability and security has all but dissipated among Iraqis, many thousands of whom are voting with their feet and fleeing the country. The height of optimism came in late 2005, when millions of Iraqis went to the polls to elect a new national assembly and a government that promised to put Iraq on the road to reconciliation and recovery. This optimism was soon dashed by the rising tide of violence.

Compounding the carnage, as well as the dilemma facing US forces trying to find an exit from Iraq, has been the inability of the new government to deal with the situation. Buffeted by rival ethnosectarian political groups, the Maliki administration that came into office in the spring of 2006 has proved indecisive, incompetent, and unable to arrest the country's slide into civil war.

The Conflicted Insurgency

The local Iraqi insurgent movement, which incorporates nationalists, remnants from the ousted Baathist regime of Saddam Hussein, and mainstream Sunni Islamist groups, remains as potent as ever. An increase in US casualties in the fall partly reflected the deployment of American forces into Baghdad in an effort to restore order and security in a capital held hostage to attacks by insurgents and rival communal militias. But attacks against US and Iraqi government forces increased in intensity and frequency throughout 2006. US control over the restive Sunni Anbar province deteriorated significantly in 2006 as a result of a paucity of troops to police the province. And, from the American perspective, the past year has seen worrisome operational advances among the insurgents. They have begun to train and field relatively effective teams of snipers; they are fielding platoon-sized units that can stand and engage US troops in lengthy fire-fights, in contrast to their usual modus operandi of hit-and-run attacks. The strength of the insurgency is underscored by its financial resilience.

The Sunni insurgency does have its share of problems, of which three are critical and unlikely to be resolved soon. First, there are too many groups with their own political agendas; the insurgency continues to lack a unified political vision of what it wants for a post-occupation Iraq. Its weakness in this area is compounded by the fact that even if it were to develop a common political vision or agenda, it would still be limited to the minority Sunni Arab community. Iraq's Kurds and Shiites have their own respective visions, neither of which have much in common with the Sunni insurgents'.

Second, as a result of this political factionalism, the Sunni insurgency is unable to present an effective negotiating strategy vis-à-vis the US-led coalition or the Iraqi government. While some groups are willing to negotiate an end to the insurgency in return for the implementation of certain demands, others remain adamant that they will never negotiate with either US forces or the Iraqi government. Others indicate that they will negotiate only with the real power in the country, the United States. Still others put forward demands that they know will not be accepted.

Third, the insurgency is split organizationally between nationalist groups and the Iraqi and foreign Islamist extremists. Some former Baathists and others have been ambivalent about the strategy promoted by Al Qaeda in Iraq, under the leadership of Abu Musab Al-Zarqawi until his death in June, to deliberately target Shiite civilians in order to promote sectarian strife. AQI itself, meanwhile, has had its share of problems, both with its ostensible parent organization Al Qaeda, and with the "mainstream" Iraqi insurgent groups.

Senior Al Qaeda leaders worried about Zarqawi's indiscriminate violence against both Iraqi Sunnis and Shiites, which they regarded as counterproductive. On July 9, 2005, Ayman al-Zawahiri, the lieutenant of Al Qaeda leader Osama bin Laden, sent Zarqawi a letter in which he asserted that the overarching strategic goal is the establishment of a caliphate. The jihad in Iraq, he said, has several incremental goals intended to contribute to this ultimate objective: expulsion of the Americans from Iraq; establishment of an Islamic authority or emirate; extension of the jihadist wave to secular countries neighboring Iraq; and extension of the jihad against Israel. Zawahiri pointed out that these intermediate goals require "popular support from the Muslim masses in Iraq and the surrounding Muslim countries."

Zawahiri's letter stressed that in the absence of such support the jihadist movement would be crushed. Therefore, the movement must avoid taking actions that the masses do not understand or endorse. With regard to the Shiites, Zawahiri knew he was treading on sensitive ground; he granted that jihadists have a right to defend themselves against the "aggressive" actions of Shiites who cooperated with the occupiers in overthrowing the Baathist regime in exchange for their assumption of power. His letter left no doubt that there is bound to be a collision between the Shiites and the model Sunni state of the future. Nevertheless, he proceeded to ask Zarqawi if it was correct for him to launch a wide-ranging assault on the Shiite community in Iraq, an assault that has raised questions and aversion among the majority of Muslims.

Another senior Al Qaeda operative, Attiyah Abdal-Rahman, wrote Zarqawi a letter in December 2005 strongly urging Zarqawi to cooperate more with other Sunni insurgent groups. In light of these problems within AQI, it is not surprising that, in January 2006, the jihadists felt compelled to create an umbrella leadership group to help coordinate their activities and gain more support. This group, the Mujahideen Shura Council (MSC), includes leaders of AQI and smaller jihadist organizations.

The Tribes Strike Back

AQI's other problem is its disintegrating relationship with the mainstream Iraqi insurgents. The problems between the two groups began in the spring of 2005 with the bullying and mistreatment of residents in small and remote towns such as Rutba in Anbar province. The inhabitants of most of these towns lacked the wherewithal to oppose the jihadist insurgents. It was only in the town of Al Qaim that locals, led by the Albu Mahal tribe, managed to kick out the jihadists in one of the first large-scale firefights between townspeople and foreign terrorists. (Whenever coalition forces made their rare and fleeting sweeps through these towns, they would disarm the locals and leave them at the mercy of the jihadists.)

However, the falling-out between the natives and the jihadists in these remote areas would most likely have had little strategic significance had relations between AQI and major Sunni tribes in the heart of Anbar province not deteriorated dramatically during the fall of 2005. In October 2005, one of the largest mainstream insurgent groups, the Islamic Army in Iraq, engaged in firefights with the jihadists. In early 2006, the jihadists began to kill tribal sheikhs and clerics, infuriating the townspeople. In the space of one month—January 2006—AQI killed four Ramadi sheikhs who had been working on a peaceful solution to the dire security situation in Ramadi and opposed Al Qaeda's presence in their town.

The killing of 70 Sunnis lining up to join the police force in Ramadi on January 5, 2006, was a major indication of the collapse of the relationship. Tribal leaders and local insurgents vowed to drive Zarqawi's militants out of Anbar. Three Ramadi-based Islamist guerrilla factions that had been financed by Zarqawi broke with him, making it harder for his forces to operate in the city. In February 2006, Sheikh Usamah al-Jadaan of the Karabilah tribe complained bitterly about the jihadists who he said were killing innocent Iraqis in the markets, schools, mosques, and churches, instead of fighting the occupation. Jadaan was killed a few months later for being so outspoken, but this did not silence the Sunni sheikhs.

The impact of the civil war on Iraqi society has been nothing short of catastrophic.

Initially, Iraqis had seen Zarqawi as beneficial to the insurgency. Zarqawi had no qualms about claiming credit for bloody attacks; this enabled local insurgent groups to pin the blame on him for the most gruesome incidents. But by mid-2006 he had begun to outlive his usefulness for many within the insurgency, particularly the Sunni tribes. Zarqawi had a big price on his head and was constantly on the run. It would not be surprising if it was disgruntled Sunnis who revealed his whereabouts to the US forces that killed him in an air strike on June 7.

Contrary to expectations that Zarqawi's death would mean the end of the jihadists, AQI returned to the fray with a vengeance. It elected a new leader, Abu Hamza al-Muhajir, allegedly a foreigner. He expressed allegiance to the head of the umbrella group, the MSC, claimed that he would follow the parent organization to the letter, redoubled his efforts to recruit more members and groups into the MSC, and quickly reached out to other Sunnis. Muhajir was instrumental in the MSC's decision later in 2006 to set up a so-called Islamic emirate in the Sunni areas of the country that the insurgents had supposedly "liberated" from US forces and the Shiite-dominated Iraqi government. This decision was met with consternation and derision among both mainstream Sunni insurgent organizations and legitimate political groups. They accused the jihadists of trying to split up Iraq like other groups were trying to do (that is, Shiite political parties and the Kurds).

AQI's political efforts under Muhajir have not succeeded in winning the group much adherence among the Sunni tribes of Anbar province. The traditional power of the tribal leaders is threatened by the Al Qaeda "emirs." Some sheikhs have also been repelled by Al Qaeda attacks aimed at Shiites, believing that they are wrong and will ultimately hurt the Sunnis. Another source of confrontation is the fact that AQI has created a burgeoning criminal enterprise that runs everything from black-market gasoline sales to extortion of police and government paychecks from salaried employees in the province. This has hit people where it matters, and has also caused AQI to run afoul of criminal enterprises run by local Iraqis.

From the spring through the summer of 2006, AQI continued unabated its assassinations and executions of Sunni tribal sheikhs, officials, and clerics. These assassinations, the organization's aggressive recruitment efforts among youth, and the increasingly oppressive jihadist control over small towns like Khaldiya and Haditha, have provoked the Anbar Sunni tribes to cooperate with one another in forming anti-jihadist militias. Tribal leaders have reached out to the government to provide them with arms to fight a mutually loathed enemy. AQI has also found itself engaged in vicious struggles with Baathists and with nationalist insurgent groups such as the 1920 Revolution Brigades.

In recent months, AQI has been slowly but surely squeezed out of sanctuaries in Anbar province as a result of action by both the tribes and American and Iraqi government forces. In particular, AQI has found itself on the receiving end of a Sunni tribal force called the Anbar Salvation Council, which promises to rid the province of foreign terrorists. A number of Al Qaeda leaders and fighters have been killed or captured, including Saudis and Syrians.

Us versus Them

Al Qaeda in Iraq has contributed immensely to making Iraq an unworkable state, to the dramatic decline in intercommunal relations, and to the country's slide into sectarian strife. But the onset of a civil war on top of the insurgency cannot be blamed solely on that organization. The year 2006 was most noteworthy for the dramatic growth of intercommunal violence, which seems to have displaced insurgent violence in its scope and ferocity. While there was the inevitable bloodletting between Kurd and Arab, and Turkmen and Kurd in and around Kirkuk and other areas in the north, the bigger problem has been a massive increase in Sunni-Shiite violence.

Civil strife in Iraq is largely ethnic and sectarian. But this is not the same as arguing that the various groups are dredging up dormant, ancient hatreds among ethno-sectarian communities and that is why they are fighting. The old theory of "ancient hatreds" to explain ethnic conflict is discredited. Rather, it is more accurate to argue that in the struggle for resources and power—including material benefits (land, money, natural resources), political power (positions in or control of government), and symbolic power (imposition of one's conception of national identity or values on the state)—political leaders in ethnically segmented states mobilize their respective communities by promoting ideologies and values that highlight the dangers posed by opposing ethnosectarian groups. The result is the promotion of an "us" versus "them" view of the world.

Transition periods in a country's political evolution almost invariably imply serious loss of power, privileges, and patronage, and the possible political marginalization or even elimination of a particular group. Historically, it has been clear that peoples or groups often fight as fiercely to protect privileges and positions of dominance as they do to try to gain further privileges. After 80 years of political domination and extraordinary privileges, the Sunnis feel that they have lost out in the new Iraq.

The Sunnis' abhorrence of the Shiites is extraordinary; it appears among groups ranging from Sunni Arab nationalists to the obviously anti-Shiite Sunni religious extremists. The distinction between the two groups in their loathing for the Shiites is subtle: Sunni Arab nationalists view many Shiites as a fifth column (tabour khamis) for Iran. Sunnis are convinced that some of the leading Shiite political parties and movements have taken over the country in order to undermine it for Iran's benefit. The religious Sunnis' animosity stems from their view of Shiites as apostates from true Islam and as historical betrayers of the Islamic community of believers.

Despite the mutual suspicions between these two communities, there was little sectarian violence in 2003, the year in which Sunni hegemony over Iraq was displaced by the empowerment of the Shiites. The year 2004 witnessed increased sectarian tensions, particularly as the anti-Shiite jihadists began to make themselves known within the insurgency and to deliberately target the Shiite community. But even in 2004 Iraqis could still talk about Sunni-Shiite cooperation against the US-led coalition, particularly in the spring of 2004 at the height of the first Falluja uprising and the first rebellion by Sadr, the anti-coalition Shiite cleric, and his ragtag militia, the Mahdi Army. The spring of 2004 constituted the high tide of Sunni-Shiite amity, a time when people from both communities were able to wax lyrical about their joint rebellion against the British in 1920 and to see their rebellious endeavor of 2004 as a repetition of history.

Sectarian Cleansing

Since the fall of 2004, it has been easy to trace the country's slow and inexorable descent into civil conflict. The increase in jihadist suicide bombings, abductions, and executions of Shiite civilians and security personnel has driven a massive wedge between the two communities, even though leaders and clerics from both have implored ordinary citizens not to fall into the trap of the extremists. The widening chasm between the two communities was reflected in support among Shiites for the US assault on Falluja in November 2004 and the alleged glee with which they welcomed the town's destruction. Meanwhile, the regularity with which Shiite civilians were killed by Sunni extremists prompted calls for self-defense and retaliation.

This was only satisfied when the Shiites managed to win the elections in January 2005 and to dominate the first elected government headed by Prime Minister Ibrahim Jaafari. Communal relations have plummeted dramatically since. First, the officially sanctioned emergence of the Shiites as the ruling element in Iraq was a massive psychological blow to the Sunnis, whose worst fears about the Shiites bubbled to the surface. Moreover, the fears of a Shiite renaissance among the wider Sunni regions of the Middle East stiffened the resolve and bloody-mindedness of the Sunnis in Iraq who, more than ever, believed they constituted the last line of defense against the heterodox Shiites. Second, the Shiites were able to dominate the security establishment and to pack these institutions with their own personnel. In addition, militias and armed groups associated with Shiite political parties in the government were now able to act with impunity. They began to target the Sunni community, a tactic that, in turn, prompted retaliation by the Sunnis and escalated the cycle of violence. By the spring of 2005 the reality of sectarian conflict in Iraq was inescapable, but the situation could not yet be termed a civil war between the two communities.

For several months now, US commanders on the ground in Iraq and high officials in Washington have been losing faith in the Maliki government.

The Iraqi-on-Iraqi communal violence that took such a horrendous toll in 2006 was accelerated by the bombing of the Al-Askariya Mosque, a Shiite shrine in the overwhelmingly Sunni city of Samarra, on February 22. In fact, many ordinary Iraqis saw the attack as the opening salvoes of the civil war. The Shiites viewed the destruction of the shrine as an attack on their identity. Many responded violently. Dozens of Sunni mosques were assaulted and many Sunnis were killed in an orgy of bloodletting following the attack. The killing continues, unrelenting, today.

US forces have acted as a brake on the slide into full-scale civil war. Some Iraqis argue, however, that it is the very presence of US troops that promotes civil war and perpetuates the Iraqis' inability to deal with their problems. The situation is rendered more bizarre by the fact that there is a seemingly ad hoc legitimization of the foreign occupation among some Sunni Arabs. Feeling threatened, they have requested the presence of US troops to guarantee their safety since they have no confidence in the Iraqi army or in security forces infiltrated by Shiite death squads.

Iraqis from the various communities are now seeking succor, support, and security within their own respective communities. People who are not of the same faith or ethnicity are seen as the "Other." Hussein claimed to have wanted to abolish sectarian and ethnic affiliation as an organizing principle, yet he practiced it by promoting Sunni Arabs and particularly those from his own area and tribe to key positions. This ethnic nepotism remained barely hidden below the edifice of a nationalist and homogenizing system, which in itself was destructive of the ethnic particularities of the Shiites and the Kurds. The violent climate of post-Hussein Iraq has only deepened the extent to which sectarian and ethnic affiliation continues to be the organizing principle of Iraqi politics.

The impact of the civil war on Iraqi society has been nothing short of catastrophic. The social fabric has frayed and is collapsing. Trust among the various communities—already in short supply because of the style of governance and social controls during Hussein's rule—has collapsed as a result of the Iraqi-on-Iraqi violence. Mixed communities have all but been destroyed by the violence, and ethnic cleansing is rampant. In late October, for example, the neighboring towns of Dhuluiya (largely Sunni) and Balad (largely Shiite) engaged in an orgy of mutual bloodletting prompted by the killing of 17 Shiite laborers from Dhuluiya by Sunni religious extremists. By the time the violence ended, the Sunnis who lived in Balad had fled to the safety of Dhuluiya, and the Shiites in Dhuluiya had fled to the safety of Balad. Tens of thousands of Iraqis have fled mixed neighborhoods to seek safety among their own. Many more Iraqis have fled to neighboring countries, including huge numbers of professionals desperately needed in Iraq.

The Failing State

The December 2005 national election—in which 77 percent of the electorate, including the Sunni Arabs, voted—was greeted as the dawn of an era of reconciliation. From the vantage point of a year's passage, that perception has proved at best premature. The chasm between the Sunnis and Shiites is reflected in the fact that neither of the Sunni coalitions—the Iraqi Accord Front or the Iraqi National Dialogue Front—would agree to join in an alliance with the United Iraqi Alliance (UIA), the principal Shiite coalition; this would have given them an absolute majority in the parliament. Indeed, it is not clear that the parties had much in common; and even if they had formed an alliance it is most likely that it would have been caught up in bitter squabbles. It is an undeniable fact that the Sunnis and Shiites see themselves as enemies. Many of the Shiite parties within the UIA see the Sunni political groups as fronts for the insurgency and the former regime; many Sunni politicians see many of the Shiite officials as fronts for Iran and the perpetrators of death-squad violence against Sunni civilians. Thus, the Sunni political fronts have

been more willing to do business with US officials in a bid to slow the seemingly inexorable empowerment of the Shiites.

Hope that their nation can turn things around has all but dissipated among Iraqis.

Maliki, a member of the Shiite Dawa Party and a compromise candidate who was eventually accepted as prime minister, came into office proposing bold new plans to end the insurgency, restore security, abolish the independent militias or integrate them into the regular armed forces, and set the country on the road to stability and recovery. All of these goals came under the rubric of an overall national reconciliation. Americans nodded approvingly. Many glum and weary Iraqis were convinced that the Maliki government was their country's last chance—that if it did not succeed over the course of its first year, the 85-year project to maintain Iraq as a nation would finally be doomed.

Unfortunately, none of Maliki's goals has been realized. His "unity" government has proved nothing more than a sectarian carve-up of the ministries. Most of the political parties view the ministries that they have been allocated as vehicles for ethno-sectarian patronage, not the formulation and implementation of policies. Indeed, jockeying for the allocation of ministries occupied much of the new government's energies in the spring of 2006 while the country was collapsing in the face of rising civil strife between Sunnis and Shiites.

Maliki also has failed to make much headway in reducing the insurgency. The hope among Iraqi government officials and the Americans that new Sunni ministers might constitute a channel to the mainstream insurgent groups—and that these could be persuaded to come forth to negotiate, lay down their arms, and join the political process—has been dashed. There have been sporadic contacts and cloak-and-dagger reports of meetings between the government and insurgents. But Maliki cannot get too far ahead of his Shiite constituency, many of whom regard all the insurgent groups as terrorists with whom one cannot negotiate. Most Shiites view the US interest in negotiating with mainstream Sunni insurgent groups as a means to dilute Shiite power. Meanwhile, many Sunni groups continue to issue communiqués that deny any interest in negotiating with the "puppet" government of Maliki.

The Militia Morass

The many militias operating in Iraq have proved to be the main sticking point. This is, in fact, one of the most important problems that any Iraqi government will have to deal with, because it goes to the heart of whether the state can maintain a monopoly over the instruments of violence, institutionalize its legitimacy, and establish security and the rule of law. Militias have been a serious issue since at least the spring of 2005. Shiite ministers—above all, Bayan Jabr al-Sulagh, who controlled the Ministry of Interior—argued emphatically that militias had a legitimate role in keeping order alongside the regular security forces. A year later in 2006, militias had become an institutionalized part of the Iraqi political and societal fabric.

Today, Iraqis of all ethno-sectarian backgrounds look to their militias or local forces as their last line of defense in a situation of dire intercommunal violence. Militias associated with Shiite political organizations have behaved with impunity, taking the law into their own hands and rounding up and killing scores of Sunnis in revenge for insurgent attacks. They also have infiltrated the official security forces and used them as fronts for acts of violence. Maliki has declared that all weapons must be in the hands of the state. He has discussed integrating militias into the armed forces or unifying the country's many security agencies into a single force.

Yet Maliki's goals remain unattainable so long as the regular security forces prove incapable of providing nation-wide security. Maliki is loath, moreover, to do anything to seriously curtail the militias of Shiite political parties, since these parties control seats in the parliament and are part of his government. In this context, he has shown considerable frustration with American insistence that he bring the largest and most dangerous of the Shiite militias, the Mahdi Army, under control. It is not clear that Maliki has the political or military wherewithal to curtail the power of that militia. Indeed, it is not even clear that the militia's ostensible leader, Sadr, actually controls the entire Mahdi Army. It seems to have grown enormously beyond his or his subordinate commanders' authority.

For several months now, US commanders on the ground in Iraq and high officials in Washington have been losing faith in the Maliki government, on which they had staked so much in the spring of 2006. They have noted, in particular, his government's failure to root out corruption, to stem the violence, and to take on the brutal militias. The insidious role of the militias is of particular concern to the United States since their provision of local protection to their respective communities and taking the law into their own hands have detracted from the buildup of effective national security forces, a stated condition for withdrawal of us troops.

Remaining Options

The failures of the Maliki government have created a deep sense of estrangement between the Iraqi and American sides. Yet both sides know they have a mutual dependence that requires them to work together even as the country slides further and further into the abyss. The Maliki government needs the continued protection of the 140,000 or so us troops in the country to prevent a deterioration into even worse civil war, to give the Iraqi leader some freedom of maneuver vis-à-vis his allies in the government, and to provide security until the Iraqi armed forces are ready to take over.

As for the Americans, despite rumors of plans to remove Maliki and replace him with a strongman or a junta, it is clear that they have little alternative but to stick with him as Washington debates options concerning the future disposition of US forces—a debate rendered more pressing by the November congressional elections that overwhelmingly repudiated the Bush administration's Iraq policy.

Among the formal reviews of military options is a study begun during the fall by the Pentagon. According to Thomas Ricks writing in *The Washington Post,* the Defense Department reviewers have concluded there are three available options, popularly termed "Go Big," "Go Home," and "Go Long." "Go Big" calls for a major increase in the US troop presence to combat the cycle of sectarian and insurgent violence. It is not clear where the United States would get the extra thousands of troops required to wage a classic counter-insurgency campaign, one that would need to be supported by effective Iraqi military forces, of which there are precious few. It is also doubtful whether the American public would support such an effort.

"Go Home" calls for a quick withdrawal of US troops. It has been rejected by the Pentagon group as likely to push Iraq's already bloody civil war into an even larger conflict that could be followed by the breakup of the country. Army General John P. Abizaid, the top US military commander for the Middle East, reinforced this view when he told the Senate Armed Services Committee in mid-November that the most likely result of immediate troop withdrawal would be an increase in the violence in Iraq. An escalated Iraqi civil war would also have immediate negative regional repercussions, as Iraq's neighbors intervened to support their favored sides and prevent the chaos from spilling into their territories.

"Go Long" is premised on the gradual drawdown of US forces in Iraq while concentrating on a massive long-term expansion of training and advisory efforts to create an effective Iraqi national army and security forces. This option envisions a series of steps that actually begins with a major but temporary increase in the US troop presence to bear more of the burden of combating the violence and to bolster the confidence of the shaky Maliki government. After some months the United States would then radically reduce its combat presence, transition away from bearing the brunt of the counterinsurgency campaign, and turn its attention to a long-term training and advisory program for the Iraqi forces so that they can undertake effective counterinsurgency.

The advantages of the "Go Long" option are that it is the only palatable one left, and it shows the Americans as helping the Iraqis to ultimately help themselves. Its drawbacks include the need for a long-term vision, patience, and the creation of a strong and well-funded cadre of trainers and advisers. The Americans would expect to be engaged in what was once referred to as "foreign internal defense" in Iraq for anywhere between five and ten years in order to create a relatively effective nonsectarian military that can reduce the intensity of sectarian, insurgent, and terrorist violence.

The Endgame

Calling the mayhem in Iraq "sectarian violence" or even "regional conflict" amounts to euphemism as a means of denial. The US and Iraqi governments' reluctance to accept the designation "civil war" does not alter the reality on the ground. Most analysts and media outlets have now accepted this dismal reality. Appreciating the fact that Iraq is in a civil war represents a necessary first step toward devising realistic policy options for designing an end to the conflict.

Historically, civil wars have ended in a variety of ways. Sometimes they end with power-sharing among the rival communities. But this requires the construction of effective institutions of state and equitable resource-sharing. Sometimes they end with the decisive victory of one side over another. But this is not possible among the various feuding groups in Iraq, unless the United States weighs in on one side against another. And whether the Americans weighed in on the side of the Shiites, the Sunnis, or even the Kurds would almost certainly have dramatic effects that would not be positive for the United States or its interests in the region.

Last but not least, civil wars sometimes end with partition, as various ethno-sectarian groups pull away from each other and form their own regions. Partition, whether occurring chaotically through bloodshed or managed by the United States and the international community, would not be pretty. Moreover, it is not clear that any of Iraq's neighbors want it. Remarkably, despite all the tragic bloodletting among Iraqis, it is also not clear that they would prefer it. Ultimately, though, partition may come to pass in spite of all efforts to prevent it.

AHMED S. HASHIM is a professor of strategic studies at the US Naval War College and a lecturer at the Kennedy School of Government at Harvard University.

Reprinted from *Current History,* January 2007, pp. 3–10. Copyright © 2007 by Current History, Inc. Reprinted with permission.

When the Shiites Rise

Iraq the Model

VALI NASR

The war in Iraq has profoundly changed the Middle East, although not in the ways that Washington had anticipated. When the U.S. government toppled Saddam Hussein in 2003, it thought regime change would help bring democracy to Iraq and then to the rest of the region. The Bush administration thought of politics as the relationship between individuals and the state, and so it failed to recognize that people in the Middle East see politics also as the balance of power among communities. Rather than viewing the fall of Saddam as an occasion to create a liberal democracy, therefore, many Iraqis viewed it as an opportunity to redress injustices in the distribution of power among the country's major communities. By liberating and empowering Iraq's Shiite majority, the Bush administration helped launch a broad Shiite revival that will upset the sectarian balance in Iraq and the Middle East for years to come.

There is no such thing as pan-Shiism, or even a unified leadership for the community, but Shiites share a coherent religious view: since splitting off from the Sunnis in the seventh century over a disagreement about who the Prophet Muhammad's legitimate successors were, they have developed a distinct conception of Islamic laws and practices. And the sheer size of their population today makes them a potentially powerful constituency. Shiites account for about 90 percent of Iranians, some 70 percent of the people living in the Persian Gulf region, and approximately 50 percent of those in the arc from Lebanon to Pakistan—some 140 million people in all. Many, long marginalized from power, are now clamoring for greater rights and more political influence. Recent events in Iraq have already mobilized the Shiites of Saudi Arabia (about 10 percent of the population); during the 2005 Saudi municipal elections, turnout in Shiite-dominated regions was twice as high as it was elsewhere. Hassan al-Saffar, the leader of the Saudi Shiites, encouraged them to vote by comparing Saudi Arabia to Iraq and implying

that Saudi Shiites too stood to benefit from participating. The mantra "one man, one vote," which galvanized Shiites in Iraq, is resonating elsewhere. The Shiites of Lebanon (who amount to about 45 percent of the country's population) have touted the formula, as have the Shiites in Bahrain (who represent about 75 percent of the population there), who will cast their ballots in parliamentary elections in the fall.

Iraq's liberation has also generated new cultural, economic, and political ties among Shiite communities across the Middle East. Since 2003, hundreds of thousands of pilgrims, coming from countries ranging from Lebanon to Pakistan, have visited Najaf and other holy Shiite cities in Iraq, creating transnational networks of seminaries, mosques, and clerics that tie Iraq to every other Shiite community, including, most important, that of Iran. Pictures of Iran's supreme religious leader, Ayatollah Ali Khamenei, and the Lebanese cleric Muhammad Hussein Fadlallah (often referred to as Hezbollah's spiritual leader) are ubiquitous in Bahrain, for example, where open displays of Shiite piety have been on the rise and once-timid Shiite clerics now flaunt traditional robes and turbans. The Middle East that will emerge from the crucible of the Iraq war may not be more democratic, but it will definitely be more Shiite.

It may also be more fractious. Just as the Iraqi Shiites' rise to power has brought hope to Shiites throughout the Middle East, so has it bred anxiety among the region's Sunnis. De-Baathification, which removed significant obstacles to the Shiites' assumption of power in Iraq, is maligned as an important cause of the ongoing Sunni insurgency. The Sunni backlash has begun to spread far beyond Iraq's borders, from Syria to Pakistan, raising the specter of a broader struggle for power between the two groups that could threaten stability in the region. King Abdullah of Jordan has warned that a new "Shiite crescent" stretching from Beirut to Tehran might cut through the Sunni-dominated Middle East.

Stemming adversarial sectarian politics will require satisfying Shiite demands while placating Sunni anger and alleviating Sunni anxiety, in Iraq and throughout the region. This delicate balancing act will be central to Middle Eastern politics for the next decade. It will also redefine the region's relations with the United States. What the U.S. government sows in Iraq, it will reap in Bahrain, Lebanon, Saudi Arabia, and elsewhere in the Persian Gulf.

Yet the emerging Shiite revival need not be a source of concern for the United States, even though it has rattled some U.S. allies in the Middle East. In fact, it presents Washington with new opportunities to pursue its interests in the region. Building bridges with the region's Shiites could become the one clear achievement of Washington's tortured involvement in Iraq. Succeeding at that task, however, would mean engaging Iran, the country with the world's largest Shiite population and a growing regional power, which has a vast and intricate network of influence among the Shiites across the Middle East, most notably in Iraq. U.S.-Iranian relations today tend to center on nuclear issues and the militant rhetoric of Iran's leadership. But set against the backdrop of the war in Iraq, they also have direct implications for the political future of the Shiites and that of the Middle East itself.

The Iranian Connection

Since 2003, Iran has officially played a constructive role in Iraq. It was the first country in the region to send an official delegation to Baghdad for talks with the Iraqi Governing Council, in effect recognizing the authority that the United States had put in power. Iran extended financial support and export credits to Iraq and offered to help rebuild Iraq's energy and electricity infrastructure. After former Prime Minister Ibrahim al-Jaafari's Shiite-led interim government assumed office in Baghdad in April 2005, high-level Iraqi delegations visited Tehran, reached agreements over security cooperation with Iran, and negotiated a $1 billion aid package for Iraq and several trade deals, including one for the export of electricity to Iraq and another for the exchange of Iraqi crude oil for refined oil products.

Iran's unofficial influence in Iraq is even greater. In the past three years, Iran has built an impressive network of allies and clients, ranging from intelligence operatives, armed militias, and gangs to, most visibly, politicians in various Iraqi Shiite parties. Many leaders of the main Shiite parties, the Supreme Council for the Islamic Revolution in Iraq (SCIRI) and Dawa (including two leading party spokesmen, former Prime Minister Jaafari and the current

prime minister, Nouri al-Maliki), spent years of exile in Iran before returning to Iraq in 2003. (SCIRI's militia, the Badr Brigades, was even trained and equipped by Iran's Revolutionary Guards.) Iran has also developed ties with Muqtada al-Sadr, who once inflamed passions with his virulent anti-Iranian rhetoric, as well as with factions of Sadr's movement, such as the Fezilat Party in Basra. The Revolutionary Guards supported Sadr's Mahdi Army in its confrontation with U.S. troops in Najaf in 2004, and since then Iran has trained Sadrist political and military cadres. Iran bankrolled Shiite parties in Iraq during the two elections, used its popular satellite television network al Aalam to whip up support for them, and helped broker deals with the Kurds. Iraqi Shiite parties attract voters by relying on vast political and social-service networks across southern Iraq that, in many cases, were created with Iranian funding and assistance.

The extent of these ties has displeased the U.S. government as much as it has caught it off-guard. Washington complains that Iran supports insurgents, criminal gangs, and militias in Iraq; it accuses Tehran of poisoning Iraqi public opinion with anti-Americanism and of arming insurgents. Washington failed to anticipate Iran's influence in Iraq largely because it has long misunderstood the complexity of the relations between the two countries, in particular the legacy of the war they fought during most of the 1980s. Much has been made of the fact, for example, that throughout that savage conflict—which claimed a million lives—Iraq's largely Shiite army resisted Iranian incursions into Iraqi territory, most notably during the siege of the Shiite city of Basra in 1982. But the war's legacy did not divide Iranian and Iraqi Shiites as U.S. planners thought; it pales before the memory of the anti-Shiite pogrom in Iraq that followed the failed uprising in 1991. Today, Iraqi Shiites worry far more about the Sunnis' domination than about Tehran's influence in Baghdad.

In addition to military and political bonds, there are numerous soft links between Iran and Iraq, forged mostly as a result of several waves of Shiite immigration. In the early 1970s, as part of his Arabization campaign, Saddam expelled tens of thousands of Iraqi Shiites of Iranian origin, who then settled in Dubai, Kuwait, Lebanon, Syria, and for the most part, Iran. Some of the Iraqi refugees who stayed in Iran have achieved prominence there as senior clerics and commanders of the Revolutionary Guards. A case in point is Ayatollah Muhammad Ali Taskhiri, who is a senior adviser to Khamenei and a doyen of the influential conservative Haqqani seminary, in Qom, where many of Iran's leading security officials and conservative clerics are educated. Taskhiri briefly returned to Najaf in 2004 to oversee the work of his Ahl al-Bayt Foundation, which has invested tens of millions of dollars in construction projects and medical facilities in southern Iraq and promotes cultural and business ties between Iran and Iraq. He is now back in Tehran, where he wields considerable power over the government's policy toward Iraq.

Throughout the 1980s and after the anti-Shiite massacres of 1991, some 100,000 Iraqi Arab Shiites also took refuge in Iran. In the dark years of the 1990s, Iran alone gave Iraqi Shiites refuge and support. Since the Iraq war, many of these refugees have returned to Iraq; they can now be found working in schools, police stations, mosques, bazaars, courts, militias, and tribal councils from Baghdad to Basra, as well as in government. The repeated shuttling of Shiites between Iran and Iraq over the years has created numerous, layered connections between the two countries' Shiite communities. As a result, the Iraqi nationalism that the U.S. government hoped would serve as a bulwark against Iran has proved porous to Shiite identity in many ways.

Ties between the two countries' religious communities are especially close. Iraqi exiles in Iran gravitated toward Iraqi ayatollahs such as Mahmoud Shahroudi (the head of Iran's judiciary), Kazem al-Haeri (a senior Sadrist ayatollah), and Muhammad Baqer al-Hakim (a SCIRI leader, killed in 2003), who oversaw the establishment of Iraqi religious organizations in Tehran and Qom. Those organizations have wielded great influence in Iran since the 1980s thanks to the role they played then in opening up the Shiites of Lebanon, who had traditionally been turned toward Najaf, to Iranian influence. Many senior clerics and graduates of the Iraqi Shiite seminaries in Iran have joined Iran's political establishment. Several judges in the Iranian judiciary; including Shahroudi, are Iraqis and are particularly close to Khamenei. And those Iraqi clerics who returned to their homeland after 2003 to take over various mosques and seminaries across southern Iraq have created an important axis of cooperation between Qom and Najaf.

So much, then, for the conventional wisdom prevailing in Washington before the war: that once Iraq was free, Najaf would rival Qom and challenge the Iranian ayatollahs. Since 2003, the two cities have cooperated. There is no visible doctrinal rift between their clerics or any exodus of dissidents from one city to the other. Grand Ayatollah Ali al-Sistani's popular Web site, www.sistani.org,

Percentage of population that is Shiite (estimated)

<10%   10–20%   20–50%   50–75%   >75%

Figure 1   Shiites in Selected Countries

94

is headquartered in Qom, and most of the religious taxes collected by his representatives are kept in Iran. Despite repeated entreaties from dissident voices in Iran, senior clerics in Najaf have kept scrupulously quiet about Iranian politics, deliberately avoiding upsetting the authorities in Qom and Tehran.

This nexus extends well beyond the elites. The opening of the shrine cities of Iraq has had an emotional impact on regular Iranians, especially on the more religious social classes that support the regime. Since 2003, hundreds of thousands of Iranians have visited the holy cities of Najaf and Karbala every year. This trend has reinforced the growing popularity of devotional piety in Iran. Over the past decade, many Iranian youth have taken to adulating Shiite saints, in particular the Twelfth Imam, the Shiite messiah. Many more Iranians recognize Ayatollah Sistani as their religious leader now than did before 2003, and many more now turn their religious taxes over to him. Although largely cynical about their own clerical leaders, many Iranians have embraced the revival of Shiite identity and culture in Iraq.

Business has followed religious fervor. The Iranian pilgrims who flock to the hotels and bazaars of Najaf and Karbala bring with them investments in land, construction, and tourism. Iranian goods are now ubiquitous across southern Iraq. The border town of Mehran, one of the largest points of entry for goods into Iraq, now accounts for upward of $1 billion in trade between the two countries. Such commercial ties create among Iranians, especially bazaar merchants—a traditional constituency of the conservative leadership in Tehran—a vested interest in the stability of southern Iraq.

Granted, the legacy of the Iran-Iraq War, Iraqi nationalism, and, especially, ethnic differences between Arabs and Persians have historically caused much friction between Iran and Iraq. But these factors should not be overemphasized: ethnic antagonism cannot possibly be all-important when Iraq's supreme religious leader is Iranian and Iran's chief justice is Iraqi. Although ethnicity will continue to matter to Iranian-Iraqi relations, now that Saddam has fallen and the Shiites of Iraq have risen, it will likely be overshadowed by the complex, layered connections between the two countries' Shiite communities.

These connections, moreover, are likely to be reinforced by the two communities' perception that they face a common threat from Sunnis. Nothing seems to bring Iraqi Shiites closer to Iran than the ferocity and persistence of the Sunni insurgency—especially at a time when their trust in Washington, which has called for disbanding Shiite militias and making greater concessions to the Sunnis, is sagging.

Sunni Scares

Just five years ago, Iran was still surrounded by a wall of hostile Sunni regimes: Iraq and Saudi Arabia to the west, Pakistan and Taliban-ruled Afghanistan to the east. Iranians have welcomed the collapse of the Sunni wall, and they see the rise of Shiites in the region as a safeguard against the return of aggressive Sunni-backed nationalism. They are particularly relieved by Saddam's demise, because Iraq had been a preoccupation of Iranian foreign policy for much of the five decades since the Iraqi monarchy fell to Arab nationalism in 1958. Baathist Iraq worried the shah and threatened the Islamic Republic. The Iran-Iraq War dominated the first decade of Ayatollah Ruhollah Khomeini's revolution, ravaged Iran's economy, and scarred Iranian society.

If there is an Iranian grand strategy in Iraq today, it is to ensure that Iraq does not reemerge as a threat and that the anti-Iranian Arab nationalism championed by Sunnis does not regain primacy. Iranian President Mahmoud Ahmadinejad and many leaders of the Revolutionary Guards, all veterans of the Iran-Iraq War, see the pacification of Iraq as the fulfillment of a strategic objective they missed during that conflict. Iranians also believe that a Shiite-run Iraq would be a source of security; they take it as an axiom that Shiite countries do not go to war with one another.

All this is small consolation for the Sunnis in the region, who remember the consequences of Iran's ideological aspirations in the 1980s—and now worry about its new regional ambitions. A quarter century ago, Tehran supported Shiite parties, militias, and insurgencies in Bahrain, Iraq, Kuwait, Lebanon, Pakistan, and Saudi Arabia. The Iranian Revolution combined Shiite identity with radical anti-Westernism, as reflected in the hostage crisis of 1979, the 1983 bombing of the U.S. Marine barracks in Beirut, and Tehran's continued support for international terrorism. In the end, the Iranian Revolution fell short of its goals, and except for in Lebanon, the Shiite resurgence that it inspired came to naught.

Some say the Islamic Republic is now a tired dictatorship. Others, however, worry about the resurgence of Iran's regional ambitions, fueled this time not by ideology but by nationalism. Tehran sees itself as a regional power and the center of a Persian and Shiite zone of influence stretching from Mesopotamia to Central Asia. Freed from the menace of the Taliban in Afghanistan and of Saddam in Iraq, Iran is riding the crest of the wave of Shiite revival, aggressively pursuing nuclear power and demanding international recognition of its interests.

Leaders in Tehran who want to create a greater zone of Iranian influence—something akin to Russia's concept of "the near abroad"—view Tehran's activities in southern Iraq as a manifestation of Iran's great-power status. Yet none of them holds on to Khomeini's dream of ruling over Iraq's Shiites. Rather, Tehran's goal in southern Iraq is to exert the type of economic, cultural, and political influence it has wielded in western Afghanistan since the 1990s. Although Tehran clearly expects to play a major role in Iraq, it may not aim—or be able—to turn the country into another Islamic republic.

Predictably, Iran's growing prominence is complicating relations between sectarian groups in the region. Sunni governments have used Tehran's ambitions as an excuse to resist both the demands of their own Shiite populations and Washington's calls for political reform. Since 2003, Sunni leaders in Egypt, Jordan, and Saudi Arabia have repeatedly blamed Iran for the chaos in Iraq and warned that Iran would wield considerable influence in the region if Iraqi Shiites came to hold the reins of power in Baghdad. The Egyptian president, Hosni Mubarak, sounded the alarm last April: "Shiites are mostly always loyal to Iran and not the countries where they live." Such partly self-serving rhetoric allows Sunni leaders to divert attention away from their own responsibility for Iraq's troubles: Egypt, Jordan, and Saudi Arabia have so far supplied the bulk of Abu Musab al-Zarqawi's army of suicide bombers. It also provides them with a subterfuge to resist U.S. calls for domestic political reform. If bringing democracy to the Middle East means empowering Shiites and strengthening Iran, they argue, Washington would be well advised to stick to Sunni dictatorships.

The Sunnis' public-relations offensive worries the Iranian leadership. Despite its growing clout, Tehran needs its neighbors' support and the goodwill of "the Arab street" to resist international pressure over its nuclear program. So far, Tehran has avoided sectarian posturing and further antagonizing Sunnis; instead, it has tried to generate support in the region by escalating tensions with the United States and Israel. Iranian leaders have routinely blamed sectarian violence in Iraq, including the bombing of the Askariya shrine, in Samarra, in February, on "agents of Zionism" intent on dividing Muslims. Meanwhile, Tehran aggressively pursues nuclear power both to confirm Iran's regional status and to minimize Washington's ability to stand in its way.

A Meeting of Minds

Iran's aspirations leave Washington and Tehran in a complicated, testy face-off. After all, Iran has benefited greatly from U.S.-led regime changes in Kabul and Baghdad. But Washington could hamper the consolidation of Tehran's influence in both Afghanistan and Iraq, and the U.S. military's presence in the region threatens the Islamic

Republic. In Iraq especially, the two governments' short-term goals seem to be at odds: whereas Washington wants out of the mess, Tehran is not unhappy to see U.S. forces mired there.

So far, Tehran has favored a policy of controlled chaos in Iraq, as a way to keep the U.S. government bogged down and so dampen its enthusiasm for seeking regime change in Iran. This strategy makes the current situation in Iraq very different from that in Afghanistan after the fall of the Taliban in late 2001, when Iran worked with the United States to cobble together the government of Hamid Karzai. Tehran cooperated with Washington at the time largely because it needed to: its Persian-speaking and Shiite clients in Afghanistan made up only a minority of the population and were in no position to protect Iran's interests. Tehran's calculus in the aftermath of the Iraq war has been different. Not only do Iran's immediate interests not align with those of the United States, but Tehran's position in Iraq is stronger than it was in Afghanistan thanks to the majority status of Shiites in Iraq. Seeing the Bush doctrine proved wrong in Iraq would be an indirect way for Iran's leaders to discredit Washington's calls for regime change in Tehran. Their recent willingness to escalate tensions with Washington over Iran's nuclear activities suggests that they believe they have largely succeeded in this goal; Iran is now stronger relative to the United States than it was on the eve of the Iraq war.

And yet, in the longer term, U.S. and Iranian interests in Iraq may well converge. Both Washington and Tehran want lasting stability there: Washington, because it wants a reason to bail out; Tehran, because stability in its backyard would secure its position at home and its influence throughout the region. Iran has much to fear from a civil war in Iraq. The fighting could polarize the region and suck in Tehran, as well as spill over into the Arab, Baluchi, and Kurdish regions of Iran, where ethnic tensions have been rising. As former Iranian Deputy Foreign Minister Abbas Maleki has put it, chaos in Iraq "does not help Iranian national interest. If your neighbor's house is on fire, it means your home is also in danger." Clearly wary, Tehran has braced itself for greater troubles by appointing a majority of its provincial governors from the ranks of its security officials and Revolutionary Guard commanders.

Two groups within Iran could help convince the Iranian leadership that cooperation with Washington is in its interest. The first are Iraqi refugees, who act as a lobby for Iraqi Shiite interests in Tehran. They have encouraged Iran to pursue talks with the United States over Iraq, partly because they view Washington and Tehran as the twin pillars of their power in Iraq. The escalation of tensions between the two governments would not serve the interests of Iraqi Shiites, and that lobby does not want to see Iraq become hostage to the international standoff over Iran's nuclear program. The second important constituency is made up of the many Iranians who are greatly concerned about the sanctity of Iraq's shrine cities. Every major bombing in Najaf and Karbala so far has claimed Iranian lives. The Iranian public expects Tehran to ensure the security of those cities; its influence has already provided Khamenei with a pretext for publicly endorsing direct talks with Washington over Iraq.

Still, Iran will actively seek stability in Iraq only when it no longer benefits from controlled chaos there, that is, when it no longer feels threatened by the United States' presence. Iran's long-term interests in Iraq are not inherently at odds with those of the United States; it is current U.S. policy toward Iran that has set the countries' respective Iraq policies on a collision course. Thus a key challenge for Washington in Iraq is to recalibrate its overall stance toward Iran and engage Tehran in helping to address Iraq's most pressing problems.

Setting the Stage

The most important issue facing Iraq in the coming months will be the constitutional negotiations, particularly regarding the questions of federalism and how oil revenues will be distributed. It was only after the U.S. ambassador to Iraq, Zalmay Khalilzad, persuaded the Shiites and the Kurds to agree to change the constitution that the Sunnis participated in the referendum to ratify it in late 2005. Since then, Washington has hoped for a deal that would bring moderate Sunnis into the political process and thus weaken the Sunni insurgency. But the prospects of such a deal are uncertain. The Shiites, the Sunnis, and the Kurds are unlikely to see the wisdom of compromise without outside pressure, and the U.S. government no longer has the political capital to force concessions or satisfy the demands of one party without risking alienating another. It is the weakening of the United States' position in Iraq that makes it necessary—more so now than in 2003—for Washington to reach out to Iraq's neighbors.

If the constitutional negotiations fail, the Sunnis could abandon the political process. Even if the Sunnis participate, bargaining with the Shiites may become more complicated, especially given signs of increasing turmoil in southern Iraq. Over the past three years, the Shiites have both participated politically and resisted the Sunni insurgency's provocations, largely because they have believed that backing U.S. policy would serve their interests. But if they were to conclude that Washington is now more eager to buy the Sunnis' cooperation than to reward them for their steadfastness, the Shiites might turn their backs on the political process. Such an upset could spark a Shiite uprising. The Shiites would not even need to pick up arms to pressure the United States; by virtue of their numbers alone, they can change the country's political balance. In January 2004, Sistani rallied hundreds of thousands of Shiites for five days of demonstrations against U.S. plans to base the first post-Saddam elections on a caucus system. Earlier this year, he called the crowds to the streets again to protest the Askariya shrine bombing—and to ensure that the U.S. government understood the extent of Shiite power.

Given its clout among the Shiites in southern Iraq, Tehran could help maintain order there while the constitutional negotiations were under way. Iran could ensure that the growing rivalry among Shiite factions such as SCIRI and Sadr's troops did not spin out of control, destabilize southern Iraq, and erode government authority in Baghdad. Keeping the Shiites together and maintaining calm in the south is of singular importance to the United States, and Iranian cooperation is crucial to achieving that goal. Iran's cooperation would help address Iraq's security and reconstruction needs, as well as buttress the central government in Baghdad.

But securing such cooperation would require the United States to address broader issues in its relationship with Iran. Tehran will end its military and financial support to Shiite militias and criminal gangs in southern Iraq only if it receives broad security guarantees from Washington. The current situation in Iraq is similar to that in Afghanistan in 2001 in the way it seems to entangle U.S. and Iranian interests—only it is more complicated and the stakes are higher. After the fall of the Taliban in Afghanistan, the United States and Iran worked closely together to bring the Northern Alliance and its Shiite component into the mainstream political process. Washington and Tehran negotiated intensely on the sidelines of the Bonn conference on the future of Afghanistan, striking deals that helped ensure the early successes of the Karzai regime. The Bonn process promised to open a new chapter in the history of U.S.-Iranian relations. But at the time, Washington had little interest in further engaging a regime it believed it would soon overthrow. It missed an important opportunity then.

Iraq's troubles today offer Washington and Tehran a second great chance not only to normalize their relations, but also to set the stage for managing future tensions between Shiites and Sunnis. The Shiites' rise to power in Iraq sets an example for Shiites elsewhere in the Middle East, and as the model is adopted or tested it is likely to exacerbate Shiite-Sunni tensions. Better for Washington to engage Tehran now, over Iraq, than wait for the problem to have spread through the region. Although Washington and Tehran are unlikely to resolve their major differences, especially their dispute over Iran's nuclear program, anytime soon, they could agree on some critical steps in Iraq: for example, improving security in southern Iraq, disbanding

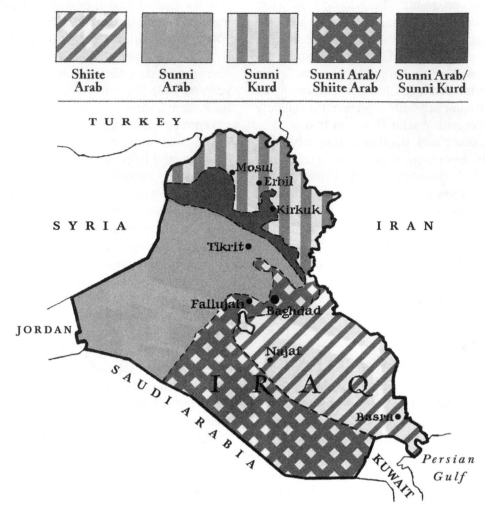

Figure 2 The Major Communities of Iraq and where they are concentrated

Note: In Baghdad and Kirkuk, no community clearly predominates.

Source: National Public Radio, www.npr.org.

Country	Percentage of population that is Shiite	Total population	Shiite population
Iran	90%	68.7 million	61.8 million
Pakistan	20%	165.8 million	33.2 million
Iraq	65%	26.8 million	17.4 million
India	1%	1,095.4 million	11.0 million
Azerbaijan	75%	8.0 million	6.0 million
Afghanistan	19%	31.1 million	5.9 million
Saudi Arabia	10%	27.0 million	2.7 million
Lebanon	45%	3.9 million	1.7 million
Kuwait	30%	2.4 million	730,000
Bahrain	75%	700,000	520,000
Syria	1%	18.9 million	190,000
UAE	6%	2.6 million	160,000
Qatar	16%	890,000	140,000

Notes: "Shiites" includes Twelver Shiites and excludes Alawis, Alevis, Ismailis, and Zaydis, among others. Percentages are estimated. Figures under 1 million are rounded to the nearest 10,000; figures over I million are rounded to the nearest 100,000.
Source: Based on data from numerous scholarly references and from governments and NGOs in both the Middle East and the West.

the Shiite militias, and convincing the Shiite parties to compromise.

But if Washington and Tehran are unable to find common ground—and the constitutional negotiations fail—the consequences would be dire. At best, Iraq would go into convulsions; at worst, it would descend into full-fledged civil war. And if Iraq were to collapse, its fate would most likely be decided by a regional war. Iran, Turkey, and Iraq's Arab neighbors would likely enter the fray to protect their interests and scramble for the scraps of Iraq. The major front would be essentially the same as that during the Iran-Iraq War, only two hundred miles further to the west: it would follow the line, running through Baghdad, that separates the predominantly Shiite regions of Iraq from the predominantly Sunni ones. Iran and the countries that supported it in the 1980s would likely back the Shiites; the countries that supported Iraq would likely back the Sunnis.

Iraq is sometimes compared to Vietnam in the early 1970s or Yugoslavia in the late 1980s, but a more relevant—and more sobering precedent may be British India in 1947. There was no civil war in India, no organized militias, no centrally orchestrated ethnic cleansing,

no battle lines, and no conflict over territory. Yet millions of people died or became refugees. British India's professional army was sliced along communal lines as the country was partitioned into Hindu-majority and Muslim-majority regions. Unable to either bridge the widening chasm between both groups or control the violence, the British colonial administrators were forced to beat a hasty retreat. As in Iraq today, the problem in India then lay with a minority that believed in its own manifest destiny to rule and demanded, in exchange for embracing the political process, concessions from an unyielding majority. The pervasive sectarian violence and ethnic cleansing plaguing Iraq today are ominous reminders of what happened in India some 60 years ago. They may also be a worse omen: if the situation in Iraq deteriorates further, the whole Middle East would be at risk of a sectarian conflict between Shiites and Sunnis.

VALI NASR is a Professor at the Naval Postgraduate School, an Adjunct Senior Fellow at the Council on Foreign Relations, and the author of *The Shia Revival: How Conflicts Within Islam Will Shape the Future*.

Letter from Afghanistan
Are the Taliban Winning?

"There is no doubt that Afghanistan has progressed enormously since 9-11, but now even the positive achievements carried out by the international community appear to be unraveling."

AHMED RASHID

In Kabul today, most Afghans, from illiterate cooks to well-educated civil servants, take it for granted that the Taliban are coming back to power. Afghans speak of yet another American betrayal, trading theories on why the United States and the international community have not been serious about combating the Taliban insurgency, stemming the flow of jihadists out of Pakistan, or devoting money and resources sufficient to rebuild the country.

Many Afghans see President Hamid Karzai as an increasingly forlorn figure, trapped in the presidential palace as events spin out of his control, grasping for political straws to stem the widespread disillusionment with his government, begging the international community for more support.

Public morale has been most affected by the revived Taliban insurgency in southern and eastern Afghanistan, areas covering one-third of the country, and by the gradual withdrawal of US troops from the insurgency-hit areas and their replacement by less well-equipped or less motivated NATO forces. On average five NATO soldiers have died every week since May, three times the casualties taken by US troops in the same period. More than 4,000 Afghans, including Taliban fighters, were killed in 2006. Some 700 have died in more than 80 suicide bombings, which until 12 months ago were almost unknown in the 27 years of conflict since the Soviet Union invaded Afghanistan.

The Taliban have been able to launch attacks involving battalion-size units of more than 1,000 men, and for the first time in their four-year-old insurgency, they now receive considerable local support. The major Al Qaeda and Taliban leaders are still at large. And the critical Pakistan-Afghanistan border zone, inhabited by the Pashtun tribes, has become the world's "terrorism central," a base area where once again terrorist attacks worldwide are planned, and training and funding are coordinated.

Afghans, including aides to Karzai, believe that the hard-line neoconservatives within the US administration never had the intention to stabilize or rebuild Afghanistan after 9-11. Iraq is not just a major distraction, sucking in eight times more American troops and seven times more money than Afghanistan has received. It is Washington's ideological and foreign policy focus, whereas stabilizing Afghanistan is a sideshow.

While Iraq has bathed in US funding for infrastructure projects (though these projects have rarely been completed), there is less electricity in Kabul now than there was under Soviet occupation in the 1980s. Afghanistan remains one of the poorest countries in the world—even though it provides 92 percent of the world's heroin, which pumps some $3 billion annually into the Afghan economy, or more than 60 percent of gross domestic product. More than five years after 9-11, and after a well-documented explosion in drug production, there is still no international agreement or adequate funding for a major anti-drug campaign that would offer Afghan poppy farmers new jobs or alternative crops to grow.

Most of the depressing developments in Afghanistan are matters of fact. Others may be matters of perception, or even falsehood. But in a largely illiterate society that for three decades has been fed a diet of violence and rumors, as well as real and imagined conspiracies and interference by neighboring countries, perceptions are all-important. For many Afghans, the perception is that the war against the Taliban is already lost.

Two Steps Back

There is no doubt that Afghanistan has progressed enormously since 9-11, but now even the positive achievements carried out by the international community appear to be unraveling. It took at least $300 million for the United Nations to hold presidential and then legislative elections in 2004 and 2005, inaugurate the parliament, and pass a new constitution. Since then parliamentarians have been killed by the Taliban and abused by warlords, and many from the south cannot go home because of the insurgency. The new constitution is in virtual abeyance across the country because implementing it is impossible.

Japan contributed $100 million to a highly successful UN-led program that collected heavy weapons from warlords and disarmed some 62,000 Afghan militiamen. But now a follow-up UN program to disarm more than 1,000 smaller illegal gangs and armed groups is at a standstill. In northern and western Afghanistan the price of weapons has doubled, as warlords and ordinary Afghans rearm to protect themselves against Taliban fighters arriving in their areas.

The rebuilding of a 70,000-man Afghan National Army by the Americans and the training of a 60,000-man police force by the Germans are going far too slowly. The army numbers just 34,000 men and is poorly equipped, lacking armor and helicopters. Now, in order to protect towns and villages in the south, the government has asked tribal chiefs to provide local guards—a return to the kind of local warlordism that the new political order was supposed to replace.

The beacon of the international aid effort in Afghanistan—restoring education and placing 5.1 million children in school—has been badly affected as the Taliban have killed teachers and students and burned down school buildings, causing 300 schools to shut down. Afghans are passionate about education. It has become the most important indicator of progress and change, and it highlights the differences between conditions today and those under the former Taliban regime—which is precisely why the Taliban are targeting schools and in particular girls' schools.

For many Afghans, Taliban bases and sanctuaries in Pakistan are at the heart of the problem. The Bush administration knows these bases and sanctuaries exist but refuses to acknowledge them. Karzai and US and NATO military commanders believe the Taliban leadership is based in Quetta, the capital of Balochistan province, just 80 miles from the Afghan border. From this safe haven the Taliban are able to recruit, organize logistics, import arms and ammunition, and carry out fund-raising.

Since 9-11 the Pakistani military and the Inter-Services Intelligence (ISI) have deliberately allowed "Talibanization" to take place along the 1,600-mile-long Pakistan-Afghanistan border, both sides of which are populated by Pashtun tribes. Tens of thousands of Afghan Taliban retreated into Pakistan after their defeat in 2001. The radical Islamic schools and parties in Pakistan, which had supported their cause since 1994, gave them shelter. And they were joined by Pakistani Taliban, young Pashtun men who had been indoctrinated by the same madrassas. Today, hundreds of Pakistani Taliban join in attacks inside Afghanistan.

Pakistan sees the Taliban as a proxy card to be kept in reserve and used to mount pressure on Karzai, so that Pakistan can regain its dominant position among the Afghan Pashtuns in the south. Islamabad also believes that Talibanization or the Islamization of Pashtun culture and politics will serve as a bulwark against secular and democraticminded Pashtun nationalism, which is reemerging in Kabul, Peshawar, and Quetta.

A Talibanized Pashtun belt will owe first loyalty to Islamabad rather than Kabul, and will counter growing Indian influence in Afghanistan, which Pakistan sees as a threat to its security. Finally, the Pakistani military, arguing that only it can combat Islamic fundamentalism, believes that the threats posed by Al Qaeda and the Taliban encourage continued international support for General Pervez Musharraf's regime and for military rule.

Angry and Bewildered

Afghans are disillusioned with the United States and the international community because they see them as providing cover for Pakistan's actions. Anti-Pakistan feeling is running at an all-time high among Afghans across the political and ethnic spectrum.

In a US Senate Foreign Relations Committee hearing on September 21, 2006, General James Jones, NATO's supreme commander, testified that the Taliban's headquarters is based in Quetta. Yet President George W. Bush did not even bring up Quetta when he hosted a dinner for Musharraf and Karzai in Washington on September 27. Jones's comments were largely ignored by the US media—infuriating many Afghans.

Tom Koenigs, the UN secretary general's special representative for Afghanistan, reported to the UN Security Council in September that "five distinct leadership centers of the insurgency can be identified." These include a Taliban northern command active in Afghanistan's northeastern provinces, a Taliban eastern command, and a Taliban southern command, as well as separate fronts established by two Taliban allies, the Islamist warlords Gulbuddin Hekmetyar and Jalaluddin Haqqani.

Although Koenigs did not openly allege that all these fronts are based in Pakistan, NATO and US intelligence place all the top leaders of these fronts—Haqqani, Hekmetyar, Taliban leader Mullah Mohammed Omar, and Mullah Dadullah, the chief commander in the south—in Pakistan. "The leadership relies heavily on cross-border fighters, many of whom are Afghans drawn from nearby refugee camps and radical seminaries in Pakistan," said the report to the Security Council. "They are trained and paid to serve as medium-level commanders, leading operations inside Afghanistan and are able to retreat back to safe havens outside the country," the report added.

The UN Security Council declined to debate Koenigs's findings, which again left Afghans angry and bewildered. Afghans were even more infuriated when Musharraf, during his September visit to Washington, waved the UN report at journalists at the White House, saying that it vindicated Pakistan's denials about providing sanctuary to the Taliban. The State Department declined to correct Musharraf's misreading of the report.

However, the ISI is cooperating fully with the United States and Britain in dealing with their domestic terrorism threat, which in Britain largely emanates from young men born in Pakistan or of Pakistani descent who now hold British citizenship. Access to information from Pakistani intelligence about potential terrorist threats has trumped concerns about Afghanistan.

Many Afghans see President Hamid Karzai as an increasingly forlorn figure, trapped in the presidential palace as events spin out of his control.

Meanwhile, the Pakistani military's controversial September 5 deal with Afghan and Pakistani Taliban in the North Waziristan tribal region has allowed Pakistani Taliban to set up a virtual Islamist state. Although Islamabad insisted the deal would prevent attacks against both Pakistani troops in Pakistan and US forces in Afghanistan, Lt. Gen. Karl Eikenberry, the commander of US forces, told me that attacks out of North Waziristan have gone up 300 percent since the deal was signed.

After promising a strategy of peace with the seven tribal agencies that border Afghanistan, the Pakistani military, under US pressure, bombed a religious school in the Bajaur tribal agency on November 1, killing 80 people believed to be extremists. The action inflamed emotions and left Pakistanis baffled by the military's vacillating tactics and apparent lack of strategy.

Pakistan's military has carried out few of the reforms promised by Musharraf after 9-11. There has been no reform of the madrassas, where radicals and militants are trained, and no serious attempt to deal with extremists. In fact, the military remains in alliance with the largest Islamic fundamentalist party that aids the Taliban—the Jamiat-e-Ullema Islam. Next year Musharraf plans to continue his alliance with these radicals when he runs for another five-year term as president.

India, Iran, the Central Asian states, Russia, and even Pakistan's longstanding ally China are looking warily at Pakistan's support of the Taliban. Most of these states have zero tolerance for Sunni Islamic radicalism of the Taliban variety and they expect the United States to contain Pakistan. If America proves unable or unwilling to do so, Washington's clout in the region will diminish substantially. Weaker countries such as those in Central Asia will move closer to China and Russia to protect themselves, instead of relying on the United States.

Failed Commitments

For many Afghans the other part of the crisis is the incompetence and corruption of the regime. President Karzai has failed to carry out tough measures against well-known drug traffickers, including several in his cabinet and parliament. Western nongovernmental organizations say corruption is epidemic, with aid money and profits from reconstruction contracts being siphoned off to senior officials. Key parts of the reform agenda that Karzai promised he would carry out after he was elected president in 2004 remain to be implemented. The lack of developmental activities in the south has resulted in part from Karzai's failure to purge corrupt or drug-trafficking officials from powerful positions. This has fuelled disillusionment among Pashtuns, the dominant ethnic group in southern and eastern Afghanistan, many of whom are now offering to fight for or at least offer sanctuary to the Taliban.

The other part of the blame rests with the international community's failure to rebuild the shattered infrastructure in the south, including roads, electricity, and water supply, and to invest in agriculture to wean farmers from growing poppies. NATO cannot combat the growing insurgency in Afghanistan unless it shows the flexibility and determination to effectively address major problems that stem from the legacy of the American failure in Afghanistan over the past five years. Turning the tide will mean that NATO has to act not just as a military alliance, but also as an economic, political, and diplomatic alliance—something it has never done before.

NATO now commands some 30,000 troops in Afghanistan drawn from 37 countries, including 8,000 American troops, while another 10,000 US troops remain under separate US command. NATO will need to use military victories as a lever to pry more money out of the European Union, the United States, and the Muslim world—money that, along with funds from Western development agencies, could be devoted to expensive infrastructure projects.

NATO also has to play a critical political role in resuscitating the Afghan government and giving it the confidence to perform better and to eliminate public corruption. At the same time, NATO needs to play a more aggressive diplomatic role in convincing Pakistan to stop supporting the Taliban.

However, as a result of the intense fighting in the south, European countries are balking at providing more troops to the NATO forces in Afghanistan. Norway, Denmark, Sweden, and others have refused to send more soldiers. France, Germany, Spain, Turkey, and Italy, which have troops stationed in the more peaceful regions of Afghanistan, are refusing to send them to the south, where British, Canadian, and Dutch forces are facing the bulk of the fighting. NATO members have also been extremely slow to come up with a reserve brigade and the necessary military equipment for their troops, especially much-needed helicopters.

Lieutenant General David Richards, the NATO commander in Afghanistan, says he is trying to persuade all NATO countries to lift the caveats that governments have imposed on their contingents, caveats that prevent troops from taking part in combat or being deployed where commanders want them. Not surprisingly, the publics, parliaments, and media in many NATO countries whose soldiers are dying in Afghanistan are up in arms—demanding that their governments recall their troops. In many European countries, public opinion equates Afghanistan with Bush's misjudged occupation of Iraq, and the dislike for Bush's policies means Afghanistan suffers as a result.

Stiff Resistance

NATO was ill prepared for the Taliban offensive in the south this past summer. When the NATO forces deployed there, they found themselves under heavy attack by the Taliban, who aimed to inflict such heavy casualties that Western publics would demand a recall of their troops. In "Operation Medusa," from September 4 to September 17, 2006, NATO forces in Kandahar's Panjwai district defeated a well-entrenched force of 1,500 Taliban who had planned to attack Kandahar city. NATO commanders say they killed a staggering 1,100 Taliban fighters, including hundreds of Taliban reinforcements who arrived from Quetta in pickup trucks.

A post-battle report compiled by NATO and Afghan intelligence showed that during the battle the Taliban had fired an estimated 400,000 rounds of ammunition, 2,000 rocket-propelled grenades, and 1,000 mortar shells. The Taliban had stocked over 1 million rounds of ammunition, much of it presumably acquired in Pakistan. "Taliban decision-making and its logistics are all inside Pakistan. There are several Taliban shuras [councils] in Quetta, each with a Pakistani ISI officer coordinating it," said Afghan Defense Minister and army chief General Rahim Wardak.

As in their comments about the war in Iraq, senior US officials have downplayed the threat of any imminent collapse of the Afghan government or defeat for NATO forces. They have insisted that all is well and the Taliban violence is only a sporadic response to NATO's wider deployment. But to many Afghans, it seems the Americans are talking about some other country, not Afghanistan.

NATO and US commanders now believe that there will be no winter lull in Taliban attacks as has happened in the past, and that suicide bombings in the cities against soft Afghan targets and concerted Taliban strikes against NATO forces will continue. Since the Panjwai battle there have been major Taliban attacks in the southern provinces of Helmand, Uruzgan, and Zabul, demonstrating that the huge losses they suffered have not demoralized the fighters.

A major problem for the West is its inability or refusal to acknowledge past failures in Afghanistan, or the country's present predicament, and to offer serious future commitments of both money and troops. Until that happens, Afghans will continue to believe that they are losing the war against the Taliban.

AHMED RASHID is a journalist who has written for the *International Herald Tribune, The Washington Post,* and *The New York Review of Books.* He is the author of *Jihad*: *The Rise of Militant Islam in Central Asia* (Penguin Books, 2002) and *Taliban* (Yale Press, 2001).

Pakistan and the Islamists

"There is more to Pakistan than General Musharraf, and sooner or later US policy makers will have to turn their attention to the state of the Pakistani state."

Husain Haqqani

Pakistan plays a contradictory role in the struggle against global Islamist terrorism—it is considered both part of the solution and part of the problem. Soon after the attacks of 9-11, Pakistan's military ruler, General Pervez Musharraf, gave up support for the Taliban regime in Afghanistan and chose to become an American ally. Pakistani support was crucial in the US effort to oust the Taliban from Kabul and pursue terrorist leaders. Indeed, most of the senior Al Qaeda figures now in American custody were arrested and handed over by Pakistan's security services.

In return for his cooperation in the war against terrorism, Musharraf has received lavish praise and generous economic and military assistance from the United States, along with the status of a major non-NATO ally. Yet Pakistan continues to be a major center for Islamist militancy, a legacy of the country's projection of itself as an Islamic ideological state and a bastion of religion-based opposition to communism during the cold war.

Radical Islamists who came from all over the world to resist the Soviet occupation of Afghanistan went on to become allies of Pakistan's military intelligence apparatus. The intelligence services then used the Islamists to fight Indian control over the disputed Himalayan territory of Kashmir, as well as to expand Pakistan's influence in Afghanistan. Musharraf's efforts, under US pressure, to contain the Islamist radicals have consistently fallen short. Partly as a result, the Taliban have surged in Afghanistan and Al Qaeda has been revitalized in the rugged region along the Pakistani-Afghan border.

Most American analysts since 9-11 have focused on Musharraf's ability to remain in power and keep up the juggling act between his alliance with the United States and his management of various domestic constituencies, including the Pakistani military and Islamist militants. Musharraf says he is dedicated to changing Pakistan from an Islamic, ideological state to a moderate Muslim country. But the imbalance between Pakistan's perceived external importance and its proven internal weakness raises fundamental questions about the dysfunction of the Pakistani state. Careful examination indicates that Musharraf's eclectic policies are aimed less at changing Pakistan's direction than at salvaging a policy paradigm—including the tolerance of the Islamists—that Pakistan's military-led oligarchy has embraced since the country's early days.

That Musharraf will be able to retain power as long as the United States and the Pakistani military continue to support him is not in doubt. Barring unforeseen events, such as assassination or incapacitation by natural causes, Musharraf seems set to preside indefinitely over a weakening state. But there is more to Pakistan than General Musharraf, and sooner or later US policy makers will have to turn their attention to the state of the Pakistani state.

A Sign of Weakness?

In the years since 9-11, Musharraf's critics have attributed his failure in rooting out Al Qaeda and the Taliban to a deliberate policy. Musharraf has time and again drawn a distinction between anti-US terrorists affiliated with Al Qaeda, who need to be fought or eliminated, and local Islamist insurgents (whether Afghan, Pakistani, or Kashmiri), who can be engaged in dialogue. India and Afghanistan have repeatedly accused Pakistan of supporting terrorists that target its two neighbors, with whom Pakistan has had disputes since it emerged as an independent country from the 1947 partition of British India. As violence has spiraled in Kabul and the Afghan countryside, Afghan President Hamid Karzai has stepped up his criticism of Pakistan's role in supporting a resurgent Taliban. "Pakistan hopes to make slaves out of us, but we will not surrender," Karzai declared in December 2006.

Under US pressure, Pakistan has intermittently applied military force against pro-Taliban and pro–Al Qaeda Pashtun tribesmen living along the Afghan border. But the tribesmen have managed to inflict heavy casualties on the Pakistani military. Last year the government agreed to a cease-fire in a controversial deal that restored the tribes' autonomy in return for a commitment that they would not provide sanctuary to enemies of Pakistan.

Musharraf's deals with the tribal leaders, whatever the intent behind them, have proved ineffective in ending militancy and terrorism. The Taliban have stepped up their attacks inside Afghanistan, and suicide bombings in Pakistan reached an all-time high within the first two months of 2007. Several press reports based on leaks by US and British intelligence sources have taken note of Al Qaeda's regrouping in Pakistan and tacit Pakistani backing for the Taliban.

In February 2007, the outgoing US ambassador to Pakistan, Ryan Crocker, attempted to resolve the apparent contradiction between Washington's publicly stated view of Musharraf as a critical US ally in the war against terrorism and the persistent intelligence reports indicating that terrorists operate and train in Pakistan with relative impunity. "Pakistan has been fighting terrorists for several years, and its commitment to counterterrorism remains firm," Crocker said during Senate hearings on his nomination as US ambassador to Iraq. Pakistan's challenge in coming to terms with Taliban fighters along its border with Afghanistan, he suggested, has to do more with a lack of capacity than a lack of will.

The Week That Was

In the last week of February, Vice President Dick Cheney made a surprise visit to Islamabad. During a meeting with Musharraf, Cheney conveyed US concerns about the Taliban's resurgence and asked for closer cooperation between the Karzai and Musharraf governments. Cheney pressed Musharraf to do more in the war against terrorism while acknowledging that Musharraf has "been closely allied with US going after Al Qaeda." There was no public sign of waning US support for, or dependence on, Musharraf.

Radical and violent manifestations of Islamist ideology are in some ways a state project gone wrong.

If Cheney needed any reminder of the threat posed by the Taliban, it came in the form of a suicide bombing at the Bagram Military Air Base near Kabul soon after Cheney's arrival from Pakistan. The week preceding Cheney's trip was especially bloody in Pakistan, too. The country was the target of seven suicide attacks within seven days, some in relatively quiet parts of the country's heartland. Seventeen people, including a senior civil judge, were killed and 30 wounded in a powerful suicide bombing at the district courts in the southwestern city of Quetta. Sixty-seven people were killed and more than 50 wounded in a fire caused by a bomb

on two coaches of the India-Pakistan *Samjhota* (reconciliation) express train. In central Punjab province, a female cabinet minister was killed by a religious fanatic who disapproved of her going unveiled.

The events of just that one week should be enough to highlight the increasing impotence of Pakistan's state machinery in the face of growing violence and internal conflict. A compilation of published figures on terrorism-related casualties indicates that 1,471 people were killed in Pakistan during 2006, up from 648 terrorism-related fatalities in the preceding year. Of these, 608 were civilians, 325 security personnel, and 538 terrorists.

Also within that fateful February 2007 week preceding Cheney's visit, amid widespread lawlessness and the increased boldness of terrorist groups, Pakistan successfully tested the latest version of its long-range nuclear-capable missile. The Hatf VI (Shaheen II) ballistic missile, launched from an undisclosed location, is said to have a range of more than 1,200 miles. According to the Pakistani military, it has the capability to hit major cities in India.

Clearly, Pakistan's supposed ability to project power externally is not matched by a strong or effective state at home. In the process of building extensive military capabilities, Pakistan's successive rulers have allowed the degradation of essential internal attributes of statehood. Indeed, a defining attribute of a state is its ability to maintain a monopoly on public coercion, or at least a preponderance of it. A proliferation of insurgents, militias, criminal gangs, and high ordinary corruption reflects the Pakistani state's weakness in this key area. There are too many non-state actors in Pakistan, ranging from religious vigilantes to criminals, who possess coercive power in varying degrees. In some instances, the threat of non-state coercion in the form of suicide bombings weakens the state's ability to deal with challenges to its authority.

The Fake Election

Two thousand and seven is an election year in Pakistan, but Musharraf has decided not to risk his position and power at a free poll. He will be "elected" president by the parliament and provincial legislatures that were seated in tainted 2002 elections, and the lawmakers will make their choice just as their term enters its last days. Some observers see Musharraf's decision as reflecting his total hold on power in Pakistan. In fact, Musharraf is consolidating his own position at the risk of further eroding the power and credibility of a state apparatus in decline.

The Pakistani constitution envisions a parliamentary system of government with directly elected legislatures at the federal and provincial levels. The president, under the constitution, is head of state and the symbol of the unity of the federation. He is elected by an electoral college comprised of the National Assembly, the Senate, and the four provincial assemblies. Under the constitutional scheme, the president derives his mandate from the mandate given by the people to their elected representatives.

The four presidents elected under the constitution since its adoption in 1973 (Chaudhry Fazal Elahi, Ghulam Ishaq Khan, Farooq Leghari, and Rafiq Tarar) were chosen by newly elected assemblies at the beginning of their five-year terms. Musharraf, on the other hand, is seeking election from assemblies whose own flawed mandate is about to end. This technical legality is not a substitute for legitimacy. Opposition political parties—notably the secular Pakistan Peoples Party led by former Prime Minister Benazir Bhutto, as well as a faction of the conservative Pakistan Muslim League led by Nawaz Sharif—are already vehemently questioning Musharraf's legitimacy.

Sharif, who was prime minister at the time of Musharraf's 1999 military coup, and Bhutto have buried their differences and joined forces in the Alliance for the Restoration of Democracy. Although both leaders are in exile at the moment, the possibility of their return to Pakistan to lead anti-Musharraf protests adds another dimension to the potential for instability in the country. Musharraf could arrest them or return them into exile, but the opposition would almost certainly be energized by the homecoming of the two politicians who led Pakistan through its weak democratic phase in the decade preceding Musharraf's military takeover. Musharraf accuses Bhutto and Sharif of corruption. But the charges, previously believed widely, have lost their significance because of the government's failure to obtain convictions against the two leaders in a court of law.

As of now Musharraf is president because he decreed himself as such, following a rigged referendum held before the legislative elections of 2002, which were deemed by international observers and the US State Department as "flawed." Then, too, Musharraf did not seek election under the terms of the constitution. He also gave himself a waiver from the constitutional bar on employees of the state (including active military officers) holding elective office.

Musharraf's term of office—if it can be called that, given that he secured the position by fiat—ends on November 16, 2007. His maneuver to secure election from the outgoing legislatures reflects an attempt to ensure that he remains president without having to seek election from new legislatures elected by the people.

Such quasi-legal maneuvers, aided by notions such as the doctrine of necessity and the concept of a military coup being its own legal justification, have been used by Pakistan's military rulers to legitimate their rule since the country's first coup in 1958. If history is any guide, Pakistan's coup makers are always politically weaker after manipulating themselves into a second term.

Pakistan's next parliamentary elections, scheduled to be held by the end of 2007, are unlikely to transform the country into a democracy or return it to civilian rule. Musharraf has made it clear that he intends to continue running the country, combining the offices of army chief and president in his own person. Musharraf has persistently rejected opposition demands that he transform himself into a civilian leader by seeking election under the constitution after retiring from the army. "At the end of the day," he has said, "I am a soldier and I love to wear the uniform. It is part of me, my second skin."

Given Pakistan's position as a critical ally in the global war against terrorism, neither the United States nor other Western nations are likely to apply serious pressure for political reform. Pakistan has been unable to evolve into a democracy six decades after being carved out of British India essentially because many of the country's leaders, including Musharraf, have assumed that the army has the rightful authority to run Pakistan. If there is a common thread running through Pakistan's checkered history, it is the army's perception of itself as the country's only viable institution, along with its deep-rooted suspicion of civilian political processes.

The Islamist Surge

The international community pays little attention to Musharraf's legitimacy problems and the democratic politicians snapping at his heels. The United States and its allies are concerned more about the rising influence of Pakistan's Islamists, who made their strongest showing in a general election during the 2002 parliamentary polls. The Islamists secured only 11 percent of the popular vote but gained 20 percent of the seats in the lower house of parliament. Since then, they have pressed for Taliban-style Islamization in the Northwest Frontier Province bordering Afghanistan, where they control the provincial administration. The Islamists' political success, made possible by restrictions on Bhutto and Sharif, flies in the face of Musharraf's repeated reassurances to the world that he intends to radically alter Pakistan's policy direction away from the recent Islamist and jihadist past.

In a major policy speech on January 12, 2002, Musharraf announced measures to limit the influence of Islamic militants at home. "No organizations will be able to carry out terrorism on the pretext of Kashmir," he declared. "Whoever is involved with such acts in the future will be dealt with strongly whether they come from inside or outside the country." But Musharraf's government has continued to make a distinction between "terrorists" (a term applied to Al Qaeda members, mainly of foreign origin) and "freedom fighters" (the officially preferred label in Pakistan for Kashmiri militants). Authorities have also remained tolerant of remnants of Afghanistan's Taliban regime, hoping to use them in resuscitating Pakistan's influence in Afghanistan in case the US-installed Karzai regime falters.

This contradiction in Pakistani policy is a structural problem, rooted in history and consistent state policy. It is not just the inadvertent outcome of decisions by some governments (beginning with that of General Mohammad Zia-ul-Haq in 1977), as is widely believed. Pakistan's leaders have played on religious sentiment as an instrument of strengthening Pakistan's identity since the country's inception. As any Pakistani elementary school student knows, Pakistan is an "ideological state," and its ideology is Islam.

Musharraf is consolidating his own position at the risk of further eroding the power and credibility of a state apparatus in decline.

Indeed, it is the military's desire to dominate the political system and define Pakistan's national security priorities that has been the most significant, though by no means the only, factor in encouraging an Islamic ideological model for Pakistan. General Zia-ul-Haq went further than others in Islamizing Pakistan's legal and educational system, but his Islamization policy was the extension of a consistent state ideology, not an aberration.

Pakistan's rulers have attempted to manage militant Islamism, trying to calibrate it so that it serves its nation-building function without destabilizing internal politics or relations with Western countries. The state has sponsored and supported Islamist groups at different times to influence domestic politics and support the military's political dominance. The Islamists have also been allies in the Pakistani military's efforts to seek strategic depth in Afghanistan and to put pressure on India for negotiations over the future of Kashmir.

Of course, relations between ideologically motivated clients and their state patrons are not always smooth. This partly explains why Pakistan's generals have not been able completely to control the Islamists since 9-11. The relationship between the army and the mosque has been forged over time, and its character has changed with the twists and turns of Pakistani history. But the alliance has been a constant.

Gradually the political commitment to an ideological state evolved into a strategic commitment to the jihadist ideology, both for regional influence and for domestic reasons. For example, the Pakistani military used Islamist idioms and the help of Islamist groups to keep out of power the elected secular leaders supported by the majority Bengali-speaking population. Bengali rebellion and brutal suppression of the Bengalis by the military followed.

In the original Pakistan's western wing, before the country was bifurcated in 1971 with the birth of an independent Bangladesh, religion was used in an effort to create national cohesion among disparate ethnic and linguistic groups. Islamic groups, both armed and unarmed, have become gradually more powerful as a result of this alliance between the mosque and the military. Radical and violent manifestations of Islamist ideology, which sometimes appear to threaten Pakistan's stability, are in some ways a state project gone wrong.

Cooperation for a Price

Pakistan's alliance with the United States has also been an important part of the ruling elite's strategy for building the Pakistani state. If Islam was the cement that would unite various ethnic and linguistic factions within Pakistan, the United States was seen as the source of funding for a country that inherited only 17 percent of British India's revenue sources in 1947. Pakistan's first indigenous military commander, General Mohammad Ayub Khan, initiated the US-Pakistan alliance when he visited Washington in 1953 and sought a deal in which Pakistan could—for the right price—serve as an anchor in an Asian alliance. Pakistan joined US-sponsored treaty organizations beginning in 1954, and the alliance flourished further once Ayub Khan took over as president in a military coup in 1958.

General Musharraf, too, has followed Ayub Khan in seeking the right price for cooperation in the war against terrorism after September 11, 2001. The United States has given Pakistan more than $10 billion in military, economic, and development assistance since 9-11 and perhaps even more in covert intelligence and military aid.

While Pakistani rulers have bargained well for military and economic aid since the 1950s, the United States has generally had to be modest in its ambitions about what it could hope to achieve. Pakistan's real or projected limitations and compulsions have repeatedly been cited during the execution stage of deals, limiting the fulfillment of American expectations. Secretary of State John Foster Dulles signed on Ayub Khan as an ally because he wanted to create a "northern tier of containment" with bases in countries immediately to the south of the Soviet Union. Pakistan received the aid it sought, but Dulles never got the largescale military bases he wanted in Pakistan. (He had to be content with listening posts and a secret facility for U-2 reconnaissance planes flying over the Soviet Union.)

Similarly, during the 1980s, Zia-ul-Haq secured aid in return for allowing the CIA to operate out of Pakistan in arming and funding the mujahideen who were bleeding Soviet forces in Afghanistan. But he did not keep his promises to the Reagan administration about limiting Pakistan's nuclear program, and went on to assert that by helping the United States, Pakistan had "earned the right to have a regime in Afghanistan to our liking." Instead of ending its involvement with arming the mujahideen once the Soviet Union left Afghanistan in 1988, as the United States desired, Pakistan played an active role in the Afghan civil war that ensued.

Ayub Khan, Zia-ul-Haq, and their military successors gave US policy makers some of what they sought but, at the same time, backed out of some of their commitments. And now it appears that the latest US attempt to buy influence and policy concessions from a Pakistani military ruler is headed in a similar direction. Whether it is a divergence of interests and lack of commitment on Musharraf's part, as his critics assert, or a lack of capacity to root out the Taliban and Al Qaeda, as

Ambassador Crocker suggests, Pakistan is unlikely to fulfill Washington's expectations in the war against terrorism. In the process, Pakistan's own internal crises will likely grow worse.

Fear and Loathing

Pakistan's military historically has been willing to adjust its priorities to fit within the parameters of immediate US global concerns. The purpose has been to ensure the flow of military and economic aid from the United States, which Pakistan considers necessary for its struggle for survival and its competition with India. Thus, Pakistan's relations with the United States have been part of the Pakistani military's policy tripod that emphasizes Islam as a national unifier, rivalry with India as the principal objective of the state's foreign policy, and an alliance with the United States as a means to defray the costs of Pakistan's massive military expenditures.

Fear and hatred of India constitute an equally important component of Pakistan's state ideology. They are also the justification for Pakistan's continuous efforts to militarily equal India—including its development of nuclear weapons. Notwithstanding periodic peace initiatives, hostility between India and Pakistan continues. And on each occasion when Pakistan's path has diverged from the one jointly charted with the United States, competition with India has been one of the causes.

Containing Indian influence in Afghanistan is one of the justifications given for tolerating the Taliban, and some members of the Pakistani ruling elite continue to see Islamist militants as an unconventional counterweight to India's preponderant power. The alliance between mosque and military helps maintain, and sometimes exaggerates, the psycho-political fears about national identity and security that help both the Islamists and the generals in their exercise of political power.

State of Decline

In an effort to become an ideological state guided by a praetorian military, Pakistan has ended up accentuating its dysfunction, especially during the past two decades. The state's disproportionate focus since 1947 on ideology, military capability, and external alliances has weakened Pakistan internally. Meanwhile, US support for the Pakistani military makes it difficult for Pakistan's weak secular civil society to assert itself, wean the country away from the rhetoric of Islamist ideology, and shift focus toward issues of real concern for Pakistan's citizens.

Today the country's institutions—from schools and universities to the judiciary—are in a state of general decline. The economy's sputtering growth depends largely on the level of concessional flows of external resources. Pakistan's gross domestic product stands at about $75 billion in absolute terms and $295 billion in purchasing power parity, making Pakistan's economy the smallest of any country that has tested nuclear weapons thus far. Pakistan suffers from massive urban unemployment, rural underemployment, illiteracy, and low per capita income. One-third of the population lives below the poverty line, and another 21 percent subsists just above it.

Shortly after independence, 16 percent of Pakistan's population was literate, compared with 18 percent of India's significantly larger population. By 2003, while India had managed to attain a literacy rate of 65 percent, Pakistan's stood at only about 35 percent. Today, Pakistan allocates less than 2 percent of its GDP to education and ranks close to the bottom among 87 developing countries in the amount allotted to primary schools. Its low literacy rate and inadequate investment in education have led to a decline in Pakistan's technological base, which in turn hampers the country's economic modernization.

With a population growing at an annual rate of 2.7 percent, the state of public health care and other social services in Pakistan is also in decline. Meanwhile, Pakistan spends ever more on defense, yet is still unable to match the conventional forces of India—which outspends Pakistan three to one, while allocating proportionally less of its burgeoning GDP to military spending. Pakistan, partly as a result, is far from developing a consistent system of government, while political polarization persists along three major, intersecting fault lines: between civilians and the military, among different ethnic and provincial groups, and between Islamists and secularists.

Weak and Well-Armed

America's alliance with Pakistan, or rather with the Pakistani military, is almost always based on some immediate concern and lacks a long-term view. This pattern of partnership has had three significant consequences for Pakistan. First, because the US military sees its ally in the context of Middle East strategy, Pakistan has become more oriented toward the Middle East, even though it is geographically and historically part of South Asia.

Second, the intermittent flow of US military and economic assistance has encouraged Pakistan's military leaders to overestimate their potential to assert power. This, in turn, has contributed to their reluctance to accept normal relations with India even after learning through repeated misadventures that Pakistan can, at best, hold India to a draw in military conflict and cannot defeat it. Even now, the bulk of US aid is going toward military equipment, including Pakistan's acquisition of additional F-16 fighter planes, sidewinder missiles, and P-3 Orion aircraft.

Third, the ability to secure military and economic aid by fitting into the current paradigm of American policy has made Pakistan a rentier state, basically living off the rents for its strategic location. Unfortunately, because of the Pakistani military's alliance with the mosque, all of these policies have served to encourage the Islamists.

Radical Islamism threatens not only US interests and global security, but also Pakistan's own viability and national cohesion. The United States perhaps could deal better with Pakistan in the long term by using its influence to help reshape the Pakistani military's ideologically limited view of Pakistan's national interest. In particular, normalization of relations with India and a return to democratic norms are likely keys to the military's permanent withdrawal from the political arena, as well as to Pakistan's long-term stability. If Pakistan does not transcend the national ideology defined by Islamist ideologues and a dominant military, it will remain a perilous entity: a dysfunctional state with nuclear weapons.

HUSAIN HAQQANI, a senior fellow at the Hudson Institute, is an associate professor and director of the Center for International Relations at Boston University. He is the author of *Pakistan: Between Mosque and Military* (Carnegie, 2005).

The Pashtun Factor: Is Afghanistan Next in Line for an Ethnic Civil War?

DANIEL CONSOLATORE

On January 15 of this year, the American news media reported yet another story of a suicide bomb attack—this one on an army convoy in which fourteen people were killed, including a Canadian diplomat. On January 16 the headlines announced a pair of attacks that killed twenty-five civilians and one soldier, and injured another four dozen people. On February 3 an operative disguised in traditional Muslim women's dress killed himself and four soldiers at an army checkpoint, and on February 7 a terrorist drove a motorcycle into a police headquarters killing thirteen uniformed men. Sadly these all would have been fairly unremarkable stories had the setting been Baghdad or Karbala in Iraq, where such bloody events have become almost commonplace. But these were just the latest in a spate of some twenty such attacks since October 2005 in Afghanistan, where suicide terrorism was almost unknown before last year.

The majority of Americans have now come to feel that sending troops to Iraq was a mistake, but Afghanistan was supposed to be different. Operations there were much more clearly a front in the war on terrorism and a justifiable response to 9/11. American troops liberated Afghan men and especially women from the hated Taliban, and the subsequent international effort to reconstruct the country and introduce democracy seemed successful and welcome. Afghans turned out in large numbers for their presidential election in fall 2004, choosing by a landslide the Bush administration's preferred candidate, the likable Hamid Karzai. Last September's parliamentary elections there were a little messier but resulted in the first truly representative governing body in Afghanistan. The very traditional, very conservative, very Muslim society even set aside 25 percent of the seats in the Wolesi Jirga, or lower house of parliament, for women and wrote protections guaranteeing women's equal status into the new constitution. There remained Taliban remnants to clean up, and Osama bin Laden and his al-Qaeda deputies were still at large but had been chased into mountain caves in Pakistan. Compared to Iraq at least, everything seemed to be going according to plan.

But suddenly a whole lot seems to be amiss. It's not clear exactly who is carrying out the suicide bombings. Some insist that, since the tactic was unknown in Afghanistan before 2005,

it certainly must be that Arabs and non-Afghan extremists are finding their way to the country from Iraq and other hot spots and importing that most effective of terrorist methods. That would be bad enough. Still worse though, spokespeople for the movement so often now referred to as the neo-Taliban insist they have hundreds of volunteers—all native Afghans—lined up ready to martyr themselves. And no doubt intentionally playing on America's uneasy memory of Vietnam, they brag that their fighters are so easily able to blindside the foreigners and "infidels" because they are welcomed by, and move unseen among the Afghan people. The violence is partly funded through the country's gargantuan opium trade which now makes up one-third of its gross domestic product, dwarfs the national budget, and may be the country's greatest challenge overall. Drugs and violence are of course tied to the intractable poverty as well—a poverty so bad that the average worker tries to feed ten people on a mere $35 a month. And while the national government struggles to purge its own ranks of corruption and provide basic public services like electricity and police protection, entrenched warlords still run some large provinces like their own private kingdoms. Most disturbing perhaps, because of the way it recalls Iraq, ethnic and sectarian violence is sprouting again in Afghanistan. Suddenly the success story in the war on terrorism is looking more and more—to borrow author Robert Kaplan's famous mouthful of pessimism—like the coming anarchy.

Just how bad is the situation in Afghanistan? By the measure that the American public is most likely to track, it's pretty bad and getting worse. There are only about 20,000 U.S. troops in the country, as compared to 139,000 in Iraq, but soldier for soldier, American service men and women are more likely to die in Afghanistan. Ninety U.S. military personnel died in Afghanistan in 2005, twice as many as in the previous year, and more than 250 were seriously wounded, up from about 200 in 2004. Some thirty NATO soldiers stationed at the outlying forts known as Provincial Reconstruction Teams, or PRTs, were also killed. Reliable reports on the number of Afghan civilians to die as "collateral damage" or direct targets have been famously difficult to come by since the U.S.-led air assault in 2001, but the explosive devices killing them are now increasingly set off by their fellow citizens and co-religionists. Eighty-seven police were killed between August and October 2005 alone, and more recently a number of schools have been torched at night by masked bands. Foreign and Afghan aid workers, as well as government officials and other public figures, have also been shot or killed by amateur but increasingly sophisticated improvised explosive devices (called IEDs).

But the growing similarity between Iraq and Afghanistan has to do with more than wandering Arabs and the drifting tactic of martyrdom, as reflected in the semantic debates among government and military officials. In private and increasingly in public, U.S. generals are now speaking of their neo-Taliban enemies as "insurgents" even though Afghan President Karzai objects to such thinking. "It's not an insurgency" he declared after one recent attack in January 2006 in a village in Helmand province. "It's terrorism," he insisted, and their choice of methods really only shows the desperation of the "enemies of Afghanistan." But to the extent that the distinction between insurgent and terrorist has any meaning, Karzai is probably more hopeful than correct. The press-grabbing suicide attacks on civilians are simply one tactic by the remaining deepest core of a native Afghan Islamist movement, determined to resist what it sees as a puppet government and its infidel foreign patrons. But not only has the movement not died away, it's being fed by the resentment of Afghanistan's main ethnic group on everything that's gone wrong and is threatening to metastasize again into a popular resistance movement, much like the Sunni Arab insurgency in Iraq.

Afghanistan has an ethnically mixed population, but there's one group at the core. As political scientist and renowned Afghanistan expert Barnett Rubin puts it: the Pashtun are the titular ethnicity of the country. That is, the word Afghan was originally nothing more than a variation of the word Pashtun, making Afghanistan literally the "land of the Pashtun." In some sense, it still is. Though no official or reliable census data exist to allow for certainty, they're typically estimated to comprise some 40 to 45 percent of the modern nation's total population. Also like Iraq's Sunni Arabs, the Pashtun have long monopolized political power at the national level, even while the other major groups—Tajik, Uzbek, and Hazara—enjoyed significant regional autonomy and distinctiveness. As often happens, occupation by a foreign power stimulated an all-Afghan solidarity in the fight against the Soviet Union during the 1980s but, as Rubin says, that very quickly gave way to a multipolar ethnic conflict after the rise of the Taliban in 1992.

The Taliban emerged from refugee camps and that half of the Pashtun population located across the line on the map that, in theory, separates modern-day Afghanistan from Pakistan. As the movement emerged as a successful fighting force, its members were embraced by the overwhelmingly Pashtun populations of the war-weary southern and eastern provinces, less for their ideology than because they were local boys who brought a semblance of stability and rule of law. There were very few Tajik, Hazara, or Uzbek Afghans in the Taliban ranks, as all of those groups had their own regional forces led by popular, often deeply loved leaders who stood in opposition to the Taliban.

The Afghan civil war that lasted through 2001 was marked by frequent massacres of surrendered soldiers and unarmed civilians of one ethnic group by troops of another. One of the worst

such incidents occurred less than ten years ago in the spring of 1997 when the Taliban briefly captured the northern city of Mazar-e-Sharif and brutalized and murdered Uzbek and Hazara civilians. When the Taliban lost the city days later, thousands of their ethnic Pashtun troops were themselves executed and buried in a mass grave. The cycle of revenge continued later that year when the Taliban retook Mazar and killed thousands more Hazara. Similar incidents occurred throughout the war, through to the months following the U.S.-led invasion in 2001 when, according to Human Rights Watch, "Pashtuns throughout northern Afghanistan . . . faced widespread abuses including killings, sexual violence, beatings, extortion, and looting." They were explicitly targeted, the group says, "because their ethnic group was closely associated with the Taliban regime."

Given all these very recent, very bloody interethnic tensions, it might not be surprising that Afghanistan is once again in danger of polarizing along ethnic lines. The Pentagon knew that this was a risk from the outset of Operation Enduring Freedom in October 2001, when it chose the Northern Alliance to serve as shock troops, because those armies and militias were all drawn from the non-Pashtun populations. When major combat ceased the top Northern Alliance warlord-generals—like the brutal Uzbek Rashid Dostum, the Tajiks Ismael Kahn and Mohammed Fahim, and the Hazara Karim Khalili—found themselves in powerful ministries of the provisional government. Predictably, the Pashtun population was wary and less than enthusiastic to see these developments, and even the rise of the Pashtun Karzai and inclusion of many Pashtuns in the new government didn't put fears of being dominated by a coalition of the other groups entirely to rest.

The few Western organizations that have been able to gauge popular feeling have found strong evidence that dissatisfaction and worry about the future is still concentrated in the "Pashtun belt"—the southern and eastern provinces of Helmand, Kandahar, Zabul, Pakhtia, Paktika, and Uruzgan. In 2005 Washington's Center for Strategic and International Studies surveyed Afghans throughout the country to find out how they felt things stood and what their expectations for the future were, in terms of justice, their financial and social well-being, and safety and security. Consistently the people of the Pashtun regions saw things significantly worse than those in the majority Tajik, Uzbek, and Hazara regions. As early as August 2003 the International Crisis Group warned of Pashtun alienation from the Karzai-led government and the international nation-building effort known as the "Bonn process." More recently, those suicide attacks that are making headlines have almost all targeted perceived Pashtun traitors and taken place in the cities and towns of those same provinces, especially in Kandahar, the largest city in southern Afghanistan.

Even more worrying are the reports filtering out of the mountainous and isolated Pashtun regions like Zabul province, where the neo-Taliban are most active. U.S. soldiers are constantly on the hunt there in so called "kinetic operations" or search-and-destroy missions, and are now encountering the enemy more and more often. Unfortunately, this isn't because they and their Afghan National Army (ANA) partners have isolated the hold-out resisters, but simply because more locals are joining up.

The soldiers themselves call Zabul the "Fallujah of Afghanistan" and, when expressing their frustrations, compare their mission to the war in Vietnam, pointing out that the enemy is again invisible and the villagers they're supposed to be fighting for lie to them and play a double game. When the troops find a weapons cache in a hamlet or nearby fields, for example, the local peasants deny any knowledge and claim they've never seen any Taliban.

There's no reason to believe, however, that U.S. troops are held in contempt quite the way they so often were in Vietnam or are in parts of Iraq, but every inadvertent civilian death, including those among Pashtuns across the border in Pakistan by predator drones, increases suspicion and resentment and hands the neo-Taliban grist for their anti-American propaganda. One journalist on the ground there reported that things have gotten so bad in Zabul that ANA Tajik and Hazara soldiers try to avoid getting off the helicopters they use to patrol the region for fear of being outnumbered by the enemy, who are literally at home in the region. In the words of Taliban spokesperson Mohammed Tanif, the sentiment prevails that the "country is occupied by foreign forces, and it affects the pure nationalist emotions of our people" This is true "especially in the southern and eastern provinces of the country." And it's those nationalist emotions in the Pashtun belt, he adds, that explain why the numbers of recruits for suicide bombing missions are increasing.

Is the Afghan nation-building project doomed to failure, and a return to civil war inevitable? That level of cynicism would require overlooking a number of promising developments of the past four and half years. Pashtuns no less than other Afghans are participating in the peaceful reconstruction effort every day by laying down their weapons, returning to their farms, building roads, digging wells, and teaching in public schools. Millions of Afghans seem to have endorsed the Bonn process by voting in the two national elections in much larger proportions than Americans go to the polls. And while an official national reconciliation program to reach out to Taliban rank and file has had limited success, the parliament itself is a forum for reconciliation where resentments are expressed with words rather than bullets.

But the suicide bombings in Afghanistan are symptomatic of a worsening situation and, if the country's largest and titular ethnic group comes to feel that they don't have a stake in the reconstruction process, those attacks may be a bellwether of an Iraq-like civil war, where wariness of one's neighbors becomes an attitude of "get them before they get us" U.S. commanders have begun to embrace, at least in rhetoric, the need to prioritize the political and psychological struggle for the "hearts and minds" of the Pashtun population. But as one expert, Paul Fishstein of the Kabul-based Afghanistan Research and Education Unit, put it when talking about U.S. "kinetic operations" in the Pashtun regions, they'll need "a more nuanced and sophisticated" approach focused on building "legitimacy for the government without creating more enemies" That is, the army and marines might have to live up to the new Pentagon directive that officially makes nurturing civil society and establishing rule of law top mission priorities. And to do that, they'll have to worry less about killing young Pashtuns and more about winning them over. If that doesn't happen, and Afghans come to feel that the neo-Taliban represent them more than Karzai and the Kabul government, then those reports of suicide bombings could become as common in Kandahar as in Karbala, and chaos will come again to Afghanistan.

DAN CONSOLATORE served as a research consultant to former Secretary of State Madeleine Albright for her forthcoming book, *The Mighty and the Almighty; Reflections on America, God, and World Affairs.* He can be reached at daniel.consolatore@gmail.com.

Again

Never again? What nonsense. Again and again is more like it. In Darfur, we are witnessing a genocide again, and again we are witnessing ourselves witnessing it and doing nothing to stop it. Even people who wish to know about the problem do not wish to know about the solution. They prefer the raising of consciousnesses to the raising of troops. Just as Rwanda made a bleak mockery of the lessons of Bosnia, Darfur is making a bleak mockery of the lessons of Rwanda. Some lessons, it seems, are gladly and regularly unlearned. Except, of course, by the perpetrators of this evil, who learn the only really enduring lessons about genocide in our time: that the Western response to it is late in coming, or is not coming at all.

Were the 1990s really that long ago? They are remembered now as the halcyon and money-happy interval between the war against Soviet totalitarianism and the war against Islamic totalitarianism, but the truth is that, even in the years immediately following the cold war, history never relented. The '90s were a decade of genocides—unimpeded (Rwanda) and partially impeded (Bosnia) and impeded (Kosovo). The relative success of those genocides was owed generally to the indifference of that chimera known as "the international community," but, more specifically, it was owed to the learning curve of an American president about the moral—and therefore the operational—difference between genocide and other foreign policy crises. The difference is simple. In the response to most foreign policy crises, the use of military force is properly viewed as a last resort. In the response to genocide, the use of military force is properly viewed as a first resort.

The notion of force as a first resort defies the foundations of diplomacy and also of common sense: A willingness to use hard power abroad must not become a willingness to use it wildly. But if you are not willing to use force against genocide immediately, then you do not understand what genocide is. Genocide is not a crisis that escalates into evil. It is evil from its inception. It may change in degree if it is allowed to proceed, but it does not change in kind. It begins with the worst. Nor is its gravity to be measured quantitatively: The intention to destroy an entire group is present in the destruction of even a small number of people from that group. It makes no sense, therefore, to speak of ending genocide later. If you end it later, you will not have ended it. If Hitler had been stopped after the murder of three million Jews, would he be said to have failed? Four hundred thousand Darfuris have already been murdered by the

Janjaweed, the Arab *Einsatzgruppen.* If we were to prevent the murder of the 400,001st, will we be said to have succeeded?

This elementary characteristic of genocide—the requirement that the only acceptable response is an immediate and uncompromising response or else we, too, will be complicit in the crime—should have been obvious after the inhumane ditherings, the wrenchingly slow awakenings to conscience, of the '90s; but the discussion of the Darfur genocide in recent years shows that this is not at all obvious. To be sure, there is no silence about Darfur. Quite the contrary. The lamentations about Darfur are everywhere now. There is eloquence, there is protest. Unlikely coalitions are being formed. Movie stars are refusing to be muzzled, and they are standing up and being counted. Even officials and politicians feel that they must have something pained and wrathful to say. These latecomers include the president of the United States.

All of this is to the good, of course. In a democratic and media-maddened society, this right-thinking din is one of the conditions of political action, as domestic pressures are increasingly significant factors in the formulation of US foreign policy. But it makes no sense—and, in this instance, it is a sophisticated form of indecency—to care about a problem without caring about its solution. During the Bosnia crisis, there were many people who cared about the ethnic cleansing and systematic rape of the Bosnian Muslims, but they insisted that it was a European problem with a European solution. They were half right: It was indeed a European problem, classically so. But it was perfectly plain to every honest observer of the genocide that there would be no European solution, and that the insistence upon such a solution amounted to a tender indifference to the problem.

The Darfur variety of the Bosnia hypocrisy is now upon us. We are told that this genocide must be stopped, now, now, never again, all it takes for the triumph of evil is for good men to do nothing, not on our watch, fight the power, we shall overcome—but stopped by us? Of course not. This is an African problem with an African solution. The African solution comes in two versions. There is the view that Darfur will be rescued from the genocide by the successful resolution of the negotiations taking place in Abuja—or, more precisely, that the people who are perpetrating the evil are the ones to whom we must look for the end of its perpetration. (At the rally on the Mall in Washington last week, Russell Simmons jammed excitedly that the Khartoum government had just accepted a draft of a peace accord. Def, indeed.) This version of the African solution does not even acknowledge the requirement of military force to halt the evil. And there is the version of the African solution that looks to the troops of the African Union to do the job. Nancy Pelosi is especially enamored of this remedy. She has boldly proclaimed that AU troops must be "given more mobility" and "freed from the restriction that limits their effectiveness," all in the name of stopping the genocide. It would be nice, wouldn't it? But, so far, the forces of the African Union have had no significant impact on the emergency. To ask them to do the job is to admit that you do not really need the job done.

Then there is the other alibi for Western inaction, the distinguished one: the belief that salvation will come from blue helmets. After the slaughters of the '90s, all of which numbered the fecklessness—and even the cynicism—of the United Nations among their causes, it defies belief that people of goodwill would turn to the United Nations for effective action. The United Nations is not even prepared to call the atrocities in Darfur a genocide. Kofi Annan says all sorts of lofty things, but everybody knows that he is only the humble servant of a notoriously recalcitrant body. Meanwhile the Sudanese regime maneuvers skillfully—what is the Chinese word for oil?—to prevent reprisals of any kind from the Security Council. And even if the United Nations were somehow to recover its ethics and its efficacy, it would take many months—in some estimates, most of a year—before a UN force could be deployed. No, they are not losing any sleep in Khartoum over the UN option.

There is also the view that this is an African problem with a European solution—but let us come to the heart of the matter. All these proposals for ending the genocide in Darfur are really proposals to prevent the United States from ending it. It appears that there is something even more terrible than genocide in this very terrible world, and it is the further use of American military power abroad. And in a Muslim country! Why, it would make

us more unpopular. Remember that in the post-September 11, post-Operation Iraqi Freedom environment, the sensitivities of Muslims—insofar as they can be clearly known and accurately predicted—must not be further offended. Never mind that they themselves give gross offense: This is a genocide committed by Muslims against Muslims that no Muslims are racing to stop. The poor Darfuris: Their plight interferes with the anti-imperialist integrity of liberals in the only country in the world with the power and the authority (yes, still) to help them. The Democrats in Washington are now clamoring for the appointment of a special envoy to Sudan. (No mention so far of Brent Scowcroft.) That is to say, they are searching for reasons to deflect the responsibility of refusing to let crimes against humanity stand. In the matter of genocide, the party of Clinton is still the party of Clinton.

But it is not only, or mainly, the Democrats who impede a US—or a US-led, or a US-NATO—campaign against the killers. This is a Republican era, after all. And the record of the Bush administration on Darfur has been disgraceful (see Marisa Katz, "A Very Long Engagement"). The president has his own uses for all the alibis. He is not inclined to order one more American soldier into action. (But would the camels of the *Janjaweed* pose a tactical challenge to us? Surely all that is required is a little shock and no awe at all.) And there are other disturbing reasons for Bush's tepidity about Darfur. One of them, again, is Sudan's oil, which suddenly confers upon this repulsive state a certain strategic prestige. And there is also the haunting memory of Sudan's previous hospitality to anti-American jihadist terrorism. In the view of the White House, then, an intervention in Darfur may be counter to American interests. So, in this crisis, too, the streets of Washington now run with realism.

All this is grotesque. Sure, interventions are always more complicated than planned (though they are rarely as poorly planned as Iraq, which must not serve as the only model); but not all interventions are quagmires waiting to happen. And the risks to American values if we fail to act against genocide are far greater than the risks to American interests if we act against it. Is Iraq now all that the United States needs to know? Will we allow Abu Ghraib and Guantánamo Bay to disqualify us from our moral and historical role in the world? Is idealism in US foreign policy only for fair weather? What is so unconscionable about nation-building anyway? Why will we never get the question of genocide right, when, in some ways, it is the easiest question of all? The discussion of Darfur, even by many people whose outrage is sincere, has become a festival of bad faith. Everybody wants to do everything but what must be done. It is the season of heartless bleeding hearts.

Somalia: Anatomy of an Unending Conflict

Ethiopian forces, with American support (if not instigation), moved into Somalia on Christmas Eve and drove away the Islamic militants who, for six months last year, had succeeded in imposing some semblance of order in the war-ravaged country. But, as Najum Mushtaq reports, Ethiopia's entry into the conflict could bring a new dimension of violence to an already complex and complicated conflict.

NAJUM MUSHTAG

Somalia is the bleeding sore of the Horn of Africa. The 16-year-old civil war in the country took another vicious turn on Christmas Eve as Ethiopia's formidable military might forced the Union of Islamic Courts (UIC) out of Mogadishu and put the internationally-backed interim government back in charge of most of South-central Somalia.

At the time of writing, America was patrolling the waters off Somalia's coast to prevent UIC militants from fleeing the country by sea, and had actually launched air strikes, killing many of them; the Ethiopian forces were cracking and killing them; and Kenya had closed its borders and vowed to stop the defeated militants from crossing over.

But this does not, however, spell the end of Somalia's woes. Nor does it mean that the Islamic movement, which had taken control of Mogadishu in June 2006 and for six months brought a semblance of order and security in the war-ravaged southern heart land of Somalia, is already history. More likely, the return of the interim government with the help of Ethiopia, which most Somalis see as their ancient foe, will add new dimensions of violence to an already complex and complicated conflict. There are three levels at which the conflict in Somalia can be analysed: the local clan dynamics which dictates the country's politics and marks the geographical and political fault-lines; the regional level where countries like Ethiopia and Kenya have to manage sizeable Somali populations of their own; and the international level which is defined by America's "war on terror." Viewing Somalia from all these three levels is a sorry sight.

The Political Landscape

The regions now comprising Somalia were decolonised in 1960. Somaliland was a British protectorate, while the rest of Somalia was an Italian domain. On the eve of decolonisation,

British Somaliland and Italian Somaliland merged as the Somali Republic on 1 July 1960.

In terms of political administration, the country is divided into three units: the autonomous regions of Puntland and Somaliland, and South-central Somalia. The last region includes the historical capital city of Mogadishu, most of the strategically vital ports and some of the more dominant clans. It is largely inhabited by sub-groups of the Hawiye clan whose militia were also dominant in the UIC. Most of the top UIC leaders are Hawiye. It is the South-central region that had fallen into the hands of the Islamic militia. The other two regions (Somaliland and Puntland) had remained fiercely resistant to UIC expansion.

All these regions are inhabited by different clans—there are six major groups. Clan affiliation is the most crucial identity marker and the cause of political divisions. State government has been weak and the process of building a nation-state has failed as the clan system continues to hold sway.

The clans of Somaliland had had an uneasy and confrontational relationship with the central government in Mogadishu and remained marginalised from power. In 1991, as the rest of the country plunged into warlordism and internecine violence after the collapse of the Siad Barre government, Somaliland declared its independence although it does not enjoy international diplomatic recognition.

By and large, Somaliland has remained at a distance from the civil war and enjoys a certain degree of stability and peace, even though it has territorial disputes with Puntland over the Sool and Sanaag regions.

All through Siad Barre's rule, the northeastern region of Puntland had also considered itself as an autonomous state. Unlike Somaliland, which asserts full independence. Puntland proclaims autonomy within Somalia which it seeks to turn into a federation.

After seven years of being a theatre in the civil war, Puntland's leaders were able to forge the trappings of an administration, and announced its autonomous status in July 1998. The American-and-Ethiopia-backed president of the transitional Somali government, Abdullahi Yusuf, belongs to a Puntland-based clan. For a brief period in the mid-1990s, under attack by Al-Ittehad, the forerunner of the UIC, Yusuf had taken refuge in Somalia's traditional "enemy" state (Ethiopia) from where be bounced back with Addis Ababa's support to head an internationally-brokered interim government in 2004.

The Rise of the UIC

From the late 1970s until his overthrow in early 1991, President Siad Barre had received US financial and military support that kept him in power. America was the major supplier of arms to Somalia. In return, the US used the military facilities that were originally meant for the Soviet Union. These bases gave Washington access to the Middle East through the Red Sea. As a result, Washington ignored warnings throughout the 1980s by human rights groups that continued support of Barre's dictatorial government would eventually lead Somalia into chaos.

As soon as the American support was withdrawn after the collapse of the Soviet Union, Barre was overthrown and different clan-based militias began to carve the country into fiefdoms. It was the political and judicial vacuum after Barre's ousting that provided space for the Islamic movements to grow.

A bewildering array of Islamic associations suddenly emerged and experienced unprecedented freedom, each purporting to represent a discrete religious doctrine. Their common denominator was the desire for an "authentic" form of Islamic governance in Somalia. However, they had an assortment of warlords to contend with. Opposition to the Islamic movements has been the defining factor in the shifting of local, regional and international allegiances in the 1990s.

For instance, the same warlords who gave the Americans a bloody nose after the famous Black Hawk Down episode in 1993, later became America's favourites in 1995 when the Islamic militia unsuccessfully launched an offensive to take over Mogadishu.

With constant wars ravaging the South-central and adjoining parts of Somalia, various warlords have received support from a number of regional and international actors. Proxyism has led to many a combination of alliances. Since then, Somalia has been without a central government. Though they failed to sustain military victories in the mid-1990s, the Islamic movements made political gains through educational institutions (madrasas), businesses and by establishing courts in different clan areas to resolve disputes and fight crimes.

The cleric-led courts have found a receptive audience in a war-fatigued country. Gradually but surely, the courts gained military and financial muscle and, after a hard fight, won decisive battles in Mogadishu in June last year when the US-backed "anti-terror" alliance of warlords were soundly defeated.

Ethiopia and Other Rivals

With a long coastline running from the Red Sea into the Indian Ocean, Somalia's strategic location places it at the centre of regional geopolitics. This central position is reinforced by the fact that the Somalis are a trans-national ethnic group, with sizeable populations in neighbouring countries in the Horn. The rise of the Islamic Courts and the emerging possibility of a hostile, fundamentalist central government in Mogadishu has caused regional tensions and spurred a competition for influence. There are historical reasons for this. In 1969, when General Siad Barre toppled Somalia's first government in a coup d'état, years of war and chaos followed. Repression of rival clans, Islamic movements and political dissidence of any kind was the hallmark of the Barre government.

Initially, Somalia was a client of the Soviets. Barre's alignment with the Soviet Union was in reaction to the American military support for Somalia's rival, Ethiopia. The Soviets established a naval base on the strategic north coast, at the mouth of the Red Sea.

The Cold War dynamics suddenly changed when Emperor Haile Selassie of Ethiopia was ousted by leftist military officers led by Col Mengistu Haile Miriam who declared the country a 'Marxist Leninist state' in 1975.

The superpowers promptly swapped their clients: the Soviet Union went for the socialist Ethiopia and America sided with the Barre regime in Somalia. Pursuing the policy of Greater Somalia and enjoying US backing, the Barre regime attacked the Somali-dominated Ogaden region of eastern Ethiopia in 1977. Ethiopia was eventually able to repel the attack with large-scale Soviet military support and 20,000 Cuban troops.

Since then, the drought-prone but resource-rich Ogaden region has been inhabited by four million Somalis and has been a bone of contention between the two countries.

The region constitutes 25% of Ethiopia's total area and is the centre of resistance by the Ogaden National Liberation Front (ONLF) and the United Western Somali Liberation Front (UWSLF) against Amhara domination.

Although Eritrea does not share a border with Somalia, its interest in the civil war stems from its military rivalry with its once "parent-country," Ethiopia. Relations between Eritrea and Ethiopia have been consistently tense since Eritrea gained its independence from Addis Alsaba in 1993 after a 30-year guerrilla war. The two countries went to war again in 1998 and after two years of violence, they agreed to a ceasefire agreement in 2000. Mutual suspicion and enmity, however, persists and Somalia's conflict provides them an avenue to continue hurting one another by proxy.

Eritrea's support for the Islamic Courts was not because of any ideological affinity or religious sentiment; the only thing Asmara shares with the Islamic militia is a warlike stance towards Ethiopia.

The Kenyan area along the Somali border, with a significant Somali population, has also been part of the Creater Somalia dream. Though the Somali rhetoric on this count has been diluted as confrontation with Ethiopia takes centre stage, Kenya is nonetheless direcdy affected by the instability in Somalia.

There are more than 150,000 Somali refugees living in camps in Kenya. Even in the capital area of Nairobi, an exclusively Somali pocket of Eastleigh is a constant source of concern for the Kenyan government. As a victim of the bombing of the American embassy in Nairobi in 2002 and other Al-Qaeda attacks, Kenya is now assuming an agressive role in flushing out the remnants of the ousted Islamic militia.

Sudan, too, has a hand in the muddle. On a number of occasions in the 1990s, the Islamic-minded government In Khartoum had tried to unify the disparate Islamic movements of Somalia to form an Islamic emirate. After the UIC took over Mogadishu in June 2006, Sudan also facilitated a shortlived agreement between the Islamic militia and Yusuf's transitional government. With the Ethiopian military propping up its client and by extension the transitional government. Sudan and other neighbouring countries remain wary of an unfriendly regime establishing control in Mogadishu.

The ideological colouring of the conflict and the jihadi jargon of the Islamic Courts has sucked many countries from beyond the Horn of Africa into the Somali conflict. A US State Department report prepared by the former US ambassador to Ethiopia, David Shinn, lists as many as 12 countries having a direct or indirect involvement in Somalia and bankrolling either the transitional government or the Islamic Courts.

Among the countries named are Djibouti, Egypt, Uganda, Tanzania, Yemen, Libya, Saudi Arabia, United Arab Emirates and Iran. The report says that not wanting to be in the bad books of the US, some of the countries, like Saudi Arabia, have publicly disassociated themselves from the radical Islamic groups.

America's Role

All said and done, it is the US itself that remains the most crucial actor in determining the future of Somalia and the region, as it has been in the past. Some of the leaders and organisations associated with the defeated Islamic Courts are on the State Department's anti-terrorism list.

America has all along attempted to influence the outcome of Somalia's civil war by funding an anti-terrorism alliance of unpopular and bickering warlords. That has left the Bush administration's Somalia policy in shreds and further tarnished the US image in Somalia, which was used by the Islamic Courts as a rallying cry to gain local support. Even in the wake of the Islamic Courts' defeat by Ethiopia, anti-US sentiment runs high in Somalia.

Though formally disengaged from the Somali conflict since the Black Hawk Down episode in 1993, America has been openly siding with the rivals of the Islamic militias. Washington sponsored last year's UN Security Council Resolution 1725, which precipitated the UIC-Ethiopia war.

It has pursued its policy of containing Islamic forces with a renewed vigour after the attacks of 11 September 2001. US-led coalition forces are anchored in the Red Sea waters off Somalia, for the purpose of blocking off international Islamic networks' support systems. Diplomatically, Washington prefers engagement through the Somalia Contact Group, which also includes Norway, Britain, Sweden, Italy, Tanzania, and the European Union. The African Union, the Arab League, a group of East African countries, and the United Nations have observer status.

The contact group continues to support the transitional government. As US assistant secretary of state, Jendayi Frazer, puts it: America "would prefer to lead from behind". Nonetheless, the Bush administration is openly working through regional powers like Ethiopia and Kenya to contain and finally defeat the Islamic Courts.

Whereas the conventional military component of that victory has been achieved, decimating the Islamic movement and its paraphernalia of support in society remains a distant goal. The militia leaders and foot-soldiers gone underground have already started to resort to the same tactics that the Taliban have been employing since the occupation of Afghanistan after the 9/11 attacks. They will be difficult to beat in that kind of war.

It would be simplistic, therefore, to approach the brewing conflict in the Horn solely from the perspective of America's post-9/11 war on terrorism. There are many layers of the present chaos in the region. Religious radicalism is but only one aspect of the turmoil that seems to engulf the region.

Ethnic and religious rivalries within several East African states have transformed into interstate conflicts which are now spilling over far beyond the region and gaining an international dimension. And Somalia is likely to find itself at the centre of this whirlpool of instability for years to come.

Call in the Blue Helmets

Peacekeeping: Can the UN cope with increasing demands for its soldiers?

Call it peacekeeping, peace-enforcement, stabilisation or anything else, but one thing is clear: the world's soldiers are busier than ever operating in the wide grey zone between war and peace.

The United Nations has seen a sixfold increase since 1998 in the number of soldiers and military observers it deploys around the world. About 74,000 military personnel (nearly 100,000 people including police and civilians, and increasing fast) are currently involved in 18 different operations—more than any country apart from the United States. And it is not just the UN that is in high demand. NATO, the European Union and the African Union (AU), as well as other coalitions of the willing, have some 74,000 soldiers trying to restore peace and stability in troubled countries. Added to their number come the more than 160,000 American, British and other troops in Iraq.

The "war on terror" is one cause of this military hyperactivity. But Jean-Marie Guéhenno, the UN's under-secretary for peacekeeping, also sees more hopeful reasons. The growing demand for blue helmets, he says, is a good sign that a number of conflicts are ending.

This is only partly true. In Congo, southern Sudan and Liberia—the UN's three biggest operations—the blue helmets are shoring up peace agreements. But in countries such as Lebanon or Côte d'Ivoire, they are at best holding the line between parties still in conflict.

One reason for the surge in UN peacekeeping is that Africa, the region most in need of peacekeepers, is least able to provide for itself. The AU is trying to improve its peacekeeping capacity, but is desperately short of resources. It has handed over its operation in Burundi to the UN. Now it wants the blue helmets to help relieve its 7,000 hard-pressed AU peacekeepers in Sudan's troubled region of Darfur.

The Sudanese government has long resisted such a deployment, accusing the UN of being an agent of the West. But under sustained international pressure to halt what Washington regards as genocide, it has grudgingly agreed to allow in a "hybrid" UN and AU force. An advance party of 24 police advisers and 43 military officers, wearing blue berets and AU armbands, has started to arrive in Darfur to test Sudan's co-operation. According to a three-phase plan, the force will be built up into a contingent of 17,000 soldiers and 3,000 police officers.

Can the UN take on another onerous peacekeeping operation? Mr Guéhenno says the world already faces two kinds of "overstretch": the military sort, in which many armed forces of many leading countries are badly strained by foreign operations; and "political overstretch", in which the world's political energies are focused on just a few acute problems while the UN is left to deal as best it can with many chronic or less visible conflicts.

Mr Guéhenno is cautious about what he can achieve in Darfur. He says he may get the soldiers, given the right political conditions, but is worried about getting enough "enablers"—the crucial specialised units and equipment that enhance the ability of a force to move and operate. These include army engineers and logisticians, field hospitals and nurses, heavy-lift aircraft and transport helicopters, as well as proper command-and-control and intelligence-gathering: in other words, the wherewithal of modern Western expeditionary forces. These capabilities are in short supply and are expensive; the few countries that have them are using them, and the others can't afford them.

In a region as vast as Darfur, an effective UN force would need to be highly mobile, and make use both of unmanned surveillance drones and special forces. It would need to sustain itself in a harsh environment, some 1,400km (870 miles) from the nearest harbour and with few airfields. Engineers could drill for water, but would be under pressure to share it with local populations and with refugees. And then there is the problem of time. On current plans it would take six to nine months to build up to full strength in Darfur. Having to merge with the AU adds further complications to the command structure.

Finding a Fire Engine

Apart from military capability, or lack of it, there is the question of political will. Who will risk their soldiers' lives, and their valuable military assets, in a faraway conflict? NATO, the world's foremost military alliance, has struggled for months to find a few thousand additional soldiers—and a few extra helicopters—to back up its troops fighting in southern Afghanistan.

By contrast, European countries moved with unusual speed when the UN appealed for its hapless mission in Lebanon to be reinforced last summer in order to end the war between Israel and Hizbullah. Within weeks of a ceasefire being called in August, French and Italian peacekeepers were coming ashore. It was the first time that sizeable Western forces had donned blue helmets since the unhappy days of the war in Bosnia.

But there were particular reasons for this. Lebanon, of course, is more easily accessible than Afghanistan or Darfur. But it is also less dangerous than southern Afghanistan, and European governments regard the Israeli-Arab conflict as much closer to their interests than the effort to pacify rebellious Pashtun tribesmen.

Kofi Annan, the former UN secretary-general, liked to say that the UN is the only fire brigade that must go out and buy a fire engine before it can respond to an emergency. The Security Council must first authorise an operation and pass a budget, and then the secretariat beseeches governments to contribute forces and arranges the means to transport them. This system has created a two-tier structure: powerful countries decide the missions (and pay for them) while poor countries such as India, Pakistan, Bangladesh, Nepal and Jordan supply the soldiers. They receive a payment for doing so; this becomes for some a subsidy for their own armed forces, while the deployment also provides their troops with training.

Idealists such as Sir Brian Urquhart, a former UN under secretary-general, believe it is high time the UN had its own "fire engine": a permanent force that could deploy quickly to stop conflicts before they spin out of control. The UN's founding fathers envisioned some kind of international army, but all proposals for a standing UN force have foundered—partly because of political objections to giving the UN too much power, partly because of the practical difficulties of recruiting, training and paying for such a force.

After the failure of the UN in the mid-1990s to stop bloodletting in Somalia, Rwanda and the Balkans, many argued it would be better for those who are properly equipped to deal with putting out the fires of conflict. In 1999, it was NATO that stopped the killing of ethnic Albanians in Kosovo, while a force led by Australia halted the conflict in East Timor. A year later, in Sierra Leone, the quick deployment of about 1,000 British soldiers helped save what was then the UN's largest peacekeeping mission from collapsing under attack by rebels of the Revolutionary United Front.

All this seemed to confirm that the UN could take on only soft peacekeeping and "observer" missions with co-operation from the warring sides. But in 2000 a panel headed by Lakhdar Brahimi recommended a complete rethink of UN peacekeeping. The United Nations, it acknowledged, "does not wage war"; but its operations nevertheless had to "project credible force" and be ready to distinguish between victim and aggressor.

Mr Brahimi's central recommendation was the creation of multinational brigades around the world ready to deploy at short notice. This idea of pre-assembling bits of the fire engine has made only fitful progress. But other proposals have been acted on. They include the creation of a more powerful headquarters to oversee the UN effort; stockpiling of equipment; compilation of lists of

Unlimited Current UN peacekeeping missions

Location	Mission Name	Year of deployment	Number of personnel*
Congo	MONUC	1999	22,167
Liberia	UNMIL	2003	18,382
Southern Sudan	UNMIS	2005	13,021
Lebanon	UNIFIL	1978	11,431
Côte d'Ivoire	UNOCI	2004	11,150
Haiti	MINUSTAH	2004	3,142
Kosovo	UNMIK	1999	4,631
Burundi	ONUB	2004	3,142
Ethiopia and Eritrea	UNMEE	2000	2,687
Timor-Leste	UNMIT	2006	1,340
Golan Heights (Israel/Syria)	UNDOF	1974	1,247
Cyprus	UNFICYP	1964	1,069
Afghanistan[a]	UNAMA	2002	850
Western Sahara	MINURSO	1991	459
Georgia	UNOMIG	1993	419
Middle East[b]	UNTSO	1948	374
Sierra Leone[a]	UNIOSIL	2006	298
India and Pakistan	UNMOGIP	1949	113

*Includes military, police and civilians

[a]Political or peace-building missions

[b]Egypt, Jordan, Israel, Lebanon and Syria

Source: United Nations

119

military officers, police and other experts who will be on *call* to join UN missions; and the meshing of peacekeeping with ordinary policing, government reform and economic development.

New missions are now much more likely to be given robust mandates authorising them to use "all necessary means" under Chapter VII of the UN Charter: in other words, aggressive military force. In places such as Congo and Haiti, the UN has even been accused of using too much force.

Since the world is likely to need large numbers of peacekeepers for the foreseeable future, a further option is being explored: "leasing" the fire engine by hiring private security companies to do more of the work. Don't expect anything to happen quickly, though. The world, and especially the Americans, has moved a long way towards the privatisation of war. But for many, the privatisation of peacekeeping is still a step too far.

The Democratic Mosaic

MARTIN WALKER

The administration of President George W. Bush has been defined by the war on terrorism, its response to the appalling terrorist attacks of September 11, 2001. But it wants to be remembered for a grander and more positive strategy, as unveiled by the president at the National Endowment for Democracy in November 2003 and further elaborated in his State of the Union address this year. This "forward strategy of freedom in the greater Middle East" seeks to promote free elections, free markets, a free press, and free labor unions to advance democracy and opportunity in 22 Arab countries, stretching from Morocco on the Atlantic coast to Oman on the shores of the Indian Ocean. The inhabitants of those countries number some 300 million, speak diverse Arabic dialects that are often mutually incomprehensible, and have long endured violence, poverty, and arbitrary rule. The United States has little choice but to attempt this daunting challenge, said Bush: "As long as the Middle East remains a place of tyranny and despair and anger, it will continue to produce men and movements that threaten the safety of America and our friends."

The grandly ambitious project is inspired partly by the Helsinki treaties of 1975, which gave crucial breathing room to human rights groups in the old Soviet bloc, and partly by the success of American policies after 1945 that led to democratic governments in Japan and West Germany. To be sure, 59 years after victory in World War II, American forces remain deployed in those two countries, and the new strategy for the Middle East may similarly depend, in part, on a U.S. military presence.

But merely to prescribe democracy is not to settle the matter, because democracy comes in such a bewildering variety of forms. There are parliamentary monarchies without any written constitution (Britain), highly centralized presidential democracies (France), federal democracies (Germany), democracies with separated powers and a venerable constitution (United States), and democracies that seem to flourish despite an effective one-party system (Japan). There are new democracies (South Korea and Taiwan), and democracies that maintain most of their essential freedoms despite the strains of war and terrorism (Israel). Some democracies have survived and deepened despite poverty (Costa Rica), violent separatist movements (modern Spain), recurrent wars (much of Europe), and deep ethnic divisions (Brazil). India's democracy has flourished despite all those challenges and the further complications of a debilitating caste system.

There are democracies so decentralized that the "central" government is almost impotent (Switzerland), and democracies so young and fragile that they exist only by means of a powerful and intrusive outside authority (Bosnia-Herzegovina). There are democracies restored from within (Spain and Portugal) and democracies born in the defeat of military dictators (Greece and Argentina); in Chile, a vigorous democratic movement eventually ended the military rule of General Augusto Pinochet, who had led a coup in 1973 to topple the elected government of Salvador Allende.

Democracy's stunning advance has bypassed the Islamic world.

Democracy, however defined, has scored some stunning advances since Allende's fall. According to Freedom House, which for 30 years has published an annual survey of political rights around the world, democracy's reach has grown ever more extensive. In 1972, the year of its first survey, Freedom House rated 43 countries as "free," 38 as "partly free," and 69 as "not free." The 2004 Freedom House survey rates 88 states as free, 55 as partly free, and 49 as not free. So the number of free countries has more than doubled over the past 30 years, the number of partly free states has grown by 17, and the number of repressive (i.e., not free) states has declined by 20. (The absolute number of states has grown over the same period.)

Democracy has proved so diverse over the past half-century that it confounds easy definition. It's a strikingly robust plant, capable of almost infinite variety. But in the Islamic world, democracy struggles on unfriendly soil. The Freedom House survey of the 47 nations with an Islamic majority found only nine electoral democracies, none of them in the Middle East. But even the electoral democracies often lack fundamental rights. Of states with an Islamic majority, Freedom House ranks only two, Senegal and Mali, as free. Why should this be? India's example suggests that the influence of colonialism is not an adequate explanation. Nor is poverty, which, in any case, is not an issue in the oil-rich states. The explanation must lie elsewhere.

Most political theory about the key components of democracy focuses on three important preconditions: the role of certain key state institutions, the strength of civil society, and socioeconomic and cultural structure. The key institutions include elections, in some form, with a secret ballot; reasonably free speech and media; and the rule of law, as administered by a tolerably independent judiciary to protect the rights of minorities. The rule of law is critical. (Without it, Thomas Jefferson's somber definition of a democracy as "nothing more than mob rule, where fifty-one percent of the people may take away the rights of the other forty-nine," might well discredit the enterprise.) It should extend to all citizens, and cover commercial as well as criminal matters; otherwise, property rights and the sanctity of contract are at risk. But the rule of law can take many forms. The countries of the European Union, for example, manage to function with fundamentally different legal systems. Most Continental nations prefer variants of the French system, in which a state-employed magistrate acts as investigator and as prosecutor before a judicial panel. The British retain trial by jury and an adversarial system in which the Crown presents the prosecution and the defense then tries to refute it.

But such distinctions between the legal forms of Western democracy are mere details by comparison with the gulf that separates Islamic law, sharia, from Western concepts of law. Although democracy can function with a state-established religion, as in Britain or Israel, the question of whether it can emerge in the shadow of sharia remains open. The difficulty is less the hudud, the stern code of punishment for fornication (flogging), theft (amputation), and adultery (stoning), than it is sharia's fundamental objection to any separation of church and state. Nor can there be much freedom of individual conscience when the penalty for converting from Islam to another religion is death. This is not to say necessarily that democracy cannot prosper under sharia, but finding an accommodation will be difficult, and is unlikely to be peaceful. It took centuries of war and dispute—and eventually the Reformation—for medieval Europe to resolve a similar clash of prerogatives between the canon law of the Roman Catholic Church and the secular law of earthly sovereigns.

The importance of civil society in the emergence of democracy has long been recognized. "Among the laws that rule human society," Alexis de Tocqueville suggested in *Democracy in America,* "there is one that seems to be more precise and clear than all others. If men are to remain civilized or to become so, the art of associating together must grow and improve in the same ration." Samuel Huntington, in his seminal *Political Order in Changing Societies* (1969), saw the insufficient development of this art as explaining the problems of "the modernizing countries of Asia, Africa and Latin America, where the political community is fragmented against itself, and where political institutions have little power, less majesty and no resiliency, where in many cases governments simply do not govern." Huntington discerned in the countries being destabilized by rapid change "a lack of civic morale and public spirit capable of giving meaning and direction to the public interest,"

Freedom in the Middle East

While there has been steady progress toward greater freedom around the world in recent decades, the Middle East still lags behind. Freedom House, a nonpartisan research organization that annually surveys the status of freedom in 192 countries, reports that only one of the 18 countries it groups in the Middle East and North Africa is rated "free," and that is Israel. Worldwide, 88 countries are rated free. The good news is that Yemen, once a refuge for Osama bin Laden, has moved from "not free" to "partly free." Six Middle Eastern countries are now partly tree. According to Freedom House, the presence or absence of elections is not decisive in rating a country. In partly free countries, "political rights and civil liberties are more limited [and] corruption, dominant ruling parties, or, in some cases, ethnic or religious strife are often the norm." Eleven countries in the region (and 49 worldwide) are considered not free.

and concluded that "the primary problem of politics is the lag in the development of political institutions behind social and economic change."

Democracy can function with a state-established religion; the question of whether it can emerge in the shadow of sharia remains open.

To give life to those political institutions, a civil society is needed, in the form, for example, of sports and hobby clubs, labor unions, cafés, and other nongovernmental and political entities within which people can gather and argue and cooperate outside state structures. All of these—and an increasingly independent news media spurred by satellite TV and the Internet, charitable bodies, and women's groups—exist throughout most of the Arab world. Not all of them are organized through the mosques, and many thrive despite political repression, the customary restraints upon a public role for women, and the competing tug of tribal tradition. In countries that are making significant steps toward representative government, such as Morocco, Jordan, Oman, Qatar, and Kuwait, civil society is blossoming fast. Those five countries, all monarchies, have sovereigns who seem prepared to enlarge the political space for their subjects. The prospects for "the art of associating together" in these states are promising, in part because long-established royal dynasties with their own religious credentials do not seem intimidated by the Islamist clerics.

Civil society is inextricably linked with socioeconomic structure, but the economic circumstances of successful democracies are widely divergent. India is an obvious example of democracy unimpeded by poverty, as is Costa Rica, with a long and exemplary record of representative government in Latin America. In the most populous countries of the Arab world, wealth is actually distributed more equitably than in the United States.

Economists measure income distribution in a state by means of the Gini index (named for Corrado Gini, the Italian statistician who devised it). The lower the index, the more evenly income is distributed in a country; the higher the index, the greater the share of wealth owned by the rich. So a fully egalitarian society would have a Gini figure of 0, and a society in which the richest person owned everything would have a figure of 100. The table gives the Gini figures for selected countries, with gross domestic product (GDP) shown in purchasing power parity. It's important to note, however, that figures for the Arab world are notoriously unreliable, and that, for the oil-rich states, a Gini index is almost meaningless because of the extraordinarily high proportion of foreign workers.

Income disparities are a crude indicator, concealing both regional differences (a low income in New York City can be relatively high in Mississippi) and many social subtleties. But the figures suggest that democracy can flourish in countries with sharp disparities of income, and survive even in countries such as Brazil, where the disparities tend toward the acute. If reasonably even levels of income distribution are a useful predictor, then many Arab countries are in promising shape.

Long-established royal dynasties with their own religious credentials seem less intimidated by the Islamist clerics.

Incomes may not be a helpful indicator, however, in analyzing a particularly distinctive characteristic of democracies— the middle class, which plays a stabilizing political role. The middle class is hard to define because income is only one factor in its

Wealth and Inequality

Country	Gini index	Per capita GDP (U.S.$)
Japan	24.9	25,130
Sweden	25.0	24,180
Yemen	33.4	790
Egypt	34.4	3,520
Britain	36.0	24,160
Jordan	36.4	3,870
Morocco	39.5	3,600
China	40.3	4,020
United States	40.8	34,320
Russia	45.6	7,100
Mexico	53.1	8,430

Parts of the Arab world may enjoy less income inequality than the United States. A low Gini index connotes low levels of income inequality.

measurement; social origin, education, career, and lifestyle all contribute to the making of a middle class. Nonetheless, there are common features. Members of the middle class have homes and savings. They make some provision for their old age. They invest in the education of their children. Thus, they have a stake in a stable future, and that provides a strong personal incentive for them to be politically active—to ensure that schools are good, that the financial system will handle their savings honestly, that police will safeguard their property, that courts will be honest, and that the government will not tax them too highly or waste their savings through inflation. They need a free press to tell them what the government and courts are doing, and freedom of speech and assembly and elections to organize their opposition if the government lets them down. In short, though it may be simplistic to say that a middle class, by definition, will demand the kinds of institutions that help sustain democracy, such institutions and a socially active and politically engaged middle class will mutually reinforce each other.

The middle class is growing fast in most Arab countries, although it's growing most quickly in the state bureaucracies. But no doubt as a consequence of the subservient role of women, the Arab middle class is not growing nearly quickly enough to cope with the stunningly high birthrates that give the region such a high proportion of young people under the age of 25. According to the United Nations Department of Economic and Social Affairs, the median age in Egypt and Algeria is now 20; in Lebanon it's 18, and in Iraq it's 17. On average, annual population growth remains about three percent in many Arab countries, compared with two percent globally.

The role of women in the Arab world points to a deeper issue: the degree to which democracy depends on culture. The long stability of Britain and the United States, the first countries to produce a mass middle class, is telling. Some political theorists suggest that the tradition of juries and common law, property rights, elected parliaments, a free press, and largely free trade, along with the low taxes permitted by a happy geography that precluded the need for a vast standing army, endowed the English-speaking world with a special predisposition to democracy. The theory is beguiling, but it turns ominous when used to suggest that some peoples and cultures are inherently antipathetic to democracy—as has been said at various times of Germans, Japanese, Indians, Africans, and Russians, and as is now being said of the Islamic world in general.

The debate on democracy's potential in the Middle East will continue, even as democracy's green shoots are evident in Oman's elections, Qatar's new constitution (which gives women the right to vote), and Jordan's and Morocco's significant steps toward representative government. But these potential democracies remain works in timid progress, proceeding under two baleful shadows. The first is the example of Iran, where a democratically elected parliament and president have been unable to establish their authority over the ayatollahs of the Guardian Council, who control the judicial system, the Pasdaran Revolutionary Guard, and the domestic security agencies, and who are deeply suspicious of democracy. As Ayatollah

Ruholla Khomeini wrote in 1977, "The real threat to Islam does not come from the Shah, but from the idea of imposing on Muslim lands the Western system of democracy, which is a form of prostitution." The second shadow is the nagging fear that a democratic election in most states of the Arab world is likely to be won by the well-organized Islamists. The army intervened in Algeria to prevent the Islamic Salvation Front from taking office after it won the elections of 1992. That triggered an insurgency in which more than 100,000 people have since died.

Still, it's not entirely clear that the separation of religion and state, a concept Islam finds difficult to embrace, is a prerequisite for democracy. The British have functioned tolerably well with an established Church of England for nearly five centuries; Germany's Christian Democratic and Christian Social Union coalitions have provided impeccably democratic government; and France's proud republican tradition of laicism has not spared the nation political anguish over the right of Muslim women to wear headscarves in school. But there's little left in modern European politics of the religious passions that unleashed war, massacres, and persecution in the 16th and 17th centuries.

Islam, at least in the Arab world, has yet to undergo its Reformation, and those Islamic states that have produced a more relaxed religious form have their own difficulties. Indonesia is a tremulous democracy, rent by ethnic as well as religious tensions, with the army constantly poised to intervene again. Malaysia, economically the most dynamic of Islamic countries, has seen Islamist extremist groups win power in two states—one of which they lost in recent elections—after years of well-funded Wahhabi proselytizing. Turkey, where a moderate Islamic party has now come peacefully to power by elec-

tion, remains the most promising example of the way in which Islam and democracy might prosper together. Since the reforms of Kemal Atatürk, Turkey has had 80 years of secular rule, 50 years of NATO membership, and now the lure of joining the European Union to strengthen its democratic commitment.

Turkey, of course, is a constant reminder that there's little in history or political theory to suggest that Islamic nations cannot become democracies. Indeed, the constitutional monarchy and parliamentary system that ruled independent Iraq from 1932 to 1958 produced the freest press, the most vibrant civil society, and the most impressive levels of health and education in the Arab world during that period. Yet Iraq was a clouded democracy: The elected prime minister, Nuri Said, was an authoritarian figure, susceptible to British influence, who routinely suspended parliaments when they proved hostile. At least the latest efforts at democratization in the Arab world take place under happier circumstances, without the looming presence of the Cold War.

President Bush's new "forward strategy of freedom" will need a great deal of international support, both political and financial, if it is to succeed, and a patient world will have to persuade a highly skeptical Arab public that the United States is resolved to achieve a fair peace settlement between Israel and the Palestinians. Ultimately, however, as the president made clear in January, his strategy rests on an act of faith: "It is mistaken, and condescending, to assume that whole cultures and great religions are incompatible with liberty and self-government. I believe that God has planted in every human heart the desire to live in freedom. And even when that desire is crushed by tyranny for decades, it will rise again."

MARTIN WALKER is editor in chief of United Press International and a former public policy fellow at the Woodrow Wilson Center.

Bringing the Wicked to the Dock

But does an international search for justice hurt or help the pursuit of peace?

Hitherto, the world's worst tyrants have usually managed to avoid being brought to court for their crimes. Some, of course, were killed. Hitler took his own life. But Stalin and Mao died in their beds. Pol Pot, responsible for the slaughter of 2m Cambodians in the 1970s, lived on in Cambodia until his death in 1998. Idi Amin, Uganda's brutal dictator, saw out his days in comfortable exile in Saudi Arabia; Ethiopia's Mengistu Haile Mariam continues to live in Zimbabwe. The list goes on. But with the spread of international justice over the past decade, the noose is tightening. It is now accepted that there can be no immunity for the worst violations of human rights, not even for heads of state.

Serbia's president, Slobodan Milosevic, was indicted for war crimes in 1999 and is likely to be sentenced to life imprisonment when his trial ends later this year. After ten years on the run, Ratko Mladic, the Bosnian Serb army chief held responsible for the Srebrenica massacre, is expected to be arrested any day. In Chile, Augusto Pinochet is finally facing a real possibility of trial 17 years after the end of his dictatorship. Hissene Habre, a ruthless ex-president of Chad, exiled in Senegal for the past 16 years, could soon be extradited to Brussels to face trial for crimes against humanity under Belgium's "universal jurisdiction" law. Polish prosecutors are preparing to bring charges against Wojciech Jaruzelski, their last communist leader. And Saddam Hussein, Iraq's former dictator, faces near-certain execution at the end of his trial before a special tribunal in Baghdad.

Debate has long raged about the best way to deal with gross violations of human rights. Is it more important to punish the perpetrators or to bring an end to the atrocities? Can one, in other words, secure both justice and peace, or are the two naturally antagonistic?

In the 1980s the concept of "truth and reconciliation" began to be the rage, and justice was relegated to the back burner. Truth-telling, perhaps encouraged by amnesties, appeared a good way of revealing the previously suppressed stories of the victims and (much less often) the perpetrators of the covert state-sponsored violence (death squads, "disappearances" and such like) in Latin America. Indeed, the first truth and reconciliation commission was set up not in South Africa, as many still believe, but in Chile, in 1990. Others followed in quick succession in El Salvador, Chad, Haiti, South Africa (1995), Ecuador, Nigeria, Peru, Sierra Leone, South Korea, Uruguay, Timor-Leste, Ghana, Panama, Congo, Liberia and Morocco, the first in the Arab world. Algeria, Afghanistan and Burundi are now considering following suit.

But for many, the idea that genocide, ethnic cleansing, torture and other such horrors should go unpunished became increasingly troubling. Under the principle of national sovereignty, nation states were supposed to have responsibility for enforcing their own criminal justice. But all too often they had shown themselves unwilling or incapable of prosecuting the worst culprits, either because those responsible were still in power, or because they had taken refuge in other countries and were now out of reach. Hence the turn to international justice.

In 1993, the UN's International Criminal Tribunal for ex-Yugoslavia (ICTY) in The Hague became the first international war-crimes tribunal to be set up since the Nuremberg and Tokyo trials after the second world war. It was followed a year later by the UN tribunal for Rwanda, based in Arusha, Tanzania. Like their post-war forebears, the two courts operate exclusively under international law and are staffed by foreign judges. Since then, five other war-crimes tribunals, all with more or less international input, have been—or are being—set up to deal with atrocities in Sierra Leone, Cambodia, Timor-Leste, Iraq and Afghanistan. Lebanon has now asked the UN for help in setting up a "tribunal of international character" to try the assassins of Rafik Hariri, the former Lebanese prime minister who was killed a year ago.

What Man Can Do to Man

The Special Court for Sierra Leone, set up jointly by the UN and the Sierra Leonean government in 2002, was the world's first "hybrid" court. Financed by voluntary contributions from UN members, it operates under international law but with a mixture of local and international judges. Based in Freetown, Sierra Leone's capital, it was also the first modern war-crimes tribunal to be based "in theatre" (ie, in the country where the crimes were committed). Desmond de Silva, the court's chief prosecutor, recounts his first visit to an amputee camp in the town four years ago: "I saw a little girl with no arms saying to her mother: 'Mummy, when will my arms grow again?' Nearby was a baby suckling at his mother's breast: neither had any arms. These were sights that said to me: do something. This is evil beyond belief."

Most conflicts, especially third-world civil ones, are marked by atrocities. But the wanton cruelty of Sierra Leone's 11-year bloodbath was particularly barbaric. Although hacking off limbs became the special trademark of the Revolutionary United Front (RUF), the main rebel group, all sides were guilty. Child soldiers, some not yet in their teens, would rip open pregnant women's stomachs after taking bets on the sex of the fetus. Women's vaginas were sewn with fishing line. Mouths were clamped shut with padlocks.

Children were forced to batter their parents to death and then eat their brains. One man was skinned alive before having his flesh picked off and eaten. Another had his heart torn out and stuffed into the mouth of his 87-year-old mother. Thousands were burned alive in their homes. In all, some 50,000-200,000 people were killed (there is no accurate count) and three-quarters of the country's 6m inhabitants were forced to flee their homes. Should such crimes really be forgiven and forgotten?

Charles Taylor, Liberia's ex-president and a notorious warlord, is regarded as one of the greatest villains of the piece. Accused of arming the RUF rebels in exchange for "blood" diamonds, he was indicted three years ago by Sierra Leone's court, but managed to flee into exile in Nigeria after the collapse of his own regime a few months later. Since then, he has been living undisturbed in a seaside villa, courtesy of President Olusegun Obasanjo. The Nigerian leader granted him asylum as part of a peace deal brokered by Nigeria, Britain and the United States. But prosecutors claim that Mr Taylor has broken the conditions of that deal by continuing to meddle in politics, in Liberia and wider afield. Both America's Congress and the European Parliament have demanded his transfer to the Special Court.

But Mr Obasanjo has said he will not hand Mr Taylor over unless requested to do so by a democratically elected Liberian government. In November, Ellen Johnson-Sirleaf was elected Liberia's new president. She may not yet have made the request; in any case, Mr Obasanjo has made no move. African leaders tend to watch each other's backs for fear that it could be their own turn next. But the pressure is building up. In November, the UN Security Council told its peacekeepers in Liberia to arrest and transfer Mr Taylor to the Special Court if he sets foot in the country. And the United States, hitherto reluctant to upset a valuable ally, has begun to speak out. "We think Obasanjo has an international responsibility and we fully expect him to carry it out," Condoleezza Rice, the secretary of state, recently told reporters.

If the Special Court does get Mr Taylor, it would be a tremendous coup both for it and for international justice. Mandated to try only "those with the greatest responsibility" for the atrocities, the court has indicted just 13 people (compared with the 162 indicted by the ICTY). The trials of nine of them—three from each of the two main rebel groups and three from the pro-government Civil Defence Force (CDF), in a demonstration of even-handedness—are already well under way. But the four chief culprits are either still at large, like Mr Taylor, or dead, like Foday Sankoh, dreaded leader of the RUF rebels. Their absence has led some critics to question the continued existence of a tribunal which many Sierra Leoneans see as irrelevant to their lives.

The court's decision to try Chief Samuel Hinga Norman, the former CDF leader, has provoked particular anger. Many Sierra Leoneans regard the former government minister, who helped oust a savage rebel junta in 1998, as a national hero. "Surely there has to be a difference between a group of thugs and killers who go round butchering people mindlessly, for no particular reason, and people trying to defend their lives, their homes and their children," protested Peter Penfold, who was British high commissioner to Sierra Leone in 1997–2000. Mr Norman should never have been indicted, Mr Penfold told the court last month. To such objections, which recur whenever an admired national leader is prosecuted, Mr de Silva is wont to reply: "You can fight on the same side as the angels and nevertheless commit crimes against humanity." Hence, again, the need for international courts.

Sierra Leone's court is in many ways regarded as a model, with its two-to-one mix of foreign and local judges, ambitious "outreach" (public relations) and victim-protection programmes, tight timetable—it expects to complete its work in under five years as opposed to the Yugoslav tribunal's 17 years—and relatively low budget, less than $30m a year, a quarter of the ICTY's. Admittedly, the competition is not exactly fierce.

The Yugoslav and Rwandan tribunals, while doing good work, are regarded as slow, costly and remote, while the special tribunals in Cambodia, with its majority of local judges, and in Iraq, where Mr Hussein's trial before an all-Iraqi bench keeps threatening to collapse in chaos, are regarded by many as counter-examples, lacking both impartiality and competence. With results so mixed, it is perhaps not surprising that people have begun questioning the need to finance such tribunals.

The Court They Love to Hate

The International Criminal Court (ICC) is the world's first permanent war-crimes tribunal. It is also the first not to have any direct UN involvement and has faced strong opposition from America. Set up in The Hague in 2002, alongside the ICTY and the UN's International Court of Justice (the much older body which rules on disputes between states), it is designed to provide a fairer, cheaper, and more effective way of dealing with the most serious violations of international humanitarian law.

Last October, it issued its first indictments—against Joseph Kony and four members of his savage Lord's Resistance Army in northern Uganda. More indictments are expected soon relating to the slaughter in Congo, where war has claimed 4m lives since 1998. The court has also been mandated by the Security Council to investigate the current horrors in Darfur, in western Sudan, and continues to keep watch on developments in five other violence-racked countries, including Côte d'Ivoire and the Central African Republic.

Yet the ICC's reach is limited. Under its statutes, it cannot bring a prosecution unless the accused's country of origin is "genuinely unable or unwilling" to do so. This is a potential minefield: Sudan, for example, insists it is perfectly capable and willing to try those responsible for Darfur and is refusing to cooperate with the court. It may not prosecute crimes committed before its inception in 2002. And it has jurisdiction only over nationals of countries which have ratified its statutes—100 have done so to date—or over those whose crimes were committed in a country which has. The exception to this rule is if the Security Council refers the matter to the ICC, as in the case of Sudan, a non-member. The ICC is further hampered by the refusal of many of the world's worst human-rights violators to sign up to it. Zimbabwe, Cuba, Uzbekistan, North Korea, Syria, Belarus and Saudi Arabia are all non-members. So are the United States, China and Russia, all three veto-wielding permanent members of the Security Council and thus able to block any Security Council referrals.

Imperfect Justice

The purpose and value of the ICC and the other ad hoc war-crimes tribunals are now, in their turn, coming under scrutiny. Critics complain that they are selective and politicised, deliver only partial justice and perpetuate the bitterness, thus preventing social and ethnic reconstruction. All too often, suggests Dominic McGoldrick, professor of public international law at Liverpool University in Britain, they are seen as an attempt by the West to impose its own concept of justice and morality on the third world.

Others, however, argue that ending impunity is vital, not only to reduce the victims' anger and resentment, which might otherwise fuel a never-ending cycle of reprisals and counter-reprisals, but also to deter further atrocities. Without justice, says Paul van Zyl of the New York-based International Centre for Transitional Justice, you may be able to bring a temporary stop to the killing, but there can be no sustainable peace.

Does deterrence work? It is easy to point to the apparent failures. Despite Nuremberg, genocide has continued. The creation of the ICTY failed to prevent the massacres in Srebrenica and Kosovo. The indictment of Mr Kony and his henchmen has not stopped the Ugandan killings. And since the referral of Darfur to the ICC, the violence there has got even worse. But to be effective, deterrence has to be credible. It works only when the potential culprits have a reasonable expectation of being apprehended and punished. It is too early to judge what effect the ICC and the other tribunals will have, says Mr van Zyl, but he adds that there is no doubt "that there is a growing trend in the world toward justice for the top dogs." He believes Mr Taylor's capture would send a very strong signal to other potential tyrants.

But what about the lower-level perpetrators—the middle-ranking officers who simply follow orders out of fear for their own lives, or the child soldiers, dragged from their homes, brutalised and forced to commit atrocities often under the influence of drugs or alcohol? Should they, too, be held accountable? Here some kind of truth-telling mechanism, backed up by traditional methods of mediation and reconciliation, might be appropriate, argues Kenneth Roth, head of Human Rights Watch, another New York-based lobby. Aimed only at the worst culprits, international justice is at best a blunt instrument. But he is adamant that blanket amnesties are generally counter-productive, except (a big exception) when used as a temporary expedient to bring warring parties to the negotiating table, with the possibility of being "undone" once peace is restored.

In Sierra Leone, Mr Roth points out, the amnesty negotiated as part of the 1999 Lomé peace agreement with the rebels did not prevent the resumption of atrocities a few months later and was therefore annulled. In war-torn northern Uganda, a five-year-old government amnesty, while successful in bringing thousands of middle- and low-ranking rebels in from the bush, has failed to get Mr Kony and his pals to lay down their arms.

Prosecution is by no means necessarily an impediment to peace, Mr Roth insists; the absence of any amnesty provision in the Dayton peace agreement on Bosnia, for example, did not stop Mr Milosevic from signing up to it (because he never dreamt that he, himself, would be prosecuted). Nor did it prevent Afghanistan's warring parties from reaching a peace agreement in Bonn. Furthermore, he says, the amnesties that have been introduced in the past are beginning to be unpicked in the courts, as in Chile in 2003, or annulled outright, as in Argentina the same year. It is now generally accepted that, under international law, amnesties can never apply to gross violations of humanitarian law.

Truth, Reconciliation and Punishment

Even South Africa's lauded truth and reconciliation process, presided over by Archbishop Desmond Tutu, provided no automatic amnesty. Under the slogan "revealing is healing", perpetrators were invited to confess to crimes committed under the three decades of apartheid, and apply for an amnesty. But if their misdeeds were deemed too heinous, amnesty could be denied. More than 7,000 applications were accepted, but 5,400 were turned down. In addition, those who refused to confess remained liable to prosecution. For a long time, it looked as if no charges would ever be brought. But now South Africa has announced that it is ready to prosecute five people (no names yet given), with 15 more likely to follow.

Reconciliation and punitive justice are both necessary in the view of Messrs Roth and van Zyl. Far from being antagonistic, the two approaches complement one another. Much depends on local circumstances. Sometimes, as in South Africa, it is better to start with truth and reconciliation, and prosecute later. At other times, as in Iraq, prosecution comes first, and truth and reconciliation may follow when or if the violence ends. Sierra Leone is the only country that has set up a truth and reconciliation commission and a war-crimes court at the same time. Locals grumble, but the wounded little country's bold experiment could set a trend.

UNIT 4
Political Change

Unit Selections

Key Points to Consider

- What are the current trends in democracy throughout the world?

- What makes Iran's politics so complicated?

- What are the sources of Turkey's political upheaval?

- What challenges does Thailand face in trying to return to civilian rule?

- What factors contribute to the tenuous peace in the Democratic Republic of Congo?

- Why have African liberation organizations found it difficult to transform into political parties?

- What are the lessons of Latin America's recent elections?

- What are the sources of leftist electoral victories in Latin America?

Student Web Site
www.mhcls.com/online

Internet References
Further information regarding these Web sites may be found in this book's preface or online.

Latin American Network Information Center—LANIC
http://www.lanic.utexas.edu
ReliefWeb
http://www.reliefweb.int/w/rwb.nsf
World Trade Organization (WTO)
http://www.wto.org

A history of authoritarian rule and the lack of a democratic political culture have hampered efforts to extend democracy to many parts of the developing world. Colonial rule was authoritarian and the colonial powers failed to prepare their colonies adequately for democracy at independence. Even where there was an attempt to foster parliamentary government, the experiment frequently failed, largely due to the lack of a democratic tradition and a reliance on political expediency. Independence-era leaders frequently resorted to centralization of power and authoritarianism, either to pursue ambitious development programs or often simply to retain power. In some cases, leaders experimented with socialist development schemes that emphasized ideology and the role of party elites. The promise of rapid, equitable development proved elusive, and the collapse of the Soviet Union discredited this strategy. Other countries had the misfortune to come under the rule of tyrannical leaders concerned

with enriching themselves and who brutally repressed anyone with the temerity to challenge their rule. Although there are a few notable exceptions, the developing world's experiences with democracy since independence have been very limited.

Democracy's "third wave" brought redemocratization to Latin America during the 1980s, after a period of authoritarian rule. The trend toward democracy also spread to some Asian countries, such as the Philippines and South Korea, and by 1990 it also began to be felt in sub-Saharan Africa. The results of this democratization trend have been mixed so far. A recent survey by Freedom House shows a slight increase in freedom around the world during 2005. The most significant finding was a slight increase in freedom in the Middle East. Although Latin America has been the developing world's most successful region in establishing democracy, widespread dissatisfaction due to corruption, inequitable distribution of wealth, and threats to civil rights have produced a left wing, populist trend in the region's politics.

Africa's experience with democracy has also been varied since the third wave of democratization swept over the continent beginning in 1990. Although early efforts resulted in the ouster of many leaders, some of whom had held power for decades, and international pressure forced several countries to hold multiparty elections, political systems in Africa range from consolidating democracies to states mired in conflict. In 2004, South Africa, the continent's biggest success story, celebrated ten years of democracy with its third round of national elections. South Africa's successful democratic consolidation stands in sharp contrast to the circumstances in other parts of the continent, especially next door in Zimbabwe, where President Mugabe continues to rule through intimidation and manipulation. Nigeria's 2007 elections were marred by allegations of fraud and corruption, tainting the country's first experience of successive civilian governments. While the Democratic Republic of Congo held elections in 2006, the peace remains tenuous.

Political change has begun in the Middle East but it will be a long-term challenge. Debate about the role of Islam, its compatibility with democracy, and the power of Islamist groups will continue to influence progress toward democracy in the region as evidenced in both Iran and Turkey. Although welcomed by many Thais, Thailand's 2006 military coup demonstrates the lingering potential for military intervention into politics and demonstrates the fragility of democracy.

While there has been significant progress toward democratic reform around the world, there is no guarantee that these efforts will be sustained. Although there has been an increase in the percentage of the world's population living under democracy, nondemocratic regimes are still common. Furthermore, some semidemocracies have elections but citizens lack civil and political rights. International efforts to promote democracy have often tended to focus on elections rather than the long-term requirements of democratic consolidation. More effective ways of promoting and sustaining democracy must be found to expand freedom further in the developing world.

The 2005 Freedom House Survey

Progress in the Middle East

AILI PIANO AND ARCH PUDDINGTON

A modest but potentially significant increase in human rights and democratic freedoms in the countries of the Arab Middle East was the most notable development in the state of world freedom during 2005. This is the principal finding of *Freedom in the World 2006,* the index of global political rights and civil liberties issued annually by Freedom House.

According to the study, one Middle Eastern country, Lebanon, showed sufficient progress to warrant an improvement in its freedom designation from Not Free to Partly Free. A similar gain was registered by the Palestinian Authority.[1] Smaller improvements were registered by Iraq, Saudi Arabia, and Kuwait. In addition to the gains registered in the Arab world, the study showed important improvements in two majority-Muslim countries in Asia: Indonesia, which moved from Partly Free to Free, and Afghanistan, which advanced from Not Free to Partly Free. Improvement was also registered in a majority-Muslim

African country—Mauritania—whose status improved from Not Free to Partly Free.

Despite these gains, the Middle East continues to lag behind other regions on the Freedom House index. Only one Middle Eastern country, Israel, has a Free ranking, while 6 countries (and one territory) register as Partly Free, with 11 countries receiving Not Free ratings. Nevertheless, the gains for 2005 represent the most significant one-year improvements for the region since *Freedom in the World* began providing annual reports on the state of world freedom in 1972. The findings are a hopeful sign that the Middle East is showing a new openness to the democratic electoral competition and free institutions that have made so profound an impact on other world regions with strong traditions of authoritarian rule.

Significant change was registered in the former Soviet Union, despite the continued poor performance of Russia, whose freedom

---

Freedom in the World

Freedom in the World is an evaluation of political rights and civil liberties in the world that Freedom House has provided on an annual basis for over 30 years. (Established in New York in 1941, Freedom House is a nonprofit organization that monitors political rights and civil liberties around the world.) The survey assesses a country's freedom by examining its record in two areas: A country grants its citizens **political rights** when it permits them to form political parties that represent a significant range of voter choice and whose leaders can openly compete for and be elected to positions of power in government. A country upholds its citizens' **civil liberties** when it respects and protects their religious, ethnic, economic, linguistic, and other rights, including gender and family rights, personal freedoms, and freedoms of the press, belief, and association. The survey rates each country on a seven-point scale for both political rights and civil liberties (1 representing the most free and 7 the least free) and then divides the world into three broad categories: Free (countries whose ratings average 1.0 to 2.5); Partly Free (countries whose ratings average 3.0 to 5.0); and Not Free (countries whose ratings average 5.5 to 7.0).

The ratings, which are the product of a process that includes a team of 24 in-house and consultant writers and 19 senior academic scholars, are not merely assessments of the conduct of governments. Rather, they are intended to reflect the real-world rights and freedoms enjoyed by individuals as the result of actions by both state and nonstate actors. Thus, a country with a benign government facing violent forces (such as terrorist movements or insurgencies) hostile to an open society will be graded on the basis of the on-the-ground conditions that determine whether the population is able to exercise its freedoms. The survey enables scholars and policy makers both to assess the direction of global change annually and to examine trends in freedom over time and on a comparative basis across regions with different political and economic systems.

For more information about Freedom House's programs and publications please visit *www.freedomhouse.org.*

Note. The findings in this essay and accompanying table reflect global events from 1 December 2004 through 30 November 2005.

Table Independent Countries, Freedom in the World 2006: Comparative Measures of Freedom

Country	PR	CL	Freedom Rating	Country	PR	CL	Freedom Rating
Afghanistan	5	5 ▲	Partly Free	East Timor *	3	3	Partly Free
Albania *	3	3	Partly Free	Ecuador *	3	3	Partly Free
Algeria	6	5	Not Free	Egypt	6	5	Not Free
Andorra *	1	1	Free	El Salvador *	2	3	Free
Angola	6	5	Not Free	Equatorial Guinea	7	6	Not Free
Antigua & Barbuda *	2	2	Free	Eritrea	7	6	Not Free
Argentina *	2	2	Free	Estonia *	1	1	Free
Armenia	5	4	Partly Free	Ethiopia	5	5	Partly Free
Australia *	1	1	Free	Fiji	4	3	Partly Free
Austria *	1	1	Free	Finland *	1	1	Free
Azerbaijan	6	5	Not Free	France *	1	1	Free
Bahamas *	1	1	Free	Gabon	6 ▼	4	Partly Free
Bahrain	5	5	Partly Free	The Gambia	5 ▼	4	Partly Free
Bangladesh *	4	4	Partly Free	Georgia *	3	3 ▲	Partly Free
Barbados *	1	1	Free	Germany *	1	1	Free
Belarus	7	6	Not Free	Ghana *	1 ▲	2	Free
Belgium *	1	1	Free	Greece *	1	2	Free
Belize *	1	2	Free	Grenada *	1	2	Free
Benin *	2	2	Free	Guatemala *	4	4	Partly Free
Bhutan	6	5	Not Free	Guinea	6	5	Not Free
Bolivia *	3	3	Partly Free	Guinea-Bissau	3 ▲	4	Partly Free
Bosnia-Herzegovina	4	3	Partly Free	Guyana *	3 ▼	3 ▲	Partly Free
Botswana *	2	2	Free	Haiti	7	6	Not Free
Brazil *	2	2 ▲	Free	Honduras *	3	3	Partly Free
Brunei	6	5	Not Free	Hungary *	1	1	Free
Bulgaria *	1	2	Free	Iceland *	1	1	Free
Burkina Faso	5	3 ▲	Partly Free	India *	2	3	Free
Burma	7	7	Not Free	Indonesia *	2 ▲	3 ▲	Free
Burundi *	3 ▲	5	Partly Free	Iran	6	6	Not Free
Cambodia	6	5	Not Free	Iraq	6 ▲	5	Not Free
Cameroon	6	6	Not Free	Ireland *	1	1	Free
Canada *	1	1	Free	Israel *	1	2 ▲	Free
Cape Verde *	1	1	Free	Italy *	1	1	Free
Central African Republic *	5 ▲	4 ▲	Partly Free	Jamaica *	2	3	Free
Chad	6	5	Not Free	Japan *	1	2	Free
Chile *	1	1	Free	Jordan	5	4	Partly Free
China	7	6	Not Free	Kazakhstan	6	5	Not Free
Colombia *	3 ▲	3 ▲	Partly Free	Kenya *	3	3	Partly Free
Comoros *	4	4	Partly Free	Kiribati *	1	1	Free
Congo (Brazzaville)	5	5 ▼	Partly Free	Korea, South *	1	2	Free
Congo (Kinshasa)	6	6	Not Free	Kuwait	4	5	Partly Free
Costa Rica *	1	1	Free	Kyrgyzstan	5 ▲	4 ▲	Partly Free
Côte d'Ivoire	6	6	Not Free	Laos	7	6	Not Free
Croatia *	2	2	Free	Latvia *	1	1 ▲	Free
Cuba	7	7	Not Free	Lebanon	5 ▲	4 ▲	Partly Free
Cyprus *	1	1	Free	Lesotho *	2	3	Free
Czech Republic *	1	1	Free	Liberia	4 ▲	4	Partly Free
Denmark *	1	1	Free	Libya	7	7	Not Free
Djibouti	5	5	Partly Free	Liechtenstein *	1	1	Free
Dominica *	1	1	Free	Lithuania *	1 ▲	1 ▲	Free
Dominican Republic *	2	2	Free	Luxembourg *	1	1	Free

(continued)

Table Independent Countries, Freedom in the World 2006: Comparative Measures of Freedom *(continued)*

Country	PR	CL	Freedom Rating	Country	PR	CL	Freedom Rating
Macedonia *	3	3	Partly Free	Singapore	5	4	Partly Free
Madagascar *	3	3	Partly Free	Slovakia *	1	1	Free
Malawi *	4	4	Partly Free	Slovenia *	1	1	Free
Malaysia	4	4	Partly Free	Solomon Islands *	3	3	Partly Free
Maldives	6	5	Not Free	Somalia	6	7	Not Free
Mali *	2	2	Free	South Africa *	1	2	Free
Malta *	1	1	Free	Spain *	1	1	Free
Marshall Islands *	1	1	Free	Sri Lanka *	3	3	Partly Free
Mauritania	6	4 ▲	Partly Free	St. Kitts & Nevis *	1	1 ▲	Free
Mauritius *	1	2	Free	St. Lucia *	1	1 ▲	Free
Mexico *	2	2	Free	St. Vincent & the Grenadines *	2	1	Free
Micronesia *	1	1	Free				
Moldova *	3	4	Partly Free	Suriname *	2 ▼	2	Free
Monaco *	2	1	Free	Swaziland	7	5	Not Free
Mongolia *	2	2	Free	Sweden *	1	1	Free
Morocco	5	4	Partly Free	Switzerland *	1	1	Free
Mozambique *	3	4	Partly Free	Syria	7	7	Not Free
Namibia *	2	2 ▲	Free	Taiwan (Rep. of China) *	1	1	Free
Nauru *	1	1	Free	Tajikistan	6	5	Not Free
Nepal	6 ▼	5	Not Free	Tanzania	4	3	Partly Free
Netherlands *	1	1	Free	Thailand *	3 ▼	3	Partly Free
New Zealand *	1	1	Free	Togo	6	5	Not Free
Nicaragua *	3	3	Partly Free	Tonga	5	3	Partly Free
Niger *	3	3	Partly Free	Trinidad & Tobago *	3	2 ▲	Free
Nigeria *	4	4	Partly Free	Tunisia	6	5	Not Free
North Korea	7	7	Not Free	Turkey *	3	3	Partly Free
Norway *	1	1	Free	Turkmenistan	7	7	Not Free
Oman	6	5	Not Free	Tuvalu *	1	1	Free
Pakistan	6	5	Not Free	Uganda	5	4	Partly Free
Palau *	1	1	Free	Ukraine *	3 ▲	2 ▲	Free
Panama *	1	2	Free	United Arab Emirates	6	6	Not Free
Papua New Guinea *	3	3	Partly Free	United Kingdom *	1	1	Free
Paraguay *	3	3	Partly Free	United States *	1	1	Free
Peru *	2	3	Free	Uruguay *	1	1	Free
Philippines *	3 ▼	3	Partly Free	Uzbekistan	7	7 ▼	Not Free
Poland *	1	1	Free	Vanuatu *	2	2	Free
Portugal *	1	1	Free	Venezuela *	4 ▼	4	Partly Free
Qatar	6	5	Not Free	Vietnam	7	5 ▲	Not Free
Romania *	2 ▲	2	Free	Yemen	5	5	Partly Free
Russia	6	5	Not Free	Zambia	4	4	Partly Free
Rwanda	6	5	Not Free	Zimbabwe	7	6	Not Free
Samoa *	2	2	Free				
San Marino *	1	1	Free				
São Tomé & Príncipe *	2	2	Free				
Saudi Arabia	7	6 ▲	Not Free				
Senegal *	2	3	Free				
Serbia & Montenegro *	3	2	Free				
Seychelles *;	3	3	Partly Free				
Sierra Leone *	4	3	Partly Free				

PR and CL stand for Political Rights and Civil Liberties, respectively; 1 represents the most-free and 7 the least-free rating.

▲ ▼ up or down indicates an improvement or a worsening, respectively, in Political Rights or Civil Liberties since the last survey.

*indicates countries that are electoral democracies.

The Freedom Rating is an overall judgement based on survey results. See the box on p.120 for more details on the survey.

The ratings in this table reflect global events from 1 December 2004 through 30 November 2005.

ranking had declined from Partly Free to Not Free in 2004. Major gains were registered by Ukraine and Kyrgyzstan, with three other former Soviet republics showing less significant progress.

Otherwise, the study found no significant regional patterns for the past year. In the case of Latin America, the absence of a discernible trend was of some significance, given the degree of political volatility that has gripped countries such as Bolivia and Ecuador, as well as the continuing assault on democratic institutions mounted by the government of Venezuela's President Hugo Chávez. Venezuela did show a decline in its freedom score, but two important countries in the region registered modest improvements: Colombia, due to a strengthening of the rule of law and a decrease in the violence stemming from the country's long-running civil war, and Brazil, as a result of the political system's responsiveness to the need to fight corruption.

Globally, the state of freedom worldwide showed a slight net improvement from 2004 to 2005. The number of countries designated as Free was 89, or 46 percent of the world's total, the same number as the previous year. Fifty-eight countries (30 percent of the total) were designated as Partly Free, a net increase of 4. Forty-five countries (24 percent of the total) earned a Not Free designation, a net decrease of 4.

An analysis of regional patterns indicates that the Middle East and North Africa continue to lag behind other world regions when overall levels of freedom are measured. Figures for countries in the Americas are 24 Free, 9 Partly Free, and 2 (Cuba and Haiti) Not Free. For Central and Eastern Europe and the former Soviet Union, the breakdown is 13 Free, 7 Partly Free, and 7 Not Free. In the Asia-Pacific region, the survey figures show 16 countries as Free (a number of which are small island states), 12 as Partly Free, and 11 as Not Free. In Sub-Saharan Africa, the breakdown is 11 Free, 23 Partly Free, and 14 Not Free. And for Western Europe, the figures are 24 Free countries and 1, Turkey, which is Partly Free.

According to the survey, outright improvements in freedom status—that is, positive movement across the threshold separating Not Free from Partly Free, or Partly Free from Free—occurred in eight countries and one territory in 2005. Lebanon moved from Not Free to Partly Free due to successful parliamentary elections in May and a general improvement in the civil-liberties climate following large-scale, nonviolent protests against Syrian domination and the subsequent withdrawal of Syrian troops. The Palestinian Authority moved from Not Free to Partly Free due to an overall improvement in the political landscape that followed the election of Mahmoud Abbas to succeed the late Yasser Arafat as the territory's president, and the enhanced freedom of movement that followed Israel's abandonment of settlements in Gaza. Indonesia moved from Partly Free to Free as a result of peaceful and relatively free elections for regional leaders and for the presidency. Despite continuing problems in various regions of the country, Afghanistan saw its status move from Not Free to Partly Free because of a strengthening of civil society and a modest improvement in the rule of law and the holding of relatively successful parliamentary elections. The Central African Republic moved from Not Free to Partly Free due to successful elections and an improvement in freedoms of expression and assembly. Mauritania improved from Not Free to Partly Free due to an enhancement of the civil-liberties environment follow-

ing the overthrow of President Taya. Trinidad and Tobago moved from Partly Free to Free because of improvements in judicial independence and economic policies that enhanced equality of opportunity. Ukraine improved from Partly Free to Free due to overall changes in the political process and the civil-liberties environment following the Orange Revolution of December 2004. Kyrgyzstan moved from Not Free to Partly Free due to relatively free presidential elections and improvements in freedoms of expression and assembly.

Only four countries registered an outright decline in status. Here the most significant development was the downgrading of the Philippines from Free to Partly Free, a decision based on a corruption scandal surrounding the election of President Gloria Macapagal-Arroyo. Nepal declined from Partly Free to Not Free due to a "palace coup" in which the king dissolved parliament and declared a state of emergency. Thailand declined from Free to Partly Free because of a progressive weakening of opposition political parties and a lack of political competitiveness. Guyana declined from Free to Partly Free because of the growing influence of the illegal narcotics trade on the country's political system.

In addition to the countries that registered a status improvement in 2004, 19 countries showed gains in freedom that were insufficient to produce a change in their overall freedom designation: Brazil, Burkina Faso, Burundi, Colombia, Georgia, Ghana, Guinea-Bissau, Iraq, Israel, Latvia, Liberia, Lithuania, Namibia, Romania, St. Kitts and Nevis, St. Lucia, Saudi Arabia, Taiwan, and Vietnam. Meanwhile, six countries experienced a decline that did not merit a status change: Congo (Brazzaville), Gabon, Gambia, Suriname, Uzbekistan, and Venezuela.

Although the United States and the majority of countries in Western Europe registered the highest possible ratings on the freedom index—a 1 for both political rights and civil liberties—*Freedom in the World 2006* noted several looming problems in a number of these established democracies. The survey pointed to the increasingly widespread use of sophisticated forms of gerrymandering in the drawing of congressional-district boundaries in the United States as a weakness in that country's political process that has reduced competitiveness in congressional elections. At the same time, the survey findings revealed that several European countries are facing significant challenges to their democracies from a failure to effectively integrate non-European immigrants socially or economically, a problem whose most vivid reflection was the rioting that afflicted France during the past year.

Note

1. The Palestinian Authority appears not in the Freedom House table of sovereign countries, but in a separate listing of related and disputed territories.

AILI PIANO is managing editor of *Freedom in the World* and a senior researcher at Freedom House. **ARCH PUDDINGTON** is director of research at Freedom House. The survey will be published in book form as *Freedom in the World 2006* (Rowman & Littlefield) in the summer of 2006.

From *Journal of Democracy*, January 2006, pp. 119–124. Copyright © 2006 by National Endowment for Democracy and The Johns Hopkins University Press. Reprinted with permission of The Johns Hopkins University Press.

Whose Iran?

LAURA SECOR

The Mahestan mall in South Tehran is sometimes called "the honeycomb" of the Basij, the Iranian youth militia, because it is here that Basijis, as the militia members are known, buy and sell banners for the Shiite festival of Ashura, as well as religious books and posters. Somber, bearded young men in collarless shirts linger over tea behind stands selling tapes of religious singers—cult celebrities who belt out tear-jerking laments for the martyrdom of Hussein and make a small fortune performing at memorial services. Omid Malekian, a 28-year-old employee of a Tehran petrochemical refinery and the son of a carpenter, was shopping at Mahestan on Dec. 16, the day after Iran's elections for city councils and for the Assembly of Experts, the 86-member clerical board that will select the next supreme leader should anything happen to the current leader, Ayatollah *Ali Khamenei*. In the 2005 presidential election, Malekian voted for the winner, *Mahmoud Ahmadinejad*, and when I asked if he was happy with the president, he answered frankly.

"Sometimes I am analyzing myself and thinking, Oh, we have done wrong," he mused. "He is very popular and friendly with the people, but sometimes when he is expressing his ideas, he doesn't think about the future or the consequences. He is a simple man."

In particular, Malekian suggested that Ahmadinejad had been incautious in his promises to improve the economy— promises he has yet to keep. There was another area, too, in which Ahmadinejad had faltered: "About the Holocaust," he said. "I don't know much about it, but from the reaction of the world, it seems he should have said something different."

Still, Malekian said that he voted for the most severe fundamentalist among the candidates running for the clerical Assembly of Experts. The campaign turned on the competition between two incumbents, Ayatollah Taqi Mesbah-Yazdi— widely reputed to be Ahmadinejad's spiritual leader—and Ayatollah Ali Akbar Hashemi Rafsanjani, the pragmatic former president who lost the presidential race to Ahmadinejad in 2005. Each hoped to increase his share of the vote and thus his power on the assembly.

South Tehran is Ahmadinejad's heartland. It is here, in the less affluent neighborhoods of the city of 14 million where he was once mayor, that he rose from the obscure end of the seven-candidate roster in 2005, only to become one of the most popular figures in the Muslim world. Because liberal-minded Iranians boycotted the 2005 presidential election, and because Ahmadinejad so adeptly played the populist card, the militants, the unemployed and the cultural conservatives of neighborhoods like this one were in the driver's seat, steering the politics of this crucial nation while their opponents warned of their presumed doctrinaire views and political naïveté.

Early on, Ahmadinejad's faction was expected to win last month's elections handily. But the results contradicted the conventional wisdom about the Iranian electorate. The president put forward his own slate of candidates for the city councils. It was trounced. By some reckonings, reformists won two-fifths of the council seats and even dominated in some cities, including Kerman and Arak. Some conservative city-council candidates did well, particularly in Tehran, but they were not the conservatives associated with Ahmadinejad: rather, they belonged to the rival conservative faction of the current Tehran mayor, Mohammad Baqer Qalibaf. And most significant, the vote for Rafsanjani for the Assembly of Experts dwarfed that of Mesbah-Yazdi by nearly two to one. By mid-January, Ahmadinejad's isolation even within his own faction was complete: 150 of 290 members of parliament, including many of Ahmadinejad's onetime allies, signed a letter criticizing the president's economic policies for failing to stanch unemployment and inflation. A smaller group also blamed Ahmadinejad's inflammatory foreign-policy rhetoric for the *United Nations Security Council* resolution imposing sanctions on Iran. As if that were not enough, an editorial in Jomhouri Eslami, a newspaper that reflects the views of the supreme leader, accused the president of using the nuclear issue to distract the public from his failed policies. Ahmadinejad's behavior was diminishing popular support for the nuclear program, the editorial warned. The Iranian political system seems to be restoring its equilibrium by showing an extremist president the limits of his power. But is it an equilibrium that can hold?

In part, last month's election results reflected the complexity of Ahmadinejad's skeptical, conditional and diverse constituency. They also demonstrated his isolation within the powerful conservative establishment, whose politics, however opaque, are determinative. At its center, Khamenei commands a faction known as the traditional conservatives. No elected leader can serve, let alone execute a policy agenda, without the acquiescence of the supreme leader and his associates. But was Ahmadinejad one of the leader's associates? Or was he, like his predecessor, Khatami, something of a political rival? The answer to this question should determine the extent to which Ahmadinejad's foreign-policy extremism and authoritarian tendencies are taken seriously as a political program. But it is a puzzle that has vexed political analysts since the president took office in August 2005, bringing with him a faction that was largely new to the post-revolutionary political scene. Composed partly of military and paramilitary elements, partly of extremist clerics like Mesbah-Yazdi and partly of inexperienced new conservative politicians, those in Ahmadinejad's faction are often called "neoconservatives." But to the extent that they have an ideology, it is less new than old, harking back to the early days of the Islamic republic. Since that time, the same elite has largely run Iranian politics, though it has divided itself into competing factions, and the act of wielding power has mellowed many hard-liners into pragmatists. Ahmadinejad's faction, on the other hand, came into power speaking the language of the past but with the zeal of the untried.

In 2005, many analysts believed that Ahmadinejad's elevation to the presidency must have been sanctioned by the supreme leader—indeed, that it reflected a hardening agenda among the traditional conservatives. He would be the "secretary" of Khamenei, a number of reformists said to me that summer in Tehran. But the way Ahmadinejad governed was nothing if not divisive. He undertook the most far-reaching governmental housecleaning since the revolution itself, reportedly replacing as many as 20,000 bureaucrats. And when it came time for the elections last month, he offered his own slates of candidates, disdaining to ally himself with the traditional conservatives or with anyone else. For the Assembly of Experts, Ahmadinejad endorsed a ticket of scholars from what is known as the Haqqani circle, a group of clerics who cleave strongly to the notion of the divine state and disdain popular sovereignty and democracy.

The senior figure in this circle, Mesbah-Yazdi, already belonged to the assembly. But in the fall of 2006, buoyed by association with the populist president, his group put forward a wave of candidates in a bid to transform the assembly. Even after the Guardian Council—an appointed body that answers to the supreme leader and that vets candidates and legislation—had disqualified almost half the proposed candidates, including most of the reformists and a large number of Mesbah-Yazdi's students, clerics associated with Mesbah-Yazdi still stood a reasonable chance of winning dozens of the 86 seats. It was here that the ideological contest of the Ahmadinejad presidency was starkest. Were the public and the leadership ready to accept Mesbah-Yazdi's brand of extremism along with the populism Ahmadinejad had served up? And what did it mean if they were not?

The 97-mile stretch of highway from Tehran southwest to Qom passes through a cratered landscape of magnificent desolation to the basin between a salt marsh and a desert at the foot of the Zagros Mountains. Middle-class, educated Tehranis often scorn and even fear Qom as the center of religious Puritanism and political repression. But for pious Shiites in Iran and elsewhere, the city is a pilgrimage destination, home to one of the holiest Shiite shrines, most of the living Shiite marjas (senior religious figures, literally "sources of imitation") and more than 50 seminaries, institutions that long pre-existed universities in Iran and where the works of the Greek philosophers have for centuries been studied alongside religious texts. Students, who number some 40,000, enter Qom at an average age of 17. Some of them continue their studies for decades, as Shiite religious learning has no set end point. Since the Islamic revolution, the seminary city has thrived as the government has spent lavishly on mosques and dormitories, nearly all with the same pale brick and blue tile facades. In recent years, Qom has absorbed waves of Shiite immigrants from Afghanistan and Iraq. There is an Iraqi bazaar not far from the holy shrine, and the sight of men in Arab dishdashas is commonplace.

Mesbah-Yazdi has a major presence here in the form of the Imam Khomeini Institute, the enormous seminary of which Mesbah-Yazdi is the head scholar. It holds Iran's most extensive library of scholarly books in English, totaling 11,200 volumes. It is the envy of the universities in Tehran. Mesbah-Yazdi, a fellow cleric told me, believed that it was important to understand Western ideas to better resist and refute them.

Born in 1934, Mesbah-Yazdi is an éminence grise among the ayatollahs of Qom, but age has not mellowed him. In the last decade he has become famous less for his learned philosophical exegeses (he posts his entry in the Routledge Encyclopedia of Philosophy on his Web site) than for his jeremiads at Friday prayers against popular sovereignty, free speech, women's rights and Islamic reform. Public execution and flogging are "a basic principle of Islam," Mesbah-Yazdi has said, and the government should regulate the content of speech "just as it checks the distribution of adulterated or contaminated foodstuffs." Because "Mesbah" sounds like the Farsi word for crocodile, he is known by his critics as Ayatollah Crocodile. (A cartoonist was once imprisoned for depicting him as a reptile, shedding crocodile tears as he strangled a dissident writer with his tail.)

At Ahmadinejad's invitation, members of Mesbah-Yazdi's Haqqani circle occupy several key government posts. But before Ahmadinejad came to power, they had been pushed mostly to the margins of Iranian politics, where they complained bitterly about the efforts of the reformist Khatami and his colleagues to advance their agenda through the elected branches of government. To the Haqqani scholars, it seemed that the reformists were challenging the doctrine of velayat-i-faqih, which is based on the sovereign power of the chief jurist, the supreme leader. "We shall wait to see what place these foxes who claim to be the supporters of reform will occupy in hell," Mesbah-Yazdi proclaimed. If Iranians believed in their supreme leader as the agent of God, second-guessing his judgment through elections was tantamount to holding a referendum on whether or not Damavand was the highest peak in Iran. What if 51 percent of the public said that it was not? "It doesn't matter what the people think," Mesbah-Yazdi was quoted as saying. "The people are ignorant sheep." He has also said, "Islam was the government of God, not the government of the people."

Mesbah-Yazdi's most open and media-friendly acolyte, Ayatollah Mohsen Gharavian, did not put the matter quite so strongly when, draped in the encompassing Iranian chador, I met with him in an unadorned office at a small seminary on one of Qom's dusty side streets.

"In the name of God, the beneficent and merciful," Gharavian intoned, "before coming to the main question and answer, I want to know where you got this chador. Is it from the United States or Iran?"

From Iran, I told him.

"Congratulations on seeing you in a very Islamic manner," Gharavian replied.

For a cleric who had been quoted as saying that despotism was not all bad and that public opinion was meaningless, Gharavian, who teaches philosophy at the Imam Khomeini Institute, did not have a severe presence. Rather, he was a big, courteous man of 54 with a reddish beard. The election to the Assembly of Experts was just a day away, and Gharavian was the hard-line candidate for the hard-line city of Qom. Still, he expected to lose, and he did lose. Amiably, he remarked that he had run and lost before, and that to win would have required a financial outlay of which he disapproved.

When it came to politics, he spoke mostly in evasions and platitudes. Democracy, he explained, was acceptable within the boundaries of Islam, and human rights were contained within Islam, but such rights should not include freedom of worship or freedom to believe things that are untrue or unwise. (His examples were the misguided beliefs of Nietzsche and Machiavelli.) The Islamic penal code required no modification in the modern era; its harshest punishments, he asserted, were no more violent than some American and European spectator sports. He appeared shocked by the suggestion that Iran held political prisoners and demanded an example. I offered the journalist Akbar Ganji, imprisoned for six years on account of his critical writings. Gharavian replied: "Did you read Mr. Ganji's manifesto? He questioned the whole establishment." Freedom of expression, he explained, did not include the freedom to "breach the peace of the society." He demanded, "Don't you have prisoners in your country?"

Mesbah-Yazdi's statements on most of these matters were a matter of public record, and they were even blunter. "If someone tells you he has a new interpretation of Islam, hit him in the mouth," he said in 2000. Two years later, he said, "The prophets of God did not believe in pluralism. They believed that only one idea was right." On Sept. 4, 1999, he said: "Killing hypocrites does not require a court order, as it is a duty imposed by the Shariah on all genuine Muslims. The order of Islam is to throw them down from a high mountain and kill them outright." He spoke the following month of the need to break the unnecessary taboo on violence.

If such a taboo existed in the Islamic republic, it had been broken. That year, a string of dissidents were murdered under suspicious circumstances. In the writings that led to his prison sentence, Ganji accused Mesbah-Yazdi of sanctifying such actions with whispered fatwas and members of the Haqqani circle of direct involvement in the murders. A member of the shadowy vigilante group Ansar-e *Hezbollah*, which had violently attacked student demonstrators in July 1999, lent credence to Ganji's claims with videotaped testimony in which he said that Mesbah-Yazdi had encouraged the group to assassinate a reformist politician. "Now, on the issue of whether I authorized the assassination of individuals," Mesbah-Yazdi declared unapologetically in March 2001, "I must say that Imam Khomeini, may God be satisfied with him, issued a decree saying that shedding Salman Rushdie's blood was a religious obligation and, therefore, he advocated resorting to violence as well."

Why Ahmadinejad would ally himself with these clerics remains something of a mystery. Contrary to popular belief, says Nasser Hadian, a political scientist at Tehran University and a childhood friend of the president, Ahmadinejad never expounded a particularly conservative moral or social agenda. Rather, says Hadian, Ahmadinejad was and continues to be inspired above all by Ali Shariati, the mid-20th-century theorist of radical Islamic egalitarianism. The president's agenda is redistributionist and anti-imperialist, Hadian says. That doesn't make him a democrat. Nonetheless, "he is basically using Mesbah," Hadian says. It is an alliance of political convenience.

Alireza Haghighi, a political scientist who teaches at the University of Toronto at Mississauga, agrees that the association between Ahmadinejad and Mesbah-Yazdi has been overstated. But in an article he wrote with his colleague Victoria Tahmasebi in International Journal, Haghighi documented yet another Ahmadinejad genesis story. Young Ahmadinejad led a politically and religiously conservative Islamist student group during the Islamic Revolution, the writers claim. When the leftist Islamist students proposed seizing the American Embassy in 1979, Ahmadinejad opposed the action as imprudent, but he suggested that if they went ahead with it, they should seize the Soviet Embassy as well. His plan rejected, Ahmadinejad found himself excluded from historic events and spurned by the Islamic left, which was at that time a powerful faction within the regime. His opposition to that faction ossified into a vendetta.

Soon after Khomeini's death, the Islamic left lost the factional battle for dominance. Its members wandered eight years in the political wilderness before returning as the reform movement. That, too, Ahmadinejad was anxious to crush. In that aspiration he would have found ample common ground with the Haqqani circle.

As president, Ahmadinejad looked to the extreme right rather than seeking allies among the traditional conservatives, and in so doing, he exposed himself politically. "They were very arrogant," Hadian said of Ahmadinejad and his camp. "They didn't want to make any compromises. He has stood against the entire political structure in Iran, not inviting any of them, even the conservatives, to be partners. You don't see them in the cabinet; you don't see them in political positions."

And for that there was a price to be paid. This fall, Rafsanjani, who had suffered a humiliating defeat at Ahmadinejad's hands in the presidential election of 2005, was reportedly persuaded to run again for the Assembly of Experts by the supreme leader or people close to him. Rafsanjani is a divisive figure in Iranian politics. He is widely perceived as a kingmaker, the power behind the rise of Khamenei to the position of supreme leader and that of Khatami to the presidency. But though he remains highly respected among clerics, Rafsanjani is not a beloved figure in Iranian public life. During his presidency, he adopted an economic liberalization program that involved extremely unpopular austerity measures; meanwhile, through pistachio exports, he had himself become one of the richest men in Iran. Political and social repression did not ease until Khatami, his successor, came into office.

Nonetheless, in the Assembly of Experts elections in December, Rafsanjani emerged as the compromise candidate of the reformists and traditional conservatives. One reformist activist described him to me as the very last line of defense against the extreme right. And Rafsanjani delivered a staggering blow, winning nearly twice as many votes as Mesbah-Yazdi. The neoconservatives, it seemed, had been slapped down much the same way the reformists had: the traditional conservatives had decided that the threat they posed was intolerable, and the voters had decided that the president associated with them could not deliver on his promises.

On the morning of Election Day, Dec. 15, there were long lines outside the polling places in central and east Tehran. A crowd milled about the front courtyard of Masjed al Nabi, a large mosque in the east. There were children, a television camera and a seller of balloons in the shape of rabbit ears. A middle-aged couple stood by the sinks normally used for ablutions; the woman wore a long, tailored raincoat and a conservative black scarf. Her husband explained that the election was very important to them. "We are choosing our future," he said through an interpreter. He was too sick, really, to move, but he had told his doctor that he could not forgo his civic duty to participate in the election.

Then I asked him if he saw big differences among the candidates for Assembly of Experts. "No," he said, "they are all the same."

What about the ones for city council?

"No," he replied. "They are all the same, too."

It is nearly impossible to have a political discussion with only one person on an Iranian street. Outside Masjed al Nabi, the first interloper was a clean-cut 35-year-old man in a plaid shirt who gave his name as Ali. "How can you say they are all the same?" he nearly shouted at the man who had been speaking. "We have candidates who are like the Taliban and others who are practically liberals. We have candidates who think women should be free and others who do not think so at all."

"I never heard of a thing like that," the first man said calmly. "The country has laws to decide these matters."

To my right, a woman in a chador heatedly exclaimed: "He's right! How can you say they are all the same? That's why we're here to vote, because they are all different. Our new president, Ahmadinejad, before the election he said women were free and equal. Now he says we should just make babies. Because he wanted our votes, he said good things."

The original couple took advantage of the hubbub to slip away. Mohammad, a 37-year-old in a running jacket, pushed his way into our circle. "I am not voting," he told me. "I want to choose my freedom. I don't want to vote for them. I'm sure that whether I vote or not, it makes no difference. I don't accept the Constitution of this country, and I hope I can change it without voting."

Ali was listening intently. "The people who are good in this thing accept the vote of the people not just for show and not just on Election Day," he told Mohammad. "Even in America it is the same; everywhere in the world it is. Everywhere in the world there are some people who are pro-democracy and others who are against it. Now people are more educated. One day, our democracy will be better than democracy in the United States, if we believe in it. We like our religion, our imams, God and Islam. We want democracy next to this. We don't believe in democracy and freedom the way it exists in other parts of the world. We want something of our own."

It was 5 o'clock when I left the crowded mosques of middle-class central and east Tehran for the deserted polling places of the affluent northern hills. In Tajrish, an election official told me that he had seen just 200 voters—far fewer than in the presidential election less than two years ago. "All the mullahs are the same," he confided. "Everything always gets worse. Ahmadinejad is like a catalyst, speeding it up. The philosophical foundation of the state is not good."

The debates among ordinary voters go to the heart of a structural weakness in the Iranian state. Founded on two conflicting ideas—the sovereignty of the people and divinely inspired clerical rule—the Islamic Republic of Iran has suffered from a decade-long crisis of legitimacy. Nothing forced that crisis quite the way the reform movement did, despite, or perhaps even because of, its cautious temperament and legalistic methods. Over the course of Khatami's presidency, Iranians were faced with an inevitable question: What use was a supreme leader in a democracy, and what use were elections in a theocracy? The rise of Ahmadinejad, then his comeuppance, have forced those questions from the other direction. How far could the conservatives go in the authoritarian direction, and if not all the way, why not?

"In a sense, many people, including myself, we believe that Mesbah is right," Sadegh Zibakalam, a reformist Tehran University professor, reflected when I visited him at his mother's home in north Tehran in December. "Trying to make an amalgam of Western, liberal, democratic ideas and Shiite theology is nonsense. It doesn't work."

Later, he added: "Either Khamenei is infallible, or he's not. If he's not, then he is an ordinary person like Bush or Blair, answerable to the Parliament and the people. If he is, then we should throw away all this nonsense about Western values and liberal democracy. Either we have Western liberal philosophy, republican government and checks and balances, or we should stick to Mesbah. But to combine them? Imam Khomeini was so popular and charismatic. People rallied behind him and believed he was infallible. We never thought, What if the supreme leader is not supported by the people? The answer to this was brilliantly made by Mesbah: to hell with them."

Zibakalam described Mesbah-Yazdi's reading of velayat-i-faqih as a radical version of the one first proposed by Ayatollah *Ruhollah Khomeini*. But when I looked back through the lectures in which Khomeini first delineated the theory in Najaf in 1970, I found a vision strikingly similar to Mesbah-Yazdi's. At that time, Khomeini had little luck with popular sovereignty. He quoted the Koran and sayings attributed to Muhammad: "The prophet has higher claims on the believers than their own selves" and "The scholars are the heirs of the prophet." The only legitimate legislation was that which had already been made by God, and this would be administered by the learned jurist, who would rule over the people like a guardian over a child.

Nine years later, from his Paris exile during the revolution, Khomeini would approve a constitution drafted by more liberal associates. It was the blueprint for a parliamentary democracy, in which a council of clergymen would play an advisory role. This draft became the basis for the debate that occupied the first Assembly of Experts, convened to revise and approve a final constitution. After much discussion of the contradictions it engendered, the experts, many of them clerics, nonetheless yoked velayat-i-faqih to the republican structure they had been handed.

To this day, the structure of the Iranian state remains too liberal for the authoritarians and too authoritarian for the liberals, but the traditional conservatives at the center of power cannot resolve this obvious paradox at the republic's heart without relinquishing their own position. The best they could do was to revise the Constitution after Khomeini's death, greatly expanding the powers of the clerical councils and of the supreme leader at the expense of the elected offices.

Clerics I spoke to from the traditional conservative camp associated with Khamenei were paternalistic in their view of the state rather than outright authoritarian. They seemed to genuinely believe in a limited form of popular sovereignty—guided, of course, by Islamic scholars so that the people would not fall into error but nonetheless necessary for the legitimacy of the state.

It was this traditional conservative establishment that the reformists, many of them clerics, hoped to transform by introducing new policies through the legal channels of the state and by persuading jurists to assimilate new ideas about rights and freedoms into their interpretations of the sacred texts. One of the leading reformist theorists, Mohammad Mojtahed Shabestari, explained to me: "Many nations have influenced our jurisprudence. We could set aside some of the decrees of Islam today and bring some Western laws to replace them. This doesn't make us infidels."

After eight years in power, the reform movement found itself blocked by the conservative establishment, hamstrung by its own mistakes and unwilling or unable to shore up the failing economy. Ahmadinejad rose in its wake, campaigning not on ideological extremism but on populist blandishments. He would ease the financial pain of his countrymen, he promised, by bringing Iran's oil wealth to the people's tables.

As Omid Malekian had intimated to me at the Mahestan shopping mall, however, this was not a promise to make lightly. The Iranian economy has been mismanaged at least since the revolution, and to fix it would require measures no populist would be willing to take. Under Ahmadinejad, inflation has risen; foreign investors have scorned Iranian markets, fearing political upheaval or foreign invasion; the Iranian stock market has plummeted; Iranian capital has fled to Dubai. Voters I talked to pointed to the prices of ordinary foodstuffs when they wanted to explain their negative feelings about the government. According to Iranian news sources, from January to late August 2006 the prices of fruits and vegetables in urban areas rose by 20 percent. A month later, during Ramadan, the price of fruit reportedly doubled while that of chicken rose 10 percent in mere days. Housing prices in Tehran have reached a record high. Unemployment is still widespread. And Ahmadinejad's approval rating, as calculated by the official state television station, had dipped to 35 percent in October.

Iran is not a poor country. It is highly urbanized and modern, with a sizable middle class. Oil revenues, which Iran has in abundance, should be channeling plenty of hard currency into the state's coffers, and in fact the economy's overall rate of growth is healthy and rising. But as Parvin Alizadeh, an economist at London Metropolitan University, explained to me, what ultimately matters is how the state spends its influx of wealth. The Iranian government has tried to create jobs swiftly and pacify the people by spending the oil money on new government-run projects. But these projects are not only overmanned and inefficient, like much of the country's bloated and technologically backward public sector; they also increase the demand for consumer goods and services, driving up inflation.

Ahmadinejad has continued this trend. He has generated considerable personal good will in poorer communities, but hardly anyone I asked could honestly say that their lives had gotten better during his presidency. He fought to lower interest rates, which drove up lending, leading to inflation and capital flight. The government cannot risk infuriating the public with the austerity measures that would be required in order to solve its deep-rooted economic problems. But as long as its short-term fixes continue to fail, the government will go on being unpopular. The last two presidents have lost their constituencies over this issue. And so officials seek to distract people from their economic woes with ideological posturing and anti-Western rhetoric. Not only has this lost its cachet with much of the Iranian public, it also serves to compound Iran's economic problems by blackening its image abroad. "Iran has not sorted out its basic problem, which is to be accepted in the international community as a respectable government," Alizadeh said. "Investors do not take it seriously. This is a political crisis, not an economic crisis."

For a Western traveler in Iran these days, it is hard to avoid a feeling of cognitive dissonance. From a distance, the Islamic republic appears to be at its zenith. But from the street level, Iran's grand revolutionary experiment is beset with fragility. The state is in a sense defined by its contradictions, both constitutional and economic. It cannot be truly stable until it resolves them, and yet if it tries to do so, it may not survive.

LAURA SECOR, an editor of the New York Times Op-Ed page, writes about international affairs.

Turkey Face West

**Rebuffed by the European Union, angered by U.S. policies
in the Middle East, and governed by an Islamist political party,
Turkey seems to have every reason to turn its back on the West.
To most Turks, however, that would be inconceivable.**

SOLI ÖZEL

In most countries, the news that one of their own has been awarded a Nobel Prize is an occasion for universal pride and self-congratulation. That was not the case when the renowned Turkish novelist Orhan Pamuk received the Nobel Prize for Literature this past October. Many Turks still angrily remembered Pamuk's controversial assertion in a Swiss newspaper in 2005 that "a million Armenians and thirty thousand Kurds have been killed in this land," which provided fodder for allegations that Ottoman Turkey had committed genocide against Armenians during and after World War I. The Turkish government scandalously put Pamuk on trial for defaming "Turkishness," provoking a public outcry in Turkey and abroad before he won acquittal in 2006. When the news of the Nobel broke, some Turks could barely hide their resentment and spite. For them the prize was simply a function of Pamuk's political views, which, in their view, he had expressed only to curry favor in the West and secure the Nobel.

Those with clearer minds rejoiced in Pamuk's accomplishment. By honoring him, the Swedish Academy had acknowledged the Western part of modern Turkey's identity. It cited his literary achievements as a master novelist who transformed the literary form and in the process helped to make East and West more intelligible to each other. Still, the unhealthy reaction by a sizable portion of the Turkish public spoke volumes about the country's current state of mind toward the West.

The West certainly has given Turks a great deal to think about. Indeed, less than two hours before the Academy notified Pamuk of the great honor he had received, the French National Assembly staged its own crude attack on freedom of expression by passing a resolution making it a crime to deny that Ottoman Turkey was guilty of genocide against the Armenians. In September came Pope Benedict XVI's infamous lecture at the University of Regensburg, in which he infuriated Muslims around the world by quoting a Byzantine emperor: "Show me just what Muhammad brought that was new, and there you will find things only evil and inhuman, such as his command

to spread by the sword the faith he preached." Then, in mid-December, came the cruelest cut of all. The European Union announced the suspension of negotiations on eight of 35 policy issues that must be addressed before Turkey can complete the long EU accession process begun in 2004, bringing accession to a virtual halt. Even worse from the Turkish perspective was the intensity with which some European states suddenly objected to Turkey's membership, a matter that presumably had been settled in 2004. Many Turks saw the decision as yet another example of the EU's double standard in its dealings with its Muslim applicant.

In the past when the Turks were upset with Europe, they turned to the United States. Ankara and Washington have a history of close relations dating to the Cold War, when the Soviet Union loomed menacingly over its southern neighbor. Turkish troops fought alongside the Americans during the Korean War, and Turkey joined NATO in 1952. In the post-Cold War era, the United States was an enthusiastic supporter of the recently completed Baku-Ceyhan pipeline that carries oil from Azerbaijan to the Turkish port of Ceyhan on the Mediterranean, making Turkey a significant energy player while reducing Western dependence on Russia. When Turkey faced a severe economic crisis in 2001, the United States used its clout to convince the International Monetary Fund to assist Ankara.

But the Iraq war opened a rift. The Bush administration was embittered by Turkey's refusal to allow the deployment of U.S. troops in the country to open a northern front against Iraq. Ankara was angered by Washington's hard-nosed policies and alarmed by the potential for upheaval among its own traditionally restive Kurdish population created by events in the Kurdish areas of Iraq. And many Turks believe, along with other Muslims, that the United States is leading a crusade against Muslims. Anti-Americanism has begun to consume the Turkish public. The latest German Marshall Fund survey of transatlantic trends found that only seven percent of Turks approve of President George W. Bush's policies.

Turkey's unique experiment in Westernization was already under intense scrutiny in the post-9/11 world, and these latest blows have led many to question whether that experiment will continue. Will the Turks drift away from the path of Westernizing modernization? The answer to this question, if it implies that Turkey may take a U-turn from its chosen path, is empathically no.

The Turkish experiment, after all, is two centuries old, having begun with the decision of Sultan Mahmud II (1784–1839) to meet the challenge of a rising Europe with a thorough reform of the Ottoman Empire. Under Mahmud and his successors, the reforms included legal equality for all subjects of the empire, extension of private property rights, reform of the educational system, and the restructuring of the military and the notoriously ponderous Ottoman bureaucracy. With the determined leadership of Kemal Atatürk, the elite that founded the Turkish Republic on the ashes of the empire in 1923 pursued a more radical modernization, with a staunch secularism as its mainstay. Religion would be subjugated to the state and relegated strictly to the private sphere. Turkey under Atatürk replaced its alphabet and civil law virtually overnight; even the way men and women dressed was reformed.

Turkish democracy traces its practical origins to 1950, when an opposition party defeated the incumbent Republican Party and peacefully assumed power. As politicians became more responsive to popular sentiment, religion returned to the public realm and the Turkish military took it upon itself to serve as the primary custodian of the secular republican order. In its name, the army staged four direct or indirect military interventions; the last of these was the so-called postmodern coup of February 28, 1997, in which it mobilized public opinion and the news media to force the resignation of a coalition government led by the Islamist Welfare Party.

Yet significant political and economic changes were under way by the beginning of the 1990s. In the past decade and a half, the country has progressed in modernizing its economy, liberalizing its political system, and deepening its democratic order. Trade, financial flows, and investment increasingly integrate Turkey into world markets. Office towers are rising over Istanbul, which has recovered the cosmopolitan reputation it enjoyed in Ottoman times. "Cool Istanbul," as the global media sometimes call it, is a center for investment capital from East and West, a gateway to Central Asia, and a magnet for affluent sophisticates drawn by its prosperity, its spectacular nightlife, and its museums and other cultural riches.

Throughout Turkey, the burgeoning market economy is rapidly breaking down traditional economic habits and drawing in ordinary Turks, breeding more individualistic attitudes and spreading middle-class values, even as many embrace religious piety. The results can be paradoxical. In a recent survey by the Turkish Economic and Social Studies Foundation, 45 percent of Turks identified themselves first as Muslims rather than Turks, up from 36 percent in 1999. Yet support for the adoption of sharia—Islamic law—fell from 21 percent to nine percent, and the percentage of women who said they wore an Islamic headscarf declined by more than a quarter, to 11.4 percent. It is no small part of the Turkish paradox that the rush toward reform

and the EU is being led by the Islamist Justice and Development Party (AKP), which won control of parliament in November 2002 and installed the current prime minister, Recep Tayyip Erdoğan, the following March.

All of these changes have been accompanied by a somewhat painful process of self-inspection. International conferences held in Turkey on the tragic fate of the Ottoman Empire's Armenian population, the status of the Kurds (the country's main ethnic minority), and the role of Islam in modern Turkey's social and political life are emblematic of the new openness. Turkish society is increasingly pluralistic. After decades of state control, there are now more than 300 television and 1,000 radio stations on the air, broadcasting everything from hard rock to Turkish folklore, from BBC reports to Islamic and Kurdish newscasts. The questioning of established dogmas has generated intense debates. Turkish modernity, long a top-down phenomenon directed by the heirs of Atatürk, is being reshaped and redefined at the societal level. Inevitably, tensions, contradictions, and disagreements over the nation's direction abound.

The Turkish debate over Westernization has never been a winner-take-all contest between supposedly pure Westernizers and retrograde Muslims. The strategic aim of Atatürk and other founding fathers of the Turkish Republic in 1923 was to be part of the European system of states, just as the Ottomans had been. Yet even among committed Westernizers there were lines that could not be transgressed, and suspicions that could not be erased when it came to dealing with the West. After all, the Republic had been founded after a bitter struggle amid the rubble of the empire against occupying Western armies. Its founding myths had an undertone of anti-imperialist cum anti-Western passion.

In his remarkable book of autobiographical essays on his hometown, Istanbul: Memories and the City (2005), Orhan Pamuk observes that "when the empire fell, the new Republic, while certain of its purpose, was unsure of its identity; the only way forward, its founders thought, was to foster a new concept of Turkishness, and this meant a certain cordon sanitaire to shut it off from the rest of the world. It was the end of the grand polyglot multicultural Istanbul of the imperial age. . . . The cosmopolitan Istanbul I knew as a child had disappeared by the time I reached adulthood."

In all his work, Pamuk reflects on the Turkish ordeal of Westernization. In Istanbul, he notes that "with the drive to Westernize and the concurrent rise of Turkish nationalism, the love-hate relationship with the Western gaze became all the more convoluted." The Republic sought to Westernize, be part of the European universe, but kept its guard up against Western encroachments and did not quite trust its partners-to-be. Today, the nationalist reflexes of Atatürk's heirs—the secularist republican elites in the military, the judiciary, the universities, and among the old professional and bureaucratic classes—arguably play as large a role in the blossoming anti-Western sentiment as the Islamist political parties and the more religious segment of the population. These old elites are keenly aware of their ebbing power amid the transformative effects of the market economy and democratization.

Yet it is also easy to overstate the degree of anti-Western animus. Ordinarily, the Turkish public sees itself as a mediator between "civilizations," to use the fashionable term of the day, and believes profoundly in its historical right to such a role. This self-confidence is a function of its long association with the West and the secular-democratic nature of its political order. As if to illustrate this sense of mission, Prime Minister Erdoğan stood on a podium in Istanbul this past November beside his Spanish counterpart, José Luis Rodríguez Zapatero—in symbolic terms, the two heirs to leadership of the contending Muslim and Christian superpowers of the past—along with UN secretary general Kofi Annan, Archbishop Desmond Tutu, and former Iranian president Muhammad Khatami, to launch the idea of an "Alliance of Civilizations."

Pope Benedict's highly publicized visit to Turkey in December offered a more surprising illustration of the limits of Turkish anti-Westernism. Erdoğan, a strong critic of the pope's Regensburg speech who also has a politician's exquisite sensitivity to the public mood, initially decided to stay away from the country while Benedict was there. Once the debate in Turkey intensified, however, those who believed that the prime minister had to meet with this important visitor gained the upper hand. Erdoğan rescheduled his departure for a NATO summit in Latvia and, in a gesture that took everyone by surprise, greeted the pope on the tarmac.

The visit itself went exceedingly well (except for the residents of Ankara and Istanbul, who suffered the torturous inconveniences of maximum security for the pope). Protest rallies organized by fundamentalist political parties failed to draw the predicted multitudes, and widely feared disruptions by radical groups did not materialize. Benedict met with Turkey's highest official religious leader, Professor Ali Erdoğan, and removed his shoes and faced Mecca to pray alongside Istanbul's most senior religious official at the famed Blue Mosque. Most remarkably, the pope, who spoke in Turkish on several occasions, reportedly told the prime minister that he looked favorably upon Turkey's accession to the EU—an extraordinary turnabout for a man who had vehemently objected to such an eventuality when he was a cardinal. His earlier vision of the EU, shared by many Europeans, was of a Christian union rather than one in which membership is obtained when objective and secular criteria are fulfilled.

It was a supreme irony that just as the pope was giving such warm messages, the EU was preparing to deliver its blow, virtually slamming the door on what has been Turkey's great national object—a project that has enjoyed the steady support of some 70 percent of the population.

Ostensibly, the break is a result of Turkey's refusal to open its seaports and airports to traffic from the Greek part of Cyprus, because of the still-unresolved conflict between it and the Turkish north. But most EU insiders acknowledge that this is a fig leaf behind which France, the Netherlands, Denmark, and other countries are trying to conceal their desire to keep Muslim Turkey out of the Union.

For many Turks (as others), entry into the EU is not just the final destination of a journey they undertook a long time ago. It is also a test of Europe's own universalist and multiculturalist claims, a symbol of the prospects for harmonious relations between different faiths. A snubbing of Turkey that is perceived as religiously based will have repercussions throughout the Muslim world, including Europe's own Muslim immigrant communities. In the words of the Newsweek correspondent in Istanbul, "Not so long ago, it seemed that Europe would overcome prejudice and define itself as an ideology rather than a geography, a way of being in the world rather than a mere agglomeration of nation-states. But that chance is now lost."

Yet it is hardly the case that all is lost for Turkey, or that it must now turn its back on the West. The transformations of recent decades have put the country firmly on a modernizing path, as the example of the governing AKP itself illustrates. Founded by current prime minister Erdoğan, Abdullah Gül (his foreign minister), and others, the AKP grew out of a split in the Islamist movement in the 1990s. Erdoğan and his allies in the younger generation broke away from the more conservative and ideological (and anti-EU) group. The AKP retained a great deal of support from the traditional constituencies of the Islamist parties. But there was now a new and dynamic constituency that made a bid for increased power in the economic and political system. Turkey's market reforms had propelled a new generation of provincial entrepreneurs who had prospered in the newly competitive and open economy. They were part of a globalizing economy, and were eager to get a bigger share of the economic pie and to pursue EU membership. Also attracted to the AKP were the recent arrivals from the countryside, who lived and worked on the periphery of the major cities and suddenly found themselves with new and different interests.

The AKP won an overwhelming majority in the 2002 parliamentary elections. The exhaustion of the established elites—in particular, their failure to manage the Turkish economy and reform the political system to make it more responsive to the demands of a fast-modernizing society—along with the electorate's desire to punish the incumbents, played a prominent role in the AKP'S success. The promise the party's rise to power held for a better, more inclusive, less corrupt future, rather than the appeal of an ideological call for an Islamic order, won the elections for the AKP. Post-election data showed that half of its support came from voters who had backed secular parties in previous elections. And in its market-oriented economic policies and acceptance of some liberal political principles, the AKP represented a break from the traditional Islamist parties of earlier decades.

Despite its numerous shortcomings (such as its habit of appointing ideological kin rather than qualified personnel to top jobs), the AKP mostly has remained true to its electoral platform, to the surprise of many abroad. Seeking to accelerate Turkey's progress through the EU accession process, it has taken big steps toward political liberalization, civilian control of the military, and consolidation of the rule of law. The example it sets therefore stands as the antithesis of the Islamic order in Al Qaeda's imagination. Still, in the eyes of many the AKP remains suspect because of its origins, its cliquish and ideologically motivated appointments, and the decidedly faith-based cultural preferences of its leading figures—whose wives, for example, wear the Islamic headscarf. Some critics even detect a dangerous tilt in Ankara's foreign policy. Particularly controversial was the visit by Khalid Meshal, a leader of Hamas, after the Palestinian elections, just when the West was trying to isolate Hamas and force it to renounce terrorism and recognize Israel's right to exist. And Turkey has drawn the ire of some in Washington for remaining on good terms with its Syrian and Iranian neighbors—a choice that may look different now that the Iraq Study Group has recommended dialogue with those two countries.

Some of the AKP's critics charge that one more term under the party will leave Turkey less secular, somewhat less democratic, and decidedly non-Western. This is unfair and untrue. Whatever its failings, the party represents something new in Turkish life. Indeed, if one were to speak of fundamentalism with respect to the AKP and its constituents, "market fundamentalism" would have to hold pride of place. The "creative destruction" of Turkey's vibrant capitalism has transformed sleepy provincial towns such as Kayseri, Denizli, Malatya, and Konya, and integrated them into the global markets. Producing consumer goods, machinery, textiles, furniture, and ceramics for export to Europe, the United States, the Middle East, and Central Asia, they have been enriched and exposed to the wider world. The new social mobility has made the conservative weft of the country's cultural fabric more visible and poignant. Partly because Turkish institutions did little to ease the transition, mobility reinforced communitarian tendencies. An ineffective state and a sluggish banking sector that was slow to reach out to credit-starved businesspeople left many Turks with nowhere to turn but to networks based on kin, faith, and community.

At the same time, the newly acquired wealth created demands for the rewards of consumer society. Women in the conservative Muslim middle classes dressed modestly and wore headscarves but eagerly shopped for the latest look at Islamic fashion shows. Seaside hotels with facilities allowing the separation of the sexes at the beach sprang up to accommodate the newly affluent. The children of the new middle classes, both sons and daughters, registered in the best of schools and often went abroad, mostly to Western countries (preferably the United States), to get their college degrees or their MBAs.

Despite the EU's crude rebuff, Turkey's multifaceted modernization will continue. The impact of global integration and ongoing economic and political reforms will still ripple through Turkish society, and the transformation will also strain Turkey's social fault lines. A widening sphere of freedom and democratic engagement brings forth demands from long-suppressed groups—from Kurds to environmentalists—and, as in all such cases, triggers a reaction. Yet these are all the birth pangs of a more modern Turkey that will remain European while redefining itself, even if Europe cannot yet grasp this process and its significance. If it manages its transformations wisely, Turkey will indeed become, as Presidents Bill Clinton and George W. Bush have both predicted, one of the key countries shaping the 21st century.

In awarding the Nobel Prize to Pamuk, the Swedish Academy cited his rendering of Istanbul's melancholy in his work. The Turkish word for this is hüzün. "The hüzün of Istanbul," Pamuk writes, "is not just the mood evoked by its music and its poetry, it is a way of looking at life that implicates us all, not only a spiritual state but a state of mind that is ultimately as life-affirming as it is negating." This hüzün, he says later, "suggests nothing of an individual standing against society: on the contrary, it suggests an erosion of the will to stand against the values and mores of the community and encourages us to be content with little, honoring the virtues of harmony, uniformity, humility."

Arguably the hüzün of Istanbul is no more. At best, it is on its way out. The cosmopolitan city of different ethnicities and religious affiliations and many languages that Pamuk knew is indeed long gone. A new cosmopolitanism, that of financial services and multinational corporations, advertisers and artists, oil men and real estate agents, is rapidly filling the gap. Individuals of all colors who partake of it exude self-confidence and are unlikely to be "content with little." They will want to take on the world.

SOLI ÖZEL, a Southeast Europe Project policy scholar at the Wilson Center in 2006, is a professor of international relations at Istanbul Bilgi University and a columnist for the newspaper Sabah.

Thailand's Elusive Equilibrium

"The challenges facing the interim administration create a difficult environment in which to undertake constitutional reform. . . ."

CATHARIN DALPINO

In the post–cold war era, military interventions in politics have fallen out of favor. Nevertheless, many in the Bangkok political class initially hailed the September 2006 intervention in Thailand as a "good coup." Those who supported the action voiced fatigue and despair over the tumultuous five-year tenure of Prime Minister Thaksin Shinawatra, the last year of which was one of stalemate between a protest movement led by anti-Thaksin groups and a leader determined to remain in power. Six months into the interim administration, many in the political elite now question whether military intervention can be a panacea for Thailand's political ills.

Supporters of the September military action maintain—not without reason—that Thaksin had turned a consolidating, if somewhat chaotic, democracy into a semi-authoritarian system through a combination of strongman tactics and financial maneuverings. In his election campaign, Thaksin had struck a populist note, proposing a national health care system and other emollients that promised economic security to a country that may have technically recovered from the 1997 Asian economic crisis but still harbored deep-seated insecurities from the shock. At the beginning of his administration in 2001, Thaksin's leadership style, which he billed as "CEO management" of the government, impressed many Thais.

Soon, however, Thaksin, a former police officer, had launched a widespread campaign against drug dealers that resulted in numerous deaths that were deemed suspicious. More objectionable to the political classes, he tightened controls on the media, in part by encouraging high-ranking officials of his party to purchase controlling interests in media groups that were critical of the government.

Anti-Thaksin sentiment expanded with popular opposition to the January 2006 sale of the Thaksin family business, Shin Corporation, to Temasek Holdings, an investment firm connected to the Singaporean government. Shin Corp., a telecommunications giant, had satellites in its portfolio, so its transfer to a foreign entity had security implications. Insult was added to injury when Thaksin, a billionaire businessman, exploited loopholes in the regulatory code that made the sale tax-free.

Another major concern in the Thaksin era was the resurgence of violence in Thailand's southernmost provinces, which have a Muslim majority population. Although the source and cause of the violence are still not completely understood, a common assumption was that Thaksin's heavy-handed approach to the south had exacerbated tensions.

To many of the prime minister's critics, the coup offered a chance for a fresh start—a means of restoring Thailand to its pre-Thaksin equilibrium, reconciling with southern Muslims, and drafting a new constitution with fewer loopholes that allow the conversion of political power to personal gain. If these hopes were overblown, even unrealistic, they were also indicative of how badly many Thais believed their political fabric had unraveled.

Western democracy promoters do not necessarily disagree with Thaksin's detractors—many had criticized his tactics while he was in power—but they point out that Thaksin had twice been elected in democratic contests, and that he had devoted more funds and attention to Thailand's rural sector than any political leader in recent years. Both sides agree, however, that freedoms were eroded in the Thaksin period. Less than a decade ago, Freedom House, an organization that monitors democratic progress, had ranked Thailand as "free," a category that generally signifies a liberal democracy. In the Thaksin years, the rating slipped to "partly free."

The campaign against drug dealers and the media crackdown were early issues, but in the summer of 2006 Thaksin raised new alarms with veiled hints that he might seek constitutional changes that would move Thailand from a parliamentary to a presidential system. While this would not in theory be undemocratic, many Thais feared that a move to such a system would enable Thaksin to institutionalize his own hold on power by shaping the Thai system to suit his purposes. These worries were exacerbated by a casual remark by the prime minister that he hoped to lead the government for another 20 years. This accounts for part of the initial support for the military intervention: some Thais believed Thaksin was in the process of planning a coup of his own, albeit one that was political rather than military.

In 2006, after the September coup, Freedom House gave Thailand a "not free" designation, the lowest possible ranking. Despite this precipitous fall, the new rating has drawn little attention in Thailand. Analysts in the country who took note of the Freedom House move saw it as proof that Western critics do not understand the complexities of the country's political problems.

This debate on democracy is vital to Thailand's future, and it would be a mistake to assume that it is not being conducted within the country as well. Although the international media tend to focus on the opinions of politicians and analysts who supported the coup, there are some who question how democracy can be strengthened when its processes have been set aside, even temporarily. They also caution that even a brief intervention risks politicizing a military that had been regarded as increasingly professional after Thailand's last episode with military rule in 1991.

Dethaksinization

Restoring democracy in Thailand will be both a short- and long-term task. International attention and pressure have centered on resumption of the electoral process. The United States was obligated by law to suspend certain security assistance programs after the coup, but it has focused its diplomatic efforts on encouraging the military-backed government to move toward early elections, which have been tentatively set for this fall. Before elections can go forward, however, the process of drafting a new constitution must be completed.

At this point it is not clear to what extent there will be consultations on the constitution, which for the 1997 charter took the form of public hearings. Whatever the substance of the new constitution, its acceptance will depend in part on the degree to which the drafters have involved and enfranchised key elements of the Thai political system, including civil society. In the meantime, an interim National Assembly, with some former elected officials representing their parties in an appointed capacity, is acting as a legislative placeholder.

To many of the prime minister's critics, the coup offered a chance for a fresh start—reconciling with southern Muslims, and drafting a new constitution with fewer loopholes.

The parties that opposed Thaksin, such as the Democrat Party, need only await the resumption of politics as usual. But the survival of Thaksin's Thai Rak Thai (TRT) party would require not only a change in the party's leadership but also a reinvention of its public image. At this juncture, it is not certain whether the Thai Rak Thai party will survive. Many in the party's inner circle were out of the country at the time of the coup, as was Thaksin himself. Several in the TRT leadership structure who were in Bangkok were arrested. Thaksin officially resigned from the party in October 2006. The TRT has not been disbanded, but it is not reckoned to be a serious force when elections resume.

While the interim government does not fear the Thai Rak Thai Party itself, it is nervous about Thaksin's possible return to Thailand. Thai leaders recently chastised the Singapore government for meeting with the former prime minister. The government has also been reluctant to lift all military controls in the provinces in north and northeastern Thailand that are the center of Thaksin's political strength.

Tensions over Thaksin's lingering political presence have been felt in government ministries as well. In late February, Finance Minister Pridiyathorn Devakula, a former central bank governor, resigned, claiming that he could not work with officials still in the ministry who had been aligned with Thaksin. This very public example of internal bureaucratic dissonance hints at a broader split across the system.

Pridiyathorn's resignation was a blow to the unity of the interim government and sparked rumors of an anticipated broader cabinet shuffle. But fissures between Thaksin's supporters and the government were already a matter of public preoccupation. A series of bombs set off in Bangkok on New Year's Eve is a case that is still to be solved, but one popular theory holds that they were detonated by pro-Thaksin forces seeking to destabilize the new government. Views on this are far from unanimous, and some Thai analysts believe the blasts were linked to tensions in the Muslim south. Either way, polls show that the bombings have lowered confidence in the new leadership. The government has warned that further attacks are possible, especially around the Buddhist New Year in April.

Unrest in the South

Beyond personnel issues, many of the actions of the military-backed government since September have been designed to reverse Thaksin policies. The first of these new directions involves the critical issue of the Muslim south, specifically relations with Thailand's three southernmost provinces: Narathiwat, Yala, and Pattani. Although Muslims are a minority amounting to only 4 percent of the population overall, in these provinces they form a majority. Three years ago, violence in the deep south reached a level of national concern, presumably engineered by a second generation of separatist movements that had been active in the 1970s and 1980s.

At the time, Thaksin's critics assumed the unrest was a response to his policies in the Muslim south, which emphasized assimilation of minorities into the Thai mainstream rather than special cultural, linguistic, or educational arrangements. A year before the violence reemerged, Thaksin had disbanded the Southern Border Provinces Administrative Center, whose functions included mediation and consultation with Muslim and other southern leaders.

But events since September suggest this hypothesis does not hold up. The appointed interim prime minister, General Surayud Chulanont, has made two major shifts in the central government's policy toward the Muslim south. He has restored the southern administrative apparatus designed to provide mediation services, and he has declared the government's willingness to negotiate with separatist groups, although precisely which groups is not clear. Both measures have brought praise from Bangkok and from southern leaders— yet the violence has not diminished. On the contrary, it has increased. The death toll for the past three years has reached nearly 2,000 Thai Muslims and Buddhists, many of them teachers and some of them clergy.

In a single weekend in February, more than 50 violent incidents, ranging from bombings to shootings to arson attacks, took place in the southern provinces. This was significant not only for the extent of the violence but also because Muslim groups publicly claimed credit for the attacks, a rare occurrence. The self-proclaimed "Warriors of the Pattani Islamic State" urged in leaflets that Muslims wage holy war against the "Siam oppressors," using Thailand's historic name to recall the period when the province of Pattani was an independent kingdom.

Although it has not quelled tensions between minority Muslims and majority Buddhists in Thailand, the new policy has succeeded in improving relations with Thailand's neighbor to the south, Malaysia. Surayud's willingness to negotiate with separatist groups has reassured his Malaysian counterpart, Prime Minister Abdullah Badawi, who has offered to facilitate talks between Bangkok and Thai Muslims. Reducing tensions in southern Thailand would improve security in Malaysia, where the northernmost provinces are a power base for the Islamic political opposition.

The Economics of Sufficiency

A second major area of concern is economic policy, and here too Thailand is attempting to move forward while addressing the past. Foreign investors were rattled in December when the government suddenly imposed currency controls designed to deflate the *baht* and slow trading of it on the international market. This was one of the first decisions under a newly proclaimed economic policy of "sufficiency," the precise definitions of which are still under discussion.

The new policy direction may be a reaction both to the 1997 Asian financial crisis, which began with the collapse of the Thai *baht,* and to Thaksin's support for free trade agreements with other nations. Negotiations on a US-Thailand free trade agreement foundered during the political crisis last year and have not gotten back on track. In any case, reaction from the Thai stock exchange to the currency controls was sharply negative—the index fell 15 percent in a day—and the decision was quickly reversed.

Another initiative that may fall under the "sufficiency" rubric is a proposed amendment to the 1999 Foreign Business Act (FBA) to prevent foreign investors from using Thai "nominees" to gain controlling interests in Thai companies. This harks back to a clause in the FBA that enabled Thaksin to sell Shin Corp. to Temasek, an issue that is still alive, not only in Thailand's economic policy but also in Thailand-Singapore relations. While Thai-Malaysian relations have improved in the post-Thaksin era, Thailand's relations with Singapore have suffered a serious downturn.

International business is taking a wait-and-see approach on the FBA, but the aggregate effect of these shifts in economic policy has been a drop in public confidence in the new government. Recent estimates indicate that Thailand's growth in gross domestic product (GDP) for 2007 could fall below 4 percent, dropping from the 5 percent rate recorded in 2006. This places Thailand behind Vietnam, Malaysia, and Indonesia in terms of projected GDP growth. In late February a poll conducted by Bangkok University showed that 54 percent of Thais surveyed did not believe the government's actions have been effective.

Adjustments are also being made in Thailand's relations in the broader Southeast Asia region. Some officials in Thailand's neighboring states in mainland Southeast Asia have privately expressed concern over Thaksin's ouster. While he was in office, Thaksin had given special attention in the form of increased trade to Cambodia, Laos, and Burma—countries with levels of economic development significantly lower than Thailand's. This was consonant with the policies of his predecessors, such as former Prime Minister Chatichai Choonhavan, who saw special economic advantage for Thailand in cultivating neighboring countries. Chatichai in the late 1980s had envisioned a "Golden Peninsula" on mainland Southeast Asia in which Thailand would be the catalyst and the center of an economic revival.

Yet some in the Thai foreign affairs community believe that Thaksin subtly undermined Thailand's relations with the Association of Southeast Asian Nations (ASEAN), challenging its focus and cohesion by setting up parallel groups such as the Asian Cooperation Dialogue. Rebalancing Thailand's relations within ASEAN will be an ongoing task. With the country preoccupied with internal political dynamics and violence in the south, Bangkok may find it difficult to concentrate on regional affairs. However, there will be two pull factors: the next ASEAN secretary general is expected to come from Thailand, and in 2008 the chairmanship of ASEAN will rotate to Bangkok.

The Next Constitution

Although some of those who supported the military intervention are now questioning its efficacy, many ordinary Thais do not feel that life under the interim government has had a negative impact on personal freedoms. There is little evidence of any widespread despair about the future. Even so, the challenges facing the interim administration create a difficult environment in which to undertake a major overhaul of the country's legal and administrative system through constitutional reform. As a result, the constitutional drafting and ratification process may slip behind schedule, and elections may be delayed. Any such delays are not likely to be lengthy, since the Thai public's desire for stability and a return to normalcy has become increasingly apparent. Nevertheless, Thailand will need to address a number of fundamental issues as it moves toward a new constitutional order.

First, constitutionalism itself needs to be strengthened. Since Thailand's system of constitutional monarchy was established in 1932, transfer of power has often been accompanied by a new constitution. The new constitution generally reflects the views of the new leaders but fails to provide the basis for an enduring political system. Indeed, since 1932 Thailand has had 17 constitutions, on average more than one every five years.

The 1997 constitution was intended to be more sustainable, and it allowed for revisions after the first five years. However, in 2002 reservations within the Thai political community over Thaksin's authoritarian tendencies raised fears that reopening the constitution would result in a less democratic system, and the opportunity to make adjustments passed. Although the 1997 constitution differed from previous charters in its attempt to require transparency and accountability from elected leaders, it was obvious by 2002 that it was unable to prevent the excesses of the Thaksin regime.

Nevertheless, some political activists and analysts in Thailand maintain that the 1997 constitution was too easily dismissed in September when the army intervened. They believe constitutionalism would have been strengthened if attention had been focused on reforming the existing charter.

Second, as Thai reformers have long urged, the judiciary needs to be strengthened. In April 2006, as anti-Thaksin protests were growing in Bangkok, King Bhumipol Adulyadej performed the routine task of swearing in a new group of administrative judges. On this occasion, however, he summoned the media and after the swearing in told the judges, "Now go do your job." This was interpreted as a charge to the Thai judiciary to be more rigorous in prosecuting corruption.

It was also seen, more broadly, as a suggestion to the Thai public that political disputes would have to be solved working through the system, the growing "people power" movement notwithstanding. Indeed, many Thais who were uncomfortable with the idea of a military intervention to depose Thaksin were equally uncomfortable with the prospect of a targeted protest forcing an elected leader to resign.

In 2006, after the September coup, Freedom House gave Thailand a "not free" designation, the lowest possible ranking.

The 1997 constitution added two new institutions to the Thai judicial system: a constitutional court and a National Counter-Corruption Commission (NCCC). A few years later both of these fledgling bodies would be asked in sequence to act on the case of Thaksin himself, charged with financial improprieties in his previous position as deputy prime minister. Thaksin was acquitted in the constitutional court by a single vote, and both institutions lost power in subsequent years. The post-September government has restored the NCCC to some degree, but there is concern that the judiciary may falter in the future over politically charged cases. An alternative view holds that the judiciary is not to blame for lax enforcement and that important corruption cases are stopped before they get to the courts.

Like democracy, judicial independence is an ideal and remains open to interpretation. It is the centerpiece of legal systems of English inheritance, where common law encourages judges to distinguish themselves through their decisions. Thailand's legal system is influenced by several traditions, but leans toward the European model of code law rather than common law. Code law systems generally feature a closer relationship between the courts and the prosecutors, and judges often advance through bureaucratic skill rather than by the strength of their judicial decisions. In the next constitution, Thailand is not likely to rewire its legal system, but special attention will need to be paid to bolstering judicial mechanisms to enforce accountability.

Toward Accountability

Third and finally, Thailand needs to clearly define appropriate civil-military relations. The 1997 constitution diminished the political role of the military by switching from an appointed upper house in the legislature to an elected one. The military supported this and other revisions as a quid pro quo: they would accept limitations on their political role if the constitution demanded—and obtained—greater accountability from elected civilian politicians. The constitution did demand greater transparency from elected officials, but enforcement mechanisms proved too weak to withstand political manipulation.

At the same time that it was becoming apparent that accountability was slipping, the Thai military was subjected to attempts by the Thaksin administration to personalize the armed forces, much as his government was also trying to personalize the civilian bureaucracy. In this way Thaksin had taken a page from the playbooks of former Prime Minister Mahathir Mohamad in Malaysia and former President Suharto in Indonesia, selecting officials and promoting them on the basis of loyalty. This practice inevitably serves to factionalize the agency in question. (In the United States, this risk is addressed through the Hatch Act, which aims to protect both civilian bureaucrats and military personnel from being pressured into partisan loyalty by elected politicians.)

In both 1991 and 2006, a significant segment of the Thai public demonstrated that it would accept a military intervention in politics when it appeared that corrupt politicians could not be removed by legal means. However, this acceptance carries with it a distinction between military intervention and direct and open-ended military rule. In 1992, when the coup leader General Suchinda Krapayoon emerged as prime minister, protests in Bangkok eventually forced his resignation.

This distinction is a complicating factor, not only in Thai civil-military relations but also in the broader Thai political environment. Western analysts typically focus on the military side of the equation and ignore or underestimate the reforms needed on the civilian political side. Significant shifts in civil-military relations in Thailand are not likely to be a matter of short-term negotiation. Rather, they will be more evolutionary, as Thailand pairs democratic progress with stronger instruments for bringing elected leaders to account.

On top of the widespread demand that democracy be restored, the lessons of the Thaksin era will be critically important (even if so far they have been less discussed) in determining how effective Thailand's next constitution will be—and how long it will last. Thaksin's initial popularity was based on a desire among the Thai people for strong and effective leadership without a strongman government. The former is to be found in linking politics accountably with the public interest, something that has often been lacking in the past 20 years of elected civilian rule. The new constitution can provide additional curbs on corruption, but this should be combined with an ongoing public dialogue about Thai political culture—about the need for the full range of actors in the Thai political system to agree on the rules of the game, and ultimately to follow those rules. Without this tacit covenant, even the best-crafted constitution is fated to come undone.

CATHARIN DALPINO is a visiting associate professor and director of Thai studies at the Edmund A. Walsh School of Foreign Service at Georgetown University. The author of *Deferring Democracy: Promoting Openness in Authoritarian Regimes* (Brookings, 2000), she was deputy assistant secretary of state for democracy, human rights, and labor from 1993 to 1997.

Reprinted from *Current History,* April 2007, pp. 180–185. Copyright © 2007 by Current History, Inc. Reprinted with permission.

Big Men, Big Fraud, Big Trouble

The deep rottenness of Nigeria's political system threatens all the economic gains this giant country has made

Ever since Sani Abacha expired in the arms of two Indian prostitutes, possibly from an overdose of Viagra, in 1998, Nigerians supposed that their worst days were behind them. The "coup from heaven," as Abacha's death was called, seemed to release the country from three decades of increasingly ruinous military dictatorships that had brought Nigeria diplomatic isolation and economic collapse. In 1999, the country made a fresh start with a new elected civilian administration led by Olusegun Obasanjo, the outgoing president. He has been lauded in the West for his economic reforms and his drive against corruption.

But the organised vote-rigging and *fraud* that characterised the state and local elections on April 14th, as well as the parliamentary and presidential polls on April 21st, suggest that Nigeria may be sliding backwards again. Nigeria's own independent observers' group has called them a "sham". The European Union, normally a master of nuance in these matters, baldly stated that the whole electoral process "cannot be considered to have been credible", and remarked that its report was the most damning it had ever issued anywhere in the world.

The opposition parties have called for a re-run of all the elections. The only people who seem happy with the charade are officials of the inept and craven Independent National Electoral Commission (INEC) and those who appointed them in the ruling People's Democratic Party (PDP). The PDP's presidential candidate, Umaru Yar'Adua, won an astonishing 70% of the vote; but few will accept the result as anything other than a *fraud*.

The consequences could be extremely destabilising in a country as fragile as Nigeria: a brittle mosaic of about 300 different ethnic groups, equally divided between Muslims, largely in the north, and Christians, mainly in the south. This is a fractious and rancorous polity at the best of times. But with a full-blown insurgency raging in the oil-producing Delta, and relations between Muslims and Christians already tense, the last thing Nigeria needed was a new government that many will regard as illegitimate.

Much protest will take place in the courts, which will proceed at their usual glacial pace. But it will also take other forms. About 200 people were killed during the elections themselves, according to EU estimates. Most of the violence has been directed against institutions that (in popular belief) connived in the results. Several INEC offices were burnt down. In the *big* cities this week, thousands of police and soldiers were on the streets in armoured cars, ready for trouble. The situation could easily get out of hand.

In many African countries all this might pass without much comment. But Nigeria matters more than most. It is Africa's most populous country, with 140m people, and, after South Africa, the continent's second-biggest economy. It vies with South Africa, too, for diplomatic and military leadership. Its peacekeepers serve throughout the continent; Nigeria provides most of the troops in Darfur, for example. A strong and stable Nigeria has become essential to the project of building an Africa that can solve its own problems.

It is also the continent's largest producer of oil, and the sixth-biggest oil-exporter in the world. It already provides 8.5% of America's imports, a figure that could rise to 10% in a few years' time. Nigeria has been proposed as the answer to the West's concerns over energy security; a dependable oil ally, away from the turbulent Middle East and Venezuela's pesky Hugo Chávez. But given the current state of affairs, the oil price has been edging up all week on fears of worse to come in Nigeria.

The country's boosters had invested heavily in a successful presidential election. They hoped that this ballot—potentially, the first constitutional transfer of power from one civilian administration to another since independence in 1960—would cap the "Nigerian renaissance". Instead, the country is sliding into grave political uncertainty. How did this happen?

The Promise of Reform

The answer is to be found largely in Mr Obasanjo's government of the past eight years. When Abacha died, Nigerians looked to Mr Obasanjo—a charismatic Christian, ex-general and former president—as the man to guide them out of the country's mess. He won an election in 1999 and, after a slow start, set about tackling many of Nigeria's long-term problems. And he achieved a good deal.

A team of younger, zealous reformers, dubbed "the seven samurai" by one diplomat, was brought in to overhaul the economy. In particular, they confronted the corruption that had seen Nigeria's leaders pocket, by some estimates, $380 billion of the country's oil wealth since independence, the equivalent of about two-thirds of all the aid given to Africa during that time. Thus the "reform programme" was born.

At the macroeconomic level, Nigeria has been hailed as a success. A forceful former finance minister, Ngozi Okonjo-Iweala, got rampant inflation down to single digits last year and built up foreign exchange reserves that now stand at around $48 billion. The country has been achieving growth rates of over 5% in the past few years. So impressive have the statistics proved to international financial institutions that Nigeria has recently won debt relief, and the country's credit rating is now good enough to let it issue bonds on the global market.

It was the anti-corruption drive, though, that caught the domestic and international imagination. Mr Obasanjo set up an agency, the Economic and Financial Crimes Commission (EFCC), which at first amazed and delighted Nigerians with its success. It was headed by a wiry and energetic former policeman, Nuhu Ribadu, whose hand-picked enforcers have recovered over $5 billion in stolen assets and successfully prosecuted the sort of people, businessmen and policemen, who most Nigerians assumed would forever remain above the law.

This was all impressive stuff. But in other respects Nigeria's old problems remain, and have even worsened under Mr Obasanjo. For a start, much of the macro-economic success is due to the high price of oil; it has made little visible difference to Nigerians' wretched daily lives. Over 70% still live on the equivalent of less than $1 a day; decaying hospitals, schools and roads tell their own stories. Bashir Borodo, the president of the Manufacturers' Association of Nigeria, reckons that in the poorer north of the country over 60% of university graduates are unemployed. And with so many people doing casual jobs, under-employment is massive too.

Besides all this, the deeply corrupt political system has remained intact and, if anything, entrenched itself under Mr Obasanjo. In Nigeria, politics is money, and money is politics. With economic activity almost totally dependent on the oil revenues that flow in through the central government coffers (over $50 billion in 2006), the surest way to enrichment is through political office—or through contracts from your best mates in those offices. Incumbency has become everything in Nigeria; to lose office is to lose almost the only means of survival, as well as immunity from prosecution. The extra cash flowing through the system from a higher oil price has merely raised the political stakes, making politicians more brazen than ever in their attempts to cling to office. Or, as Mr Obasanjo said himself, these elections were "do or die" time for his ruling PDP.

The result, as the EFCC's Mr Ribadu puts it, is "not even corruption. It's gangsterism. It's organised crime." That is particularly true of local and state politics, where most of the money is actually disbursed. The problem is most acute in the five or six oil-rich Delta states. There the local elections on April 14th were replaced by something more like organised thuggery, with PDP gunmen beating up opponents, intimidating voters, snatching ballot boxes and stuffing them with pre-marked ballots. Winning candidates piled up huge victories on high turnouts in places where the ballot papers had never even arrived.

The rewards for such rigging can be impressive. In 2006, for instance, the governor of Rivers State, Peter Odili, had a budget of $1.33 billion to spend, considerably more than the budgets of some other west African countries, such as Mali and Niger. Moreover, Mr Odili had far fewer people to spend his money on.

Not that much of the money is actually spent on them. An almost total lack of transparency hides where most of the money goes, but a Human Rights Watch report managed to catalogue some items in the Rivers State budget for last year. The governor's office spent $65,000 a day on transport and travel and over 1.5 billion naira ($11.5m) on new cars; two new helicopters cost 5 billion naira, on top of the previous year's new jet; about 1.3 billion naira went on gifts and catering. By contrast, the capital budget for the health sector was 2.8 billion naira, in a state with some of the poorest, least healthy and worst-educated people in Africa.

Gangster Politics

When farcical election exercises deny people the opportunity to vote their politicians out of office, it is not surprising that many take up arms to get their share of the oil money, through kidnapping and illegal bunkering of oil. Political resistance slips easily into plain gangsterism. But the politicians, in turn, will employ the gangsters to do some kidnapping and bunkering for them. It is good business; over 100 foreign oil-workers have been kidnapped and ransomed in the past year alone, at about $500,000 a time. In much of the Delta it has now become difficult to distinguish between politicians, gangsters and insurgents. The charade of the state elections on April 14th will only have added to the bitterness and hostility in the region, making early resolution of the Delta insurgency even less likely than before.

On the day of the presidential election money-politics could be seen in action in central Kano, the dusty, dilapidated industrial capital of the north. There, in the local government area of Fagge, the PDP had budgeted 35m naira for political "mobilisation" and the main opposition party, the All Nigerian Peoples' Party (ANPP), 40m naira. In one ward, Fagge A, the PDP, according to one of its operatives, had budgeted

594,000 naira ($4,650) for 21,000 registered voters and 35 ballot boxes. Thus each "independent" presiding officer at the polling station was given 3,000 naira and his clerk 2,000 naira. Each policeman was getting 1,000 naira. That left payments of about 200 naira ($1.57) per voter—whose votes, far from being secret, were inked with a thumb on the ballot in front of party agents. Multiple voters, who will have registered several times with sympathetic election officials, might vote ten times, at a reduced bulk rate of 100 naira—still picking up a tidy 1,000 naira each.

The friendly officials are paid for a variety of services, one of which is not to scrutinise the register too closely. Hasia, for example, had just voted with the registration card of her mother, who had already voted herself. Hasia had the second of her mother's two cards. She has probably not even reached the legal voting age of 18. Her card clearly identified its owner as being 60 years old, but this had not proved a problem with the right official.

All day PDP and ANPP party agents were negotiating spot-prices on votes, rather like the oil markets that grease the rotten political machines. But at least there was voting in Kano state. To the north, in Katsina, Mr Yar'Adua's home state—which he had to win comfortably—it was more like the Delta, with ballot papers arriving very late or not at all. And, curiously, remarkably few presidential ballot papers arrived at the polling stations, leading many voters to conclude that they had already been filled in elsewhere.

In his own quest to hang on to the rewards of office, in 2005 Mr Obasanjo started a campaign to alter the constitution to allow him to run for a third term. Huge bribes, of up to 50m naira, were offered to parliamentarians to vote for the change, but the Senate bravely voted against it last year. Since then, Mr Obasanjo has misused every means at his disposal to ensure that his own PDP *men* win the state houses and the presidency, knocking his opponents out of the race by bringing charges of corruption against them from the EFCC.

So even the straight-talking Mr Ribadu's outfit has now been politicised. It has used high-handed and unconstitutional means to smear Mr Obasanjo's opponents and keep their names off the ballot papers. The EFCC has done some good work in the past. But, like the elections themselves, its credibility has been mortgaged to political expediency.

The charitable interpretation of Mr Obasanjo's behaviour is that he has to act this way to "preserve" the reform programme. If that is so, he has badly miscalculated; the reform programme has itself become a casualty of the rotten politics.

Can Nigeria expect anything better from Mr Yar'Adua, if he is sworn in as president on May 29th? Probably not. Despite a reputation for personal honesty, the obscure northern governor comes to power as a creature of Mr Obasanjo's PDP clique. With few obvious credentials for the job, apart from being the younger brother of Mr Obasanjo's former

vice-president, he was hand-picked by the president against the will of many in the party. And Mr Obasanjo will retain considerable formal power as the party chairman. At least Mr Yar'Adua is a northern Muslim, taking over the presidency from a Christian southerner.

As a free-marketeer, he has pledged to continue the reforms of his master. But he will come to power with even less legitimacy than Mr Obasanjo had after his own flawed election victory in 2003. This will cause huge difficulties for him, especially if Nigeria's disillusioned Western backers give the country a wider berth.

Progress by Saxophone

Nigerian politics does not have to be like this. Given a chance, good state governors do emerge. In Cross Rivers, for instance, on the border with Cameroon, Donald Duke has effected an impressive transformation over the past eight years.

In the state capital, Calabar, the streets have no pot-holes. According to the state government, every village is connected to the national grid and everyone has access to clean water. There is almost no litter. Remarkably, instead of the fleet of blacked-out SUVs that normally idle outside governors' offices, ready to whisk the *big* man a few hundred metres down the road, outside Mr Duke's office stand brand new garbage lorries from Germany.

Moreover, Cross Rivers has no oil wealth. Mr Duke has achieved all this on a fraction of the money available to his neighbours. Instead, he has frozen official salaries, cleverly exploited existing resources and taken on debt. In partnership with private investors, he is also responsible for Tinapa, the largest retail and business development in west Africa. It contains several new giant studios to grab a large slice of the $200m-300m a year "Nollywood" film industry, which churns out, by some estimates, more films than either of its rivals in Los Angeles or Bombay.

The other key to the state's success is Mr Duke's love of the saxophone. Every Sunday evening he performs in his house with his band. And instead of trying to micro-manage his succession, rig the state elections and prepare for endless court battles, when he leaves office at the end of May Mr Duke is going off to America for a music course. It is an unusual example of a politician who is willing to let go.

But if honest and good leaders can make a difference, the only sure way to break the corrosive link between money and politics in Nigeria is to encourage a private sector that is vigorous enough to give people other ways to make money. As last week's vote-rigging showed, Nigeria is bursting with energetic entrepreneurial talent. But trying to start a business from scratch is almost impossible. Capital scarcely exists. Although banks are required by law to set aside one-tenth of their pre-tax profits for small business start-ups, few loans are actually made.

The biggest impediment of all to economic activity in Nigeria is the country's feeble and erratic power supply. All businesses have to have expensive generators that can double the cost of a start-up; they then have to employ people just to scuttle around grabbing whatever scarce diesel fuel they can find to supply the generators. Two weeks before the election, the ramshackle national Power Holding Company (known to Nigerians as Please Hold Candle) managed to churn out just half the electricity that the country produced in 1960 for about half as many people. If the new president could do just one thing to improve Nigeria's political and economic prospects, it would be the full electrification of his country.

"It is totally false", wrote Chinua Achebe, Nigeria's greatest writer, 24 years ago, to suggest that Nigerians are fundamentally different from any other people in the world. Nigerians are corrupt because the system under which they live today makes corruption easy and profitable; they will cease to be corrupt when corruption is made difficult and inconvenient. The trouble with Nigeria is simply and squarely a failure of leadership.

Congo's Peace
Miracle or Mirage?

"Impunity has been to some extent the glue of the peace process. This fact could undermine the country's fragile stability."

Jason K. Stearns

On March 22 this year, the worst fighting that Kinshasa has ever seen broke out between government forces and supporters of the opposition. Hundreds of people lay dead in the streets and opposition leader Jean-Pierre Bemba announced his departure into exile. Yet some diplomats in the capital played down the violence as a hiccup in the peace process. "We think," one of them told me, "these are the death throes of the old war, not the beginning of a new one."

Many in the international community feel the same way: too much has been accomplished in the more than four years since the signing of a comprehensive peace agreement in Pretoria, South Africa, for war to break out again. Indeed, the Democratic Republic of Congo, once divided among half a dozen warring factions, is now united. A national army has been created. The eight foreign nations at one time involved in the conflict have withdrawn their forces.

Most importantly, in 2006, presidential, national, and provincial assembly elections took place in the first multiparty polls since 1965. The logic of guns, so the saying goes in Kinshasa, has been replaced by the logic of ballots. The incumbent Joseph Kabila (who had assumed the presidency after the assassination of his father, Laurent Kabila, in 2001) won the 2006 presidential race, and his coalition now dominates parliament and most of the provincial assemblies. There have been other successes: the country has a new, improved constitution; Congo's administration and army have been largely unified; security in parts of the country has improved dramatically.

The peace process, however, has been only partially successful. The elections did eviscerate some rebel groups, but, as the recent fighting demonstrates, new fault lines have emerged. Many reforms have been cosmetic: the Congolese state is unified but remains deeply corrupt and abusive. The administration provides almost no social services to the population. And the integrated army is the largest human rights abuser in the country, terrorizing the people it is supposed to protect.

Herein lies the paradox of the transition's success: in order to avoid alienating anyone and to keep the shaky political process going, a blind eye has been turned to high levels of corruption and abuse. Impunity has been to some extent the glue of the peace process. This fact could undermine the country's fragile stability.

Peace on Kabila's Terms

The war in Congo has been one of the bloodiest of modern times, leaving an estimated 4 million dead, largely from disease and hunger. The conflict dates back to 1996, when a coalition of regional powers, including Rwanda, Uganda, Angola, and Eritrea, backed an invasion by a rebel group led by Laurent Kabila. They toppled the dying dictator Mobutu Sese Seko, installing Kabila as head of state in May 1997. Fighting resumed in 1998 when Kabila asked his Rwandan patrons to leave the country. The Rwandans reinvaded, creating a proxy rebel group in the east. Five years of conflict drew in eight countries and spawned a dozen different Congolese armed groups.

The 2002 peace deal succeeded where its many predecessors had failed, offering each signatory something better than the status quo. The timing had much to do with this. After years of fighting, Rwanda, Uganda, and Zimbabwe were withdrawing their troops from the country, making a military victory for the remaining belligerents almost impossible. For the Congolese Rally for Democracy (RCD) and the Movement for the Liberation of Congo (MLC), Rwanda and Uganda's respective proxy forces, the deal provided a lifeline and lucrative positions in the transition. The agreement also elevated the smaller, auxiliary parties—political opposition groups, civil society, and three small rebel movements—from minor players to high-ranking positions. Finally, by offering

Joseph Kabila the presidency and command of the transition, it presented him with peace on his terms and a good chance of winning the elections.

On the face of it, the deal provided relatively equal terms to the principal belligerents. Kabila had to share power with four vice presidents, and all positions in the executive branch, legislature, and security services were divided among the signatories. However, since Kabila controlled the central state apparatus and most of the country's revenue—in particular from the mining areas of Katanga and the Kasais—many aspects of the agreement amounted not so much to power-sharing as to an integration of the other parties into Kabila's administration.

While the army command, for example, was given to the RCD, the powerful *maison militaire*—the head of state's cabinet of military advisers—controlled army funds and decision making during the first part of the transition. The 10,000-strong presidential guard was an added asset for Kabila, since it fell under his direct control. Similarly, the political opposition took control of the ministry of mines, but businessmen still had to get presidential approval for major deals. Positions in other institutions—such as the central bank; the supreme court; the two largest state-owned mining companies, MIBA and Gecamines; and the intelligence service—were not shared among the signatories, despite promises in the peace deal. Kabila simply refused.

This, of course, did not go down well with Kabila's rivals. The RCD withdrew from the transition process in August 2004; the MLC threatened to do the same in January 2005. However, in both cases, with the international community's help, Kabila was able to call their bluff. Real retreat would have forced them into the isolation of their rebel strongholds where, without the military backing of their former patrons, their future would have been questionable. They would also have foregone Kinshasa's opulence: each vice president was allocated $250,000 dollars per month for himself and his staff. Both the MLC and the RCD had 7 ministers and 118 parliamentarians each, making $4,000 and $1,500 per month respectively (several times more than judges' or doctors' salaries). Some of the directors of state companies, most of whose jobs were finally shared out by 2005, made as much as $20,000 a month. As a dissident RCD member lamented: "They couldn't get their hand out of the sugar bowl."

The international community, which funds over half of the country's budget, has refrained from criticizing Congolese leaders too harshly.

The weakness of the political parties also favored Kabila. The belligerents had been motivated by self-interest, not by ideology; once in the transition, each leader tried to fend for himself. Indeed, five MLC ministers defected to Kabila's camp, as did Olivier Kamitatu, the party's secretary general. Three RCD ministers left their party. This political advantage helped Kabila during the election campaign. He controlled state radio and television; in violation of electoral law, they broadcast mostly Kabila campaign advertisements and coverage. He deployed his presidential guard to the country's main airports, where they harassed rival candidates as they arrived or departed. Riot police in Kinshasa prevented large demonstrations from taking place; given the anti-Kabila sentiment in the capital, protests would have been favorable to the president's rivals. In perhaps the most heavy-handed incident, authorities arrested the private security guard of presidential hopeful Oscar Kashala in May 2006 for an alleged coup plot that was never substantiated.

On August 20, 2006, the day the results of the first round of the presidential election were announced, events offered a glimpse of what might have happened had the transition not worked out in Kabila's favor. Kabila failed to obtain a clear majority, sending him into a runoff with Bemba, head of the MLC and one of the vice presidents. While the exact chain of events that day is not completely clear, Kabila's presidential guard launched a frontal attack on Bemba's residences in Kinshasa with tanks and hundreds of troops.

The international community, which was spending more than $2 billion a year on the UN peacekeeping mission in Congo and aid to the country, did not want to ruffle any feathers—in particular not those of Kabila, the head of state to whom ambassadors were accredited. The International Committee for Supporting the Transition, a group of donors and countries in the region that backed the peace process, had up to that point avoided discussing the threat posed by the presidential guard. When Kabila's guard did become a problem in August 2006, the committee denounced the violence but refrained from pointing fingers. The bias shown toward Kabila in the transition agreement was problematic in that it assumed he would win the election. In hushed conversations, diplomats wondered what would happen if the incumbent were to lose the runoff. But Kabila did not lose, and the polls themselves were relatively free and fair. The president won by a wide margin, garnering 2.5 million votes more than his rival.

Regional Shifts

One of the most important achievements of the peace process has been a realignment of relations in the region. The two main rebel movements, the RCD and the MLC, were created by Rwanda and Uganda, respectively, and relied heavily on their patrons for military survival. During the 2002 peace talks in the South African luxury resort Sun City, both countries came under increasing pressure from donors that supplied more than half of their budgets. Criticism increased after successive UN investigations revealed high-level involvement by Rwanda and Uganda in the looting of timber and minerals from eastern Congo. Perhaps the most damning indictment of their presence in Congo came when the two countries clashed in Kisangani in 1999 and 2000. The fighting over diamonds, in a town more than 300 miles from their borders, rendered absurd their claim that their intrusion in Congo was strictly for self-defense.

In 2002, the United States abstained for the first time in a vote by the International Monetary Fund on renewing loans for Rwanda. Shortly thereafter, under direct pressure from South African President Thabo Mbeki, Kabila and Rwandan President Paul Kagame signed an agreement for Rwandan troops to leave eastern Congo. Kabila was supposed to demobilize Rwandan rebels, now regrouped as the Democratic Forces for the Liberation of Rwanda, whom he had funded and supported during the war.

Under pressure from donors, and less threatened by a weakened rebel resistance, Rwanda slowly shifted its foreign policy from military confrontation to one of diplomacy and cooperation. High Rwandan and Congolese officials held discreet talks. Meanwhile, Rwanda's relations with Uganda thawed considerably. Even its relations with the former Hutu rebels who had come to power in Burundi in 2005 became cordial.

There is a good chance of antigovernment unrest bubbling up in the capital and other western towns.

The logic expressed by Rwanda's leaders was clear, if somewhat quixotic: they want Rwanda to become the service hub of the region, the "Singapore of Africa," an ambitious aspiration for a desperately poor, landlocked country. As part of this effort, Kagame has courted investors, including the Los Angeles Chamber of Commerce and Wal-Mart. He has also recognized the need to clean up appearances—a Rwanda open for business cannot be seen as stoking conflict in Congo.

The impact this realignment had on the RCD was evident. Without Rwanda, the rebels lost their military backbone. After the withdrawal of the Rwandan Defense Forces in July 2002, the RCD almost collapsed as Mai-Mai militias supported by Kinshasa took large chunks of its territory. After it was forced into the political process, the RCD's organizational weaknesses also became apparent. Rwanda had run the rebels as a proxy movement and had never allowed a strong political organization to emerge, focusing instead on military strength. During the war, Rwanda had replaced the RCD's leader four times in five years. Divisions quickly emerged during the transition as many RCD officials distanced themselves from the hard-line Hutu and Tutsi leadership.

Relations between Kigali and Kinshasa did not improve overnight, and the improvement was endangered by a hefty dose of brinksmanship. At the beginning of the transition, both Rwanda and the rebels wanted to keep their options open. According to several rebel sources, high-ranking RCD officers were encouraged to refuse army integration in order to remain as a reserve force. The leader of these dissidents was Brigadier General Laurent Nkunda, a Congolese Tutsi and former intelligence officer in the Rwandan army. In May 2004, as UN investigations later confirmed, Rwanda was involved in a mutiny by the dissidents that captured the town of Bukavu for several days. When Kabila overreacted by sending thousands of troops, sparking brutal fighting, Rwanda briefly reinvaded in November 2004.

Although relations appear to be on the mend today, the brinksmanship is likely to continue. Kagame says he speaks regularly with Kabila on the phone, and both sides now insist that their former rival no longer poses a threat. But Kabila, accused of being a Rwandan stooge himself during the election campaign, is afraid of being seen as pro-Kigali. Kagame was not invited to Kabila's inauguration ceremony, and many Congolese officers still accuse Rwanda of hegemonic ambitions in their country. The UN has evidence that Nkunda is continuing to recruit in Rwandan refugee camps, probably with government consent.

Buying Peace

At times, Congo seems condemned to eternal negotiations. The state does not have a monopoly on violence. Its army is desperately weak. And the 17,000 UN peacekeepers present in the country will not carry out the messy counterinsurgency operations necessary in the east, since they lack the will to sustain the casualties such operations would entail. Left with no choice, the government is forced to bargain with warlords.

It is not surprising, therefore, that, in the words of a human rights worker in Kinshasa, "impunity greased the gears of the transition." In contrast with peace processes elsewhere, justice and reconciliation have ranked low on the list of priorities in Congo. After some talk of an international tribunal for war crimes, it was left out of the 2002 accord. A truth and reconciliation commission was created, but its leadership, too, was divided among the former belligerents, who have little interest in exposing crimes committed during the war.

The absence of justice has ended up rewarding criminal behavior. Six militia leaders from the Ituri region were promoted to the rank of general in 2005 and thirty-two others were offered ranks of colonel, including some of the most notorious human rights offenders in the country. Following an international outcry, some of these warlords were arrested, including Thomas Lubanga, who was the first person to be tried at the International Criminal Court in The Hague. However, as soon as these leaders were removed, others sprang up to replace them. Even Nkunda, the RCD dissident, is currently engaged in negotiations for positions for himself and dozens of fellow officers.

Government officials tend to blame the impunity problem on a weak army and justice system, but it is also closely linked to members of the political elite. Patronage networks permeate the police and army. During the first two years of the transition, this allowed officers to embezzle, according to some estimates, over half of the payroll, or $3 million each month. Powerful generals and politicians in Kinshasa shield their protégés in the field from accusations. The civilian population has borne the consequences of this impunity. According to UN human rights reports, the Congolese national army is the worst abuser. UN observers documented 344 murders and 349 rapes carried out by members of the police and army in 2006. Since the UN presence is thinly spread across the country, this is just the tip of the iceberg. In addition, mismanagement of the army has allowed 14,000 to 18,000 militiamen to continue terrorizing the population in the east. In 2006, half a million people were displaced because of fighting there.

Turning a Blind Eye

Impunity has also devastated public administration, rendering it incapable of even providing social services. According to a UN estimate, more than $1 billion is embezzled in the customs sector alone each year. Again, these losses can be attributed in part to predatory patronage networks that permeate the state to the highest level. In 2004, a parliamentary audit of state companies revealed the complicity of six ministers and Kabila's chief of staff in embezzlement and graft. The state auditor has compiled evidence of colossal mismanagement that leaves about one-third of the budget improperly accounted for. Despite this evidence, not a single official was tried for corruption during the transition.

Although it is too early to make predictions about how the incoming government will perform, many of the figures in it are familiar. Part of the reason for this is that, in contrast with peace deals in countries such as Liberia, the settlement in Congo has kept power largely in the hands of the former belligerents. The elections only allowed for a limited infusion of new faces into the political elite. With the notable exception of Prime Minister Antoine Gizenga, the leader of the Unified Lumumbist Party, most ministers in the new government were in office during the transition. The most important ministries—interior, defense, foreign affairs, reconstruction, finance, and planning— are all occupied by former belligerents. More important, the president and his powerful entourage have remained the same. This raises doubts about the extent to which the government will be willing or able to crack down on the corruption and abuses that they sanctioned and were at times complicit in during the past three years.

The international community, which funds over half of the country's budget, has refrained from criticizing Congolese leaders too harshly. In contrast to Liberia, the Balkans, and East Timor, where serious efforts were made to exclude human rights abusers from security forces through a vetting process, in Congo there has been little talk of accountability. Good governance has also been shelved since Security Council members refused to mandate the UN mission to form a donors group to crack down on corruption. Some donors saw impunity as a necessary evil, needed to keep the transition together. As one diplomat explained: "If we start bringing people to justice, where do we stop? Some of the worst abusers are at the top."

The elections appear to have accentuated donor frailty. During the transition, donors pressured the interim government through the International Committee for Supporting the Transition. They seem more reluctant to do so today with a new, sovereign government. None of the embassies denounced the massacre of 100 civilians in the far western province of Bas Congo in January 2007. And, despite the condemnation of the fighting in Kinshasa, the French development minister arrived in the capital shortly after it broke out to sign an aid package worth $300 million with Kabila.

Another reason for donors' reticence has to do with economic interests. Congo is enormously rich in copper, tin, diamonds, and gold. With the end of the hostilities, the country is opening up to business again. Two of the world's largest mining companies, BHP Billiton and AngloAshanti, have bought large concessions and begun operations. US-based Phelps Dodge has acquired one of the world's largest copper concessions, Tenke Fungurume. Embassies in Kinshasa have been involved in helping to negotiate deals for companies based in their countries. In the absence of strong domestic lobbies for Congo, this has discouraged donors from speaking out too boldly about abuses.

The Fallout of Elections

If the transition was a mixed bag of successes and failures, where does it leave us now? Congo in 2006 held its first multiparty elections in 40 years. Kabila's coalition, the Alliance for the Presidential Majority, emerged victorious. Besides winning the presidential race, his coalition won around two-thirds of the seats in parliament, allowing Prime Minister Gizenga to form an Alliance government. The coalition replicated its victory in the elections of senators and governors by provincial assemblies—although allegedly with the help of hefty bribes—winning 10 of the 11 governorships and a majority in the upper house of the national legislature.

Yet the elections, for all their success, have created new divisions and risks. Whereas, during the war, the east was the center of conflict, the west is now also becoming a source of concern. In coming years, there is a good chance of antigovernment unrest bubbling up in the capital and other western towns. Discontent with Kabila was evident in the elections, which revealed a divided country. Kabila won over 80 percent of the vote in the east, while Bemba won by similar margins in five western provinces. Anti-Kabila sentiment runs high in these provinces, since his government administered Bas Congo and Kinshasa for six years without successfully addressing poverty and social woes there. Unemployment is close to 80 percent, and many families eat only once a day. These frustrations are accentuated by ethnic bias—Kabila and his close advisers are from the Swahili-speaking east. Kabila himself is perceived as a foreigner, since he grew up in Tanzania and speaks stilted French and poor Lingala, the language of the west.

This is the Congolese paradox: a state that is perceived as crushingly brutal, yet is deeply weak.

Another factor stirring up urban unrest in the west is the political marginalization of the opposition, which is largely based in the west and the center. Although Bemba won 42 percent of the popular vote, his opposition coalition, the Union for the Nation, is too weak in the national assembly to challenge the ruling Alliance. Bemba's coalition has a majority in four provincial assemblies, but many of its members were bought out during gubernatorial elections, limiting his control to one provincial government. The sidelining of the opposition could push its supporters into the streets, provoking unruly protests and riots in western cities.

A first sign of this took place in Bas Congo on January 31, 2007, when opposition supporters demonstrated against corruption in the gubernatorial elections. The spiritual leader of a local religious sect, Bundu dia Kongo, had been a candidate on the losing opposition ticket. A melee broke out between his supporters and the police, and several people on each side were killed. Feeling under siege, the governor brought in the army. In the ensuing bloodshed, policemen and soldiers killed more than a hundred civilians.

The Kinshasa fighting in March 2007 was different. This time the government's opposition was armed; Bemba had a guard of 400 to 500 soldiers in the capital. Both sides had indicated they would be willing to negotiate a solution that would guarantee Bemba's safety while downsizing his militia. Hardliners in both camps won out and forced a confrontation, plunging the capital into brutal fighting. According to one human rights group, 330 people were killed; other estimates go as high as 500. While the security situation is now stable, the government seems less and less tolerant of dissent. Dozens of opposition members have been rounded up in Kinshasa under dubious charges of espionage and treason, and several television stations belonging to the opposition have been shut down.

The opposition, however, may lack the unity and strength to galvanize the population. Bemba will go into exile, and there is no clear leader to replace him. The opposition is full of former followers of the late dictator Mobutu, and none of them have Bemba's stature. The lack of lucrative positions to pass around will also weaken his coalition; some allied parties already have protested the MLC's hoarding of the few senatorial and governor positions the opposition can claim.

A Crushing Weakness

After the elections, the defining feature of the Congolese state remains its weakness. This ailment, the result of decades of misrule, affects public administration, the security services, courts, the parliament, and political parties. While most donors perceive governance to be a technical problem, patronage is deeply political. Weakness has become a strategy of rule, as elites undermine institutional checks and balances in order to continue to profit from procurement contracts, mining deals, and customs fraud. In the meantime, the government provides almost no social services—health care and education are mostly paid for by their users, churches, and nongovernment organizations. Infrastructure rehabilitation is carried out almost exclusively by donors. Of the state's own revenues, the bulk of what is not embezzled is spent on salaries.

The weakness of the state contrasts with its omnipresence. There are about half a million civil servants in the country and another 200,000 policemen and soldiers. Few of them make a living wage—the official monthly salary of a soldier is $22 a month, while a doctor makes less than $100—forcing them to look for other ways to make money. In a 2005 World Bank survey, when asked what they would do to the state if it were a person, many answered: "Kill him." This is the Congolese paradox: a state that is perceived as crushingly brutal, yet is deeply weak.

This weakness is in many ways the biggest obstacle to peace in the country. It allows small militias, which should constitute a law-and-order problem, to press the government for negotiations, only for other commanders to spring up later with new demands. It turns the security forces and public administration into predators, causing rampant abuse. And it depletes the budget of valuable resources needed to rebuild the country.

While many sub-Saharan states are fragile and corrupt, Congo's situation is particularly bad. There are 100,000 demobilized soldiers in the country, many of whom are about to finish a year-long donor program that provided them with meager earnings. There are still thousands of militiamen in the east, operating as warlords in their fiefdoms, as well as an enormous presidential guard. The ranks of the opposition are packed with former rebels and Mobutists who, deprived of lucrative positions in the state, could use civil unrest to bring the government to its knees.

The international community played a crucial role in making elections happen. But the donors' track record in peacebuilding is not nearly as good as in peacemaking: they lose focus quickly, and the new government is eager to make a show of its sovereignty. In addition, with costly peacekeeping operations moving into gear in Sudan, Lebanon, and

Somalia, the temptation to declare victory and go home will be great.

There are no silver bullets for Congo's recovery. It is clear that the country will not be able to rise out of the trap of poverty, corruption, and war unless the Congolese leadership itself wants to. In order for this to happen, the government needs to be held accountable for its actions by the parliament, the courts, and the media. In short, democratic institutions need to work.

The international community needs to help in this process. A first step will be coming to an understanding with the new government on terms for the huge international investment there. The billion-dollar question will be: How do you implement reforms that go against entrenched interests of the ruling elite? After the scandals and failures of the first two post-independence republics, Congo's Third Republic has begun with many questions and few answers.

JASON K. STEARNS, based in Kenya, is a senior analyst with the International Crisis Group. From 2002 to 2004 he served with the UN mission in the Democratic Republic of Congo.

Africa: How We Killed Our Dreams of Freedom

How did it all go so wrong? Across the continent, liberation movements that fought against colonial rule proved unable to sustain democratic governance. We cannot keep blaming the past; we have to examine ourselves, argues *William Gumede*

WILLIAM GUMEDE

Zimbabwe's Zanu-PF has become the symbol of the descent of African liberation movements into brutal dictatorship.

The great Tunisian writer Albert Memmi noted this phenomenon back in 1957. In *The Coloniser and the Colonised,* he wrote of the tendency of liberation movements, once in power, to mimic the brutality and callousness of former rulers. Backsliding liberation movements in Algeria, Angola, Ghana, Kenya, Namibia and other countries have left in their wake the lost hopes and shattered dreams of millions.

In the inner sanctum of South Africa's ruling African National Congress they have coined a word for it: "Zanufication." As Zimbabweans flee across the border to avoid police brutality or the hardships of an economy in free fall (inflation at more than 1,700 per cent and shortages of basic foodstuffs), they whisper it in hushed tones, a warning.

A senior national executive member of the ANC, Blade Nzimande, warned recently: "We must study closely what is happening in Zimbabwe, because if we don't, we may find features in our situation pointing to a similar development."

Unions, sections within civil society and church groups daily inveigh against the South African government's head-in-the-sand policy towards Zimbabwe and President Thabo Mbeki's "quiet" diplomacy. The Congress of South African Trade Unions (Cosatu) has complained to the South African Broadcasting Corporation, the public broadcaster, over its failure to cover the Zimbabwean meltdown. Although the ANC in South Africa and Zanu-PF are light years apart, the spectre of "Zanufication" haunts South Africa, raising the question: "Is there something inherent in the political culture of liberation movements that makes it difficult for them to sustain democratic platforms?"

The problem for liberation struggles was establishing a democratic culture. All governments must be kept on their toes

The irony is that it is the leaders of former heroic liberation movements who have become stumbling blocks to building a political culture on the African continent based on good governance. The former South African president Nelson Mandela and President Thabo Mbeki enthusiastically proclaimed in 1994 that the end of official apartheid was the dawn of a new era. Yet many liberation movement leaders—Mugabe is a good example—still blame colonialism for the mismanagement and corruption on their watch.

Obviously, the legacy of slavery and colonialism, and now unequal globalisation, are barriers to development. However, to blame the west for Zimbabwe's recent problems is not reasonable. Yet the diplomacy of South Africa, from which most African countries take their cue, is based on this assumption. Initially ANC leaders also bought in to this, but thankfully, on Zimbabwe, Mbeki is increasingly isolated. True to his contrarian and stubborn nature, he still argues that because Zimbabwe was given a raw deal by the British, Mugabe's regime should not be criticised publicly. In terms of land, for example, black Zimbabweans did indeed receive a raw deal, yet that is not the whole story. The Zimbabwean government was idle for at least a decade; when it finally implemented a land reform programme, this consisted of giving fertile land to cronies who subsequently left the land fallow.

The story is similar elsewhere on the continent. As African liberation movements came to power, their supporters were keen to overlook shortcomings. The feeling was that a new, popularly elected democratic government needed to be given an extended chance. Liberation movements were seen as the embodiment of the nation as a whole.

In South Africa, criticism of the ANC by supporters has always been muted. "You cannot criticise yourself," an ANC veteran once admonished me. There has also been a fear that criticising the government gives ammunition to powerful opponents. When a top ANC leader, Chris Nissen, broke rank and publicly criticised a party official's errant behaviour, he was warned: "Do not wash the family's dirty linen in public."

As a journalist—active in the liberation struggle—I, too, gave in to this principle in the heady days after South Africa's first non-racial democratic elections in 1994: "Let's not criticise too much; let's give the new government a fighting chance." But that was a grave mistake. All governments must be kept on their toes. The problem for most liberation movements is how to establish a democratic culture.

During a liberation struggle, decision-making is necessarily left in the hands of a few. Dissent and criticisms are not allowed lest they expose divisions within the movement, which could be exploited by the colonial enemy. But if non-criticism continues during the first crucial years of power, it becomes entrenched, part of a political culture. In the early liberation years, governments often operate as if under siege. Critics are marginalised, making later criticism almost impossible.

Take, for example, the South African government's initial inaction on the Aids pandemic. Mbeki embarked on a fatal policy of denial. Many ANC supporters knew he was wrong but kept quiet, in case they were seen as supporting western governments or big pharmaceutical companies bent on perpetuating Africa's underdevelopment. Many activists preferred to reserve their misgivings about government policy, rather than be placed in the camp of the "neo-colonialists."

In Zimbabwe, Mugabe brutally quashed rebellions in the 1980s, killing thousands in the Matabeleland region. No regional liberation movement said anything about it. The silence of Zanu-PF critics laid the foundations for his reign of terror.

In many African countries—with South Africa the exception—the state is virtually the only employer after liberation. Patronage can be used to reward or sideline critics.

The cold war, during which many African governments started their life, reinforced the siege mentality of "them against us" among African liberation movements. Mugabe continues to blame imperialism. So, when the UK or Australia attacks Zimbabwe, African neighbours will fall silent: they don't want to be seen supporting their former masters.

Similarly, Mbeki's silence on Zimbabwe is partly because he does not want to be associated with the "colonial" powers. South Africa's first strong political statement on Zimbabwe during the current crisis, by the deputy foreign affairs minister Aziz Pahad, one of Mbeki's closest personal friends, was to attack the South African media for giving too much attention to the western perspective on Zimbabwe. This was after Tony Blair had called for sanctions against Zimbabwe and Australian leaders had bemoaned South Africa's silence.

Blair's criticism had the effect of silencing Zanu-PF's opponents in the country. About to launch a final assault against Mugabe, they felt they had to soft-pedal so that the president could not paint them as stooges of the west. One of the main problems of the opposition Movement for Democratic Change (MDC) has been to fight

The Nation by Numbers

100,000
people gathered to watch Bob Marley perform on independence day, 18 April 1980

20%
real growth of economy in first year of independence

20,000
numbers killed during Mugabe's crackdown on Matabeleland in the 1980s

70%
of farmland still owned by white farmers in 2000, 20 years after independence

1 million
dead people on the Zimbabwean electoral role in 2002

18%
proportion of population made homeless by "Operation Murambatsvina" slum clearances, starting 2005

56%
of population earn less than $1 a day

52 years
since average income was as low as today

Research by Sarah O'Connor

off propaganda coming from Mugabe and the media that they are fronts for the west.

That is why it is so important for Mbeki to stand up and publicly condemn Zanu-PF. It would make it far harder to see the conflict in Zimbabwe through the distorting "Africa v the west" prism. Mbeki should follow the lead of Archbishop Desmond Tutu and state clearly that Zimbabwe under Robert Mugabe represents the worst backsliding of African liberation movements.

There is also a problem with the cult of the leader. Members of liberation movements defer too readily to leaders and many African countries famously retained colonial-era "insult laws" by which criticism of the president (which, in Zimbabwe, includes poking fun at him) can attract a lengthy jail sentence. Thus leaders can remain in power for decades and die in office if they are not violently pushed out of power. That is why Mandela felt it important to leave after only one term. That is also why the grass-roots democracy movements mushrooming on the African continent invariably demand that presidents limit their terms in office.

Colonial-era "insult laws" often meant criticism of the president could earn a jail sentence

How Mugabe's Violence Will Free Us

Wilf Mbanga is happy that the world has witnessed the tyranny

When President Robert Mugabe's brutal thugs, in police uniforms, thrashed opposition and civic group leaders a few weeks ago, little did they realise they were actually striking blows for freedom from the old tyrant's rule. Gruesome pictures of the battered leaders flashed around the world on the internet and were widely used in newspapers and on television.

International condemnation, muted over the past ten years by South Africa's monstrous protection of Mugabe, grew to a crescendo. The violence, perpetrated against defenceless citizens, brought Mugabe's brutality against his own people to wide public attention.

Although all foreign correspondents had been barred from the country and though the efforts of local journalists were severely hampered, the word—and the pictures—got out, galvanising anti-Mugabe feelings even in Africa, where leaders have been reluctant to condemn him because of his liberation credentials.

Mugabe—once the world's blue-eyed African, lauded for his eloquence and statesmanship—has finally been recognised as a dangerous megalomaniac. In the words of the president of the African Union, President John Kufuor of Ghana: "We are embarrassed by what is going on in Zimbabwe."

For the past eight years or so, South Africa has conned the world into believing that it has been working behind the scenes to solve the problems in Zimbabwe. But President Thabo Mbeki's "quiet diplomacy" is now derisively referred to as "pussyfoot diplomacy". The early response from that government to atrocities that all could clearly see was a vague statement from the deputy foreign minister Aziz Pahad about obeying rule of law.

However, other voices within South Africa have been vociferous in their condemnation of Mugabe—notably the leader of the opposition Democratic Alliance, Tony Leon, Archbishop Desmond Tutu, Cardinal Wilfred Napier, the powerful trade-union body Cosatu, and a number of student groups.

Inside Zimbabwe, the beatings have been a significant catalyst. People cowed by years of intimidation and weighed down by economic hardship are now angry. Anger has conquered fear. Within Zanu-PF itself, the two groups shadow-boxing for pole position to succeed Mugabe, led by Joyce Mujuru and Emmerson Mnangagwa, have come into the open, courting media attention.

Both the Mujuru and Mnangagwa factions agree Mugabe should not continue beyond the presidential elections scheduled for 2008, but not because they have suddenly seen the light and want a democratic Zimbabwe. They are motivated by self-interest: the EU's travel restrictions are irksome and the economic meltdown is destroying their business empires.

The two factions hate each other, yet neither is strong enough on its own to win a general election. Both know they will need the support of the opposition MDC, because of its local support base and because it holds the key to international recognition and donorfunded reconstruction of the economy.

Mugabe, meanwhile, wants to continue in power. He is a wily politician and we should not underestimate his machinations.

Despite his failed diplomacy, what Mbeki does will be important. His political and economic muscle will determine the ultimate outcome. Tragically for most Zimbabweans, three million of whom live in squalor and fear in South Africa, Mbeki wants to see Zanu-PF continue to rule Zimbabwe—albeit a reformed Zanu-PF.

He is working on it. The recent meetings in Johannesburg between the two countries' vice-presidents is evidence of that. There will be a role for the MDC in a new Zimbabwe, but it is clear Mbeki will exert his considerable influence to avoid an MDC—dominated government on his northern border. He mistrusts the party and fears its trade-union influence.

Wilf Mbanga was founder of Zimbabwe's Daily News, which was closed down by the government in 2003

The anti-colonial struggle was often violent, and few liberation movements have attempted to restore a culture of non-violence. Thus it is no surprise that Mugabe finds it easy to use violence against his people: the colonial state apparatus was attuned to that purpose. Once violence is used, it is used again. Even the idea of an opposition—internal or external—is a difficult concept for many. Mugabe's Zanu coerced the Patriotic Front (PF), the other major liberation movement in Zimbabwe, to merge with it in the 1980s, hence the name Zanu-PF. This eliminated a possible opposition force.

The resurgence of an opposition is due partly to a generational change in the country's politics. Many of the MDC's supporters are young and have experienced Zanu-PF mainly as a party in government that exploits its people. They are not impressed by past liberation credentials.

The articulate MDC spokesman Nelson Chamisa is not yet 30 years old. In South Africa, it is young activists in the Treatment Action Campaign and their leader Zackie Achmat who have been responsible for forcing the government to adopt more responsible Aids policies. Zwelinzima Vavi, leader of Cosatu, says: "We are not prepared to be merely 'yes-leader' workers' desks."

The sad truth, however, is that waiting for another generation before there can be real change is costly, even deadly, for ordinary Africans, not least Zimbabweans.

WILLIAM GUMEDE is a former deputy editor of the Sowetan newspaper. His book, "Thabo Mbeki and the Battle for the Soul of the ANC" will be republished by Zed later this year.

The Year of the Ballot

**"If governments and the international community learn from
and act on the lessons of 2006, the hope of a stable, developed,
and thriving region will be much closer to becoming a reality. . . . "**

Jorge Castañeda and Patricio Navia

Between December 2005 and December 2006, 11 Latin American countries held presidential elections. In addition to the two most populous nations of Brazil and Mexico, Colombia, Peru, Venezuela, Chile, Bolivia, Ecuador, Haiti, Costa Rica, and Nicaragua chose new leaders or reelected incumbents. Argentina was the only large country without an election in 2006 (it will have one in October 2007). Altogether, 80 percent of the Latin American population went to the polls last year. In fact, 2006 marked the first time in history that so many nations in the region held elections in the same year.

In most countries, the institutions of democracy remain fragile nevertheless. With Hugo Chávez's December 3 reelection in Venezuela closing out the electoral season, Latin American democracies today are sailing out to an uncertain future. In recent years, three South American countries (Argentina, Bolivia, and Ecuador) have had their presidents abruptly forced out of office. Odds are that some of the leaders elected in 2006 will eventually face similar situations.

Fortunately, however, there are five lessons from the electoral experiences of the past year that, if they are absorbed, should help consolidate Latin America's democracies. First, the election results indicate there is still hope for the embattled neoliberal model in the region. Second, the demand for broader inclusion remains very strong. Thus, third, social spending does matter. Fourth, there cannot be stable democracy without an accountable, open, and competitive political party system. And fifth, the left remains very potent in Latin America. If democracy is to fulfill the high expectations associated with it and gain full consolidation as the only game in town, strong and accountable left-wing parties must be accommodated.

The Democratic Fiesta

Incumbent governments could hardly have found a more convenient time to face elections. Latin America experienced its fourth consecutive year of economic growth in 2006. Between 1995 and 2003, the region's economies grew by an annual average of 2.2 percent. In 2004, its economic output increased by 5.7 percent. According to the International Monetary Fund, growth in 2005 was 4.4 percent, despite much lower figures for Brazil (2.3 percent) and Mexico (3 percent). The IMF estimates growth for 2006 at 4.8 percent, with Mexico (4.4 percent) and Brazil (3.2 percent) again underperforming. In a region where economic performance in the past 25 years has been mediocre at best, the 2004–2006 period was a notable exception.

The 2006 "democratic fiesta," as elections are referred to in the region, is also notable for the widespread respect shown for electoral results and the accompanying consolidation of independent and autonomous election oversight institutions. A number of races were extremely close, but with the exception of Mexico, all the losing candidates accepted defeat.

Costa Rica's election was decided by a razorthin margin of 0.3 percent. Still, defeated candidate Otton Solís accepted the results, and Oscar Arias, the social democrat and Nobel Peace Prize laureate who governed from 1986 to 1990, was sworn in as president. In Peru, the first-round election also produced a very close result for the runnerup. Christian Democrat Lourdes Flores came in 0.5 percent behind the former left-wing populist president Alan García (1985–1990). After a partial recount, García was declared the winner and went on to win the presidency in a June 4 runoff.

Mexico was the only country where official results were disputed. The losing candidate, leftist former Mexico City Mayor Andrés Manuel López Obrador, made accusations of fraud. Legislators with López Obrador's Party of the Democratic Revolution (PRD) staunchly opposed the swearing-in of the election winner, a conservative National Action Party (PAN) politician, thereby threatening the stability of Mexico's democracy. Fortunately, Felipe Calderón managed to be sworn in and assumed power on December 2.

Today, democratic elections in Latin America are better organized, more transparent, and more legitimate than when transitions to democracy first began in the 1980s and 1990s. Though under attack by the resurgence of populist politicians, representative democracy continues to be the mechanism of choice for selecting leaders in the region.

Table 1   2006 Presidential Election Results in Latin America

Country	Election date	Leading right-wing candidate vote %	Leading left-wing candidate vote %	Other candidates' vote %	Turnout (% of registered voters)
Bolivia	Dec. 18, 2005	28.6	53.7*	17.7	84.5
Chile	Dec. 11, 2005	25.4	46.0	28.6	84.5
Chile runoff	Jan. 15, 2006	46.5	53.5*	—	87.7
Costa Rica	Feb. 5, 2006	3.5	40.9*	55.6	65.2
Haiti	Feb. 7, 2006	12.4	51.2*	36.4	59.3
Colombia	May 28, 2006	62.3*	22.0	15.7	45.1
Peru	April 9, 2006	30.6	23.8	45.6	88.7
Peru runoff	June 4, 2006	52.6*	47.4	—	87.7
Mexico	July 2, 2006	36.4*	35.3	28.3	58.9
Brazil	Oct. 1, 2006	41.6	48.6	9.2	81.0
Brazil runoff	Oct. 29, 2006	39.2	60.8*	—	81.0
Nicaragua	Nov. 7, 2006	29.0	38.1*	32.9	61.2
Ecuador	Oct. 15, 2006	26.8	22.8	50.4	72.2
Ecuador runoff	Nov. 26, 2006	43.3	56.7*	—	75.5
Venezuela	Dec. 3, 2006	36.9	62.9*	0.2	74.9

*Election winner.

Table 1 shows the 15 presidential elections (counting run-offs) in 11 different Latin American countries. Based on their self-identification, candidates can be classified on a right-left continuum. Naturally, these self-definitions might be considered simplistic, but they allow for an understandable classification. As shown, leftist candidates tended to do better than right-wing candidates in 2006.

As Table 2 shows, incumbent candidates and parties also did fairly well. In six countries, the incumbent candidate—or the candidate from the incumbent party—won. In three other cases, the outgoing president had no candidate to support. Thus, only two incumbent parties were defeated. The scandal-ridden Social Christian Party in Costa Rica and the weak centrist Alliance for the Republic in Nicaragua lost. The respectable economic performance of most countries helped incumbents retain power. But incumbency strength should also be understood as an endorsement of the policies implemented by the outgoing leaders—for the most part committed to free trade.

We believe Latin American democracies will consolidate if they adequately react to the five lessons that the 2006 election season underscored. Learning from political experience could help publics and elites better understand the hurdles that newly elected leaders will face as they seek to fulfill their campaign promises and take on the challenges that have proved too difficult for past leaders in the region to overcome.

Neoliberalism Lives

The first lesson to draw from the past year's elections is that there is still hope for the beleaguered neoliberal economic model in Latin America. Candidates who advocate policies such as supporting free trade, attracting foreign investment, pro-moting privatization, and balancing the budget are not certain electoral losers. In fact, they often win, albeit by slim margins. Many Latin American voters—in some cases solid majorities—continue to support neoliberal economic policies.

In Chile, Michelle Bachelet, a socialist who pledged to continue the neoliberal policies promoted by her left-wing predecessor Ricardo Lagos, won in a runoff to become that country's first woman president. Although her election represented a radical change in terms of gender, it constituted a strong signal of continuity in terms of economic policies.

In Peru, although the most free-market-friendly candidate (Flores) ended up third in the first round, the new president has advocated the adoption of several free-market economic policies, including a free trade agreement with the United States. Drawing on Peru's historic strains with Chile, García campaigned on a promise to embrace the same aggressive pursuit of foreign markets as Chile has, in order to defeat Chile as the economic leader of South America's Pacific Rim. The anti-globalization candidate, nationalist and populist Ollanta Humala, lost. He turned out to be more a candidate of frustration than of hope. Hope in Peru was associated with García's partial embrace of neoliberal policies.

In Mexico, the candidate most closely associated with neoliberal policies came from behind to rob the anti-globalization candidate of an expected electoral victory. Calderón's strong defense of neoliberalism was comparable only to that of Alvaro Uribe, the incumbent president of Colombia, who easily won reelection. In Costa Rica, Arias won despite having promised to ratify the Central American Free Trade Agreement (CAFTA) with the United States. Solís, the anti-globalization candidate, failed to transform his opposition into a successful electoral appeal.

Table 2 Recent Economic Growth and Ideological Positioning of Outgoing and Incoming Presidents in Latin America

Country	2005 GDP Growth %	2006 GDP Growth %	Previous President	New President
Bolivia	4.1	4.1	Eduardo Rodriguez, not elected	Evo Morales, left
Chile	6.3	5.2	Ricardo Lagos, moderate left	Michelle Bachelet, moderate left*
Costa Rica	5.9	6.5	Abel Pacheco, moderate right	Oscar Arias, moderate left
Haiti	1.8	2.5	Boniface Alexandre, not elected	René Préval, moderate left*
Colombia	5.2	5.2	Alvaro Uribe, right	Alvaro Uribe, right*
Peru	6.4	6.5	Alejandro Toledo, center	Alan García, moderate left
Mexico	3.0	4.4	Vicente Fox, moderate right	Felipe Calderón, moderate right*
Brazil	2.3	3.2	Lula da Silva, moderate left	Lula da Silva, moderate left*
Nicaragua	4.0	3.7	Enrique Bolaños, moderate right	Daniel Ortega, left
Ecuador	4.7	4.4	Alfredo Palacio, moderate left	Rafael Correa, left
Venezuela	9.3	7.5	Hugo Chávez, left	Hugo Chávez, left*

*Incumbent candidate/party reelected. *Source for economic data:* IMF, "Regional Economic Outlook: November 2006"

In Brazil, although President Luiz Inácio Lula Da Silva has not been a committed champion of neoliberal policies, the opposition candidate did not promise to implement radically different policies. At a snail's pace, all Brazilian politicians are embracing neoliberal policies and implementing reforms consistent with the so-called Washington Consensus. The recently reelected Lula put it bluntly in a December 12, 2006, interview: "It's a question of how much gray hair you have. If you're on the right you move a bit toward the center, and whoever belongs to the left gradually becomes a social democrat. . . . And there's no other possible explanation: if you know a very adult person who considers himself belonging to the left, it's because he has problems. If you know a young person on the right, he has problems."

In Bolivia, Venezuela, Nicaragua, and Ecuador, the winning candidates last year were self-declared opponents of neoliberalism. But President Rafael Correa of Ecuador has promised not to reverse the dollarization of that country's economy. In Nicaragua, the victorious former president Daniel Ortega actively catered to foreign investors, so badly needed by his country's ailing economy. In addition to Venezuela's Chávez, who has emerged as the region's champion of anti-neoliberalism, Bolivian President Evo Morales has gone furthest in expanding the state into the private sector. Yet, as also happens to be the case in Venezuela, the state in Bolivia historically has had limited capacity to provide social services. Thus, not all efforts by Morales to strengthen state capacity should automatically be associated with an unjustified preference for bureaucratic

employment. Even ardent neoliberals believe there must be a state capable of providing some public services.

Many Latin American voters—in some cases solid majorities—continue to support neoliberal economic policies.

Several newly elected Latin American presidents have publicly expressed their discontent with neoliberal policies, but we should consider more the policies they implement than the speeches they give at regional summits and improvised press conferences. Candidates might claim they dislike free trade initiatives, as García did in Peru, or oppose the dollarization of the economy, as Correa did in Ecuador, but when pressed to spell out specific policies they are far more conciliatory and stop short of reversing neoliberal initiatives. And, as the case of Chile's "socialist neoliberalism" (a social free market economy, as they call it) best exemplifies, policies implemented do not necessarily coincide with rhetoric used in election campaigns and even in government.

The "Left-outs" Want In

The second lesson made clear by the election results is the continued popular demand for social inclusion. Latin America's historically obstinate levels of inequality are often ignored by policy makers, who tend to pay necessary but excessive attention to absolute levels of economic growth. As Latin America has enjoyed a good run of economic expansion in recent years, the persistent levels of inequality have resurfaced as a colossal, unmet challenge.

Thus, candidates who look like and share the experiences of the majority of the population tend to do better than those who are members of the elite or have a difficult time connecting with the electorate on a personal level. There are also implications for governance. Bachelet's election in Chile, for example, can be explained by the correct mix of continuity in economic policies and change in the means of governing. Chile has transitioned from a male, top-down, technocratic approach to politics to a more inclusive, bottom-up approach, with a more personal touch. A pediatrician by training, Bachelet often explained during her campaign that no medical treatment could be successful without fully incorporating the patients into the process. Her focus on building a stronger civil society and facilitating mechanisms for popular participation reflects her success at combining continuity in policies with a more inclusive strategy for pursuing them.

Although it is often confused with populism, social inclusion is a welcome result of a well-functioning democracy. People want to elect others who look like them, share their experiences, or at least can relate to their own lives. Elitist agreements in support of democracy that were ratified and implemented with a top-down approach have been replaced across Latin America by demands to take broader social concerns into consideration. Voters want to have not only a vote but also a say in what type of candidates make it onto the ballots and win elections.

In a region where populism has always threatened stability, a message of social inclusion remains fertile ground for populist candidates. But populism should be seen as itself a symptom of social exclusion. Countries where social exclusion has been poorly addressed tend to see the emergence of more successful populist leaders. Whereas populism has not emerged in Costa Rica or Chile, for example, populist candidates have been successful in Peru, Venezuela, and Ecuador. Countries that have made progress on social inclusion have also seen the appeal of populist leaders dramatically reduced. Even in Mexico, where inequality remains a big problem, López Obrador's populist rhetoric won him only 35 percent of the vote. Populist appeals do not automatically make for election winners.

Yet it is easier for populists to win if the alternative candidate belongs to the landed traditional oligarchy. Personal background matters. For example, had the right-wing candidate in Mexico been a member of the oligarchy (as right-wing candidates in Brazil, Chile, and Ecuador were), he would have found it more difficult to win. The fact that Calderón is a mestizo with a convincing middle-class background helped him symbolically embody the message of social inclusion. Correa, the left-wing candidate in Ecuador, won in part because he was closer to the people than was his opponent, Alvaro Noboa, a banana entrepreneur, free-market advocate, and Ecuador's wealthiest man. Had Correa, a mestizo-looking former economics professor, been the advocate of free-market policies, he still could have

won his election campaigning as the people's candidate against the candidate of the elites.

Because of the effect of mass media, representative democracy in societies marked by historical patterns of exclusion will tend to produce leaders who are much more personally identified with the ethnic and social makeup of the majority of their national populations. In industrialized democracies, candidates who are closer and more connected to the people have an unquestionable advantage in electoral campaigns. Thus, it will be more common to see candidates like Morales (who is ethnically and socially representative of the majority of Bolivians) than candidates like Gonzalo Sánchez de Losada (who belongs to the social and economic elite and does not share the ethnic background of most Bolivians) in future elections in the region.

Fighting Poverty Wins Votes

The third lesson that Latin American democracies need to heed is that social programs matter. Candidates from parties and coalitions that have implemented effective social programs—usually targeted at the poor by subsidizing demand—do better than candidates who promote trickle-down economics. Rather than the old, inefficient practice of subsidizing gas, utilities, or tortilla prices for all, programs that subsidize demand make gas, utilities, or tortillas cheaper only for those with lower incomes. While a trickle-down approach concentrates exclusively on generating employment through economic growth, a sound demand-driven subsidy uses state resources to help level the playing field in favor of those at the bottom end of the income distribution. Targeted social programs implemented effectively and efficiently are rewarded in Latin America with large shares of votes.

The Bolsa Familia program in Brazil, for instance, was partially responsible for Lula's reelection victory. The program, aimed at subsidizing the poorest Brazilian families, allowed Lula to cultivate a strong electoral base in the impoverished northeast. Whereas Lula cruised to victory in 2002 with strong support from the industrial south, in 2006 it was the impoverished *nordeste* that made the difference. In Mexico, the Progresa-Oportunidades program housed at the Social Development Ministry has been markedly successful at assigning earmarked spending in education, health, and nutrition to the poorest families. Similar programs in Chile and Colombia have helped incumbent parties and coalitions build electoral support among the marginalized poor.

Most countries in Latin America have replaced broad supply-side price supports with demand-side subsidies targeted at the poorest quintiles of their population. Yet only those countries where there is sufficient state capacity to implement such programs have seen significant poverty reduction and improvements in quality of life. In countries where there is more limited state capacity, like Peru or Ecuador, the elimination of supply-side subsidies has actually ended up hurting the poor. This is especially true among the unorganized poor. Thus, without appropriate state capacity, countries lacking sufficient social networks (such as political parties, labor unions, or neighborhood organizations) find it difficult to implement social programs targeted at helping exclusively the poor.

In Venezuela, a country with limited state capacity, President Chávez has developed a parallel state through the so-called *misiones,* initiatives aimed at bringing social services to the poor. Because the state bureaucracy is still overcrowded with machine politicians from the ancient twoparty regime, Chávez has implemented a model inspired by the Cuban Revolution to bring social services—and state presence—to impoverished urban and rural communities. Not surprisingly, Chávez's confident electoral campaign was built on the premise that the overwhelming majority of Venezuela's poor would turn out to vote for his reelection. According to the most recent report by the Latin American and Caribbean Economic Commission—based on disputed government figures—poverty in Venezuela fell from 49.4 percent in 1999 to 37.1 percent in 2005. Extreme poverty declined from 21.7 percent to 15.9 percent in the same period. There are reasons to believe figures have been tampered with to hide a more mediocre performance in poverty reduction. But there is no doubt that Chávez has built strong support among the poor even with mediocre poverty-reduction initiatives.

Countries without the appropriate state capacity have failed to build successful social programs. Despite the strong economic growth observed in Peru since 2000, poverty actually increased from 48.6 percent to 51.1 percent between 1999 and 2004. Although extreme poverty decreased from 22.4 percent to 18.9 percent during the same period, the inability of the state to effectively use its resources to help alleviate poverty might help explain the emergence of strong populist candidates. They have capitalized on the frustration of a large segment of Peruvians who can see economic growth benefit others while excluding them.

Parties Are Central

The fourth lesson from electoral experience is that the political party system matters. Countries with stronger, more established political party systems tend to have more legitimate elections. Because there are rules that can strengthen the party system and make it more transparent, Latin American countries should focus on institutional design. Competitive and accountable party systems are not the automatic result of democracy. In fact, as the 2006 elections showed, several Latin American countries, such as Colombia, Venezuela, and Costa Rica, have seen their traditionally strong party systems deteriorate. In other countries, like Mexico and Brazil, existing parties have grown stronger but are less accountable. In several countries, a *partidocracia* (political party oligopoly) has weakened and restricted democracy.

Countries where social exclusion has been poorly addressed tend to see the emergence of more successful populist leaders.

Political parties often enjoy such a negative standing that many presidential candidates seek to distance themselves from parties. We tend to see candidates trying to highlight their personal qualities and minimize their links with political parties. Often, independent candidates find it easier to build reform and anti-corruption platforms precisely because they are not identified with parties. Even worse, some aspirants are dissuaded from running for office precisely because they cannot manage the intricate and sometimes corrupt inner workings of the political party apparatus.

The Latin American electorate often welcomes outsiders as candidates. True, in some cases outsiders find it much more difficult, or even impossible, to run on a playing field tilted in favor of candidates nominated by political parties. But the popularity of outsiders—as well as the efforts by insiders to portray themselves as outsiders—reflects a profound structural problem with the quality and reputation of the political party system.

The role of political parties in societies can be compared to that of hospitals. Whereas one would prefer to interact little with hospitals and physicians, we expect them to be good, transparent, efficient, and honest. Societies cannot function well without hospitals. But underperforming, inefficient, corrupt, and self-serving hospitals will also end up hurting countries. The same can be said of political parties and politicians.

In democratic institutional design, one size does not fit all. In fact, the party system is often endogenous to the country's history and past political developments. Yet some institutional features in general can be adopted to strengthen party systems and to make them more transparent. Social, ethnic, historical, and even religious cleavages can explain the emergence and survival of different party systems. Historically informed institutional engineering can help foster the stability of a party system and encourage cooperation among existing parties.

A reasonable institutional design should not attempt to create a new and different party system. Instead, a fine-tuning approach should be adopted to implement changes that will help existing parties become more accountable, responsive, and prone to form stable coalitions. In particular, presidents who command minority support in the legislature must be able to form coalitions that will allow them to build legislative majorities to advance their agendas. Institutional changes can help promote coalition formation and stability. In addition to reducing the number of seats in every district (Brazil's state of São Paulo constitutes a single electoral district with 70 members elected to the Chamber of Deputies), holding presidential elections concurrently with legislative elections (which still does not happen in several Central American countries and in Colombia and Venezuela) should be the norm. Because the public pays more attention to presidential than to legislative elections, when they are held concurrently, presidential candidates can earn the loyalty of candidates for congress who want to associate themselves with popular presidential aspirants. Concurrent elections promote party discipline and thus help strengthen the party system.

Also, institutional features that foster transparency and accountability must be introduced. Political parties tend to legislate to make it difficult for other parties to enter the electoral arena (most notably in Mexico), thus consolidating a party oligopoly. Parties are also prone to favor increased public funds for electoral campaigns, while opposing increased transparency in how private funds are obtained and how all funds are spent. Moreover, parties strive to restrict access to funds for challengers who are not part of the party oligopoly. Reforms that foster more competition among existing parties and lower entry barriers for new parties will help strengthen the party system. A more competitive party system on a more level playing field will increase the legitimacy of democracy, improve the quality of legislation passed, and make politicians more accountable to the electorate. When candidates do not run away from the parties in elections, democracy will be more consolidated.

The Left Is Here to Stay

The fifth and final lesson of the 2006 election year is that, at the end of the day, the left is strong in Latin America. Left-wing parties did well, better than in the past, in all countries. Even in those countries where conservative candidates won presidential elections, as in Mexico and Colombia, left-wing parties did better than they had ever done before. In Mexico, the PRD garnered 30 percent of the votes and seats in the Chamber of Deputies, significantly higher than in the 2003 midterm election, and 35 percent of the presidential vote, twice what it got in 2000.

In Colombia, the presidential candidate of the Alternative Democratic Pole, Carlos Gaviria, obtained a surprisingly high 22 percent of the vote. His coalition had received only 8 percent of the vote in the parliamentary election held in March. Although this loose progressive coalition has yet to evolve into an institutional party, its electoral strength has helped the Colombian democratic left become a major player capable of challenging the historic two-party system in that country.

Some left-wing parties in the region are reformist. Others continue to embrace a failed economic model. Yet, because the left is strong, there is no sense in hoping it will never win. It makes more sense to help foster the renewal of responsible left-wing parties. Successful left-wing experiences should be promoted so that other left-wing parties can adapt them to their own national realities. The experience of Chile since the 1990s has already informed other left-wing parties. Ecuador's Correa, for example, has cited Chile as a model of what he intends to do to promote growth and reduce poverty. (He visited Chile shortly after being elected.)

Likewise, the policies of Lula in Brazil and Tabaré Vázquez in Uruguay have inspired pragmatic thinking among left-wing leaders in other countries. Because the left will likely continue to receive electoral support, fostering the growth of a moderate, growth-oriented, and democratic left should be an international priority.

Democracy Tested

With good reason, many who have studied Latin America for a long time were overjoyed to see that the debate over political developments in the region in 2006 centered around ballots rather than bullets. It is a tremendous accomplishment for the region to see elections as the only legitimate political game in town. Yet we know that elections are the easy part of the democratic process. Democratic consolidation and stability take much more effort than holding a democratic election.

As newly elected governments in Latin America implement their policies and attempt to expand economic growth, reduce poverty, and tackle the deep inequalities that persist in their nations, the region's democratic structures will be put to a test. If governments and the international community learn from and act on the lessons of 2006, the hope of a stable, developed, and thriving region will be much closer to becoming a reality when Latin America's independence bicentennial is commemorated in 2010.

JORGE CASTAÑEDA, the foreign minister of Mexico from 2000 to 2003, is a professor of politics and Latin American and Caribbean studies at New York University. PATRICIO NAVIA teaches global studies at NYU and political science at Diego Portales University in Chile.

Reprinted from *Current History*, February 2007, pp. 51–57. Copyright © 2007 by Current History, Inc. Reprinted with permission.

The Lost Continent

For decades, Latin America's weight in the world has been shrinking. It is not an economic powerhouse, a security threat, or a population bomb. Even its tragedies pale in comparison to Africa's. The region will not rise until it ends its search for magic formulas. It may not make for a good sound bite, but patience is Latin America's biggest deficit of all.

MOISÉS NAÍM

Latin America has grown used to living in the backyard of the United States. For decades, it has been a region where the U.S. government meddled in local politics, fought communists, and promoted its business interests. Even if the rest of the world wasn't paying attention to Latin America, the United States occasionally was. Then came September 11, and even the United States seemed to tune out. Naturally, the world's attention centered almost exclusively on terrorism, the wars in Afghanistan, Iraq, and Lebanon, and on the nuclear ambitions of North Korea and Iran. Latin America became Atlantis—the lost continent. Almost overnight, it disappeared from the maps of investors, generals, diplomats, and journalists.

Indeed, as one commentator recently quipped, Latin America can't compete on the world stage in any aspect, even as a threat. Unlike anti-Americans elsewhere, Latin Americans are not willing to die for the sake of their geopolitical hatreds. Latin America is a nuclear-weapons free zone. Its only weapon of mass destruction is cocaine. In contrast to emerging markets like India and China, Latin America is a minor economic player whose global significance is declining. Sure, a few countries export oil and gas, but only Venezuela is in the top league of the world's energy market.

Not even Latin America's disasters seem to elicit global concern anymore. Argentina experienced a massive financial stroke in 2001, and no one abroad seemed to care. Unlike prior crashes, no government or international financial institution rushed to bail it out. Latin America doesn't have Africa's famines, genocides, an HIV/AIDS pandemic, wholesale state failures, or rock stars who routinely adopt its tragedies. Bono, Bill Gates, and Angelina Jolie worry about Botswana, not Brazil.

But just as the five-year-old war on terror pronounced the necessity of confronting threats where they linger, it also underscored the dangers of neglect. Like Afghanistan, Latin America shows how quickly and easy it is for the United States to lose its influence when Washington is distracted by other priorities. In both places, Washington's disinterest produced a vacuum that was filled by political groups and leaders hostile to the United States.

No, Latin America is not churning out Islamic terrorists as Afghanistan was during the days of the Taliban. In Latin America, the power gap is being filled by a group of disparate leaders often lumped together under the banner of populism. On the rare occasions that Latin American countries do make international news, it's the election of a so-called populist, an apparently anti-American, anti-market leader, that raises hackles. However, Latin America's populists aren't a monolith. Some are worse for international stability than is usually reported. But some have the potential to chart a new, positive course for the region. Underlying the ascent of these new leaders are several real, stubborn threads running through Latin Americans' frustration with the status quo in their countries. Unfortunately, the United States'—and the rest of the world's—lack of interest in that region means that the forces that are shaping disparate political movements in Latin America are often glossed over, misinterpreted, or ignored. Ultimately, though, what matters most is not what the northern giant thinks or does as much as what half a billion Latin Americans think and do. And in the last couple of decades, the wild swings in their political behavior have created a highly unstable terrain where building the institutions indispensable for progress or for fighting poverty has become increasingly difficult. There is a way out. But it's not the quick fix that too many of Latin America's leaders have promised and that an impatient population demands.

The Left Turn That Wasn't

In the 1990s, politicians throughout Latin America won elections by promising economic reforms inspired by the "Washington Consensus" and closer ties to the United States. The Free Trade Area of the Americas offered hope for a better economic future for all. The United States could count on its neighbors to the south as reliable international allies. In Argentina, for example, the country's political and military links with the United States were so strong that in 1998, it was invited to become part of a select group of "major non-NATO allies." Today, however, President Néstor Kirchner nurtures a 70-percent approval rating by lobbing derision and invective against the "empire" up north. His main ally abroad is Venezuelan President Hugo Chávez, not George W. Bush. Nowadays, running for political office in Latin America openly advocating privatization, free trade, or claiming the support of the U.S. government is political suicide. Denouncing the corruption and inequality spurred by the "savage capitalism" of the 1990s, promising to help the poor and battle the rich, and disparaging the abusive international behavior of the American superpower and what is seen as its "globalization" ruse is a political platform that has acquired renewed potency throughout the region. In nearly every country, these ideas have helped new political leaders gain a national following and in Argentina, Bolivia, and Venezuela, even to win the presidency. In most other countries, notably in Mexico, Peru, Ecuador, and Nicaragua, proponents of these views enjoy wide popular support and are a fundamental factor in their countries' politics.

Latin America can't compete on the world stage in any way, not even as a threat.

So what happened? The first alarm bells sounded with the election in rapid succession of Chávez in Venezuela in 1998, Luiz Inácio "Lula" da Silva in Brazil in 2002, Kirchner in Argentina in 2003, and Tabaré Vázquez in Uruguay in 2004. All of them represented left-of-center coalitions and all promised to undo the "neoliberal excesses" of their predecessors. All of them also stressed the need to reassert their nations' independence from the United States and limit the superpower's influence.

Yet, none of these new presidents really delivered on their more extreme campaign promises, especially their plans to roll back the economic reforms of the 1990s. Brazil's Lula has followed an orthodox economic policy, anchored in painfully high interest rates and the active promotion of foreign investments. In Argentina, the only significant departure from the economic orthodoxy of the 1990s has been the adoption of widespread price controls and a disdainful attitude toward foreign investors.

In Venezuela, the rhetoric (and sometimes the deeds) are more in line with rabid anti-American, antifree trade, and anti-market postures. Chávez routinely denounces free-trade agreements with the United States: He has been known to say that "[c]apitalism will lead to the destruction of humanity," and that the United States is the "devil that represents capitalism." Chávez's anti-trade posture conveniently glosses over the reality that Venezuela enjoys a de facto free trade agreement with the United States. In fact, America is the top market for Venezuela's oil. During Chávez's tenure, Venezuela has become one of the world's fastest-growing markets for manufactured American products. And even the capitalist devils that are the objects of Chávez's wrath aren't suffering as much as might be expected. As the *Financial Times* reported in August, "Bankers traditionally face firing squads in times of revolution. But in Venezuela, they are having a party." Local bankers close to the regime are reaping huge profits. Foreign bankers who cater to the wealthy return from trips to Caracas with long lists of newly acquired clients in need of discreet "asset management" abroad.

Although some of these populist leaders have so far failed to live up to the radical economic changes they promised on the campaign trail, the gaps between incendiary rhetoric and actual practice have been far narrower in the region's foreign policies—especially in Venezuela and its relations with the United States. President Chávez, easily the world's most vocal anti-American leader, has called President George W. Bush, among other things, a "donkey," "a drunkard," and "an assassin." Not even Osama bin Laden has spouted such vitriol. Chávez has embraced Cuban leader Fidel Castro as his mentor and comrade-in-arms, and in so doing, he has become the region's most visible leader since Che Guevara. Like Che, Chávez often seems hell-bent on sparking an armed confrontation to further his revolution; he calls Saddam Hussein a "brother," and is arming new local militias with 100,000 AK-47s to repel the "imminent" U.S. invasion. His international activism now routinely takes him around the world. In Damascus this summer, Chávez and Syrian President Bashar Assad issued a joint declaration stating that they were "firmly united against imperialist aggression and the hegemonic intentions of the U.S. Empire."

The main concern is not just that Chávez is developing close ties with prominent U.S. foes worldwide, but rather his efforts to refashion the domestic politics of his neighboring countries. His persona and his message are certainly attractive to large blocs of voters in other countries. Politicians elsewhere in Latin America who emulate him and his platforms are gaining popularity, and it's hard to imagine that Chávez is refraining from using his enormous oil wealth to support their political ascendancy. The international concern about trends in Latin America peaked in late 2005, as 12 presidential elections were scheduled for the ensuing months. In several countries—Bolivia, Costa Rica, Ecuador, Mexico, Nicaragua, and Peru—leftist candidates with Chávez-sounding platforms stood a good chance of winning.

Yet that expectation did not come to pass. So far, the only election where a Chávez ally has won is Bolivia. There, Evo Morales, the leader of the coca growers, announced that he would become "the United States' worst nightmare," and quickly proceeded to enter into a close alliance with Venezuela and Cuba. But the election of Chávez-backed candidates turned out to be more the exception than the rule. Surprisingly, running for office with too close an identification with Chávez or his policies has become an electoral kiss of death. Not even his promises of supplying cheap oil and financial aid if his candidate won were enough to compensate for the strong voter backlash against a foreign president openly trying to influence the outcome of national elections.

But the electoral defeat of candidates running on platforms perceived to be too extreme or too close to Chávez does not mean that the ideas they represent are unappealing. Latin American voters are aggrieved, impatient, and eager to vote for new candidates who offer a break with the past and who promise a way out of the dire present.

If Not Left, Then Where?

Since the late 1990s, Latin American political systems have been rocked by a wide variety of frustrations. Therefore lumping the different types of discontent under generic "leftist" or "populist" monikers is misleading. Indeed, in today's Latin America, some of the grievances are clearly anti-market, while others are rooted in dissatisfactions caused not by overreliance on the market but by governmental overreach. Curbing corruption, for example, is a strong political demand that is unlikely to be satisfied by increasing the economic activities controlled by an already overwhelmed and corrupt public sector. Other grievances unite the far left and the far right. Economic nationalists who resent the market-opening reforms that allow foreign products to displace locally made ones include both right-wing business groups who profited handsomely from the protectionism, as well as leftist labor leaders who have seen their ranks shrink as local factories went out of business, unable to compete with foreign imports.

The responses to these political demands have also been varied. Some leaders, like Chávez and Kirchner, are behaving in a traditional, populist fashion, relying on massive and often wasteful public spending, on prices kept artificially low through governmental controls, or the scapegoating of the private sector to cement their popularity. Many others, however, like Lula in Brazil, Vicente Fox in Mexico, Alvaro Uribe in Colombia, or Ricardo Lagos in Chile have been models of more responsible economic governance and have shown a willingness to absorb the costs of unpopular but necessary economic policies.

What unites almost all Latin American countries, however, are two long-standing trends that multiply and deepen the variety of the grievances that are sprouting throughout the region: Prolonged mediocre economic performance, and the decay of traditional forms of political organization, and political parties in particular.

Latin America has suffered from slow economic growth for more than a quarter-century. Episodes of rapid growth have been short lived and often ended in painful financial crashes with devastating effects on the poor and the middle class. Economic growth in Latin America has been slower than it was in the 1960s and 70s, worse relative to all other emerging markets in the world, and unremittingly less than what the region itself needs to lift the poor standard of living of most of the population. This economic disappointment has become increasingly unacceptable to voters who have been promised much and gotten little and who have become better informed than ever about the standards of living of others at home and abroad. Latin Americans are fed up. Naturally, the frustrations produced by the wide gap between expectations and reality and between the living standards of the few who have so much and the many who have almost nothing create fertile ground for the fractious politics that make governing so difficult. Inevitably, political parties, and especially those in power, have suffered tremendous losses in loyalty, credibility, and legitimacy. Some of this disrepute is well deserved and often self-inflicted, as most political parties have failed to modernize their thinking or replace their ineffectual leaders. Corruption, patronage, and the use of politics as the fastest route for personal wealth are also rampant.

But it is also true that governing in a region where the political attitudes of large swaths of the population are imbued with rage, revenge, and impatience, and where the machinery of the public sector is often broken, is bound to end in failure. Because the region is resource-rich, the most

Latin American Merchandise Exports
(as a percentage of world total)

Foreign Direct Investment into Latin America
(as a percentage of world total)

Shrinking Share. Latin America's economic clout continues to slide.

Sources for Charts, Bottom: Economic Commission for Latin America and the Caribbean; Top: World Trade Organization

common explanation for poverty amid so much imagined wealth is corruption. End the corruption and the standard of living of the poor will more or less automatically improve, goes the thinking. This assumption of course ignores the fact that a nation's prosperity depends more on being rich in competent public institutions, rule of law, and a well-educated population than in exportable raw materials.

Moreover, while the widespread presence and ravaging effects of corruption are indisputable, the reality is that poverty in Latin America owes as much, if not more, to the region's inability to find ways to compete more effectively in a globalized economy than to the pervasive thievery of those in power. It is hard to argue that China or India or the fast-growing economies of East Asia are substantially less corrupt than Latin America. Yet their growth rates and their ability to lift their populations out of poverty have been better than those of Latin America. Why? The fact is that the region's democracy and activist politics make its wages too high to compete with the low-wage Asian economies. Latin America's poor educational systems and low level of technological development make it unable to compete effectively in most international markets where success is driven by know how and innovation. With its high wages and low technology, Latin America is having a hard time fitting into the hypercompetitive global economy. That fact gets far less attention than others that are more urgent, visible, or politically popular. Yet many of these problems—unemployment, poverty, slow economic growth—are manifestations of national

economies that are ill-suited to prosper under the conditions prevalent in today's world.

The Waiting Game

Like all fundamental development problems, Latin America's global competitive shortcomings cannot be reduced simply or quickly. The specific reasons behind a country's disadvantageous position in the global economy vary. Alleviating them requires simultaneous efforts on many fronts by different actors over a long period. And herein lies a central difficulty besetting all attempts to create positive, sustained change in Latin America: They all take more time than voters, politicians, investors, social activists, and journalists are willing to wait before moving on to another idea or another leader.

Latin America's most important deficit is patience. Unless the patience of all influential actors is raised, efforts will continue to fail before they are fully tested or executed. Investors will continue to ignore good projects that cannot offer quick returns, governments will only pick policies that can generate rapid, visible results even if they are unsustainable or mostly cosmetic, and voters will continue to shed leaders that don't deliver soon enough.

Reducing the patience deficit is impossible without alleviating Latin America's most immediate and urgent needs. But it is a mistake to assume that sustainable improvements will only occur as a result of radical, emergency measures. Large-scale social progress will require years of sustained efforts that are not prematurely terminated and replaced by a new, "big-bang" solution. Continuous progress demands the stability created by agreement on a set of basic shared goals and ideas among major political players. In the past, this patience was either ruthlessly forced on the population by military governments or induced by the adoption of a similar ideology shared by influential social groups. Both approaches are highly problematic and not viable in the long run.

Therefore, rather than seeking ideological consensus or forcing ideological hegemony, Latin Americans should build from what exists and seems to be working, rather than dismiss what already exists just because its champions are political competitors. Only those individuals and organizations who are able to bridge ideological divides and bring together different approaches will fix Latin America's long-standing problems. And give them time.

It's not as though there's no precedent for this kind of progressive governance. Former Presidents Fernando Henrique Cardoso in Brazil and Lagos in Chile integrated different ideological perspectives and developed pragmatic approaches to balance conflicting demands. Both came from socialist backgrounds and while in office made enormous and often successful efforts to fight poverty and improve social conditions. But they were also quite sensitive about the need to maintain economic stability—which often meant painful cuts in public spending—and to foster an attractive business environment for investors. Although neither Cardoso nor Lagos was able to drastically overhaul his nation's poor social conditions, both easily rank among the most effective and successful presidents of the last decade—anywhere. They made far more progress in alleviating poverty in their countries than any of the more strident Latin American revolutionaries whose radical efforts on behalf of the poor so often ended up creating only more poverty and inequality.

With its high wages and low technology, Latin America is having a hard time fitting into the global economy.

It is natural for Latin American citizens and politicians to be captivated by promises that seem too good to be true. People who find themselves in dire straits naturally want extreme, quick solutions. Latin Americans have been experimenting with brutal, heavy handed swings in their political economies since the 1970s. Yet, this search for silver-bullet solutions, though understandable given the grave problems of the region, is mistaken. Latin Americans must learn that, precisely because their illnesess are so acute, the solutions must be, paradoxically, more tempered. It might seem counterintuitive to reject the promises of the men and women offering radical change for a region so used to failure and neglect. But it may be the only way to lift millions out of poverty. And in the process, get Latin America back on the map.

MOISÉS NAÍM is editor in chief of *Foreign Policy*.

UNIT 5

Population, Development, Environment and Health

Unit Selections

Key Points to Consider

- How will current population trends produce demographic change?

- What are the implications of these trends?

- Why are developing countries likely to suffer even greater effects of global warming?

- Do rich countries bear some responsibility for natural disasters in the developing world?

- How might healthcare in developing countries be addressed more comprehensively?

- What trends are apparent in the fight against HIV/AIDS?

- How does illness contribute to poverty?

Student Web Site
www.mhcls.com/online

Internet References
Further information regarding these Web sites may be found in this book's preface or online.

Earth Pledge Foundation
  http://www.earthpledge.org
EnviroLink
  http://envirolink.org
Greenpeace
  http://www.greenpeace.org
Linkages on Environmental Issues and Development
  http://www.iisd.ca/linkages/
Population Action International
  http://www.populationaction.org
The Worldwatch Institute
  http://www.worldwatch.org

Although growth has slowed considerably since the 1960s, world population is still growing at the rate of approximately 75 million per year, with most of this increase taking place in the developing world. The average fertility rate (the number of children a woman will have during her life) for all developing countries is 2.9 while for the least developed countries the figure is 5.0. Increasing population complicates development efforts, puts added stress on ecosystems, and threatens food security. Population migration patterns are also increasingly shaped by trends in population growth in both the industrialized countries and the developing world.

World population surpassed 6 billion toward the end of 1999 and, if current trends continue, could reach 9.8 billion by 2050. Even if, by some miracle, population growth was immediately reduced to replacement level, the developing world's population would continue to grow for decades. Approximately one-third of the population in the developing world is under the age of 15, with that proportion jumping to 42 percent in the least-developed countries. The population momentum created by this age distribution means that it will be some time before the developing world's population growth slows substantially. Some developing countries have achieved progress in reducing fertility rates through family planning programs, but much remains to be done. At the same time, reduced life expectancy, especially related to the HIV/AIDS epidemic, is having a significant demographic impact in parts of the developing world, especially sub-Saharan Africa.

Over a billion people live in absolute poverty, as measured by a combination of economic and social indicators. As population increases, it becomes more difficult to meet the basic human needs of the developing world's citizens. Indeed, food scarcity looms as a major problem among the poor as population increases, production fails to keep pace, demand for water increases, per capita crop land shrinks, and food prices rise. Periodic drought, worsened by climate change, also reduces food supply often necessitating emergency relief.

Larger populations of poor people also place greater strains on scarce resources and fragile ecosystems. Deforestation for agriculture and fuel, as well as to meet demand for timber, has reduced forested areas and contributed to erosion, desertification, and global warming. Intensified agriculture, particularly for cash crops, has depleted soils necessitating increased fertilization, which is costly and also produces runoff that contributes to water pollution.

Economic development, regarded by many as a panacea, has not only failed to eliminate poverty but has exacerbated it in some ways. Ill-conceived economic development plans have diverted resources from more productive uses. If developing countries try to follow Western consumption patterns, sustainable development will be impossible. Furthermore, economic growth without effective environmental policies can lead to the need for more expensive clean-up efforts in the future.

Divisions between North and South on environmental issues emerged at the 1992 Rio Conference on Environment and Development. The conference highlighted the fundamental differences between the industrialized world and developing countries over causes, of and solutions to global environmental problems. Developing countries pointed to consumption levels in the North as the main cause of environmental problems, and called on the industrialized countries to pay most of the costs of environmental programs. Industrialized countries sought to convince developing countries to conserve their resources in their drive to modernize and develop. Tensions have further sharpened on the issues of climate change and greenhouse gas emissions. The Johannesburg Summit on Sustainable Development, a follow-up to the Rio conference, grappled with many of these issues, achieving some modest success in focusing attention on water and sanitation needs. The importance of environmental issues to developing countries has been highlighted by the recent report on climate change that indicates that poor countries will pay a disproportionate share of the cost of global warming.

Poverty and rapid urbanization also contribute to the spread of disease. Environmental factors account for about one-fifth of all diseases in developing countries and also make citizens more vulnerable to natural disasters. Hazardous waste also represents a serious health and environmental risk. Improving access to affordable health care would contribute to reducing poverty among the world's poor. The challenges of global health require a comprehensive approach that targets not only high profile diseases, but also pays attention to issues like training and retaining health care workers. The HIV/AIDS epidemic in particular has focused attention on public health issues, especially in Africa. Africans account for 70 percent of the over 40 million AIDS cases worldwide. Aside from the human tragedy that this epidemic creates, the development implications are enormous. The loss of skilled and educated workers, the increase in the number of orphans, and the economic disruption that the disease causes will have a profound impact in the future.

Booms, Busts, and Echoes

How the biggest demographic upheaval in history is affecting global development

DAVID E. BLOOM AND DAVID CANNING

For much (and perhaps most) of human history, demographic patterns were fairly stable: the human population grew slowly, and age structures, birth rates, and death rates changed very little. The slow long-run growth in population was interrupted periodically by epidemics and pandemics that could sharply reduce population numbers, but these events had little bearing on long-term trends.

Over the past 140 years, however, this picture has given way to the biggest demographic upheaval in history, an upheaval that is still running its course. Since 1870 death rates and birth rates have been declining in developed countries. This long-term trend toward lower fertility was interrupted by a sharp, post–World War II rise in fertility, which was followed by an equally sharp fall (a "bust"), defining the "baby boom." The aging of this generation and continued declines in fertility are shifting the population balance in developed countries from young to old. In the developing world, reductions in mortality resulting from improved nutrition, public health infrastructure, and medical care were followed by reductions in birth rates. Once they began, these declines proceeded much more rapidly than they did in the developed countries. The fact that death rates decline before birth rates has led to a population explosion in developing countries over the past 50 years.

Even if the underlying causes of rapid population growth were to suddenly disappear, humanity would continue to experience demographic change for some time to come. Rapid increases in the global population over the past few decades have resulted in large numbers of people of childbearing age (whose children form an "echo" generation). This creates "population momentum," where the populations of most countries, even those with falling birth rates, will grow for many years, particularly in developing countries.

These changes have huge implications for the pace of economic development. Economic analysis has tended to focus on the issue of population numbers and growth rates as factors that can put pressure on scarce resources, dilute the capital-labor ratio, or lead to economies of scale. However, demographic change has important additional dimensions. Increasing average life expectancy can change life-cycle behavior affecting education, retirement, and savings decisions—potentially boosting the financial capital on which investors draw and the human capital that strengthens economies.

Demographic change also affects population age structure, altering the ratio of workers to dependents. This issue of *F&D* looks at many facets of the impact of demographic change on the global economy and examines the policy adjustments needed in both the developed and the developing world.

Sharp Rise in Global Population

The global population, which stood at just over 2.5 billion in 1950, has risen to 6.5 billion today, with 76 million new inhabitants added each year (representing the difference, in 2005, for example, between 134 million births and 58 million deaths). Although this growth is slowing, middle-ground projections suggest the world will have 9.1 billion inhabitants by 2050.

These past and projected additions to world population have been, and will increasingly be, distributed unevenly across the world. Today, 95 percent of population growth occurs in developing countries. The populations of the world's 50 least developed countries are expected to more than double by the middle of this century, with several poor countries tripling their populations over the period. By contrast, the population of the developed world is expected to remain steady at about 1.2 billion, with declines in some wealthy countries.

The disparity in population growth between developed and developing countries reflects the considerable heterogeneity in birth, death, and migration processes, both over time and across national populations, races, and ethnic groups. The disparity has also coincided with changes in the age composition of populations. An overview of these factors illuminates the mechanisms of population growth and change around the world.

Total fertility rate. The total world fertility rate, that is, the number of children born per woman, fell from about 5 in 1950 to a little over 2.5 in 2006 (see Figure 1). This number is projected to fall to about 2 by 2050. This decrease is attributable largely to changes in fertility in the developing world and can be ascribed to a number of factors, including declines in infant mortality rates, greater levels of female education and increased labor market opportunities, and the provision of family-planning services.

Infant and child mortality decline. The developing world has seen significant reductions in infant and child mortality over the

(total fertility rate; children per woman)

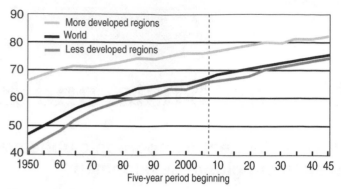

Figure 1 Smaller Families. Fertility rates are tending to converge at lower levels after earlier sharp declines.

Source: United Nations, *World Population Prospects,* 2004.

(life expectancy in years)

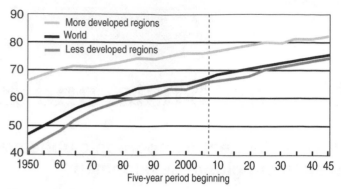

Figure 2 Living Longer. Life expectancy is continuing to rise, but there are big differences between rates in well-off and poorer countries.

Source: United Nations, *World Population Prospects,* 2004.

past 50 years. These gains are primarily the result of improved nutrition, public health interventions related to water and sanitation, and medical advances, such as the use of vaccines and antibiotics. Infant mortality (death prior to age 1) in developing countries has dropped from 180 to about 57 deaths per 1,000 live births. It is projected to decline to fewer than 30 by 2050. By contrast, developed countries have seen infant mortality decline from 59 deaths per 1,000 live births to 7 since 1950, and this is projected to decline further still, to 4 by 2050. Child mortality (death prior to age 5) has also fallen in both developed and developing countries.

Life expectancy and longevity. For the world as a whole, life expectancy increased from 47 years in 1950–55 to 65 years in 2000–05. It is projected to rise to 75 years by the middle of this century, with considerable disparities between the wealthy industrial countries, at 82 years, and the less developed countries, at 74 years (see Figure 2). (Two major exceptions to the upward trend are sub-Saharan Africa, where the AIDS epidemic has drastically lowered life expectancy, and some of the countries of the former Soviet Union, where economic dislocations have led to significant health problems.) As a result of the global decline in fertility, and because people are living longer, the proportion of the elderly in the total population is rising sharply. The number of people over the age of 60, currently about half the number of those aged 15 to 24, is expected to reach 1 billion (overtaking the 15–24 age group) by 2020 and almost 2 billion by 2050. The proportion of individuals aged 80 or over is projected to rise from 1 percent to 4 percent of the global population by 2050.

"A new UN report says that in 2007 the worldwide balance will tip and more than half of all people will be living in urban areas."

Age distribution: working-age population. Baby booms have altered the demographic landscape in many countries. As the experiences of several regions during the past century show, an initial

fall in mortality rates creates a boom generation in which high survival rates lead to more people at young ages than in earlier generations. Fertility rates fall over time, as parents realize they do not need to give birth to as many children to reach their desired family size, or as desired family size contracts for other reasons. When fertility falls and the baby boom stops, the age structure of the population then shows a "bulge" or baby-boom age cohort created by the nonsynchronous falls in mortality and fertility. As this generation moves through the population age structure, it constitutes a share of the population larger than the cohorts that precede or follow. This creates particular challenges and opportunities for countries, such as a large youth cohort to be educated, followed by an unusually large working-age (approximately ages 15–64) population, with the prospect of a "demographic dividend," and characterized eventually by a large elderly population, which may burden the health and pension systems (see Figure 3).

Migration. Migration also alters population patterns. Globally, 191 million people live in countries other than the one in which they were born. On average during the next 45 years, the United Nations projects that over 2.2 million individuals will migrate annually from developing to developed countries. It also projects that the United States will receive by far the largest number of immigrants (1.1 million a year), and China, Mexico, India, the Philippines, and Indonesia will be the main sources of emigrants.

(ratio of working-age to non-working-age population)

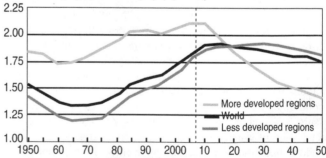

Figure 3 Tracking the Bulge. Developing countries are nearing the peak of their opportunity to benefit from a high ratio of workers to dependents.

Source: United Nations, *World Population Prospects,* 2004.

Urbanization. In both developed and developing countries, there has been huge movement from rural to urban areas since 1950. Less developed regions, in aggregate, have seen their population shift from 18 percent to 44 percent urban, while the corresponding figures for developed countries are 52 percent to 75 percent. A new UN report says that in 2007 the worldwide balance will tip and more than half of all people will be living in urban areas. This shift—and the concomitant urbanization of areas that were formerly peri-urban or rural—is consistent with the shift in most countries away from agriculturally based economies.

The existence and growth of megacities (that is, those with 10 million or more residents) is a late-20th-century phenomenon that has brought with it special problems. There were 20 such cities in 2003, 15 in developing countries. Tokyo is by far the largest, with 35 million people, followed by (in descending order) Mexico City, New York, São Paulo, and Mumbai (all with 17 to 19 million). Cities in general allow for economies of scale—and, most often, for a salutary mix of activities, resources, and people—that make them centers of economic growth and activity and account, in some measure, for their attractiveness. As continued movement to urban areas leads to megacities, however, these economies of scale and of agglomeration seem to be countered, to some extent, by problems that arise in transportation, housing, air pollution, and waste management. In some instances, socioeconomic disparities are particularly exacerbated in megacities.

What Is the Impact on Economies?

The economic consequences of population growth have long been the subject of debate. Early views on the topic, pioneered by Thomas Malthus, held that population growth would lead to the exhaustion of resources. In the 1960s, it was proposed that population growth aided economic development by spurring technological and institutional innovation and increasing the supply of human ingenuity. Toward the end of the 1960s, a neo-Malthusian view, focusing again on the dangers of population growth, became popular. Population control policies in China and India, while differing greatly from each other, can be seen in this light. Population neutralism, a middle-ground view, based on empirical analysis of the link between population growth and economic performance, has held sway for the past two decades. According to this view, the net impact of population growth on economic growth is negligible.

Population neutralism is only recently giving way to a more fine-grained view of the effects of population dynamics in which demographic change does contribute to or detract from economic development. To make their case, economists and demographers point to both the "arithmetic accounting" effects of age structure change and the effects of behavioral change caused by longer life spans (see box).

Arithmetic accounting effects. These effects assume constant behavior within age and sex groups, but allow for changes in the relative size of those groups to influence overall outcomes. For example, holding age- and sex-specific labor force participation rates constant, a change in age structure affects total labor supply.

As a country's baby-boom generation gets older, for a time it constitutes a large cohort of working-age individuals and, later, a large cohort of elderly people. The span of years represented by the boom generation (which determines how quickly this cohort moves

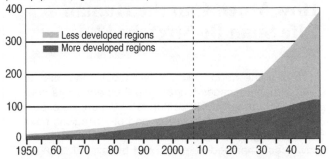

(world population, aged 80+; millions)

Figure 4 Retiree Boom. The number of people living past 80 is projected to rise sharply, but labor shortages could drive up living costs for retirees.

Source: United Nations, *World Population Prospects,* 2004.

through the age structure) and the size of the population bulge vary greatly from one country to another. In all circumstances, there are reasons to think that this very dynamic age structure will have economic consequences. A historically high proportion of working-age individuals in a population means that, potentially, there are more workers per dependent than previously. Production can therefore increase relative to consumption, and GDP per capita can receive a boost.

Life cycle patterns in savings also come into play as a population's age structure changes. People save more during their working-age years, and if the working-age cohort is much larger than other age groups, savings per capita will increase.

Behavioral effects. Declining rates of adult mortality and the movement of large cohorts through the global population pyramid will lead to a massive expansion in the proportion of elderly in the world population (see the projections for 2050 in Figure 4). Some simple economic projections show catastrophic effects of this aging. But such projections tend to be based on an "accounting" approach, which assumes that age-specific behavior remains unchanged and ignores the potentially significant effects of behavior change.

The aging of the baby-boom generation potentially promotes labor shortages, creating upward pressure on wages and downward pressure on the real incomes of retirees. In response, people may adjust their behavior, resulting in increased labor force participation, the immigration of workers from developing countries, and longer working lives. Child mortality declines can also have behavioral effects, particularly for women, who tend to be the primary caregivers for children. When the reduced fertility effect of a decrease in child mortality is in place, more women participate in the workforce, further boosting the labor supply.

The Missing Link

Demographic effects are a key missing link in many macroeconomic analyses that aim to explain cross-country differences in economic growth and poverty reduction. Several empirical studies show the importance of demographics in explaining economic development.

East Asia's baby boom. East Asia's remarkable economic growth in the past half century coincided closely with demographic change in the region. As infant mortality fell from 181 to 34 per 1,000 births between 1950 and 2000, fertility fell from six to two children per

How Much Can the Human Life Span Be Stretched?

In most of the world, children born today can expect to live for many decades longer than their ancestors born in the 19th or early 20th centuries. In Japan, life expectancy at birth is now 82 years, and other regions have also made great progress as medical and public health advances, improved nutrition, and behavioral changes encouraged by improved education have combined to reduce the risk of death at all ages. But how far can these increases in longevity go?

Continuing increases in life expectancy in low-mortality populations have led some demographers to forecast further gains. Kenneth Manton, Eric Stallard, and H. Dennis Tolley, for example, estimate that populations with extremely healthy lifestyles—that is, with an absence or near-absence of risk factors such as infectious disease, smoking, alcohol abuse, and obesity, and the presence of health-promoting behaviors such as a healthy diet and exercise—could achieve a life expectancy of between 95 and 100 years.

But others have reached different conclusions. Nan Li and Ronald Lee estimate that life expectancy in the United States will rise from a 1996 figure of 76.3 to 84.9 by 2050, with that in Japan rising from 80.5 to 88.1. S. Jay Olshansky, Bruce Carnes, and Aline Desesquelles predicted in 1990 that life expectancy at birth would not surpass 85 years, even in low-mortality settings. Death rates, they argued, would not fall sufficiently for life expectancy to rise rapidly, and earlier increases were driven largely by dramatic reductions in infant and child mortality, which could not recur (Samuel Preston, on the other hand, observes that 60 percent of the life expectancy increase in the United States since 1950 is due to mortality declines in people over the age of 50). Perhaps more important, they saw no reason why the future should necessarily mirror the past—new threats to health such as influenza pandemics, antibiotic resistance, and obesity could reverse gains made in recent decades; technological improvements could stall and the drugs needed to counter the diseases of aging might not be found; and environmental disasters, economic collapse, or war could derail health systems at the same time that they weaken individuals' ability to protect their own health.

legalization of contraceptives in 1979, Ireland saw a sharp fall in the crude birth rate. This led to decreasing youth dependency and a rise in the working-age share of the total population. By the mid-1990s, the dependency burden in Ireland had dropped to a level below that in the United Kingdom.

Two additional demography-based factors also helped fuel economic growth by increasing labor supply per capita. First, while male labor force participation rates remained fairly static, the period 1980–2000 saw a substantial increase in female labor force participation rates, particularly among those aged between 25 and 40. Second, Ireland historically had high emigration levels among young adults (about 1 percent of the population a year) because its economy was unable to absorb the large number of young workers created by its high fertility rate. The loss of these young workers exacerbated the problem of the high youth dependency rate. The decline in youth cohort sizes and rapid economic growth of the 1990s led to a reversal of this flow, resulting in net in-migration of workers, made up partly of return migrants and also, for the first time, substantial numbers of foreign immigrants.

Continued high fertility in sub-Saharan Africa. Demographic change of a very different type can account for slow economic development. Much of sub-Saharan Africa remains stalled at the first stage of a demographic transition. Fertility rates actually increased a bit from the 1950s through the 1970s and only recently have begun a slow fall. As swollen youth cohorts have entered the labor force, an inadequate policy and economic environment in most countries has prevented many young people from being able to engage in productive employment. The existence of large dependent populations (in this case, of children) has kept the proportion of working-age people low, making it more difficult for these economies to rise out of poverty.

Looking to the Future

Based on the indicators that are available, we can make a few important points:

- *All signs point to continued but slowing population growth.* This growth will result in the addition of roughly 2.5 billion people to the world population, before it stabilizes around 2050 at about 9 billion. Managing this increase will be an enormous challenge, and the economic consequences of failing to do so could be severe.

- *The world's population is aging rapidly.* The United Nations predicts that 31 percent of China's population in 2050—432 million people—will be age 60 or older. The corresponding figures for India are 21 percent and 330 million. No longer can aging be thought of as just a developed-world phenomenon.

- *International migration will continue, but the extent is unclear.* The pressures that encourage people to migrate—above all, the lure of greater economic well-being in the developed countries—will undoubtedly persist, but the strength of countervailing policy restrictions that could substantially stanch the flow of migrants is impossible to predict.

- *Urbanization will continue, but the pace is also hard to predict.* Greater economic opportunities in the cities will surely continue to attract migrants from rural areas, but environmental and social problems may stymie growth.

woman. The lag between falls in mortality and fertility created a baby-boom generation: between 1965 and 1990, the region's working-age population grew nearly four times faster than the dependent population. Several studies have estimated that this demographic shift was responsible for one-third of East Asia's economic growth during the period (a welcome demographic dividend).

Labor supply and the Celtic Tiger. From 1960 to 1990, the growth rate of income per capita in Ireland was approximately 3.5 percent a year. In the 1990s, it jumped to 5.8 percent, well in excess of any other European economy. Demographic change contributed to the country's economic surge. In the decade following the

Getting the Focus Right

Rapid and significant demographic change places new demands on national and international policymaking. Transitions from high mortality and fertility to low mortality and fertility can be beneficial to economies as large baby-boom cohorts enter the workforce and save for retirement. Rising longevity also tends to increase the incentives to save for old age.

The ability of countries to realize the potential benefits of the demographic transition and to mitigate the negative effects of aging depends crucially on the policy and institutional environment. Focusing on the following areas is likely to be key:

Health and nutrition. Although it has long been known that increased income leads to improved health, recent evidence indicates that good health may also be an important factor in economic development. Good nutrition in children is essential for brain development and for allowing them to become productive members of society. Health improvements—especially among infants and children—often lead to declines in fertility, above and beyond the heightened quality of life they imply. Focusing on the diseases of childhood can therefore increase the likelihood of creating a boom generation and certain positive economic effects. Countries wishing to accelerate fertility declines may benefit from focusing on access to family-planning services and education about fertility decisions.

> **"The ability of countries to realize the potential benefits of the demographic transition and to mitigate the negative effects of aging depends crucially on the policy and institutional environment."**

Education. Children are better able to contribute to economic growth as they enter the workforce if they have received an effective education. East Asia capitalized on its baby boom by giving its children a high-quality education, including both general schooling and technical skills, that equipped them to meet the demands of an ever-changing labor market. Ireland also profited from its baby boomers by introducing free secondary schooling and expanding tertiary education.

Labor market institutions. Restrictive labor laws can limit a country's ability to benefit from demographic change, particularly when they make it unduly difficult to hire and fire workers or to work part-time. International outsourcing, another controversial subject, may become an increasingly important means of meeting the demand for labor.

Trade. One way that East Asian countries provided their baby-boom cohorts with productive opportunities was by carefully opening up to international trade. By providing a new avenue for selling the region's output, this opening helped countries avoid the unemployment that could have arisen. We have found that open economies benefit much more from demographic change than the average, and that closed economies do not derive any statistically significant benefit from age structure changes.

Retirement. Population aging will require increased savings to finance longer retirements. This will likely affect financial markets, rates of return, and investment. In addition, as more people move into old age, health care costs will tend to increase, with the expansion of health care systems and growth in long-term care for the elderly. As nontradable, labor-intensive sectors with a low rate of technical progress, health care and elder care may slow economic growth. The ability of individuals to contribute to the financing of their retirement may be hampered by existing social security systems, many of which effectively penalize individuals who work beyond a fixed retirement age.

Although demographic changes are generally easier to predict than economic changes, the big picture outlook is nonetheless unclear. Indeed, many forces that affect the world's demographic profile are highly unpredictable. Will an outbreak of avian flu or another disease become pandemic, killing many millions and decimating economies? What happens if these diseases are, or become, drug-resistant? Conversely, scientific advances in areas such as genomics, contraceptive methods, or vaccines for diseases such as AIDS or malaria could save and improve millions of lives. Global warming and other environmental change could completely alter the context of demographic and economic predictions. Or—to take things to extremes—wars could result in massive premature mortality, thereby rendering irrelevant most predictions about demographic and related economic changes.

References

Bloom, David E., and David Canning, 2004, "Global Demographic Change: Dimensions and Economic Significance," in *Global Demographic Change: Economic Impacts and Policy Challenges,* proceedings of a symposium, sponsored by the Federal Reserve Bank of Kansas City, Jackson Hole, Wyoming, August 26–28, pp. 9–56.

Lee, Ronald, 2003, "The Demographic Transition: Three Centuries of Fundamental Change," *Journal of Economic Perspectives,* Vol. 17 (Fall), pp. 167–90.

National Research Council, 1986, *Population Growth and Economic Development: Policy Questions* (Washington: National Academies Press).

DAVID E. BLOOM is Professor of Economics and Demography and **DAVID CANNING** is Professor of Economics and International Health at the Harvard School of Public Health.

Malaria, the Child Killer

A special report by the BBC focus on Africa on the devastating effects of the disease on Africa's population and economy.

We are driving through the desert of Sudan's Dafur region when we spot in the distance two girls searching for water. They are orphans of the war, and have well developed malaria. Using all their energy signalling to us, they flail their arms, and with each rotation of the shoulder it seems they may fall over.

Death by malaria begins with cyclical attack of fever, shaking chills, sweating, dizziness, vomiting, diarrhoea and muscle pain. In the final states the liver and kidneys fail and the person enters a comma and eventually dies.

Debilitated by malaria shaking, the girls are gaunt, desiccated, visibly destroyed by the disease, literally dying in the Darfur sun the girls quiver with fever. Their faces are empty, heavy-eyed, absent of even the most basic human wonder.

This process of dying happens to someone in Africa every 30 seconds, according to the United Nation Children's agency, UNICEF.

Africa bears the vast majority of the human and economic cost of malaria worldwide, between 2 million to 3 million people die from the disease every year, about 90 per cent of which are in Africa, mostly young children and pregnant women.

At least one in five infants on the continent is born with the malaria parasite and the disease is the leading cause of death among children under five.

While HIV/AIDS kills more adults, malaria is the biggest killer of children worldwide. Yet work to find an AIDS vaccine receives seven times more funding than Malaria vaccine research.

In April 2000, African leaders signed the Abuja Declaration, committing their countries to specific malaria control achievements by this year. The declaration stated: "By 2005, at least 60 per cent of those suffering from malaria will have prompt access to be able to use correct, affordable and appropriate treatment." It also said: "At least 60 per cent of those at risk of malaria should benefit from insecticide-treated mosquito nets." But most African nations still struggle with ineffective treatments, and the World Health organisation (WHO) reports that today mosquito nets are used by less than five per cent of Africans at risk.

Annually malaria costs African countries between US$10 billion to US$12 billion in lost domestic product even though it could be controlled, perhaps even eradicated, for a fraction of that amount.

A cross Africa, as in much of the developing world, poor people suffer the most from malaria. It is both a disease of poverty and a cause of poverty. Economic growth in countries with high level of malaria transmission is significantly lower than countries without malaria. African families at risk from malaria are estimated to spend up to 25 per cent of their income on direct malaria prevention and treatment. Although the cost of a mosquito net is low between Western standards (about US$2.33), the price is beyond the reach of Africa's poorest residents.

Poverty aside, African countries have been further plagued by a strong resurgence of the disease over the last ten years, in large part due to mosquitoes developing parasite developing resistance to many antimalarial drugs.

Resistance to Chloroquine, the cheapest and most widely used antimalaria, is now common throughout Africa. Yet international donors still subsidise and fund chloroquine therapy programmes. "Donors must stop wasting their money funding drugs that don't work, medicines Sans Frontiers says in a report.

Resistance to sulfadoxine-pyrimethamine, often the first and least expensive alternative to choloroquine is also increasing in east and southern Africa.

International organisations are urging Western governments to support multi-drug combinations based on artemisinin, a herb extract used in China for centuries but little know in the West.

But artemisinin is not yet produced in large enough quantities to be reasonably priced and many African nations are stuck, unable to afford the only drug combinations prevent to be effective.

Western donors have been hesitant to promote the treatment claiming a lack of funds—artemisinin is currently ten times more expensive than chloroquine. But advocacy groups argue that international funding priorities must change to recognise the forgotten epidemic, and are urging Western donors to create subsidies for antimalarial like artemisinin. Without subsidies, they argue, in areas with insufficient government and private purchasers, a large proportion of residents at risk from malaria will be unable to afford appropriate courses of antimalaria therapies.

International efforts to contain or even eradicate the disease have received a boost in recent years with a US$4.7 billion pledge by donors over five-years to the UN global fund for AIDS, tuberculosis and malaria.

The drugs company GloxoSmithKline claims it is close to producing a malaria vaccine in a joint venture with the malaria Vaccine initiative. The vaccine prevented almost 60 per cent cases in children during trials in Mozambique. But the earliest a vaccine is expected to be ready for sale in 2010.

Malaria has been a non-issue in North America and Europe since world War II, when DDT came into use as a cheap and highly effective insecticide.

In a massive public health campaign, tiny amounts of DDT were sprayed on the inside walls of houses. This indoor Residual Spraying (IRS) method was so successful that malaria was eradicated in Europe and the US within a few years.

Following success in the West, in the 1950s the WHO launched a programme to eradicate malaria using DDT. But the sheer resources, manpower and transport needed to mount serious campaigns in Africa mean that it was never sincerely target. Funding for eradication wanted as the US and Europe became malaria-free, but by the 1970s rates of malaria began to rise again in Africa.

Ever since there has been a raging DDT debate. In many countries environmentalist concerns about the consequence of extensive DDT use in agriculture led to its banning for all uses, including public health. As a consequence, poorer African countries that want to but cannot fund their own DDT-based programme are reliant on foreign donors, who now prefer funding insecticide-treated nets to DDT. But critics say mosquito nets show limited success in reducing malaria when compared to DDT programmes, and argue it is a question of quantity: the amount of DDT used to control pests on a large farm may suffice to control mosquitoes in a small country. South Africa almost eradicated the disease through a mosquito-control programme using DDT.

Many African nations are increasing resources for malaria control. Conscious of the drain on their economies, the first against malaria is now seen to be an important element of national poverty reduction strategies for malaria-endemic countries. Many African nations have reduced taxes on insecticides, mosquito nets and the materials use to make them.

Malaria advocacy efforts are even beginning to make in roads into pop culture, with a two-day superstar-packed concert held in Senegal in March in support of battle to eradicate the disease.

There is even an on-line malaria game, created to help educate children. On www.nobelprize.org you can run around with Speedy Ann the mosquito, who sport a digital human smell detection meter to help her find humans to bite. "It's not my fault", says Speedy Ann in the games introduction, making it clear that she did not create the epidemic." I only spread the disease.

Why We Owe So Much to Victims of Disaster

At the G8 summit, Brown and Blair should think of our debts to Africans, not theirs to us. We have stolen their share of the planet's resources.

ANDREW SIMMS

If you want to know how to tackle global warming, try the simple wisdom of Wilkins Micawber in Dickens's David Copperfield. "Annual income twenty pounds, annual expenditure nineteen pounds nineteen and six, result happiness," he said. "Annual income twenty pounds, annual expenditure twenty pounds ought and six, result misery."

It is rarely understood this way, but climate change is really a problem of debt. Not a cash debt, but an ecological one. Environmentally, we're living way beyond our means, spending more than the bank of the earth and the atmosphere can replace in our accounts. It is this debt—not the hole in the nation's public spending plans—that ought to have been the subject of the election campaign. And it is this debt—not the financial debts of poor nations to rich—that should guide the thinking of the Chancellor and other western leaders as they approach the G8 summit in July.

Gordon Brown and Tony Blair have set Africa and global warming as the summit's key themes. Yet newly released documents reveal one of the government's more embarrassing oversights. It was agreed at an international summit, more than three years ago, to create a special pot of money to help poor countries cope with climate change. Britain, alone among major European aid donors, has failed to contribute to the "Least Developed Countries Fund".

For years, we have been pilfering from the natural resource accounts of the rest of the world. When the people of Asia, Africa and Latin America decide they want to spend their fair share of nature's equity, either it won't be there or we could be on the verge of a crash in its already overstretched banking system. If the whole world wanted to live like people in the UK, we would need the natural resources of three more planets. If the US were the model, we would need five.

It's not just that we owe these countries for our profligate use of the planet's resources. It is also that they suffer the worst effects of our overuse. The most vulnerable people in the poorest countries—particularly children and women—are in effect paying the interest on our ecological debts. According to the World Disasters Report, the number of mostly climate-related disasters rose from just over 400 a year in 1994–98 to more than 700 a year in 1999–2003, with the biggest rise in the poorest countries.

The sight of a Mozambican woman giving birth in a tree during the great storms of 2000 is seared into the world's consciousness. Mozambique was desperately poor and burdened with debt payments. The floods were the worst for 150 years. Not only had its potential to develop been mismanaged by western creditors, Mozambique was left more vulnerable because it had to choose between preparing for disasters or spending its meagre resources on health and education. Now, in a warming world, Africa's rainfall, so crucial to its farming, is about to become even more erratic.

The story is similar outside Africa. In the mid- to late 1990s, at the height of the Jubilee 2000 debt cancellation campaign, nearly half the Jamaican government's spending went on debt service. The island is rich in natural resources, but it was getting harder for it to earn a living from exporting crops such as sugar and bananas. Yet, under pressure from the IMF and the World Bank, the money available for social programmes in Jamaica was halved.

Angela Stultz-Crawle, a local woman who ran a project in Bennetlands, Kingston to provide basic health and education services, saw the consequences at first hand: reductions in health programmes, in education, in road repairs, in lights. "Just walking around," she said, "you see people living in dirt yards, scrap-board houses. It is repaying. Every day you hear the government come out and say, 'Oh, we have met our IMF deadlines, we have paid,' and everyone claps." Again, Jamaica is particularly vulnerable to the extreme weather that climate change will make more frequent. Last year alone, two major hurricanes, Ivan and Charley, skirted its shores.

So across the developing world, the poorest people suffer from two crises, to neither of which they contributed: financial debt (which their governments are repaying) and ecological debt (which our governments aren't repaying).

In case after case—the IMF-approved kleptocracy of Mobutu's Zaire, the collusion with corruption, asset-stripping and violence in Nigeria's oilfields—the responsibility for financial debts lies at least as much in western capitals as in developing countries in the south. Yet, to win paltry debt relief, poor countries had to swallow the economic-policy equivalent of horse pills. Even the Financial Times commented that the IMF "probably ruined as many economies as they have saved". Yet we still expect poor countries to repay most of their debts, despite the effects on their people's lifestyles. Rich countries, faced with ecological debt, will not even give up the four-wheel-drive school run.

The widening global gap in wealth was built on ecological debts. And today's economic superpowers soon became as successful in their disproportionate occupation of the atmosphere with carbon emissions as they were in colonial times with their military occupation of the terrestrial world. Until the Second World War, they managed this atmospheric occupation largely through exploiting their own fossil-fuel reserves. But from around 1950 they became increasingly dependent on energy imports. By 1998, the wealthiest fifth of the world was consuming 68 per cent of commercially produced energy; the poorest fifth, 2 per cent.

In 2002, many rich countries were pumping out more carbon dioxide per person than they were a decade earlier, when they signed the UN Framework Convention on Climate Change. Now, with Africa and climate change at the top of the G8 summit agenda, there couldn't be a better time for a little paradigm shift. If Blair and Brown want to show leadership, they could relabel the G8 as the inaugural meeting of the ecological debtors' club, and start discussing how to pay back their creditors down south.

But is there any chance that the advanced industrial economies could make the cuts in consumption needed to clear their debts? Perhaps we should ask the women recently seen reminiscing about VE Day, women who during the world war had to keep house under severe constraints. After all, global warming is now described as a threat more serious than war or terrorism. Drawing on articles in Good Housekeeping, and on guides with such titles as Feeding Cats and Dogs in Wartime or Sew and Save, they enormously reduced household consumption—use of electrical appliances, for example, dropped 82 per cent—while at the same time dramatically improving the nation's health.

The ecological debt problem of climate change, if it is to be solved, will still require a proper global framework, eventually giving everybody on the planet an equal entitlement to emit greenhouse gases, and allowing those who under-emit to trade with those who wish to over-emit. But such efforts will be hollow unless the argument to cut consumption can be won at household level.

To refuse the challenge would be the deepest hypocrisy. We have demanded that the world's poorest countries reshape their economies to pay service on dodgy foreign debts. It would be an appalling double standard now to suggest that we couldn't afford either to help developing countries adapt to climate change, or to cut our emissions by the 80–90 per cent considered necessary.

The language of restraint on public spending permeates our public discourse, yet the concept of living within our environmental means still escapes mainstream economics. That will have to change. "Balancing nature's books" could be the simple language that enables the green movement to resonate with the public. Imagine opening a letter from the bank over breakfast to learn that, instead of your usual overdraft, you had an ecological debt that threatened the planet. I wouldn't want to be there when the bailiffs called for that one.

ANDREW SIMMS's Ecological Debt: the health of the planet and the wealth of nations is published this month by Pluto Books ([pounds sterling]12.99 from www.plutobooks.com)

The Challenge of Global Health
Beware What You Wish For

LAURIE GARRETT

Less than a decade ago, the biggest problem in global health seemed to be the lack of resources available to combat the multiple scourges ravaging the world's poor and sick. Today, thanks to a recent extraordinary and unprecedented rise in public and private giving, more money is being directed toward pressing heath challenges than ever before. But because the efforts this money is paying for are largely uncoordinated and directed mostly at specific high-profile diseases—rather than at public health in general—there is a grave danger that the current age of generosity could not only fall short of expectations but actually make things worse on the ground.

This danger exists despite the fact that today, for the first time in history, the world is poised to spend enormous resources to conquer the diseases of the poor. Tackling the developing world's diseases has become a key feature of many nations' foreign policies over the last five years, for a variety of reasons. Some see stopping the spread of my, tuberculosis (TB), malaria, avian influenza, and other major killers as a moral duty. Some see it as a form of public diplomacy. And some see it as an investment in self-protection, given that microbes know no borders. Governments have been joined by a long list of private donors, topped by Bill and Melinda Gates and Warren Buffett, whose contributions to today's war on disease are mind-boggling.

Thanks to their efforts, there are now billions of dollars being made available for health spending—and thousands of nongovernmental organizations (NGOS) and humanitarian groups vying to spend it. But much more than money is required. It takes states, health-care systems, and at least passable local infrastructure to improve public health in the developing world. And because decades of neglect there have rendered local hospitals, clinics, laboratories, medical schools, and health talent dangerously deficient, much of the cash now flooding the field is leaking away without result.

Moreover, in all too many cases, aid is tied to short-term numerical targets such as increasing the number of people receiving specific drugs, decreasing the number of pregnant women diagnosed with HIV (the virus that causes AIDS), or increasing the quantity of bed nets handed out to children to block disease-carrying mosquitoes. Few donors seem to understand that it will take at least a full generation (if not two or three) to substantially improve public health—and that efforts should focus less on particular diseases than on broad measures that affect populations' general well-being.

The fact that the world is now short well over four million health-care workers, moreover, is all too often ignored. As the populations of the developed countries are aging and coming to require ever more medical attention, they are sucking away local health talent from developing countries. Already, one out of five practicing physicians in the United States is foreign-trained, and a study recently published in JAMA: The Journal of the American Medical Association estimated that if current trends continue, by 2020 the United States could face a shortage of up to 800,000 nurses and 200,000 doctors. Unless it and other wealthy nations radically increase salaries and domestic training programs for physicians and nurses, it is likely that within 15 years the majority of workers staffing their hospitals will have been born and trained in poor and middle-income countries. As such workers flood to the West, the developing world will grow even more desperate.

Yet the visionary leadership required to tackle such problems is sadly lacking. Over the last year, every major leadership position on the global health landscape has turned over, creating an unprecedented moment of strategic uncertainty. The untimely death last May of Dr. Lee Jong-wook, director general of the World Health Organization (WHO), forced a novel election process for his successor, prompting health advocates worldwide to ask critical, long-ignored questions, such as, Who should lead the fight against disease? Who should pay for it? And what are the best strategies and tactics to adopt?

The answers have not been easy to come by. In November, China's Dr. Margaret Chan was elected as Lee's successor. As Hong Kong's health director, Chan had led her territory's responses to SARS and bird flu; later she took the helm of the WHO'S communicable diseases division. But in statements following her election, Chan acknowledged that her organization now faces serious competition and novel challenges. And as of this writing, the Global Fund to Fight AIDS, Tuberculosis, and Malaria remained without a new leader following a months-long selection process that saw more than 300 candidates vie for the post and the organization's board get mired in squabbles over the fund's mission and future direction.

Few of the newly funded global health projects, meanwhile, have built-in methods of assessing their efficacy or sustainability. Fewer still have ever scaled up beyond initial pilot stages. And nearly all have been designed, managed, and executed by residents of the wealthy world (albeit in cooperation with local personnel and agencies). Many of the most successful programs are executed by foreign NGOS and academic groups, operating with almost no government interference inside weak or failed states. Virtually no provisions exist to allow the world's poor to say what they want, decide which projects serve their needs, or adopt local innovations. And nearly all programs lack exit strategies or safeguards against the dependency of local governments.

As a result, the health world is fast approaching a fork in the road. The years ahead could witness spectacular improvements in the health of billions of people, driven by a grand public and private effort comparable to the Marshall Plan—or they could see poor societies pushed into even deeper trouble, in yet another tale of well-intended foreign meddling gone awry. Which outcome will emerge depends on whether it is possible to expand the developing world's local talent pool of health workers, restore and improve crumbling national and global health infrastructures, and devise effective local and international systems for disease prevention and treatment.

Show Me the Money

The recent surge in funding started as a direct consequence of the HIV/AIDS pandemic. For decades, public health experts had been confronted with the profound disparities in care that separated the developed world from the developing one. Health workers hated that inequity but tended to accept it as a fact of life, given that health concerns were nested in larger issues of poverty and development. Western AIDS activists, doctors, and scientists, however, tended to have little experience with the developing world and were thus shocked when they discovered these inequities. And they reacted with vocal outrage.

The revolution started at an international AIDS meeting in Vancouver, Canada, in 1996. Scientists presented exhilarating evidence that a combination of anti-HIV drugs (known as antiretrovirals, or ARVS) could dramatically reduce the spread of the virus inside the bodies of infected people and make it possible for them to live long lives. Practically overnight, tens of thousands of infected men and women in wealthy countries started the new treatments, and by

mid-1997, the visible horrors of AIDS had almost disappeared from the United States and Europe.

But the drugs, then priced at about $14,000 per year and requiring an additional $5,000 a year for tests and medical visits, were unaffordable for most of the world's HIV-positive population. So between 1997 and 2000, a worldwide activist movement slowly developed to address this problem by putting pressure on drug companies to lower their prices or allow the generic manufacture of the new medicines. The activists demanded that the Clinton administration and its counterparts in the G-8, the group of advanced industrial nations, pony up money to buy ARVS and donate them to poor countries. And by 1999, total donations for health-related programs (including HIV/AIDS treatment) in sub-Saharan Africa hit $865 million—up more than tenfold in just three years.

In 2000, some 20,000 activists, scientists, doctors, and patients gathered in Durban, South Africa, for another international AIDS conference. There, South Africa's former president, Nelson Mandela, defined the issue Of ARV access in moral terms, making it clear that the world should not permit the poor of Harare, Lagos, or Hanoi to die for lack of treatments that were keeping the rich of London, New York, and Paris alive. The World Bank economist Mead Over told the gathering that donations to developing countries for dealing with HIV/AIDS had reached $300 million in 1999—0.5 percent of all development assistance. But he characterized that sum as "pathetic," claiming that the HIV/AIDS pandemic was costing African countries roughly $5 billion annually in direct medical care and indirect losses in labor and productivity.

In 2001, a group of 128 Harvard University faculty members led by the economist Jeffrey Sachs estimated that fewer than 40,000 sub-Saharan Africans were receiving ARVS, even though some 25 million in the region were infected with HIV and perhaps 600,000 of them needed the drugs immediately. Andrew Natsios, then director of the U.S. Agency for International Development (USAID), dismissed the idea of distributing such drugs, telling the House International Relations Committee that Africans could not take the proper combinations of drugs in the proper sequences because they did not have clocks or watches and lacked a proper concept of time. The Harvard faculty group labeled Natsios' comments racist and insisted that, as Sachs put it, all the alleged obstacles to widespread HIV/AIDS treatment in poor countries "either don't exist or can be overcome," and that three million people in Africa could be put on ARVS by the end of 2005 at "a cost of $1.1 billion per year for the first two to three years, then $3.3 billion to $5.5 billion per year by Year Five."

Sachs added that the appropriate annual foreign-aid budget for malaria, TB, and pediatric respiratory and diarrheal diseases was about $11 billion; support for AIDS orphans ought to top $1 billion per year; and HIV/AIDS prevention could be tackled for $3 billion per year. In other words, for well under $20 billion a year, most of it targeting sub-Saharan Africa, the world could mount a serious global health drive.

What seemed a brazen request then has now, just five years later, actually been eclipsed. HIV/AIDS assistance has effectively spearheaded a larger global public health agenda. The Harvard group's claim that three million Africans could easily be put on ARVS by the end of 2005 proved overoptimistic: the who's "3 by 5 Initiative" failed to meet half of the three million target, even combining all poor and middle-income nations and not just those in Africa. Nevertheless, driven by the HIV/AIDS pandemic, a marvelous momentum for health assistance has been built and shows no signs of abating.

More, More, More

In recent years, the generosity of individuals, corporations, and foundations in the United States has grown by staggering proportions. As of August 2006, in its six years of existence, the Bill and Melinda Gates Foundation had given away $6.6 billion for global health programs. Of that total, nearly $2 billion had been spent on programs aimed at TB and HIV/AIDS and other sexually transmitted diseases. Between 1995 and 2005, total giving by all U.S. charitable foundations tripled, and the portion of money dedicated to international projects soared 80 percent, with global health representing more than a third of that sum. Independent of their government, Americans donated $7.4 billion for disaster relief in 2005 and $22.4 billion for domestic and foreign health programs and research.

Meanwhile, the Bush administration increased its overseas development assistance from $11.4 billion in 2001 to $27.5 billion in 2005, with support for HIV/AIDS and other health programs representing the lion's share of support unrelated to Iraq or Afghanistan. And in his 2003 State of the Union address, President George W. Bush called for the creation of a $15 billion, five-year program to tackle HIV/AIDS, TB, and malaria. Approved by Congress that May, the President's Emergency Plan for AIDS Relief (PEPFAR) involves assistance from the United States to 16 nations, aimed primarily at providing ARVS for people infected with HIV. Roughly $8.5 billion has been spent to date. PEPFAR'S goals are ambitious and include placing two million people on ARVS and ten million more in some form of care by early 2008. As of March 2006, an estimated 561,000 people were receiving ARVS through PEPFAR-funded programs.

The surge in giving has not just come from the United States, however. Overseas development assistance from every one of the nations in the Organization for Economic Cooperation and Development (OECD) skyrocketed between 2001 and 2005, with health making up the largest portion of the increase. And in 2002, a unique funding-dispersal mechanism was created, independent of both the UN system and any government: the Global Fund to Fight AIDS, Tuberculosis, and Malaria. The fund receives support from governments, philanthropies, and a variety of corporate-donation schemes. Since its birth, it has approved $6.6 billion in proposals and dispersed $2.9 billion toward them. More than a fifth of those funds have gone to four nations: China, Ethiopia, Tanzania, and Zambia. The fund estimates that it now provides 20 percent of all global support for HIV/AIDS programs and 66 percent of the funding for efforts to combat TB and malaria.

The World Bank, for its part, took little interest in health issues in its early decades, thinking that health would improve in tandem with general economic development, which it was the bank's mission to promote. Under the leadership of Robert McNamara (which ran from 1968 to 1981), however, the bank slowly increased direct investment in targeted health projects, such as the attempted elimination of river blindness in West Africa. By the end of the 1980s, many economists were beginning to recognize that disease in tropical and desperately poor countries was itself a critical impediment to development and prosperity, and in 1993 the bank formally announced its change of heart in its annual World Development Report. The bank steadily increased its health spending in the following decade, reaching $3.4 billion in 2003 before falling back to $2.1 billion in 2006, with $87 million of that spent on HIV/AIDS, TB, and malaria programs and $250 million on child and maternal health. The bank, along with the International Monetary Fund (IMF), the OECD, and the G-8, has also recently forgiven the debts of many poor nations hard-hit by AIDS and other diseases, with the proviso that the governments in question spend what would otherwise have gone for debt payments on key public services, including health, instead.

When the Asian tsunami struck in December 2004, the world witnessed a profound level of globalized generosity, with an estimated $7 billion being donated to NGOS, churches, and governments, largely by individuals. Although health programs garnered only a small percentage of that largess, many of the organizations that are key global health players were significantly bolstered by the funds.

In January 2006, as the threat of avian influenza spread, 35 nations pledged $1.9 billion toward research and control efforts in hopes of staving off a global pandemic. Since then, several G-8 nations, particularly the United States, have made additional funding available to bolster epidemiological surveillance and disease-control activities in Southeast Asia and elsewhere.

And poor nations themselves, finally, have stepped up their own health spending, partly in response to criticism that they were under-allocating public funds for social services. In the 1990s, for example, sub-Saharan African countries typically spent less than 3 percent of their budgets on health. By 2003, in contrast, Tanzania spent nearly 13 percent of its national budget on health-related goods and services; the Central

African Republic, Namibia, and Zambia each spent around 12 percent of their budgets on health; and in Mozambique, Swaziland, and Uganda, the figure was around 11 percent.

For most humanitarian and health-related NGOS, in turn, the surge in global health spending has been a huge boon, driving expansion in both the number of organizations and the scope and depth of their operations. By one reliable estimate, there are now more than 60,000 AIDs-related NGOS alone, and there are even more for global health more generally. In fact, ministers of health in poor countries now express frustration over their inability to track the operations of foreign organizations operating on their soil, ensure those organizations are delivering services in sync with government policies and priorities, and avoid duplication in resource-scarce areas.

Pipe Dreams

One might think that with all this money on the table, the solutions to many global health problems would at least now be in sight. But one would be wrong. Most funds come with strings attached and must be spent according to donors' priorities, politics, and values. And the largest levels of donations are propelled by mass emotional responses, such as to the Asian tsunami. Still more money is needed, on a regular basis and without restrictions on the uses to which it is put. But even if such resources were to materialize, major obstacles would still stand in the way of their doing much lasting good.

One problem is that not all the funds appropriated end up being spent effectively. In an analysis prepared for the second annual meeting of the Clinton Global Initiative, in September 2006, Dalberg Global Development Advisors concluded that much current aid spending is trapped in bureaucracies and multilateral banks. Simply stripping layers of financing bureaucracy and improving health-delivery systems, the firm argued, could effectively release an additional 15–30 percent of the capital provided for HIV/AIDS, TB, and malaria programs.

A 2006 World Bank report, meanwhile, estimated that about half of all funds donated for health efforts in sub-Saharan Africa never reach the clinics and hospitals at the end of the line. According to the bank, money leaks out in the form of payments to ghost employees, padded prices for transport and warehousing, the siphoning off of drugs to the black market, and the sale of counterfeit—often dangerous—medications. In Ghana, for example, where such corruption is particularly rampant, an amazing 80 percent of donor funds get diverted from their intended purposes.

Another problem is the lack of coordination of donor activities. Improving global health will take more funds than any single donor can provide, and oversight and guidance require the skills of the many, not the talents of a few compartmentalized in the offices of various groups and agencies. In practice, moreover, donors often function as competitors,

and the only organization with the political credibility to compel cooperative thinking is the WHO. Yet, as Harvard University's Christopher Murray points out, the WHO itself is dependent on donors, who give it much more for disease-specific programs than they do for its core budget. If the WHO stopped chasing such funds, Murray argues, it could go back to concentrating on its true mission of providing objective expert advice and strategic guidance.

This points to yet another problem, which is that aid is almost always "stovepiped" down narrow channels relating to a particular program or disease. From an operational perspective, this means that a government may receive considerable funds to support, for example, an ARV-distribution program for mothers and children living in the nation's capital. But the same government may have no financial capacity to support basic maternal and infant health programs, either in the same capital or in the country as a whole. So my-positive mothers are given drugs to hold their infection at bay and prevent passage of the virus to their babies but still cannot obtain even the most rudimentary of obstetric and gynecological care or infant immunizations.

Stovepiping tends to reflect the interests and concerns of the donors, not the recipients. Diseases and health conditions that enjoy a temporary spotlight in rich countries garner the most attention and money. This means that advocacy, the whims of foundations, and the particular concerns of wealthy individuals and governments drive practically the entire global public health effort. Today the top three killers in most poor countries are maternal death around childbirth and pediatric respiratory and intestinal infections leading to death from pulmonary failure or uncontrolled diarrhea. But few women's rights groups put safe pregnancy near the top of their list of priorities, and there is no dysentery lobby or celebrity attention given to coughing babies.

The HIV/AIDS pandemic, meanwhile, continues to be the primary driver of global concern and action about health. At the 2006 International AIDS Conference, former U.S. President Bill Clinton suggested that HIV/AIDS programs would end up helping all other health initiatives. "If you first develop the health infrastructure throughout the whole country, particularly in Africa, to deal with AIDS," Clinton argued, "you will increase the infrastructure of dealing with maternal and child health, malaria, and TB. Then I think you have to look at nutrition, water, and sanitation. All these things, when you build it up, you'll be helping to promote economic development and alleviate poverty."

But the experience of bringing ARV treatment to Haiti argues against Clinton's analysis. The past several years have witnessed the successful provision of antiretroviral treatment to more than 5,000 needy Haitians, and between 2002 and 2006, the prevalence of HIV in the country plummeted from six percent to three percent. But during the same period, Haiti actually went backward on every other health indicator.

Part of the problem is that most of global HIV/AIDS-related funding goes to stand-alone programs: HIV testing sites, hospices and orphanages for people affected by AIDS, ARV-dispersal stations, HIV/AIDS education projects, and the like. Because of discrimination against people infected with HIV, public health systems have been reluctant to incorporate HIV/AIDs-related programs into general care. The resulting segregation has reinforced the anti-HIV stigma and helped create cadres of healthcare workers who function largely independently from countries' other health-related systems. Far from lifting all boats, as Clinton claims, efforts to combat HIV/AIDS have so far managed to bring more money to the field but have not always had much beneficial impact on public health outside their own niche.

Diamonds in the Rough

Arguably the best example of what is possible when forces align properly can be found in the tiny African nation of Botswana. In August 2000, the Gates Foundation, the pharmaceutical companies Merck and Bristol-Myers Squibb, and the Harvard AIDS Initiative announced the launching of an HIV/AIDS treatment program in collaboration with the government of Botswana. At the time, Botswana had the highest HIV infection rate in the world, estimated to exceed 37 percent of the population between the ages of 15 and 40. The goal of the new program was to put every single one of Botswana's infected citizens in treatment and to give ARVS to all who were at an advanced stage of the disease. Merck donated its anti-HIV drugs, Bristol-Myers Squibb discounted its, Merck and the Gates Foundation subsidized the effort to the tune of $100 million, and Harvard helped the Botswanan government design its program.

When the collaboration was announced, the target looked easily attainable, thanks to its top-level political support in Botswana, the plentiful money that would come both from the donors and the country's diamond wealth, the free medicine, and the sage guidance of Merck and Harvard. Unlike most of its neighbors, Botswana had an excellent highway system, sound general infrastructure, and a growing middle class. Furthermore, Botswana's population of 1.5 million was concentrated in the capital city of Gaborone. The national unemployment rate was 24 percent—high by Western standards but the lowest in sub-Saharan Africa. The conditions looked so propitious, in fact, that some activists charged that the parties involved had picked an overly easy target and that the entire scheme was little more than a publicity stunt, concocted by the drug companies in the hopes of deflecting criticism over their global pricing policies for AIDS drugs.

But it soon became apparent that even comparatively wealthy Botswana lacked sufficient health-care workers or a sound enough medical infrastructure to implement the program. The country had no medical school: all its physicians were foreign trained or immigrants. And although Botswana did have a nursing school, it still suffered an acute nursing shortage because South Africa and the United Kingdom were actively recruiting its English-speaking graduates. By 2005, the country was losing 60 percent of its newly trained health-care workers annually to emigration. (In the most egregious case, in 2004 a British-based company set up shop in a fancy Gaborone hotel and, in a single day, recruited 50 nurses to work in the United Kingdom.)

By 2002, the once-starry-eyed foreigners and their counterparts in Botswana's government had realized that before they could start handing out ARVS, they would have to build laboratories and clinics, recruit doctors from abroad, and train other health-care personnel. President Festus Mogae asked the U.S. Peace Corps to send doctors and nurses. Late in the game, in 2004, the PEPFAR program got involved and started working to keep HIV out of local hospitals' blood supplies and to build a network of HIV testing sites.

After five years of preparation, in 2005 the rollout of HIV treatment commenced. By early 2006, the program had reached its goal of treating 55,000 people (out of an estimated HIV-positive population of 280,000) with ARVS. The program is now the largest such chronic-care operation—at least per capita—in the world. And if it works, Botswana's government will be saddled with the care of these patients for decades to come—something that might be sustainable if the soil there continues to yield diamonds and the number of people newly infected with HIV drops dramatically.

But Kwame Ampomah, a Ghana-born official for the Joint UN Programme on HIV/AIDS, based in Gaborone, now frets that prevention efforts are not having much success. As of 2005, the incidence of new cases was rising eight percent annually. Many patients on ARVS may develop liver problems and fall prey to drug-resistant HIV strains. Ndwapi, a U.S.-trained doctor who works at Princess Marina Hospital, in Gaborone, and handles more of the government's HIV/AIDS patients than anyone else, also frets about the lack of effective prevention efforts. In slums such as Naledi, he points out, there are more bars than churches and schools combined. The community shares latrines, water pumps, alcohol—and HIV. Ndawpi says Botswana's future rests on its ability to fully integrate HIV/AIDS care into the general health-care system, so that it no longer draws away scarce doctors and nurses for HIV/AIDS-only care. If this cannot be accomplished, he warns, the country's entire health-care system could collapse.

Botswana is still clearly somewhat of a success story, but it is also a precariously balanced one and an effort that will be difficult to replicate elsewhere. Ampomah says that other countries might be able to achieve good results by following a similar model, but "it requires transparency, and a strong sense of nationalism by leaders, not tribalism. You need leaders who don't build palaces on the Riviera. You need a clear health system with equity that is not donor-driven. Everything is unique to Botswana: there is a sane leadership system in Gaborone. So in Kenya today maybe the elite can get ARVS with their illicit funds, but not the rest of the country. You need a complete package. If the government is corrupt, if everyone is stealing money, then it will not work. So there is a very limited number of African countries that could replicate the Botswana experience." And despite the country's HIV/AIDS achievements and the nation's diamond wealth, life expectancy for children born in Botswana today is still less than 34 years, according to CIA estimates.

Brain Drain

As in Haiti, even as money has poured into Ghana for HIV/AIDS and malaria programs, the country has moved backward on other health markers. Prenatal care, maternal health programs, the treatment of guinea worm, measles vaccination efforts all have declined as the country has shifted its health-care workers to the better-funded projects and lost physicians to jobs in the wealthy world. A survey of Ghana's health-care facilities in 2002 found that 72 percent of all clinics and hospitals were unable to provide the full range of expected services due to a lack of sufficient personnel. Forty-three percent were unable to provide full child immunizations; 77 percent were unable to provide 24-hour emergency services and round-the-clock safe deliveries for women in childbirth. According to Dr. Ken Sagoe, of the Ghana Health Service, these statistics represent a severe deterioration in Ghana's health capacity. Sagoe also points out that 604 out of 871 medical officers trained in the country between 1993 and 2002 now practice overseas.

Zimbabwe, similarly, trained 1,200 doctors during the 1990s, but only 360 remain in the country today. In Kadoma, eight years ago there was one nurse for every 700 residents; today there is one for every 7,500. In 1980, the country was able to fill 90 percent of its nursing positions nationwide; today only 30 percent are filled. Guinea-Bissau has plenty of donated ARV supplies for its people, but the drugs are cooking in a hot dockside warehouse because the country lacks doctors to distribute them. In Zambia, only 50 of the 600 doctors trained over the last 40 years remain today. Mozambique's health minister says that AIDS is killing the country's health-care workers faster than they can be recruited and trained: by 2010, the country will have lost 6,000 lab technicians to the pandemic. A study by the International Labor Organization estimates that 18–41 percent of the health-care labor force in Africa is infected with HIV. If they do not receive ARV therapy; these doctors, nurses, and technicians will die, ushering in a rapid collapse of the very health systems on which HIV/AIDS programs depend.

Erik Schouten, HIV coordinator for the Malawi Ministry of Health, notes that of the country's 12 million people, 90,000 have already died from AIDS and 930,000 people are now infected with HIV. Over the last five years, the government has lost 53 percent of its health administrators, 64 percent of its nurses, and 85 percent of its physicians—

mostly to foreign NGOS, largely funded by the U.S. or the British government or the Gates Foundation, which can easily outbid the ministry for the services of local health talent. Schouten is now steering a $270 million plan, supported by PEPFAR, to use financial incentives and training to bring back half of the lost health-care workers within five years; nearly all of these professionals will be put to use distributing ARVS. But nothing is being done to replace the health-care workers who once dealt with malaria, dysentery, vaccination programs, maternal health, and other issues that lack activist constituencies.

Ibrahim Mohammed, who heads an effort similar to Schouten's in Kenya, says his nation lost 15 percent of its health work force in the years between 1994 and 2001 but has only found donor support to rebuild personnel for HIV/AIDS efforts; all other disease programs in the country continue to deteriorate. Kenya's minister of health, Charity Kaluki Ngilu, says that life expectancy has dropped in her country, from a 1963 level of 63 years to a mere 47 years today for men and 43 years for women. In most of the world, male life expectancy is lower than female, but in Kenya women suffer a terrible risk of dying in childbirth, giving men an edge in survival. Although AIDS has certainly taken a toll in Kenya, Ngilu primarily blames plummeting fife expectancy on former President Daniel arap Moi, who kept Kenyan spending on health down to a mere $6.50 per capita annually. Today, Kenya spends $14.20 per capita on health annually still an appallingly low number. The country's public health and medical systems are a shambles. Over the last ten years, the country has lost 1,670 physicians and 3,900 nurses to emigration, and thousands more nurses have retired from their profession.

Data from international migration-tracking organizations show that health professionals from poor countries worldwide are increasingly abandoning their homes and their professions to take menial jobs in wealthy countries. Morale is low all over the developing world, where doctors and nurses have the knowledge to save fives but lack the tools. Where AIDS and drug-resistant TB now burn through populations like forest fires, health-care workers say that the absence of medicines and other supplies leaves them feeling more like hospice and mortuary workers than healers.

Compounding the problem are the recruitment activities of Western NCOS and OECD-supported programs inside poor countries, which poach local talent. To help comply with financial and reporting requirements imposed by the IMF, the World Bank, and other donors, these programs are also soaking up the pool of local economists, accountants, and translators. The U.S. Congress imposed a number of limitations on PEPFAR spending, including a ceiling for health-care-worker training of $1 million per country. PEPFAR is prohibited from directly topping off salaries to match government pay levels. But PEPFAR-funded programs, UN agencies, other rich-country government agencies, and NGOS routinely augment the base salaries of local staff with benefits such as housing and education subsidies, frequently bringing their employees' effective wages to a hundred times what they could earn at government-run clinics.

Usaid's Kent Hill says that this trend is "a horrendous dilemma" that causes "immense pain" in poor countries. But without tough guidelines or some sort of moral consensus among UN agencies, NGOS, and donors, it is hard to see what will slow the drain of talent from already-stressed ministries of health.

Going Dutch?

The most commonly suggested solution to the problematic pay differential between the wages offered by local governments and those offered by international programs is to bolster the salaries of local officials. But this move would be enormously expensive (perhaps totaling $2 billion over the next five years, according to one estimate) and might not work, because of the problems that stem from injecting too much outside capital into local economies.

In a recent macroeconomic analysis, the UN Development Program (UNDP) noted that international spending on HIV/AIDS programs in poor countries doubled between 2002 and 2004. Soon it will have doubled again. For poor countries, this escalation means that by the end of 2007, HIV/AIDS spending could command up to ten percent of their GDPS. And that is before donors even begin to address the healthcare-worker crisis or provide subsidies to offset NGO salaries.

There are three concerns regarding such dramatic escalations in external funding: the so-called Dutch disease, inflation and other economic problems, and the deterioration of national control. The UNDP is at great pains to dismiss the potential of Dutch disease, a term used by economists to describe situations in which the spending of externally derived funds so exceeds domestic private-sector and manufacturing investment that a country's economy is destabilized. UNDP officials argue that these risks can be controlled through careful monetary management, but not all observers are as sanguine.

Some analysts, meanwhile, insist that massive infusions of foreign cash into the public sector undermine local manufacturing and economic development. Thus, Arvind Subramanian, of the IMF, points out that all the best talent in Mozambique and Uganda is tied up in what he calls "the aid industry," says that foreign-aid efforts suck all the air out of local innovation and entrepreneurship. A more immediate concern is that raising salaries for health-care workers and managers directly involved in HIV/AIDS and other health programs will lead to salary boosts in other public sectors and spawn inflation in the countries in question. This would widen the gap between the rich and the poor, pushing the costs of staples beyond the reach of many citizens. If not carefully managed, the influx of cash could exacerbate such conditions as malnutrition and homelessness while undermining

any possibility that local industries could eventually grow and support themselves through competitive exports.

Regardless of whether these problems proliferate, it is curious that even the most ardent capitalist nations funnel few if any resources toward local industries and profit centers related to health. Ministries of health in poor countries face increasing competition from NGOS and relief agencies, but almost none from their local private sectors. This should be troubling, because if no locals can profit legitimately from any aspect of health care, it is unlikely that poor countries will ever be able to escape dependency on foreign aid.

Finally, major influxes of foreign funding can raise important questions about national control and the skewing of health-care policies toward foreign rather than domestic priorities. Many governments and activists complain that the U.S. government, in particular, already exerts too much control over the design and emphasis of local HIV/AIDS programs. This objection is especially strong regarding HIV-prevention programs, with claims that the Bush administration has pushed abstinence, fidelity, and faith-based programs at the expense of locally generated condom- and needle-distribution efforts.

Donor states need to find ways not only to solve the human resource crisis inside poor countries but also to decrease their own dependency on foreign health-care workers. In 2002, stinging from the harsh criticism leveled against the recruitment practices of the NHS (the United Kingdom's National Health Service) in Africa, the United Kingdom passed the Commonwealth Code of Practice for the International Recruitment of Health Workers, designed to encourage increased domestic health-care training and eliminate recruitment in poor countries without the full approval of host governments. British officials argue that although the code has limited efficacy, it makes a contribution by setting out guidelines for best practices regarding the recruitment and migration of health-care personnel. No such code exists in the United States, in the EU more generally, or in Asia—but it should.

Unfortunately, the U.S. Congress has gone in the opposite direction, acceding to pressure from the private health-care sector and inserting immigration-control exemptions for health-care personnel into recent legislation. In 2005, Congress set aside 50,000 special immigration visas for nurses willing to work in U.S. hospitals. The set-aside was used up by early 2006, and Senator Sam Brownback (R-Kans.) then sponsored legislation eliminating all caps on the immigration of nurses. The legislation offers no compensation to the countries from which the nurses would come—countries such as China, India, Kenya, Nigeria, the Philippines, and the English-speaking Caribbean nations.

American nursing schools reject more than 150,000 applicants every year, due less to the applicants' poor qualifications than to a lack of openings. If it fixed this problem, the United States could be entirely self-sufficient in nursing. So why is it fairing to do so? Because too few people want to be nursing professors, given that the salaries for full-time nurses are higher. Yet every year Congress has refused to pass bills that would provide federal support to under funded public nursing schools, which would augment professors' salaries and allow the colleges to accept more applicants. Similar (although more complex) forms of federal support could lead to dramatic increases in the domestic training of doctors and other health-care personnel.

Jim Leach, an outgoing Republican member of the House of Representatives from Iowa, has proposed something called the Global Health Services Corps, which would allocate roughly $250 million per year to support 500 American physicians working abroad in poor countries. And outgoing Senator Bill Frist (R-Tenn.), who volunteers his services as a cardiologist to poor countries for two weeks each year, has proposed federal support for sending American doctors to poor countries for short trips, during which they might serve as surgeons or medical consultants.

Although it is laudable that some American medical professionals are willing to volunteer their time abroad, the personnel crisis in the developing world will not be dealt with until the United States and other wealthy nations clean up their own houses. OECD nations should offer enough support for their domestic health-care training programs to ensure that their countries' future medical needs can be filled with indigenous personnel. And all donor programs in the developing world, whether from OECD governments or NGOS and foundations, should have built into their funding parameters ample money to cover the training and salaries of enough new local healthcare personnel to carry out the projects in question, so that they do not drain talent from other local needs in both the public and the private sectors.

Women and Children First

Instead of setting a hodgepodge of targets aimed at fighting single diseases, the world health community should focus on achieving two basic goals: increased maternal survival and increased overall life expectancy. Why? Because if these two markers rise, it means a population's other health problems are also improving. And if these two markers do not rise, improvements in disease-specific areas will ultimately mean little for a population's general health and well-being.

Dr. Francis Omaswa, leader of the Global Health Workforce Alliance—a WHO-affiliated coalition—argues that in his home country of Zambia, which has lost half of its physicians to emigration over recent years, "maternal mortality is just unspeakable. "When doctors and nurses leave a health system, he notes, the first death marker to skyrocket is the number of women who die in childbirth. "Maternal death is the biggest challenge in strengthening health systems," Omaswa says. "If we can get maternal health services to perform, then we are very nearly perfecting the entire health system."

Maternal mortality data is a very sensitive surrogate for the overall status of health-care systems since pregnant women survive where safe, clean, round-the-clock surgical facilities are staffed with well-trained personnel and supplied with ample sterile equipment and antibiotics. If new mothers thrive, it means that the health-care system is working, and the opposite is also true.

Life expectancy, meanwhile, is a good surrogate for child survival and essential public health services. Where the water is safe to drink, mosquito populations are under control, immunization is routinely available and delivered with sterile syringes, and food is nutritional and affordable, children thrive. If any one of those factors is absent, large percentages of children perish before their fifth birthdays. Although adult deaths from AIDS and TB are pushing life expectancies down in some African countries, the major driver of life expectancy is child survival. And global gaps in life expectancy have widened over the last ten years. In the longest-lived society, Japan, a girl who was born in 2004 has a life expectancy of 86 years, a boy 79 years. But in Zimbabwe, that girl would have a life expectancy of 34 years, the boy 37.

The OECD and the 0-8 should thus shift their targets, recognizing that vanquishing AIDS, TB, and malaria are best understood not simply as tasks in themselves but also as essential components of these two larger goals. No health program should be funded without considering whether it could, as managed, end up worsening the targeted life expectancy and maternal health goals, no matter what its impacts on the incidence or mortality rate of particular diseases.

Focusing on maternal health and life expectancy would also broaden the potential impact of foreign aid on public diplomacy. For example, seven Islamic nations (Afghanistan, Egypt, Iraq, Pakistan, Somalia, Sudan, and Yemen) lose a combined 1.4 million children under the age of five every year to entirely preventable diseases. These countries also have some of the highest maternal mortality rates in the world. The global focus on HIV/AIDS offers little to these nations, where the disease is not prevalent. By setting more encompassing goals, government agencies such as USAID and its British counterpart could both save lives in these nations and give them a legitimate reason to believe that they are welcome members of the global health movement.

Legislatures in the major donor nations should consider how the current targeting requirements they place on their funding may have adverse outcomes. For example, the U.S. Congress and its counterparts in Europe and Canada have mandated HIV/AIDS programs that set specific targets for the number of people who should receive ARVS, be placed in orphan-care centers, obtain condoms, and the like. If these targets are achievable only by robbing local health-care workers from pediatric and general health programs, they may well do more harm than good, and should be changed or eliminated.

In the philanthropic world, targeting is often even narrower, and the demand for immediate empirical evidence of success is now the norm. From the Gates Foundation on down to small family foundations and individual donors, there is an urgent need to rethink the concept of accountability. Funders have a duty to establish the efficacy of the programs they support, and that may require use of very specific data to monitor success or failure. But it is essential that philanthropic donors review the relationship between the pressure they place on recipients to achieve their narrow targets and the possible deleterious outcomes for life expectancy and maternal health due to the diversion of local health-care personnel and research talent.

Systems and Sustainability

Perched along the verdant hillsides of South Africa's KwaZulu-Natal Province are tin-roofed mud-and-wood houses, so minimal that they almost seem to shiver in the winter winds. An observant eye will spot bits of carved stone laying flat among the weeds a few steps from the round houses, under which lay the deceased. The stones are visible evidence of a terrifying death toll, as this Zulu region may well have the highest HIV prevalence rate in the world.

At the top of one hill in the Vulindlela area resides Chief Inkosi Zondi. A quiet man in his early 40s, Zondi shakes his head over the AIDS horror. "We can say there are 40,000 people in my 18 subdistricts," he says. "Ten thousand have died. So about 25 percent of the population has died." In this rugged area, only about ten percent of the adults have formal employment, and few young people have much hope of a reasonable future. Funerals are the most commonplace form of social gathering. Law and order are unraveling, despite Chief Zondi's best efforts, because the police and the soldiers are also dying of AIDS.

In such a setting, it seems obvious that pouring funds into local clinics and hospitals to prevent and treat HIV/AIDS should be the top priority. For what could be more important than stopping the carnage?

But HIV does not spread in a vacuum. In the very South African communities in which it flourishes, another deadly scourge has emerged: XDR-TB, a strain of TB so horribly mutated as to be resistant to all available antibiotics. Spreading most rapidly among people whose bodies are weakened by HIV, this form of TB, which is currently almost always lethal, endangers communities all over the world. In August 2006, researchers first announced the discovery of XDR-TB in KwaZulu-Natal, and since then outbreaks have been identified in nine other South African provinces and across the southern part of the continent more generally. The emergence of XDR-TB in KwaZulu-Natal was no doubt linked to the sorry state of the region's general health system, where TB treatment was so poorly handled that only a third of those treated for regular TB completed the antibiotic therapy. Failed therapy often promotes the emergence of drug-resistant strains.

There is also an intimate relationship between HIV and malaria, particularly for pregnant women: being infected with one exacerbates cases of the other. Physicians administering ARVS in West Africa have noticed a resurgence of clinical leprosy and hepatitis C, as latent infections paradoxically surge in patients whose HIV is controlled by medicine. HIV-positive children face a greater risk of dying from vaccine-preventable diseases, such as measles, polio, and typhoid fever, if they have not been immunized than do those nonimmunized children without HIV. But if financial constraints force health-care workers to reuse syringes for a mass vaccination campaign in a community with a Vulindlela-like HIV prevalence, they will almost certainly spread HIV among the patients they vaccinate. And if the surgical instruments in clinics and hospitals are inadequately sterilized or the blood-bank system lacks proper testing, HIV can easily spread to the general population (as has happened in Canada, France, Japan, Kazakhstan, Libya, Romania, and elsewhere).

As concern regarding the threat of pandemic influenza has risen worldwide over the last two years, so has spending to bolster the capacities of poor countries to control infected animal populations, spot and rapidly identify human flu cases, and isolate and treat the people infected. It has become increasingly obvious to the donor nations that these tasks are nearly impossible to perform reliably in countries that lack adequate numbers of veterinarians, public health experts, laboratory scientists and health-care workers. Moreover, countries need the capacity to coordinate the efforts of all these players, which requires the existence of a public health infrastructure.

At a minimum, therefore, donors and UN agencies should strive to integrate their infectious-disease programs into general public health systems. Some smaller NCOS have had success with community-based models, but this needs to become the norm. Stovepiping should yield to a far more generalized effort to raise the ability of the entire world to prevent, recognize, control, and treat infectious diseases and then move on to do the same for chronic killers such as diabetes and heart disease in the long term. Tactically, all aspects of prevention and treatment should be part of an integrated effort, drawing from countries' finite pools of health talent to tackle all monsters at once, rather than dueling separately with individual dragons.

David de Ferranti, of the Brookings Institution, reckons that meeting serious health goals—such as getting eight million more people on ARVS while bringing life expectancies in poor countries up to at least the level of middle-income nations and reducing maternal mortality by 15–20 percent—will cost about $70 billion a year, or more than triple the current spending.

Even if such funds could be raised and deployed, however, for the increased spending to be effective, the structures of global public health provision would have to undergo a transformation. As Tore Godal, who used to run the neglected-diseases program at the WHO, recently wrote in Nature, "There is currently no systemic approach that is designed to match essential needs with the resources that are actually available." He called for a strategic framework that could guide both donations and actions, with donors thinking from the start about how to build up the capabilities in poor countries in order to eventually transfer operations to local control—to develop exit strategies, in other words, so as to avoid either abrupt abandonment of worthwhile programs or perpetual hemorrhaging of foreign aid.

In the current framework, such as it is, improving global health means putting nations on the dole—a $20 billion annual charity program. But that must change. Donors and those working on the ground must figure out how to build not only effective local health infrastructures but also local industries, franchises, and other profit centers that can sustain and thrive from increased health-related spending. For the day will come in every country when the charity eases off and programs collapse, and unless workable local institutions have already been established, little will remain to show for all of the current frenzied activity.

Laurie Garrett is Senior Fellow for *Global Health* at the Council on Foreign Relations and the author of *Betrayal of Trust: The Collapse of Global Public Health*.

A Lifelong Struggle for a Generation

Global Aids Campaign International AIDS conference, Toronto: the global AIDS industry needs to think strategically to meet the challenges of the next 25 years

Alex de Waal

The global AIDS industry put on its sixteenth bi-annual show in Toronto from 13–18 August 2006. The conference theme was "Time to Deliver"—with reference to the ever-more-ambitious pledges to tackle the AIDS pandemic made by world leaders, culminating in the G8 commitment at Gleneagles in 2005 to provide universal Aids treatment by 2010. But for the 30,000 participants who thronged Toronto's Metro Convention Centre, the speeches and debates were less important than the chance to meet and network. The crowded stalls set up by the activist groups in the "Global Village" and the sleek suites of the pharmaceutical companies in the main exhibition hall showed the breadth of the constituency mobilised by the virus barely twenty-five years since the first AIDS cases were diagnosed. This was as much a global trade fair as scientific conference.

One of the great success stories of the AIDS industry has been the creation of powerful anti-retroviral drugs

---

Indeed, AIDS is a global industry. International aid for AIDS topped $8bn in 2005, more than twenty times what it commanded ten years ago. By volume, that still makes it a small business in comparison to the other sectors that warrant such international gatherings. If world leaders indeed recognize AIDS as one of the greatest catastrophes of our time, that recognition is still largely rhetorical, in comparison to what is spent on arms or oil. Far, far more is spent on domestic healthcare in developed nations; more on cosmetics. But the AIDS industry is now big enough

and influential enough for us to legitimately ask: What are the products that it manufactures?

A Double Achievement

The AIDS industry has had two great successes. The first—and biggest—is medicines. The international AIDS conferences began as a forum where scientists could meet to compare notes about a frightening new disease. Since the early 1980s, more has been learned about the human immunodeficiency virus than about any other pathogen in history. Anti-retroviral therapy can, properly administered, make HIV infection a chronic and treatable condition rather than a death sentence. The fact that anti-retrovirals are now accepted as a normal regimen in developed countries, available to all, shows how sky-high are the expectations of the drugs industry.

In any other age, such progress would have been regarded as miraculous. The pace of roll-out in poor countries is lagging, but is still far faster than was dreamed of even in 2001, when Western governments and United Nations agencies were still debating whether any AIDS treatment would ever be possible in sub-Saharan Africa.

The world's, and AIDS professionals', expectations are still stellar. Virologists have long been warning that the extraordinary capacity of HIV to mutate and evade the normal evolutionary pressures towards lower virulence means that we must continually develop new lines of drugs to cope with the drug-resistant strains of HIV that are sure to evolve. In 2005 there was a scare over drug-resistant HIV in New York, and resistant cases emerge regularly in other parts of the world. Meanwhile, scientific opinion is still divided over whether a vaccine will be possible, ever.

The second great success is the unprecedented way in which a fatal, sexually-transmitted infection has not been an occasion for repression and control. Historically, public-health emergencies have led to crackdowns on civil liberties, and early indications were that sex workers, migrants, gay men and drug-users would all feel the full force of the repressive state. Give governments a free hand, and we see the coercive apparatus out in force.

For example, all African armies which have the capacity to enforce compulsory HIV testing of soldiers do so, and most of them automatically discharge any soldier found to be HIV-positive. Many governments admire Cuba's highly repressive—and so far, effective—approach to controlling AIDS, through population testing and the isolation of the infected. Some public health professionals regret the way in which AIDS has been "exceptional."

For example, they argue that the individual's right to privacy has been sanctified, overriding the right of that individual's sexual partners to know his or her HIV status. Better, they assert, to have obligatory testing and partner tracing, sacrificing some confidentiality and risking the stigmatisation of those identified as HIV-positive, in order to help stop onward transmission.

The debate on human rights, confidentiality, stigma and testing rages on without conclusion. Some of the worst-hit countries, like Botswana (more than one in four adults has HIV), have introduced routine testing, which puts the burden on the individual patient to opt out of an HIV test, which is otherwise a routine activity. But epidemiological efficacy is not the only criterion for public-health policy. What about rights and democracy? What has been the political impact of the first-ever rights-based approach to tackling an epidemic?

A Liberal Dynamic

The AIDS pandemic coincided with global liberalisation. Indeed, it's possible that the increased movement of people and the relaxation of state and social control systems that accompanied the end of state socialism in many parts of the world, and apartheid in South Africa, actually facilitated the transmission of HIV. But it's also clear that the rights-based approach has helped to entrench political liberalism. In almost every country, civil-society organisations are leading the way in defining the problem, setting up prevention and care programmes, and mobilising people living with HIV and AIDS. It is particularly marked in Africa, where NGOs are represented on the "country coordinating mechanisms" whereby the Global Fund to Fight AIDS, TB and Malaria identifies the projects it will support.

The board of the Global Fund also includes people living with HIV and Aids; Peter Piot, executive director of Unaids, regularly meets with AIDS activists. An African activist who is blocked from directly influencing her government through parliament or the ministry of health may have more success through the roundabout route of linking up with international AIDS agencies, which can bring much more direct and powerful leverage to bear on the national government.

The global AIDS industry has done superbly well in giving a platform to activists across the world. Still faced with stigmatisation and discrimination, these activists need all the help they can get. Slowly the battle for the rights of people living with HIV and Aids is being won.

A Long-Wave Event

What is less clear is whether the fight against the virus is being won. The combination of pharmaceuticals and activists has led to some immense breakthroughs in providing treatment to the afflicted. But there is much less evidence for progress on preventing new infection and on providing care and support to the tens of millions of children affected by AIDS. Although HIV prevalence rates appear to have stabilised in many African countries, there is little reason for self-congratulation — a 10% adult prevalence rate still represents an immense human tragedy. Today less than 5% of African children affected by AIDS receive any support from national governments or international agencies.

Missing are organised political interests to promote HIV prevention and assistance to children. Pharmaceutical companies have clear financial incentives in developing and selling new drugs. People living with HIV and AIDS have clear incentives in expanding cheaper treatment. Governments of highly affected countries need no special programmes to help them respond to the political threats posed by AIDS they have smartly, if often surreptitiously, made sure treatment is available for the elite.

But at the moment there's no reward to a government that cuts down the number of new HIV infections. The standard measure of HIV level in a population is prevalence—the overall number of people infected. The link between new infections and overall prevalence is a complicated one, depending on the numbers of people dying, migration rates, and technical aspects of how statistics for the prevalence rate are estimated. And if the rate of new infections begins to fall, it can take six or eight years before that registers in prevalence data—enough to switch off any politician's interest. Rapid and reliable tests for new infections are available but rarely used so the most important indicator of success or failure in tackling AIDS is simply not being measured. If we are not measuring it, we cannot reward the policies that make a difference.

Children affected by unmeasured statistics are the hidden face of the epidemic. We are moved by the 14m children orphaned, but their harrowing stories of distress are not a factor in governments' calculations. There is still no serious commitment by national governments in poor countries, or from international donors, to mobilise the kinds of resources needed to provide for the basic welfare of children in societies affected. Perhaps the time lag between action today and measurable results is simply too long to attract political leaders concerned with winning the next election.

The HIV/AIDS pandemic is a long-wave event. After a quarter of a century, it has still not reached its peak. Only when political leaders are ready to act with similar generation-long time horizons, can we expect serious action to overcome it. And only when political interests are served by such long-term actions, can we expect leaders to act. The global Aids industry has come a long way: it needs to plan for its next twenty-five years.

Reversal of Fortune

Why Preventing Poverty Beats Curing It

Anirudh Krishna

Lifting people out of poverty has become a mantra for the world's political leaders. The first U.N. Millennium Development Goal is to halve the number of people whose income is less than $1 per day, currently about 1 billion people. And, in the past decade, millions around the world have been pulled out of poverty by economic growth, effective development aid, and sheer hard work.

Four years ago, I set out to discover which countries—and which local communities—were doing the best job of ending poverty. Using a varied sample of more than 25,000 households in 200 diverse communities in India, Kenya, Peru, Uganda, and the U.S. state of North Carolina, my colleagues and I traced which households have emerged from poverty and attempted to explain their success. At first, the data were very encouraging. In 36 Ugandan communities, 370 households (almost 15 percent of the total) moved out of poverty between 1994 and 2004. In Gujarat, India, 10 percent of a sample of several thousand households emerged from poverty between 1980 and 2003. In Kenya, 18 percent of a sample of households rose out of poverty between 1980 and 2004.

Looking at these figures, one could be forgiven for feeling a sense of satisfaction. But pulling people out of impoverishment is only half the story. Our research revealed another, much darker story: In many places, more families are falling into poverty than are being lifted out. In Kenya, for example, more households, 19 percent, fell into poverty than emerged from it. Twenty-five percent of households studied in the KwaZulu-Natal province of eastern South Africa fell into poverty, but fewer than half as many, 10 percent, overcame poverty in the same period. In Bangladesh, Egypt, Peru, and every other country where researchers have conducted similar studies, the results are the same. In many places, newly impoverished citizens constitute the majority of the poor. It's a harsh fact that calls into question current policies for combating poverty.

All sorts of factors—including financial crises and currency collapse—can push people into poverty. But our research indicates that the leading culprit is poor healthcare. Tracking thousands of households in five separate countries, my colleagues and I found that health and healthcare expenses are the leading cause for people's reversal of fortune. The story of a woman from Kikoni village in Uganda is typical. She and her husband lived relatively well for many years. "Then my husband was sick for 10 years before he died, and all the money that we had with us was spent on medical charges," she said. "My children dropped out of school because we could not pay school fees. Then my husband died. I was left with a tiny piece of land. Now I cannot even get enough food to eat."

Among newly poor households in 20 villages of western Kenya, 73 percent cited ill health and high medical costs as the most important cause of their economic decline. Eighty-eight percent of people who fell into poverty in 36 villages in Gujarat placed the blame on healthcare. In Peru, 67 percent of recently impoverished people in two provinces cited ill health, inaccessible medical facilities, and high healthcare costs. When families are hit by a health crisis, it's often hard to recover. In China, one major illness typically reduces family income by 16 percent. Successive illnesses ensure an even faster spiral into lasting poverty. Surveys in several African and Asian countries show that a combination of ill health and indebtedness has sent tens of thousands of households into poverty, including many that were once affluent. The phenomenon exists in the rich world as well; half of all personal bankruptcies in the United States are due to high medical expenses.

Millions of people are living one illness away from financial disaster, and the world's aid efforts are ill-suited to the challenge. An intense focus on stimulating economic growth isn't enough. Healthcare is not automatically better or cheaper where economic growth rates have been high. In Gujarat, a state in India that has achieved high growth rates for more than a decade, affordable healthcare remains a severe problem, and thousands have fallen into poverty as a result. Healthcare in fast growing Gujarat is no better than in other, often poorer, states of India. Indeed, Gujarat ranked fourth from the bottom among 25 states in terms of proportion of state income spent on healthcare. Perversely, rapid economic growth often weakens existing social safety nets and raises the danger of backsliding. In places as diverse as rural India, Kenya, Uganda, and North Carolina, we observed how community and family support crumbles as market-based transactions overtake traditional networks.

As economic growth helps lift people out of poverty, governments must stand ready to prevent backsliding by providing affordable, accessible, and reliable healthcare. Japan's recent history offers hope that enlightened policy can prevail. At 4 percent, Japan's poverty rate is among the lowest in the world. Sustained economic growth undoubtedly helped, but so too did an entirely different set of policies. Quite early in the country's post-World War II recovery, Japanese officials recognized the critical relationship between illness, healthcare services, and poverty creation, and they responded by implementing universal healthcare as early as the 1950s.

Regrettably, that insight hasn't traveled nearly as well as Japan's many other exports. It's well past time that political leaders put as much effort into stopping the slide into poverty as they do easing the climb out of it.

Anirudh Krishna is assistant professor of public policy and political science at Duke University.

UNIT 6

Women and Development

Unit Selections

Key Points to Consider

- Has there been progress on the women's agenda established at the 1994 International Conference on Population and Development?

- In what ways does educating girls contribute to development?

- What threatens women's political participation in Iraq?

- How has women's political participation in Afghanistan been increased?

- What tensions are illustrated in the debate about Muslim women and the wearing of the veil?

- In what areas have women made the most gains in public life?

- How might a larger political role for women pay dividends?

Student Web Site

www.mhcls.com/online

Internet References

Further information regarding these Web sites may be found in this book's preface or online.

WIDNET: Women in Development NETwork
  http://www.focusintl.com/widnet.htm
Women Watch/Regional and Country Information
  http://www.un.org/womenwatch/

Courtesy of Daniel Bayona (morguetile.com)

There is widespread recognition of the crucial role that women play in the development process. Women are critical to the success of family planning programs, bear much of the responsibility for food production, account for an increasing share of wage labor in developing countries, are acutely aware of the consequences of environmental degradation, and can contribute to the development of a vibrant civil society and good governance. Despite their important contributions, however, women lag behind men in access to health care, nutrition, and education while continuing to face formidable social, economic, and political barriers. Women's lives in the developing world are invariably difficult. Often female children are valued less than male offspring, resulting in higher infant and child mortality rates. In extreme cases, this undervaluing leads to female infanticide.

Those females who survive frequently face lives characterized by poor nutrition and health, multiple pregnancies, hard physical labor, discrimination, and perhaps violence.

Clearly, women are central to any successful population policy. Evidence shows that educated women have fewer and healthier children. This connection between education and population indicates that greater emphasis should be placed on educating women. In reality, female school enrollments are lower than those of males because of state priorities, family resources that are insufficient to educate both boys and girls, female socialization, and cultural factors. Although education is probably the largest single contributor to enhancing the status of women and thereby promoting development, access to education is still limited for many women. Sixty percent of children worldwide who are not enrolled in school are girls. Education for women provides improved health, better wages, and greater influence in decision making which benefits not only women but the broader society.

Women make up a significant portion of the agricultural workforce. They are heavily involved in food production, from planting to cultivation, harvesting, and marketing. Despite their agricultural contribution, women frequently do not have adequate access to advances in agricultural technology or the benefits of extension and training programs. They are also discriminated against in land ownership. As a result, important opportunities to improve food production are lost when women are not given access to technology, training, and land ownership commensurate with their agricultural role.

The industrialization that has accompanied the globalization of production has meant more employment opportunities for women, but often these are low-tech, low-wage jobs. The lower labor costs in the developing world that attract manufacturing facilities are a mixed blessing for women. Increasingly, women are recruited to fill these production jobs because wage differentials allow employers to pay women less. On the other hand, expanding opportunities for women in these positions contributes to family income. The informal sector, where jobs are smaller scale, more traditional, and labor-intensive, has also attracted more women. These jobs are often their only employment option, due to family responsibilities or discrimination. Clearly, women also play a critical role in economic expansion in developing countries. Nevertheless, women are often the first to feel the effects of an economic slowdown. The consequences of the structural adjustment programs that many developing countries have had to adopt have also fallen disproportionately on women. When employment opportunities decline because of austerity measures, women lose jobs in the formal sector and faced increased competition from males in the informal sector. Cuts in spending on health care and education also affect women, who already receive fewer of these benefits. Currency devaluations further erode the purchasing power of women.

Because of the gender division of labor, women are often more aware of the consequences of environmental degradation. Depletion of resources such as forests, soil, and water are much more likely to be felt by women who are responsible for collecting firewood and water and who raise most of the crops. As a result, women are an essential component of successful environmental protection policies but they are often overlooked in planning environmental projects.

Enhancing the status of women has been the primary focus of several international conferences. The 1994 International Conference on Population and Development (ICPD) focused attention on women's health and reproductive rights and the crucial role that these issues play in controlling population growth. The 1995 Fourth World Conference on Women held in Beijing, China, proclaimed women's rights to be synonymous with human rights.

As women have become more active in public life, greater attention has been focused on increasing their political influence. A larger political role for women will not only contribute to an emphasis on issues most important to women, but also lead to an increase in women leaders which may produce significant benefits in reducing conflict, promoting reconciliation, and fighting corruption.

There are indications that women have made progress in some regions of the developing world. The election of Ellen John-Sirleaf as president of Liberia and Africa's first female head of state is the most visible indicator of a trend toward greater political involvement for women in Africa. In the Middle East, the 2002 Arab Human Development Report highlighted the extent to which women in the region lagged behind their counterparts in other parts of the world. The influence of religious conservatives threatens to limit women's political participation in Iraq, raising further concerns about whether that country can be a model for democratic reform in the region. While there has been some progress recently, the gap in gender equality between the Middle East and the rest of the world remains large. There remains a wide divergence in the status of women worldwide, but the recognition of the valuable contributions they can make to society is increasing the pressure to enhance their status.

Ten Years' Hard Labour

More money and less ideology could improve the reproductive health of millions

A decade ago, the world's leaders met in Cairo at the International Conference on Population and Development (ICPD). There, they crafted a plan to achieve "reproductive health and rights for all" by 2015. That plan was wide-ranging—from more contraception and fewer maternal deaths to better education for girls and greater equality for women. But more than just setting targets, the ICPD plan also aimed to change the way those at the sharp end of making policy and delivering services thought about reproduction. It wanted to move away from a focus on family planning (and, by extension, government policies on population control) towards a broader view of sexual health, and systems and services shaped by individual needs.

Over the past week, hundreds of government officials, public-health experts and activists met in London to mark the anniversary of the ICPD and to take stock of progress towards achieving its goals. On paper, that progress has been impressive. Governments around the world have introduced legislation that reflects the ICPD's aims. But when it comes to turning policy into practice, "mixed success" is the verdict of a report card just released by Countdown 2015, a coalition of voluntary bodies involved in the field.

Take contraception, for example. According to the United Nations' Population Fund (UNFPA), 61% of married couples now use contraception, an 11% increase since 1994. This has helped push global population growth down from 82m to 76m people a year over the past decade. But in some places—particularly in sub-Saharan Africa and parts of Asia—birth rates remain high (see chart). That has spurred some governments to offer incentives to those who have fewer children, and others to inflict penalties on those who do not.

Sometimes, a high birth rate is a result of people wanting large families. But often it is due to a lack of affordable contraception. UNFPA estimates that 137m women who want to use contraception cannot obtain it. As Amare Bedada, the head of the Family Guidance Association of Ethiopia, points out, "We don't need to tell our clients about contra-

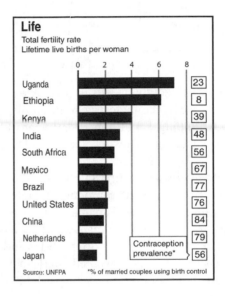

Life
Total fertility rate
Lifetime live births per woman

Uganda	23
Ethiopia	8
Kenya	39
India	48
South Africa	56
Mexico	67
Brazil	77
United States	76
China	84
Netherlands	79
Japan	56

Contraception prevalence*

Source: UNFPA   *% of married couples using birth control

ception. They see their plots of land diminishing, and they tell us they want to limit their family size."

Maternal health is another area where much more needs to be done. Poor women still die in huge numbers from the complications of pregnancy and childbirth. According to UNFPA, 920 women die for every 100,000 live births in sub-Saharan Africa. In Europe, by contrast, the figure is 24 (see the chart on the last page of this article). However, these numbers are, at best, only rough estimates gleaned from hospital statistics. Many women go uncounted because they never reach the health-care system for treatment in the first place.

Plenty of studies have shown what it takes to reduce maternal sickness and death. Good ante-natal health care is vital. So are cheap and simple drugs, such as oxytocin, to prevent haemorrhaging during birth. Trained midwives (or "birth attendants" as they are known in medical parlance) help, too. And so do local emergency obstetric centres that can handle complicated deliveries. Some countries, such as Sri Lanka, have managed to cut maternal mortality by careful spending on such measures. The challenge is to translate these successes to other places.

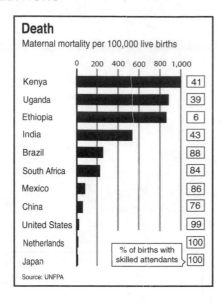

Death
Maternal mortality per 100,000 live births

Kenya	41
Uganda	39
Ethiopia	6
India	43
Brazil	88
South Africa	84
Mexico	86
China	76
United States	99
Netherlands	100
Japan	100

% of births with skilled attendants

Source: UNFPA

Yet another subject that needs to be tackled more effectively is youth sex. The largest generation of teenagers in history—a whopping 1.3 billion 10–19-year-olds—is now making its sexual debut. How it behaves, and what it learns, is crucial.

The ICPD plan was the first international agreement to acknowledge the sexual and reproductive rights of teenagers. A few countries, such as Panama, have introduced laws to safeguard some of these. In many others, youth-friendly programmes have sprung up to offer advice and assistance on thorny issues such as unwanted pregnancy and sexually transmitted diseases—now soaring worldwide at 340m infections a year.

Such programmes, of course, are complicated by fierce—if probably futile—battles in many countries over whether young people should be having sex at all. These play out in international skirmishes over abstinence versus condoms for the young, parental consent to contraception and abortion, and what, if any, sex education should be provided by the state.

Sex and Money

One significant obstacle to tackling these problems is money, or rather the lack of it. Ten years ago, the ICPD estimated the cost of implementing its recommended programmes at $18.5 billion by 2005—or $23.7 billion in today's dollars. The goal was to mobilise one-third of that money from rich donors, and the rest from developing countries themselves. But current spending is well below the mark.

Few poor countries have earmarked enough of their budgets to meet their citizens' reproductive-health needs. Nor have donors lived up to expectations. In 2003, they spent an estimated $3.1 billion on reproductive health. Although contributions have increased over recent years, with a few European countries, such as the Netherlands, chipping in

more, and private donors, such as the Gates Foundation, entering the field, this is still far off even the inflation-devalued $6.1 billion expected from donors by 2005.

Reproduction, it seems, is no longer a sexy subject. As Steve Sinding, the head of the International Planned Parenthood Federation (IPPF), points out, donor interest in the past was stimulated largely by fears of a population crisis. When the Cairo Conference reframed the issues in terms of women's health and reproductive rights, that demographic rationale was lost, taking funding with it.

Moreover, there are other causes competing for international funding, most notably AIDS. At the time of the Cairo Conference, 20m people were infected with HIV, the virus that causes AIDS. Today, that number has doubled. Indeed, AIDS threatens to derail the ICPD strategy. For, although billions of dollars are now pouring in to fight the disease, much of this money is going into AIDS-specific programmes that do not address reproductive health more broadly.

As Nafis Sadik, a former head of UNFPA and now the UN secretary-general's special envoy for HIV in Asia, observes, ten years ago those working in family planning shied away from the field of HIV, with its heavy burden of social stigma. Today, the roles are reversed, as reproductive health is engulfed in a storm of religious and political controversy. One consequence is that organisations concerned with fighting AIDS are failing to make use of valuable infrastructure and expertise already on the ground in places where the disease hits hardest. Given that more than half of HIV infections in sub-Saharan Africa are among women, and that for many African women family-planning services are their main contact with the formal health-care system, such services need to be drafted into the wider battle against HIV. Many family-planning clinics already offer HIV testing and counselling, as well as condoms (against the double whammy of unwanted pregnancy and HIV infection), and also a broad based message of sexual health.

What the field of reproductive health lacks in resources, however, it makes up in ideology. Over the past ten years, battles have broken out between contending views of sexuality, pitting religious conservatives—primus inter pares, the Vatican—against social liberals. The fight has become particularly fierce since the election of George W. Bush as America's president. Mr Bush's socially conservative views are reflected in the way America, the world's leading donor for reproductive health, spends its money at home and abroad.

Breeding Trouble

The main battles are over abortion. Austin Ruse, the president of the Catholic Family and Human Rights Institute (C-FAM), an American Christian lobby group, argues that the shift in talk from fertility control to reproductive rights and services is just code for making abortion universally available. He regards this as wrong, and believes that the ICPD plan of action and those agencies which support it—particularly UNFPA—should be opposed at every turn by a growing coalition of "pro-family" groups worldwide. "Over the next five years, I see everything coming our way, especially on the question of abortion," says Mr Ruse.

UNFPA, not surprisingly, has a different view. Thoraya Obaid, its head, reckons that those who oppose the ICPD plan of action are not just against legalising abortion, but are fighting against women's rights in general. She points to the text of the plan, which states that abortion should never be promoted as a form of family planning and that women should be helped to avoid abortion through better access to contraception. (It also says that those who have sought abortions are entitled to the best possible medical treatment to deal with the complications.)

All sound stuff, but trouble lies in the plan's statement that abortion policy should be up to national governments to decide. Since 1994, more than a dozen countries have liberalised their laws on abortion (with a couple of countries tightening them up). But none of this comes without a fight, often led by the Catholic Church. Kenya has seen a particularly nasty debate over the past six months. There have been street protests, graphic television "docudramas" showing the perils of abortion, and even the arrests of health-care workers who are alleged to have performed more than a dozen abortions whose fetuses recently ended up in a ditch outside Nairobi. The government, which was looking at its abortion laws as part of a broader constitutional review, has made no changes to the current provision, which bans abortion unless the mother's life is at stake.

In many developing countries, Christian anti-abortion groups such as America's Human Life International—a sister organisation to C-FAM—have been pitching in to help organise resistance to changes in abortion laws. But American officials have entered the fray as well. Delegates to regional meetings held in Latin America during the past year to re-affirm their commitment to the ICPD plan of action have complained about pressure from American officials to reject the plan's calls for broad-based reproductive rights and services.

While pressure by the Catholic Church and other opponents of legal abortion can shape official policy, Tim Black, the head of Marie Stopes International (MSI), a voluntary organisation providing reproductive services, argues it does little to stop women seeking abortions, legal or illegal. Surveys from hospitals in Ethiopia, Uganda and Kenya suggests that anywhere from 20-50% of maternal deaths are due to complications resulting from unsafe backstreet abortions. But these numbers are challenged by the opponents of abortion, who argue that it is a rare phenomenon

in the developing world, and that legalising it will make it more common.

The American government's views on abortion are expressed in the Mexico City Policy, which was re-introduced by Mr Bush in 2001. This policy, first implemented by Ronald Reagan in 1984, forbids American government funding of foreign organisations which in any way promote, endorse or advocate abortion. American law has banned foreign assistance for the direct performance of abortions since 1973. But the Mexico City Policy, or "Global Gag Rule" as its critics often refer to it, means that groups which want to perform abortions with money from other sources must also toe the United States' line, or else forfeit American assistance.

Opponents of this policy argue that it imposes on foreigners restrictions which are unconstitutional in America. Indeed, Frances Kissling, the head of Catholics for a Free Choice, an American voluntary organisation which opposes banning abortion, argues that Mr Bush is flexing his conservative muscles abroad—and therefore appeasing his supporters at home—precisely because he cannot deliver a domestic anti-abortion agenda. Last week, for example, a court in New York declared unconstitutional a ban on so-called partial-birth abortion that Mr Bush signed into law in 2003.

Several prominent family-planning organisations, such as MSI and the IPPF, have refused to agree to the Mexico City Policy, saying it compromises their ability to offer women in poor countries the full range of services available in the rich world. In Ethiopia, for example, these groups have had to trim their services and shelve expansion plans as a result of losing both money and contraceptive supplies from the American government.

Such arguments, however, cut little ice with Jeanne Head, the United Nations representative for National Right to Life, an American anti-abortion group. As she puts it, "if they refuse these funds and they can't keep functioning, then they don't care about these women, they only care about abortion. I think the blame lies on the organisations, not on the US government."

John Kerry has said he will rescind the Mexico City Policy if elected. The Democratic candidate has also promised to restore American funding to UNFPA. This has been withheld by the Bush administration for the past three years under a piece of legislation called the Kemp-Kasten amendment. This amendment authorises the president to restrict funding to any group that "supports or participates in the management of a programme of coercive abortion or involuntary sterilisation."

The White House accuses UNFPA of abetting coercive reproductive practices in China—a claim that UNFPA denies. Several international delegations, including ones from Britain's parliament and the American State Department, have investigated UNFPA's activities in China and failed to find evidence to support such allegations. On the contrary, they argue that where UNFPA operates, policies in China are improving. But these findings are contested. The Bush administration says UNFPA has yet to mend its ways, and refuses to pay the $34m appropriated by Congress. The agency says it has managed to fill the gap this year, from big donors such as Britain, which is raising its annual contribution to £20m ($36m), and tiny ones such as Afghanistan, which chipped in $100.

But making up the money is the easy part. Today's battles over abortion, abstinence and condoms are casting a pall over the field, and complicating what is already a formidable task. Making sex safer and reproduction less risky in the 21st century requires all the tools to hand. Policies that restrict people's choices should not be a fact of life.

Educating Girls, Unlocking Development

"Compelling evidence, accumulated over the past 20 years . . . , has led to an almost universal recognition of the importance of focusing on girls' education as part of broader development policy."

RUTH LEVINE

One of the most important public policy goals in the developing world is the expansion and improvement of education for girls. Vital in its own right for the realization of individual capabilities, the education of girls has the potential to transform the life chances of the girls themselves, their future families, and the societies in which they live. Girls with at least a primary school education are healthier and wealthier when they grow up and their future children have much greater opportunities than they otherwise would; even national economic outcomes appear to be positively influenced by expanded girls' education.

Unlike some development outcomes that depend on multiple factors outside the control of policy makers (either in developing countries or among donor nations), significant improvement in girls' education can be achieved through specific government actions. Expansion of basic education, making school infrastructure and curriculum more girl-friendly, and conditional cash transfers and scholarships to overcome household barriers have all been used to improve key outcomes, with demonstrable success. Lessons from regions that have made rapid advances with girls' education, and from programs that have introduced successful financing and teaching innovations, can be applied to accelerate progress.

While public policy can make the difference, policies that ignore important gender-related constraints to education at the primary and, particularly, at the postprimary educational levels can have the opposite effect, reinforcing existing patterns of gender discrimination and exclusion. Those patterns are often deep-seated. Families in many societies traditionally have valued schooling less for girls than for boys. In most households, the domestic workload falls more to females than to males, leaving less time for school. If families are struggling to find income, the demand for girls' help around the house (or in wage labor) may increase. Many parents believe that the return on educational investments varies according to gender—particularly if

girls, when they marry, leave their parents' households to join the husbands'.

When girls in developing countries do enroll in school, they frequently encounter gender-based discrimination and inadequate educational resources. Large numbers of girls in sub-Saharan Africa drop out, for example, when they reach puberty and the onset of menstruation simply because schools lack latrines, running water, or privacy. Parental concerns about girls' security outside the home can limit schooling where girls are vulnerable in transit and male teachers are not trusted. And in some countries, cultural aversion to the education of girls lingers. Afghanistan's Taliban insurgents, who believe that girls' education violates Islamic teachings, have succeeded in closing numerous schools, sometimes by beheading teachers. Afghanistan is an extreme case, but a reminder nonetheless of the challenges that remain on the path toward achieving the high payoffs from girls' education.

The Benefits

Why is the schooling of girls so critical? Education in general is among the primary means through which societies reproduce themselves; correspondingly, changing the educational opportunities for particular groups in society—girls and minority groups—is perhaps the single most effective way to achieve lasting transformations. A considerable body of evidence has shown that the benefits of educating a girl are manifested in economic and social outcomes: her lifetime health, labor force participation, and income; her (future) children's health and nutrition; her community's and her nation's productivity. Most important, education can break the intergenerational transmission of poverty.

Female participation in the formal labor market consistently increases with educational attainment, as it does for males. In at least some settings, the returns to education of girls are superior to those for boys. Several studies have shown that primary schooling increases lifetime earnings by as much as 20 percent for girls—higher than for their brothers. If they stay in secondary school, the returns from education are 25 percent or higher.

The inverse relationship between women's education and fertility is perhaps the best studied of all health and demographic phenomena. The relationship generally holds across countries and over time, and is robust even when income is taken into account. Completion of primary school is strongly associated with later age at marriage, later age at first birth, and lower lifetime fertility. A study of eight sub-Saharan countries covering the period from 1987 to 1999 found that girls' educational attainment was the best predictor of whether they would have their first births during adolescence.

Another study examined surveys across the developing world to compare female education and fertility by region. The higher the level of female education, the lower desired family size, and the greater the success in achieving desired family size. Further, each additional year of a mother's schooling cuts the expected infant mortality rate by 5 to 10 percent.

Maternal education is a key determinant of children's attainment. Multiple studies have found that a mother's level of education has a strong positive effect on daughters' enrollment—more than on sons and significantly more than the effect of fathers' education on daughters. Studies from Egypt, Ghana, India, Kenya, Malaysia, Mexico, and Peru all find that mothers with a basic education are substantially more likely to educate their children, especially their daughters.

Children's health also is strongly associated with mothers' education. In general, this relationship holds across countries and time, although the confounding effect of household income has complicated the picture. One study, for instance, compared 17 developing countries, examining the relationship between women's education and their infants' health and nutritional status. It found the existence of an education-related health advantage in most countries, although stronger for postneonatal health than for neonatal health. (In some countries the "education advantage" did appear to be eliminated when controlling for other dimensions of socioeconomic status.)

Other studies have found clear links between women's school attainment and birth and death rates, and between women's years of schooling and infant mortality. A 1997 study for the World Bank, which focused on Morocco, found that a mother's schooling and functional literacy predicted her child's height-for-age, controlling for other socioeconomic factors.

Although the causal links are harder to establish at the macrolevel, some researchers have made the attempt, with interesting results. For example, in a 100-country study, researchers showed that raising the share of women with a secondary education by 1 percent is associated with a 0.3 percent increase in annual per capita income growth. In a 63-country study, more productive farming because of increased female education accounts for 43 percent of the decline in malnutrition achieved between 1970 and 1995.

In short (and with some important nuances set aside), girls' education is a strong contributor to the achievement of multiple key development outcomes: growth of household and national income, health of women and children, and lower and wanted fertility. Compelling evidence, accumulated over the past 20 years using both quantitative and qualitative methods, has led to an almost universal recognition of the importance of focusing on girls' education as part of broader development policy.

The Trends

Given the widespread understanding about the value of girls' education, the international community and national governments have established ambitious goals for increased participation in primary education and progress toward gender parity at all levels. The Millennium Development Goals (MDG), approved by all member states of the United Nations in 2000, call for universal primary education in all countries by 2015, as well as gender parity at all levels by 2015.

There is good news to report. Impressive gains have been made toward higher levels of education enrollment and completion, and girls have been catching up rapidly with their brothers. As primary schooling expands, girls tend to be the main beneficiaries because of their historically disadvantaged position.

The rate of primary school completion also has improved faster for girls than for boys, again in large part because they had more to gain at the margins. Across all developing countries, girls' primary school completion increased by 17 percent, from 65 to 76 percent, between 1990 and 2000. During the same period, boys' primary completion increased by 8 percent, from 79 to 85 percent. Global progress is not matched, however, in every region. In sub-Saharan Africa, girls did only slightly better between 1990 and 2000, with primary completion increasing from 43 to 46 percent. (The primary completion rate for boys went in the opposite direction, from 57 to 56 percent.)

The overall good news about girls' progress must be tempered by realism, and a recognition that the goal is not to have boys' and girls' educational attainment "equally bad." Today, a mere nine years from the MDG deadline, it is clear that the important improvements over the past several decades in the developing world—in many instances, unprecedented rates of increase in primary school enrollment and completion—still leave a large number of poor countries very far from the target. While girls are making up ground rapidly, in many of the poorest countries the achievements on improved gender parity must be seen in the context of overall low levels of primary school completion.

An estimated 104 million to 121 million children of primary school age across the globe are not in school, with the worst shortfalls in Africa and South Asia. Completion of schooling is a significant problem. While enrollment has been increasing, many children drop out before finishing the fifth grade. In Africa, for example, just 51 percent of children (46 percent of girls) complete primary school. In South Asia, 74 percent of children (and just 63 percent of girls) do so.

Low levels of enrollment and completion are concentrated not only in certain regions but also among certain segments of the population. In every country completion rates are lowest for children from poor households. In Western and Central Africa, the median grade completed by the bottom 40 percent of the income distribution is zero, because less than half of poor children complete even the first year of school.

The education income gap also exacerbates gender disparities. In India, for example, the gap between boys and girls from the richest households is 2.5 percent, but the difference for children from the poorest households is 24 percent.

Girls are catching up quickly in most countries, but the level they are catching up to is still quite low.

In some countries the main reason for low educational attainment is that children do not enroll in school. In Bangladesh, Benin, Burkina Faso, Ivory Coast, India, Mali, Morocco, Niger, and Senegal, more than half of children from the bottom 40 percent of the income distribution never even enroll. Elsewhere, particularly in Latin America, enrollment may be almost universal, but high repetition and dropout rates lead to low completion rates. In both cases poor students are much more likely not to complete school.

In many countries the rural/urban education gap is a key factor explaining education differentials. In Mozambique, the rural completion rate is 12 percent, while at the national level 26 percent of children complete school. Burkina Faso, Guinea, Madagascar, Niger, and Togo all demonstrate a similar pattern. In rural areas, the gender gap in completion is pronounced in Africa: in Benin, Burkina Faso, Guinea, Madagascar, Mozambique, and Niger, a mere 15 percent of girls who start primary school make it to the end.

Policy makers increasingly are recognizing the importance of addressing the special needs and vulnerabilities of marginal populations, even in relatively well-off countries with education levels that, on average, look quite good. As my colleagues Maureen Lewis and Marlaine Lockheed at the Center for Global Development highlight in a forthcoming book, girls who are members of marginalized groups—the Roma in Eastern Europe, the indigenous populations in Central America and elsewhere, the underprivileged castes and tribes in India—suffer a double disadvantage. Low educational attainment for girls is an obvious mechanism through which historical disadvantage is perpetuated. In Laos, for example, more than 90 percent of men in the dominant Laotai group are literate, while only 30 percent of the youngest cohort of women belonging to excluded rural ethnic groups can read and write.

Beyond the primary school enrollment and completion trends, a complex problem is the quality of education. Although measurement of learning outcomes is spotty at best, analyses of internationally comparable assessments of learning achievement in mathematics, reading, and science indicate that most developing countries rank far behind the industrialized nations. This is all the more of concern because the tests are taken by the children in school who, in low-enrollment countries, are the equivalent in relative terms to the top performers in the high-enrollment developed nations. The data on national examinations is equally alarming. Student performance on national exams in South Asian and African countries shows major gaps in acquisition of knowledge and skills.

Thus, the picture of progress and gaps is a complex one: rapid improvements relative to historical trends, but far off the ideal mark in the poorest countries. Girls are catching up quickly in most countries, but the level they are catching up to is still quite low. In many nations, the "lowest hanging fruit" has already been reached; for all children, and for girls in particular, the ones now

out of school come from the most economically and socially disadvantaged backgrounds, and will be the hardest to reach. Finally, even among those children in school, evidence about poor learning outcomes should be cause for alarm.

The Challenges

The central imperative for improving educational opportunities and outcomes for girls in the low enrollment countries, including in sub-Saharan Africa and parts of South Asia, is to improve overall access and the quality of primary schooling. In doing so, planners and policy makers should ensure that they are not perpetuating barriers to girls' participation.

Getting to universal primary education (either enrollment or the more ambitious goal of completion) in sub-Saharan Africa and South Asia will require large-scale expansion in physical infrastructure, the number of teachers, and teaching/learning materials. Moreover, it will require fundamental improvements in the education institutions: more attention to learning outcomes rather than enrollment numbers, greater incentives for quality teaching, and more responsiveness to parents. This is a huge agenda. The donor and international technical community can support it, but it must be grounded in the political commitment of national and subnational governments.

Secondary to the "more and better education for all" agenda, and of particular relevance in countries that have already made significant progress so that most children go to school, is the need to understand and address the needs of particular disadvantaged groups, where gender differentials are especially pronounced. Beyond the efforts to reach children from poor and rural households, public policy makers need to understand and pay attention to ethnic and linguistic minorities, reaching them with tailored approaches rather than simply an expansion of the types of educational opportunities provided to the majority population. In addressing this challenge, policy makers must accept that reaching these key populations implies higher unit costs, as well as the adoption of potentially controversial measures, such as bilingual curriculum.

Finally, success in moving close to universal primary school enrollment generates its own new challenges. As more children complete primary school, the private benefits, in higher wages, decline (though the social benefits remain high). Private rates of return—perceived and real—cease to be seen as much of a reason for sending children to primary school, unless there is access to postprimary education. In addition, both the expansion of the existing education systems in many developing countries and the "scaling-up" of other public sector functions (such as health services, water management, and general public administration) require a larger cadre of educated and trained workers, the products of postprimary education. For these reasons, attention must be given to expanded opportunities for girls at the secondary level.

While international attention and goal-setting have been directed almost exclusively at the primary level, and the donor community has been persuaded by arguments about greater economic returns from primary education and the potentially regressive effects of investments at the secondary level, a large agenda remains unattended. It is at the secondary level that many of the microeconomic, health, and fertility outcomes of girls' education are fully realized. And common sense alone suggests that the large (and growing) cohort of children moving through primary schooling will create unsustainable pressures for postprimary education opportunities. If those are severely rationed, as they are in much of sub-Saharan Africa, the negative feedback to parents who sacrificed to send their children through primary school may be profound. Sorting out the design, financing, and institutional arrangements for effective secondary schooling—that is also responsive to labor market demand—is an essential part of good policy making today.

The Way Forward

Beyond general expansion of enrollment, governments can get out-of-school children into school by crafting specific interventions to reach them, and by increasing educational opportunities (formal and informal) for girls and women. In designing these initiatives, success depends on understanding and taking into account powerful demand-side influences that may constrain girls' school participation.

Specific interventions have been shown, in some settings, to get hard-to-reach children into school. These include eliminating school fees, instituting conditional cash transfers, using school feeding programs as an incentive to attend school, and implementing school health programs to reduce absenteeism. Several interventions have proved particularly successful where girls' participation is low. These include actions that increase security and privacy for girls (for example, ensuring that sanitation facilities are girl-friendly), as well as those that reduce gender-stereotyping in curriculum and encourage girls to take an active role in their education.

While few rigorous evaluations have been undertaken, many experts suggest that literacy programs for uneducated mothers may help increase school participation by their children. Adult literacy programs may be particularly useful in settings where there are pockets of undereducated women, such as ethnic or indigenous communities.

It is tempting for policy makers to focus on specific programmatic investments. But sustained improvements in education are impossible to achieve without improving the way in which key institutions in the sector function, and without increasing parental involvement in decisions affecting their children's education. Many countries with poorly performing educational systems suffer from institutional weaknesses, including low management capacity, nontransparent resource allocation and accounting practices, and substandard human resources policies and practices. Incentive structures that fail to reward good performance create and reinforce the most deleterious characteristics of weak institutions.

Parents who are well informed of policies and resource allocations in the education sector and who are involved in decisions regarding their children's schooling exert considerable influence and help contribute solutions. Involved communities are able to articulate local school needs, hold officials accountable, and mobilize local resources to fill gaps when the government response is inadequate.

In Benin, Burkina Faso, Guinea, Madagascar, Mozambique, and Niger, a mere 15 percent of girls who start primary school make it to the end.

A Modest Proposal

Donor agencies have been at the leading edge of the dialogue about the importance of girls' education, often providing the financial support, research, and political stimulus that may be lacking in countries that have more than their hands full with the basics of "Education for All." There is a broad consensus in the international donor community about the value of girls' education, and innovations have been introduced through donor-funded programs under the auspices of UNICEF, the World Food Program, the US Agency for International Development, and other key agencies. These have been valuable contributions, and have supported the work of champions at the national and local levels.

The donor community could come together now to accelerate progress in a very particular way. Working with both governments and nongovernmental organizations in countries where specific excluded groups—ethnic and/or linguistic minorities—have much poorer education outcomes, donors could finance the design, introduction, and rigorous evaluation of targeted programs to improve access to appropriate educational opportunities, with a particular emphasis (if warranted by the baseline research) on the needs and characteristics of girls. While different bilateral and multilateral donors could take the lead in funding specific types of programs or working in particular countries on the challenge of the "doubly disadvantaged," a shared learning agenda could be coordinated across agencies to generate much more than the spotty anecdotes and case studies on which we currently depend.

The learning agenda would include three components: first, the enduring questions to be examined—for example, determining the most effective strategies to improve learning outcomes among children who come from households where the language spoken is not the language of instruction; second, the use of methods that permit observed results to be attributed to the program; and third, the features that will ensure maximum credibility of the evaluations, such as independence, dissemination of results (whether the findings are favorable or not), and wide sharing of the data for reanalysis.

Just as education can transform individuals' lives, learning what works can transform the debates in development policy. The beneficiaries in developing countries would include not only girls who receive the education they deserve and need, but also families and communities and future generations thereby lifted over time out of poverty.

RUTH LEVINE is director of programs and a senior fellow at the Center for Global Development.

Women, Islam, and the New Iraq

Isobel Coleman

The Impact of Sharia

Article 14 of Iraq's new constitution, approved in a nationwide referendum held on October 15, states that Iraqis are equal before the law "without discrimination because of sex." Yet the constitution also states that no law can be passed that contradicts the "established rulings" of Islam. For this reason, the new document has been condemned by critics both inside and outside Iraq as a fundamental setback for a majority of Iraq's population—namely, its women. According to Isam al-Khafaji, an Iraqi scholar, the document "could easily deprive women of their rights." Yanar Muhammad, a leading secular activist and the head of the Organization of Women's Freedom in Iraq, worries that the Islamic provision will turn the country "into an Afghanistan under the Taliban, where oppression and discrimination of women is institutionalized."

These criticisms are not without merit, and the ambiguity of the new constitution is a cause for concern. The centrality of Islamic law in the document, however, does not necessarily mean trouble for Iraqi women. In fact, sharia is open to a wide range of understanding, and across the Islamic world today, progressive Muslims are seeking to reinterpret its rules to accommodate a modern role for women.

Iraq's constitution does not specify who will decide which version of Islam will prevail in the country's new legal system. But the battle has already begun. Victory by the progressives would have positive implications for all aspects of the future of Iraq, since women's rights are critical to democratic consolidation in transitional and war-torn societies. Allowing a full social, political, and economic role for women in Iraq would help ensure its transition to a stable democracy. Success for women in Iraq would also reverberate throughout the broader Muslim world. In every country where sharia is enforced, women's rights have become a divisive issue, and the balance struck between tradition and equality in Iraq will influence these other debates.

In many Islamic countries, reformers have largely abandoned attempts to replace sharia with secular law, a route that has proved mostly futile. Instead, they are trying to promote women's rights within an Islamic framework. This approach seems more likely to succeed, since it fights theology with theology—a natural strategy in countries with conservative populations and where religious authority is hard to challenge. Now that the United States has helped midwife an Islamic state in Iraq, U.S. officials would, for similar reasons, be wise to move beyond their largely secular interlocutors. If Washington still hopes to create a relatively liberal regime in Iraq, it must start working with progressive religious Muslims to advance the role of women through religious channels.

Rethinking the Law

Sharia is the body of Islamic law that was developed by religious scholars (*ulama*) after the death of the Prophet Muhammad. Meant to provide moral and legal guidance to Muslims, sharia is based on the Koran and the Sunna (the recorded traditions or customs of the Prophet). The Koran has about 80 verses concerning legal issues, many of which refer to the role of women in society and to important family issues, such as marriage, divorce, and inheritance.

Because neither the Koran nor the Sunna cover most day-to-day issues, however, after the death of the Prophet the *ulama* created other means for addressing them. As a last measure, qualified legal scholars could study a question, apply independent reasoning (*ijtihad*), and issue a nonbinding fatwa. In the eleventh century, however, to consolidate their control, the Sunni *ulama* crystallized their legal judgments into various schools of Islamic jurisprudence and banned *ijtihad*. With the gates of independent interpretation closed, the traditionalists imposed their own conservative positions on mainstream Islamic jurisprudence, and these have remained largely frozen for almost a millennium.

Some scholars, however, have continued to search for Islamic answers to the questions of modern life. Contrary to the claims of secularists who deny the compatibility of Islam and modern notions of women's rights, Islamic attitudes on the question actually vary quite widely. According to "Islamic feminists," Islam is actually a very progressive religion for women, was radically egalitarian for its time, and remains so in some of its Scriptures. They contend that Islamic law has evolved in ways that are inimical to gender equality not because it clearly pointed in that direction, but because of selective interpretation by patriarchal leaders and a mingling of Islamic teachings with tribal customs and traditions. Islamic feminists now seek to revive the equality bestowed on women in the religion's early years by rereading the Koran, putting the Scriptures in context, and disentangling them from tribal practices.

Among the pioneers of Islamic feminism are the Moroccan writer Fatema Mernissi and the Pakistani scholar Riffat Hassan—although neither is entirely comfortable with the label. In fact, many religious progressives prefer to distance themselves from the term "feminism" and the Western cultural baggage it brings. These scholars simply see themselves as Muslims pursuing rights for women within an Islamic discourse. Their movement already spans the globe, is growing, and is increasingly innovative. Many of its leading lights are actually men, distinguished Islamic scholars such as Hussein Muhammad in Indonesia, whose high status gives them particular credibility.

The Islamic feminists tend to focus their work on the sensitive area of family law, since it is the area of jurisprudence that has the greatest impact on women's daily lives—and since it also leaves much room for interpretation. Take, for example, the Koran's stipulations on inheritance. One contested verse states that on her parents' death, a daughter should receive half of what her brother inherits. Progressives, however, point out that at the time of the Prophet, giving a woman any inheritance was a radical departure from Arab practice. (Indeed, it was a radical notion in much of the West as well until the twentieth century.) The progressives also note that the rule made sense in traditional Islamic societies, where women had no financial obligations, only financial rights. But today, they argue, when many Muslim women do earn a living and men do not always provide the necessary support, it is important to adapt the law to changing circumstances.

Contrary to the claims of some secularists, Islamic attitudes on women's rights vary widely.

The Koran, like the Bible, also includes many multilayered, seemingly contradictory passages, and Islamic feminists tend to emphasize different verses than the traditionalists. On the sensitive subject of polygamy, for example, one verse of the Koran says, "Marry those women who are lawful for you, up to two, three, or four, but only if you can treat them all equally." Later in the same chapter, however, the Koran reads, "No matter how you try you will never be able to treat your wives equally." Many Muslim scholars today read the two verses together, as an effective endorsement of monogamy. Many tribal communities, on the other hand, focus on the former verse alone and cite it as a justification for having multiple wives.

The rules on veiling are similarly inconclusive. Progressive Muslims point out that nowhere does the Koran actually require the veiling of all Muslim women. Veiling was simply a custom in pre-Islamic Arabia, where the hijab was considered a status symbol (after all, only women who did not have to work in the fields had the luxury of wearing a veil). When the Koran mentions veils, it is in reference to Muhammad's wives. The "hijab verse" reads, "Believers, do not enter the Prophet's house . . . unless asked. And if you are invited . . . do not linger.

And when you ask something from the Prophet's wives, do so from behind a hijab. This will assure the purity of your hearts as well as theirs." In the Prophet's lifetime, all believers (men and women) were encouraged to be modest. But the veil did not become widespread for several generations—until conservatives became ascendant.

What all this suggests for Iraq is that sharia is not inherently inimical to women's rights. It also suggests that the question of who gets to interpret sharia is critical—especially on areas such as gender equality, where the letter of the law is vague.

Status Anxiety

For nearly 50 years, Iraq's personal-status law provided women with some of the broadest legal rights in the region. The law, enacted in 1959, included several progressive provisions loosely derived from various schools of Islamic jurisprudence. It set the marriage age at 18 and prohibited arbitrary divorce. It also restricted polygamy, making that practice almost impossible (the code required men seeking a second wife to get judicial permission, which would only be granted if the judge believed the man could treat both wives equally). And it required that men and women be treated equally for purposes of inheritance. When he was challenged by clerics over this provision, Abdul Karim Kassem, the Iraqi prime minister at the time, responded that the verse in the Koran calling for a daughter's inheritance to be half that of a son's was only a recommendation, not a commandment.

Religious scholars were unhappy with the code from the beginning, largely because it imposed a unified standard on Iraq's population without allowing for the differences among its various religious sects. Shiite clerics, in particular, viewed it as another aspect of unwanted Sunni oppression. But the legislation played an important role in modernizing the role of women in Iraqi society. Under secular, albeit brutal, Baathist rule, Iraqi women made significant advances in numerous areas, including education and employment.

With the overthrow of Saddam Hussein in March 2003, Shiite leaders quickly made clear that they expected the new Iraq to be an Islamic state. One of their first priorities was to try to annul the personal-status law. In December 2003, a conservative contingent on the U.S.-appointed Iraqi Governing Council (IGC) voted behind closed doors for Resolution 137, which canceled Iraq's existing family laws and placed such issues under the rules of sharia. Abdul Aziz al-Hakim, the Shiite leader of the powerful Supreme Council for the Islamic Revolution in Iraq (SCIRI), held the rotating chairmanship of the IGC at the time of the vote.

Resolution 137 was worryingly vague about exactly what form of Islamic regulation would replace the old legislation, although the decree seemed to imply that each Islamic community would be free to impose its own rules on issues such as marriage, divorce, and other important family matters. This ambiguity worried not only women's groups, but also those who feared that such an Islamic free-for-all would exacerbate sectarian tensions.

Women's organizations and moderates across the country quickly mobilized against the new regulation. They held rallies, press conferences, and high-level meetings with the American authorities to make their concerns known. They even gained the support of several moderate Islamic clerics. L. Paul Bremer, the head of the Coalition Provisional Authority, ultimately vetoed the IGC's resolution. But the intentions of Iraq's powerful conservative Shiite leaders—to broadly assert sharia over a whole range of legal questions—had been made clear.

Mosque and State

This determination was soon directed at a new target: Iraq's constitution. Sharia quickly became one of the most contentious issues facing the drafting committee. Moderate Shiite leaders such as Grand Ayatollah Ali al-Sistani insisted that they did not want to replicate Iran's theocratic system (in which clerics run most aspects of the government). But after years of brutal suppression by Saddam, the Shiites were nonetheless determined to give Islam a central role in Iraq's reconstituted state. In an August 2003 statement, Sistani announced, "The religious constants and the Iraqi people's moral principles and noble social values should be the main pillars of the coming Iraqi constitution."

The Kurds and secular Sunnis were equally adamant about keeping religion out of government. Speaking to a reporter in early 2005, Kurdish leader Jalal Talabani (shortly before he became president of Iraq) insisted, "We will never accept any religious government in Iraq. Never. This is a red line for us. We will never live inside an Islamic Iraq." Maysoon al-Damluji, president of the Iraqi Independent Women's Group, worried that "the interpretation of sharia law will take us backward." But with polls showing that a majority of Iraqis endorsed sharia, there was never really any question of whether Islam would be in the constitution; the real debate was over how much weight to give it.

Secular Iraqi women were marginalized during the drafting process. The composition of the constitutional committee reflected the results of the January 2005 national elections: about half of its 55 members came from the Shiite United Iraqi Alliance (uia), and another quarter came from the Democratic Patriotic Alliance of Kurdistan. Of the eight women on the committee, five represented the UIA, two were Kurdish representatives, and only one, Dr. Rajaa al-Khuzai, was an independent.

The new constitution makes Islam Iraq's state religion and a basic source for legislation.

The committee spent months arguing over whether Islam would be *the* source of legislation for the country (as the religious parties wanted) or *a* source (a compromise sought by the Kurds and other secularists). The disagreement had not been resolved by the time the original August 15 deadline passed, and the debate spilled over into the extension period. Conservative Shiite leaders remained intransigent and threatened to scuttle talks if Islam did not get a central place in the constitution. As the arguments dragged on, U.S. Ambassador Zalmay Khalilzad finally intervened to avoid a stalemate. To gain concessions in other areas, he supported provisions that strengthened Islam's influence. Ultimately, the Kurds acquiesced too, both because they had other priorities to defend and because they recognized that conservative Shiites were not going to capitulate.

Article 2 of the final version of the constitution makes Islam the official religion of the state, cites it as a basic source of legislation, and says that no law can be passed that contradicts its "undisputed" rulings. Interpreting this provision will fall to the Supreme Court, which the new constitution says may include clerics; their number and method of selection were not specified, but will be defined by a subsequent law that must be approved by a two-thirds majority of parliament.

Secularists and women's advocates are also worried about Article 39, the section dealing with personal-status law. As foreshadowed by the battle in the IGC, Article 39 deems Iraqis "free in their personal status according to their religions, sects, beliefs, or choices," but leaves it up to subsequent legislation to define what this means. If Shiite leaders truly meant for the provision to give Iraqis the freedom of choice—allowing Shiites to live under Shiite law and Sunnis to live under Sunni law—then the progressive 1959 code may also be kept on the books for those who want it. Allowing such freedom could lead to a confusing but relatively benign system (not unprecedented in the region), under which Iraqis with legal questions could choose among different codes and court systems—Sunni, secular, or Shiite—depending on which they thought would give them the most favorable treatment.

Many secular Iraqis worry, however, that Article 39 will lead instead to an Iranian-style theocracy, which would severely limit women's rights in particular. Adnan Pachachi, the former Iraqi foreign minister and a secular Sunni leader, told *The New York Times* in August that although he agreed with much of the new constitution, he was troubled by its more overtly Islamic provisions. "They want to inject religion into everything, which is not right," he said. "I cannot imagine that we might have a theocratic regime in Iraq like the one in Iran. That would be a disaster."

Indeed, Iran's theocracy has been a disaster on multiple fronts, including women's rights. In the aftermath of the 1979 revolution, Iran's new government quickly suspended the country's progressive family law, disallowed female judges, and strongly enforced the wearing of the hijab. Within a few months, sharia rulings lowered the marriage age to nine, permitted polygamy, gave fathers the right to decide who their daughters could marry, permitted unilateral divorce for men but not women, and gave fathers sole custody of children in the case of divorce. Over the intervening years, Iranian activists, including some conservative religious women, have managed to soften some of the harshest inequalities. But anything approaching the Iranian system would still represent a major setback for Iraq's women.

Skeptics might wonder whether the legal debate in Iraq really matters. After all, most Middle Eastern countries have elegant constitutions guaranteeing many rights and freedoms to their citizens, yet lack the sorts of strong institutions that could defend those rights with any consistency. And indeed, Iraq may slide down this path over time. In the short term, however, the heavy U.S. presence there ensures that the political process will emphasize constitutional provisions and the rule of law. Moreover, according to an analysis by Nathan Brown, a George Washington University professor and a constitutional expert, Iraq's constitution has fewer loopholes for limiting basic freedoms than those of Iraq's neighbors. The new document also designates certain institutions, such as the Human Rights Commission and the Federal Supreme Court, to defend individual rights. Although the structural details of these bodies remain to be determined by Iraq's legislature, there is still reason to hope they will effectively defend Iraqis' freedoms.

Learning from Others

No matter how effective such institutions turn out to be, the fact remains that the new constitution makes sharia supreme in Iraq. If moderates hope to advance women's rights, therefore, they will have to do it within an Islamic framework.

Fortunately, there are good precedents for such a process. Morocco, for example, recently revised its personal-status code (*moudawana*) but claimed to be doing so on Islamic grounds. The reforms were the result of over a decade of pressure from progressive Moroccan nongovernmental organizations (NGOS), which pushed to raise the marriage age from 15 to 18, abolish polygamy, equalize the right to divorce, and give women the right to retain custody of their children. Such efforts were opposed by religious groups. But Morocco's modernizing young king, Muhammad VI (who claims to be a direct descendent of the Prophet), backed the reformers and appointed a committee to examine potential changes to the *moudawana*. In October 2003, he formally presented parliament with a set of sweeping revisions to the family law, defending the changes with copious references to the Koran. In fact, both religious and secular supporters of the reforms used the language of religion and Islamic jurisprudence to advocate gender equality, and despite conservative opposition, parliament approved the changes.

Indonesia provides another example of how progressive change can come from within Islam. A group called Fatayat, the women's wing of the country's largest grass-roots organization (known as Nahdlatul Ulama), now trains its members in Islamic *fiqh* (jurisprudence) so that they can hold their own in religious debates. An NGO known as P3M (the Indonesian Society for Pesantren and Community Development) also uses *fiqh* to encourage Indonesia's many *pesantren* (religious schools) to promote women's reproductive health and family planning. And Musdah Mulia, the chief researcher at Indonesia's Ministry of Religious Affairs, caused a sensation in 2004 by calling for important changes to sharia in areas such as marriage, polygamy, and the wearing of the hijab—changes that she defended through meticulous references to Islamic jurisprudence. Her controversial recommendations have not yet been enacted, but they have sparked an important debate across Indonesian society that may eventually lead to significant changes.

An organization known as Women Living Under Muslim Laws (WLUML) provides another, transnational example of how women are pushing for change from within Islam. Founded in 1984 to oppose the harsh interpretation of sharia emerging in Algeria, WLUML functions by giving information on progressive Islamic systems around the world to local activists, who use the information to fight for greater freedoms. The network remains up and running today, providing women's groups around the world with powerful Islamic justifications for gender equality.

Turning Numbers into Influence

In Iraq, unlike in many other Muslim nations, women will have a strong advantage in their fight for equality: namely, a provision in the new constitution that guarantees them 25 percent of the seats in parliament. This quota is the product of intense lobbying by women's groups, who feared being left out of the new Iraqi politics. It also has some grounding in Iraqi history. The Baathists gave women the vote and the right to run for office in 1980; within two decades, women had come to occupy 20 percent of the seats in Iraq's rubber-stamp parliament (compared to a 3.5 percent average in the region) and some prominent cabinet positions. After the invasion, U.S. policymakers were sympathetic to women's concerns that they would lose their political position in an election process dominated by conservative Shiites. Washington also wanted to support Iraqi women without directly challenging religious convictions. Instituting a quota seemed a good way to do both.

The process started with the Transitional Administrative Law, the interim constitution issued by the Americans and the IGC in 2004, which stated that women should constitute no less than a quarter of the members of the National Assembly. In the run-up to the January 2005 elections, political parties were required to field electoral slates on which every third candidate was a woman. As a result, women captured 31 percent of the seats.

At the time of the elections, some Western commentators pointed to this high level of female representation as evidence that a grand social and cultural transformation was under way in Iraq. With so many women in parliament, they reasoned, Iraq's new government would have to take a progressive stance on women's rights in drafting the new constitution and limit the role of religion. But assuming that merely having women in government would produce liberal legislation was a mistake. After all, nearly half of the women elected had run on the UIA list, and they have toed their party's conservative Shiite line.

When the constitution-drafting process began, progressive women, sensing that they would lose the battle over Islam, focused on holding on to their 25 percent quota in parliament. Several women leaders actually hoped to expand the quota (a few mentioned 40 percent as their goal) and apply it to other decision-making positions as well. But conservatives responded by attempting to have the quota phased out altogether after two rounds of elections. In the end, the quota did make it into the final draft of the constitution, which will give women in Iraq one of the highest levels of representation in the world (after all, women make up less than 15 percent of the U.S. Congress). Many of these seats may continue to be filled by female conservatives unlikely to support progressive legislation on women's issues in the near term. Over time, however, these same legislators may start advancing women's rights within an Islamic context.

The future of Islamic feminism in Iraq will depend on politicians such as Salama al-Khafaji, a dentist turned politician who is also a devout Shiite. After losing her son in an ambush, Khafaji was rated the most popular female politician in Iraq in a survey conducted in June 2005 (and was ranked the 11th most popular politician overall). As a member of the IGC, she incurred the wrath of secular women's groups by voting for Resolution 137. But Khafaji (who has pursued her political ambitions despite the objections of her husband, who divorced her as a consequence) defended her position by arguing that Islamic rules actually provide better protection to women in divorce and custody proceedings than does secular law. Khafaji sees herself as a positive force for change on women's issues; as she told a journalist last November, "I have Islamic ideas on justice, but I am moderate." And her ability to work with both secular and Islamic parties could make her an effective legislator.

The status of women in the future Iraq will also depend in large part on the strength of the country's judicial system. Here, too, there is reason for guarded optimism; although Iraq's court system needs significant reform, it does include many qualified lawyers and judges (although their expertise lies mostly in secular law, not sharia). Iraq also has a tradition of women serving as judges. The country's first female judge, Zakia Hakki, was appointed in 1959 (she is currently a prominent member of parliament). Today, women are widely accepted as judges in the Kurdish north and in the more secular parts of Baghdad.

Assuming that merely having women in government would produce liberal legislation was a mistake.

But keeping women on the bench elsewhere will not be easy, as the story of Nidal Nasser Hussein illustrates. In 2003, the U.S. authorities appointed her the first female judge in the Shiite holy city of Najaf. The decision was met with widespread outrage. Several senior clerics quickly issued fact was saying that under Islamic law only men can be judges, and angry protesters showed up at her swearing-in ceremony. In the face of such unexpected opposition, the senior U.S. commanding officer in Najaf decided to delay Hussein's appointment indefinitely, and she has yet to take her seat on the bench. As conservatives consolidate their control in the Shiite south, such conflicts are likely to intensify. Iraqi women should respond by invoking Islamic scholars who argue in favor of female judges.

Although having the right judges on the bench will determine the formal rights of Iraqi women over the long term, in the short term religious vigilantes, who are forcing their own fundamentalist views on Iraq's besieged population, are having the

greatest impact. Over the past two years, various towns in both Shiite and Sunni areas have fallen into the hands of extremists who are imposing stringent restrictions there, such as requiring women to wear full-length veils, forbidding music and dancing, and enforcing strict segregation of the sexes in public. Many of these vigilantes are unemployed, undereducated followers of demagogues such as Muqtada al-Sadr. But at least some are reportedly also members of the police force in several southern cities (notably Basra). As their activities suggest, the greatest danger to Iraqi women stems not from any legal restrictions, but from lawlessness.

Friends in High Places

Although the status of Iraqi women will ultimately depend on Iraqis themselves, the United States can still play a constructive role. Washington should start by identifying and cultivating Islamic feminists within Iraq's mainstream religious parties. These women (and men) may not want to cooperate with the United States at first, and some of them will hold anti-American views. But these individuals wield far more political influence than the secular but marginalized Iraqi leaders who are popular in Washington, and the United States must learn how to work with them.

Indeed, the United States should work with Iraqi women across the religious spectrum in order to cultivate new leaders. Thanks to the quota system, there is no question that Iraqi women will continue to play a significant role in national politics in the years ahead, and Washington should help ensure that it is a moderating one. Most of the women elected to parliament will be new to politics. The United States should provide them with technical training (through organizations such as the National Democratic Institute for International Affairs, an NGO that provides practical assistance to leaders advancing democracy) and help them to network across sectarian lines. Iraqi politicians should also be encouraged to work with their more moderate Iranian counterparts. The current U.S. policy of excluding Iranian parliamentarians and activists from U.S.-funded conferences in the region is counterproductive and should be abandoned.

The United States should also assist with judicial reform. This means not only helping the courts modernize technologically, but also training judges, especially women, in modern Islamic jurisprudence. These training programs could be developed in partnership with the leading institutions of Islamic jurisprudence throughout the region, and they should be open to judges from across the Muslim world.

To help women defend their rights, Washington should also educate Iraqis about what their rights are—both under the new constitution and under sharia. A recent Freedom House report assessing women's rights in 17 Arab countries found that with the exception of Saudi Arabia, each has a constitution that formally mandates gender equality. The problem in these countries, however, is that the governments make little effort to inform the people of their rights. To avoid such a scenario in Iraq, the United States should support educational programs and a nationwide media campaign to promote better understanding of Iraqis' freedoms, under both the constitution and other laws. Washington should also encourage open dialogue on various interpretations of sharia governing personal-status laws. Religious scholars and international Islamic groups, such as Sisters in Islam and WLUML, should be invited to join and inform the discussions, which should be widely broadcast through media outlets such as Radio Al-Mahabba (a U.S.-funded Iraqi station dedicated to raising awareness on women's rights).

In the long term, female education may be the best way to advance the status of women. During the difficult decade of the 1990s, school-enrollment rates for girls in Iraq declined significantly, making Iraq one of the few countries in the world today where mothers are generally better educated than their daughters. Although reliable literacy figures are hard to come by, most observers agree that Iraq now has one of the worst gender literacy gaps in the world. As Iran, with its female literacy rate of more than 70 percent, has shown, educated women inevitably become effective advocates for their own rights. The United States should therefore champion female education in Iraq at all levels—primary, secondary, and tertiary—and promote adult-literacy programs for women.

In the next year, a new Iraqi parliament will be elected with the power to write laws that will shape the country for the next generation. Washington must therefore do everything it can to aid Iraqi women's groups and programs designed to help women leaders there. Efforts such as the U.S.-funded legal-education program at the University of Baghdad, where women make up 40 percent of the participants in rule-of-law seminars, should be expanded to other universities and cities across Iraq. Washington should also consider establishing a women's college in Baghdad, which could become a center of learning and critical thinking for the entire region.

The United States should also start channeling a significant portion of its reconstruction dollars to Iraqi businesswomen. Economic empowerment is a good way to boost the status of women. Despite the enormous sums of American aid flowing into Iraq, the U.S. mission in Baghdad has so far resisted having an adviser on gender issues on the ground in Iraq—where programs to support women are actually implemented. As a result, its many gender initiatives have not been nearly as effective as they could have been.

Although the United States has now missed this and several other important opportunities to promote the role of women in post-Saddam Iraq, the imposition of sharia there was virtually inevitable. But the resurgence of Islamic law in Iraq need not be a disaster for women. Although it may well mean a short-term setback in certain rights enjoyed under Saddam, in the long run, Iraqis may manage to build a more equitable society that accommodates both Islamic principles and a modern role for women. This outcome is far from guaranteed, but it is also not too much to hope for.

ISOBEL COLEMAN is a Senior Fellow and Director of the Women and U.S. Foreign Policy Program at the Council on Foreign Relations.

Women and Warlords

ANN JONES

To the Bush bunch, an election seems to equal "democracy." Yet five months after elections in Iraq, that country has no government. And nine months after parliamentary elections in Afghanistan, it's unclear who the new legislature represents and where it's headed.

I recently visited the Afghan Parliament, just finishing its third month in session, to interview twenty members of the lower house who seem to many Afghans to be the last, best hope for a democratic future. They are certainly not typical. Standard issue parliamentarians are familiar mujahedeen commanders and cronies previously defeated, discredited and driven from the country. But these twenty parliamentarians are different: They're women.

Trumpeted as "the first democratically elected Parliament in over thirty years," this one was planned at the December 2001 Bonn conference that followed the fall of the Taliban, and was brought into being at fabulous expense by an army of some 130,000 internationally paid election workers. The United States' inexplicable pressure to invite those mujahedeen commanders to Bonn plays out now in a Parliament where every other member is a former jihadi, and nearly half are affiliated with fundamentalist or traditionalist Islamist parties, including the Taliban.

The presence of so many of the country's notorious bad guys is certainly the most peculiar feature of this "democratic" Parliament (another is the new Parliament building itself, which has plenty of room for prayer mats but no office space). One international analyst reports that among the 249 members of the Wolesi Jirga (lower house) are forty commanders (warlords) of armed militias, twenty-four members of criminal gangs, seventeen drug traffickers and nineteen men facing serious allegations of war crimes and human rights violations. The deputy chairman of the Afghan Independent Human Rights Commission charges that "more than 80 percent of winning candidates in provinces and more than 60 percent in the capital, Kabul, have links to armed groups." Plenty of parliamentarians parade around town in armored cars packed with bodyguards flourishing automatic weapons. "How can I stand up to that?" asked one woman delegate. "I am only one small lady arriving on the bus."

Warlords and criminals got into Parliament by the usual tactics: intimidation, bribery, theft and the occasional murderous assault. Many spent lavishly on campaigns, running up six-figure bills despite an official spending cap of about $15,000

(750,000 afghanis). Many gave away coveted products—from cell phones to motor bikes—to inspire voter loyalty. Some allegedly stuffed ballot boxes, using voter-registration cards confiscated from women. The highest percentages of women's votes were recorded in precisely those provinces where women are not allowed to leave the house. In Kandahar province, brimming ballot boxes were returned from women's voting centers, although few women had been seen visiting the polls.

The presence on the ballot of the usual suspects—especially the commanders who wrecked the country—kept many voters from last September's polls. (The low voter turnout, also attributed to widespread disillusionment with President Hamid Karzai, further dims the democratic credentials of the new Parliament.) But many voters filed a protest vote that produced Parliament's other startling statistic: Better than one in four members of the Wolesi Jirga is a woman.

What made that result possible is a national policy of "affirmative discrimination," a quota system endorsed and encouraged by the international community. The Afghan Constitution of 2004 provides that "from each province on average at least two female delegates shall have membership to the Wolesi Jirga." That's a total of sixty-eight women, or 27 percent of the lower house, a figure that catapults Afghanistan into the ranks of nations with the highest proportion of female representation. Sweden is number one, with 44 percent, and Afghanistan a respectable number twenty. (The United States, at roughly 15 percent, is a conspicuous disgrace.)

Surprisingly, when the votes were counted last September, nineteen women had received enough votes to win seats even without the quota system. In Herat, Fauzia Gailani, a political unknown who runs a gym for women, took first place, though she faced rivals backed by the former mujahedeen commander and provincial governor (and current Cabinet minister) Ismail Khan. In Farah province, second place went to Malalai Joya, the young woman who, as a delegate to the constitutional loya jirga in 2004, became dangerously famous for denouncing the warlords and war criminals in President Karzai's Cabinet.

One female parliamentarian insists the warlords 'won't oppose women or liberals on everything. They will pick their battles.'

The performance of female candidates for the provincial councils, elected at the same time, was even more amazing. Women won the most votes in three provinces (Balkh, Ghazni and Kunduz) and won seats in eighteen of thirty-four provinces. In Kabul women won ten seats, two more than the quota prescribed. And this despite the fact that most female candidates had little money or time to spend on campaigning, while husbands and social customs kept many from campaigning at all. Many reported death threats. A rival parliamentary candidate attacked Dr. Roshanak Wardak's home in Wardak province with automatic weapons and rockets. A local warlord is suspected in an attack in Nuristan that seriously wounded parliamentary candidate Hawa Nuristani and three of her staff just days before the election. Both women won.

From the time the election results were announced last fall, commentators worried aloud about what would happen when women met warlords. The smart, cynical money was on the warlords, while international NGOs and UN agencies hastened to offer the women coaching and technical support. But after the Wolesi Jirga was in session three months, its chairman (and former presidential candidate), Yunus Qanooni, told this reporter that there are strong and outspoken parliamentarians on both sides of the gender gap. He thinks the women are doing just fine. On the whole, the women members are better educated than the men, many of whom are illiterate; and most have careers as teachers, doctors or civil servants, while taking care of five children (on average) at home.

Qanooni argues that because Parliament is a new institution, both men and women should receive international training. Maybe in communication skills: Men complain that women interrupt them. Women say men need lessons in "democratic conversation."

During the first full-scale parliamentary debate—on the issue of whether women parliamentarians would be allowed to travel abroad without *mahrams* (male escorts)—women held their own. "We no longer cross the desert by camel, you know," said Shinkai Karokhail. "We take airplanes." Warlords asked, "Why are these women yelling at us?" Qanooni quickly sent the issue to an administrative committee.

Women parliamentarians, who were expected to quail before the warlords, already claim to be changing them for the better. Unfortunately, the female quota system gave warlords the chance to buy loyalty in exchange for protection and financial support. One female parliamentarian claims off the record that "half the women in Parliament belong to some warlord." So when a female parliamentarian reports that some well-known war criminal has become "a very good man," it's hard to know what to make of her opinion.

Nevertheless, the independent Kabul member Karokhail says it's possible to work with the commanders. "They're called warlords," she says, "but they've survived by being very shrewd factional leaders. Politicians. They won't oppose women or liberals on everything. They will pick their battles, and we will pick ours." And Roshanak Wardak notes that the ground has shifted. "The commanders could be outside running around with the Taliban and Al Qaeda, but they're inside talking to us," she says. "They used to be gunmen, but what good is a gun in the Parliament?"

That's the hopeful view. But skeptics in the international community note the ease with which Afghan thugs adopt Western vocabulary. Armed militia commanders talk peace and democracy, and fundamentalist mullahs spout feminism. Internationals say, "The leopard doesn't change its spots." In the parliamentary cafeteria, women members caucus over cups of tea. In the corridor strolls gray-bearded parliamentarian Abdul Rasul Sayyaf, Islamic cleric and scholar, militia commander, leader of the Wahhabi fundamentalist faction, friend of Osama bin Laden, accused war criminal and the purported choice of President Karzai (read Bush) for chairman of the Wolesi Jirga. Optimists take his narrow loss to Qanooni (himself a former mujahid and right hand to the assassinated national hero Ahmed Shah Massoud, but no extremist) as a sign of political change.

But the strolling Sayyaf is trailed day after day by fellow parliamentarians from the provinces. They parade in cloaks and shawls, their turbans tightly wrapped or trailing tails, their beards dyed jet black or bright red in the fashion of this or that part of the countryside. Unmistakably, they are drawn to the scent of power. But if Sayyaf lost, why are they still following him?

The answer lies outside the walls of Parliament, in the countryside. There, in the south and east, where warfare that followed the American bombardment of 2001 has never stopped, violence increases every day. Schools have been attacked; teachers beheaded. It is estimated that in Kandahar 200 schools have closed; in Helmand 165; in Zabul all but five of 170. Murders are reported almost every day: police officers, village officials, former political or military leaders. Americans say the attackers are Taliban, though many Afghans say the Taliban are busy working as drivers or translators for Americans who don't know their history. Others say the attackers are drug smugglers, inciting insecurity to cover their illegal operations. But many Afghans say that the same familiar militia men are behind the violence, settling old scores.

In a sense, the countryside is supposed to belong to parliamentarians. Every Thursday they're expected to visit their constituents and report problems back to Kabul. Women members generally have less money and more obstacles to travel, but most of them go. Dr. Gulalai Noor Safi sets off by car over the arduous Salang Pass. Safora Yalkhani boards a battered bus to Bamiyan. Roshanak Wardak takes me into the mountains of Wardak in a Russian jeep for meetings with village elders and Kuchi nomads huddling around grass-fed fires. At Abdura, twenty male elders recite the needs of the village. *A school.* More than 250 boys meet daily in a field, weather permitting. A like number of girls stay home. *A clinic.* Pregnant women walk all day to reach Dr. Roshanak's surgery, and then they walk back with their newborns. *Jobs.* Twenty-five able-bodied young men have gone to work in Iran, leaving families behind. This village is lucky enough to have water, supplied most of the year by mountain snowmelt. They've terraced and cultivated small plots, but the rocky soil yields only enough food to last the villagers fifteen days. Then men must find paid work to feed their families. Looking out across the rocky, high-desert waste, one wonders where.

"Why don't they pool their resources and build a school?" I ask Dr. Roshanak. "They have no resources," she says. "I think you cannot understand what it is to have nothing."

Making justice for such villagers throughout the country—who so far have seen no benefits of the reported billions in foreign aid to Afghanistan—is the job that many women parliamentarians are undertaking. As more and more posh palaces of drug lords and corrupt officials rise in the capital, women members speak in Parliament of the deep and widening chasm between rich and poor. Warlords claim benefits for their own fiefdoms, but women—and Chairman Qanooni—press for equality among all regions and ethnic groups.

Current power struggles don't bode well. In late April President Karzai—Afghanistan's own "unitary executive"—won confirmation for twenty of his twenty-five Cabinet nominees, including a previously unknown personal adviser to replace veteran Foreign Minister Abdullah Abdullah. Among the losers were the culture minister, attacked for permitting women and "racy" Indian films to appear on state TV, and Suraya Raheem Sabarnag, named to be women's affairs minister—Karzai's only female nominee. An anonymous Karzai aide explained that women don't need "special appointments" to the Cabinet or the courts because they're already represented in Parliament.

Clearly, the only effective challenge to Karzai came not from Yunus Qanooni and colleagues but from right-wing jihadis who'd like to do away with female TV performers and ministers altogether. Karzai bowed to them (again) in naming the over-aged Islamic cleric Fazle Hadi Shinwari to continue as Chief Justice of the Supreme Court and effective head of the judiciary system. (Shinwari, who is on record opposing women on TV and equal education for girls, forced the first women's affairs minister from office by charging her with blasphemy, an offense punishable by death.)

How can women parliamentarians stand up to that? Maybe they're not meant to accomplish something like justice—or democracy—for Afghanistan. Maybe the new Parliament is just another foreign invention, like Kabul's new luxury hotel, designed to gratify the international community while serving no constructive Afghan purpose. Or maybe the new Parliament, such as it is, simply belongs already to the bad old boys.

ANN JONES (www.annjonesonline.com) is the author of *Kabul in Winter: Life Without Peace in Afghanistan* (Metropolitan).

Test Your Knowledge Form

We encourage you to photocopy and use this page as a tool to assess how the articles in *Annual Editions* expand on the information in your textbook. By reflecting on the articles you will gain enhanced text information. You can also access this useful form on a product's book support Web site at *http://www.mhcls.com/online/*.

NAME:

DATE:

TITLE AND NUMBER OF ARTICLE:

BRIEFLY STATE THE MAIN IDEA OF THIS ARTICLE:

LIST THREE IMPORTANT FACTS THAT THE AUTHOR USES TO SUPPORT THE MAIN IDEA:

WHAT INFORMATION OR IDEAS DISCUSSED IN THIS ARTICLE ARE ALSO DISCUSSED IN YOUR TEXTBOOK OR OTHER READINGS THAT YOU HAVE DONE? LIST THE TEXTBOOK CHAPTERS AND PAGE NUMBERS:

LIST ANY EXAMPLES OF BIAS OR FAULTY REASONING THAT YOU FOUND IN THE ARTICLE:

LIST ANY NEW TERMS/CONCEPTS THAT WERE DISCUSSED IN THE ARTICLE, AND WRITE A SHORT DEFINITION:

We Want Your Advice

ANNUAL EDITIONS revisions depend on two major opinion sources: one is our Advisory Board, listed in the front of this volume, which works with us in scanning the thousands of articles published in the public press each year; the other is you—the person actually using the book. Please help us and the users of the next edition by completing the prepaid article rating form on this page and returning it to us. Thank you for your help!

ANNUAL EDITIONS: Developing World 08/09

ARTICLE RATING FORM

Here is an opportunity for you to have direct input into the next revision of this volume.
We would like you to rate each of the articles listed below, using the following scale:

1. **Excellent: should definitely be retained**
2. **Above average: should probably be retained**
3. **Below average: should probably be deleted**
4. **Poor: should definitely be deleted**

Your ratings will play a vital part in the next revision.
Please mail this prepaid form to us as soon as possible.
Thanks for your help!

RATING	ARTICLE
	1. How to Help Poor Countries
	2. The Utopian Nightmare
	3. Africa's Village of Dreams
	4. Today's Golden Age of Poverty Reduction
	5. Development as Poison
	6. Why God Is Winning
	7. Climbing Back
	8. The India Model
	9. Industrial Revolution 2.0
	10. The Protection Racket
	11. Social Justice and Global Trade
	12. Cotton: The Huge Moral Issue
	13. "We Need Trade Justice, Not Free Trade"
	14. Ranking the Rich
	15. Foreign Aid II
	16. Making Aid Work
	17. Food Sovereignty: Ending World Hunger in Our Time
	18. Crisis of Credibility
	19. Without Consent: Global Capital Mobility and Democracy
	20. The End of War?
	21. Iraq's Civil War
	22. When the Shiites Rise
	23. Letter from Afghanistan
	24. Pakistan and the Islamists

RATING	ARTICLE
	25. The Pashtun Factor: Is Afghanistan Next in Line for an Ethnic Civil War?
	26. Again
	27. Somalia: Anatomy of an Unending Conflict
	28. Call in the Blue Helmets
	29. The Democratic Mosaic
	30. Bringing the Wicked to the Dock
	31. The 2005 Freedom House Survey
	32. Whose Iran?
	33. Turkey Face West
	34. Thailand's Elusive Equilibrium
	35. Big Men, Big Fraud, Big Trouble
	36. Congo's Peace
	37. Africa: How We Killed Our Dreams of Freedom
	38. The Year of the Ballot
	39. The Lost Continent
	40. Booms, Busts, and Echoes
	41. Malaria, the Child Killer
	42. Why We Owe So Much to Victims of Disaster
	43. The Challenge of Global Health
	44. A Lifelong Struggle for a Generation
	45. Reversal of Fortune
	46. Ten Years' Hard Labour
	47. Educating Girls, Unlocking Development
	48. Women, Islam and the New Iraq
	49. Women and Warlords

BUSINESS REPLY MAIL
FIRST CLASS MAIL PERMIT NO. 551 DUBUQUE IA

POSTAGE WILL BE PAID BY ADDRESSEE

McGraw-Hill Contemporary Learning Series
501 BELL STREET
DUBUQUE, IA 52001

NO POSTAGE
NECESSARY
IF MAILED
IN THE
UNITED STATES

ABOUT YOU

Name   Date

Are you a teacher? ☐ A student? ☐
Your school's name

Department

Address   City   State   Zip

School telephone #

YOUR COMMENTS ARE IMPORTANT TO US!

Please fill in the following information:
For which course did you use this book?

Did you use a text with this ANNUAL EDITION? ☐ yes ☐ no
What was the title of the text?

What are your general reactions to the Annual Editions concept?

Have you read any pertinent articles recently that you think should be included in the next edition? Explain.

Are there any articles that you feel should be replaced in the next edition? Why?

Are there any World Wide Web sites that you feel should be included in the next edition? Please annotate.

May we contact you for editorial input? ☐ yes ☐ no
May we quote your comments? ☐ yes ☐ no

Ollscoil na hÉireann, Gaillimh

3 1111 40211 4183